Noncooperative Approaches to the Theory of Perfect Competition

Academic Press Rapid Manuscript Reproduction

This is a volume in
ECONOMIC THEORY, ECONOMETRICS, AND MATHEMATICAL ECONOMICS
A Series of Monographs and Textbooks
Consulting Editor: KARL SHELL
A complete list of titles in this series appears at the end of this volume.

Noncooperative Approaches to the Theory of Perfect Competition

Edited by

Andreu Mas-Colell

Department of Economics
Harvard University
Boston, Massachusetts

1982

ACADEMIC PRESS
A Subsidiary of Harcourt Brace Jovanovich, Publishers

New York London
Paris San Diego San Francisco São Paulo Sydney Tokyo Toronto

ACADEMIC PRESS, INC.
111 Fifth Avenue, New York, New York 10003

United Kingdom Edition published by
ACADEMIC PRESS, INC. (LONDON) LTD.
24/28 Oval Road, London NW1 7DX

Library of Congress Cataloging in Publication Data
Main entry under title:

Noncooperative approaches to the theory of perfect competition.

(Economic theory, econometrics, and mathematical economics)
"The essays of this symposium originally appeared in the Journal of economic theory, volume 22, number 2 (April 1980) and are reprinted here with only minor changes"--
Includes index.
1. Competition--Congresses. I. Mas-Colell, Andreu. II. Series.
HB238.N66 1982 338.6'048 82-13936
ISBN 0-12-476750-8

PRINTED IN THE UNITED STATES OF AMERICA

82 83 84 85 9 8 7 6 5 4 3 2 1

Contents

Contributors

Numbers in parentheses indicate the pages on which the authors' contributions begin.

Pradeep Dubey (225, 249), *Yale University, New Haven, Connecticut 06520*
J. Jaskold Gabszewicz (213), *Center for Operations Research and Econometrics, Université Catholique de Louvain, Louvain-la-Neuve 1348, Belgium*
Edward J. Green[1] (37), *Department of Economics, Princeton University, Princeton, New Jersey 08544*
Oliver D. Hart[2] (165), *Churchill College, Cambridge, England*
Louis Makowski (91, 105), *Department of Applied Economics, University of Cambridge, Cambridge CB3 9DE, England*
Andreu Mas-Colell[3] (1, 225), *Department of Economics, University of California, Berkeley, Berkeley, California 94720*
William Novshek (127, 199), *Economics Department, Stanford University, Stanford, California 94305*
Joseph M. Ostroy (65), *Department of Economics, University of California, Los Angeles, Los Angeles, California 90024*
Roy Radner (17), Bell Laboratories, Murray Hill, New Jersey 07974
Kevin Roberts[4] (141), *St. Catherine's College, Oxford, England*
Martin Shubik (225), *Yale University, New Haven, Connecticut 06520*
Hugo Sonnenschein (127), *Princeton University, Princeton, New Jersey 08540*
J.-F. Thisse (213), *Center for Operations Research and Econometrics, Université Catholique de Louvain, Louvain-la-Neuve 1348, Belgium*

[1]Present address: *California Institute of Technology, Pasadena, California 91125*

[2]Present address: *Department of Economics, London School of Economics, Aldwych, London, England*

[3]Present address: *Department of Economics, Harvard University, Cambridge, Massachusetts 02138*

[4]Present address: *Department of Economics, University of Warwick, Coventry, England*

Preface

This volume is a reprinting of the April 1980 issue of the Journal of Economic Theory, which was entirely devoted to a symposium on ''Non-Cooperative Approaches to the Theory of Perfect Competition.'' I wish to acknowledge the permission and encouragement for this project of the editor of the journal, Professor Karl Shell. Participant authors have had an opportunity to correct missprints and minor mistakes but not to make substantive revisions. The index has been prepared by Mr. Xavier Vives.

Andreu Mas-Colell
August 1982

Noncooperative Approaches to the Theory of Perfect Competition: Presentation

ANDREU MAS-COLELL

University of California, Berkeley, California 94720

Received December 28, 1979

1. INTRODUCTION

Modern Walrasian economics (as presented, for example, in Debreu's "Theory of Value" or Arrow and Hahn's "General Competitive Analysis") provides an analysis of the decentralized economic coordination problem under the hypothesis that prices are publicly quoted and are viewed by economic agents as exogenously given. If we regard this as the Hypothesis of Perfect Competition, then modern Walrasian economics is a theory of perfect competition only in the sense of examining the consequences of the Hypothesis but not in that of giving a theoretical explanation of the Hypothesis itself. It is the latter line of enquiry which will interest us here.

The received body of economic doctrine abounds with theories of perfect competition (see Stigler [19]). The 19th-century contributions of Cournot [2] and Edgeworth [4] are remarkable cases in point. It was precisely in order to explain perfect competition (in terms of the insignificance of individual economic agents) that they, respectively, invented the concepts that modern game theorists call Noncooperative Equilibrium and the Core.

Under the impetus of the rediscovery of the Core concept by game theorists, Edgeworth's theory of perfect competition has been subject to extensive and rigorous elaboration in the last two decades (see Hildenbrand [9] for a presentation of the current state of the "art"). Nothing of this sort has happened with Cournot's equilibrium concept. Although his partial-equilibrium example is widely known and highly attuned to the ways economists informally think about competition, it has proven resistant to generalization. This situation is beginning to change. In the last few years, several papers have laid the groundwork for what we shall call the Noncooperative Theory of Perfect Competition (e.g., Gabszewicz and Vial [5], Hart [7], Novshek and Sonnenschein [11], Shubik [18], Shapley [17], Dubey and Shapley [3], Jaynes, Okuno and Schmeidler [12]), and to them we shall now add the contributions to this Symposium volume.

The Symposium was conceived as a vehicle for the joint publication of a

Reprinted from *Journal of Economic Theory* **22**, No. 2, 121–135 (April 1980)
ISBN 0-12-476750-8

number of papers already extant. It has not therefore developed from an a priori specified research agenda. The papers presented here are nonetheless all related and bear upon one another in diverse and interesting ways. Thus it was hoped that a useful service would be provided by bringing them out together.

One could distinguish three progressively more specific senses in which the notion of noncooperative equilibrium is understood when applied to the analysis of markets. At the first, most general level, noncooperation means simply that economic agents cannot rely upon any agreement being binding on other agents. A concomitant notion of noncooperative equilibrium follows. The second level is associated with noncooperative game theory. The trading process is formalized as a game where economic agents have well-defined strategies and trading outcomes depend on those strategies in a precisely specified manner. Then a noncooperative equilibrium (sometimes called a conjectural equilibrium) is a combination of strategies with the property that no agent has an incentive to modify them given conjectures he has on the reaction of other agents. The conjectures of primary interest to us are the stationary ones, i.e., every agent takes the strategies played by others as given. They were used by Cournot and are of great theoretical importance. (In fact, they are the sole meaningful ones in noncooperative game theory.) It has been suggested (by Shapley) that a good term for the noncooperative equilibrium in this second sense (i.e., when a game is explicit) would be strategic equilibrium. At the third level of specificity, it is understood that the noncooperative strategies are of the same nature as in Cournot's own work, i.e., quantities demanded or supplied.

The game theoretic notion of Noncooperative Equilibrium (see Harsanyi [6]) is rich in possibilities. In particular, it allows for the explicit analysis of cooperation. In a static model the contrast between cooperation and noncooperation is sharp. As indicated in the last paragraph, noncooperation (resp. cooperation) means that binding agreements are not (resp. are) possible. However, in a dynamic situation (an infinite repetition of the static model, for example) the distinction is blurred. Dynamic strategies allow for actions contingent upon past histories and therefore it may be possible to enforce agreements noncooperatively by the use of deterrence strategies. Thus, the noncooperative equilibrium of the dynamic situation provides a useful analytical tool to determine the prevalence of the cooperative or noncooperative mode of behavior in the static situation.

As might be expected, the size of the market relative to individual agents will be a key explanatory variable for the tendency of noncooperative behavior to approximate perfect competition. Directly or indirectly, every paper in the Symposium bears upon this central theme. It could also be argued that the number of agents plays an even more fundamental role. Just as Walrasian economics demands an explanation of its basic hypothesis and noncooperative theory provides a framework for it, the latter demands an explanation of the maintained noncooperative hypothesis. It accords with intuition that the number of agents will be a crucial consideration. As a research project, this goes well beyond Cournot although, as was pointed out in the last paragraph, not necessarily beyond general noncooperative theory. The papers by Green and Radner in the Symposium represent a beginning in this direction.

At least as instructive as the positive theoretical results obtained are the new cases of market failures identified in various Symposium contributions (e.g., Roberts, Hart, Makowski). Indeed, a familiar characteristic of perfect competition research does not fail to appear here: the closer one examines the concept of perfect competition the stronger are found to be the conditions for its validity. The horizon of perfect-competition prerequisites seems to be ever receding. Surely, the central position the concept of perfect competition has enjoyed since the 18th century is not about to falter. But the emphasis should be on its centrality as an organizing concept and certainly not as an innocuous descriptive category for the real world.

Almost every paper in the Symposium looks explicitly at perfect competition as a limit case of imperfect, or monopolistic, competition. Unfortunately, a powerful theory of the latter subject is still missing, but perhaps one can hope that some of the methods developed in this Symposium will take us a step closer.

A traditional requirement of perfect competition is the "transparency of markets," i.e., some appropriate form of perfect information about market conditions. The general tenor of the Symposium papers is to accept this requirement without close scrutiny and to embody it at the modeling stage. Imperfect information as a source of imperfect competition has been extensively investigated (Rothschild [16] is still a useful reference).

The Symposium papers can be classified into three general categories:

(i) The papers by Green and Radner analyze the noncooperative equilibria of repeated games for partial equilibrium models which closely resemble Cournot's original example. Thus, these papers study the robustness of Cournot's result when the choice of cooperation vs noncooperation is made endogenous.

(ii) The papers by Dubey, Dubey, Mas–Colell, and Shubik, Gabszewicz and Thisse, Hart, Novshek, Novshek and Sonnenschein, and Roberts are concerned with *static* noncooperative equilibria in general equilibrium models with large numbers of small agents.

(iii) The contribution of Ostroy and the two by Makowski seek to characterize the domain of validity of the Hypothesis of Perfect Competition by a deepening of the complementary notion that monopoly power is absent. They provide a noncooperative theory of perfect competition which does not rely on the number of agents in any explicit way and which has its intellectual roots more in the marginal productivity theory of distribution than in Cournot. In spite, or because, of this their papers interact in subtle and pervasive ways with the other contributions to the Symposium.

2. Cooperation versus Noncooperation

Suppose that a number N of firms produce a homogeneous good and face a given demand function. With the quantity produced as the strategic variable, the static cooperative (i.e., cartel) solution involves producing a quantity that maximizes the sum of profits, while the noncooperative solution is the classical one described by Cournot. Which outcome is more likely will depend upon many particulars of the market being studied, but surely two relevant circumstances are: (i) the number of firms, and (ii) the coordination possibilities open to firms. The theory of repeated games provides a method for modeling their impact. Indeed, suppose that the market game will be repeated M times. Then firm production strategies for the M periods are specified in advance and can be made contingent on past histories. Thus, a potentially large (depending on M) amount of bargaining moves can be embodied in the independent specification of strategies.

Radner and Green each discuss instances of such repeated market games. Of course, there are many differences between their models. A particularly important one is that the payoff criterion of Radner is the average profit over the M periods, while Green adopts a discounted sum of profits (payoffs), the discount rate being positive but perhaps very small.

In the context of a linear example, Radner examines the following intuition: for a fixed number of firms N the larger is M the more numerous are the coordination possibilities available and therefore the more stable the cartel agreement will be. On the other hand, for a fixed $M < \infty$ the larger is N the more difficult it is to coordinate, and, therefore, the more likely it is that noncooperation prevails and that the outcome will resemble the Cournot equilibrium which, being N large, will in turn be close to the Walrasian Equilibrium. The first thing needed for a rigorous analysis is a solution concept. Suppose we were to adopt as such the (perfect) noncooperative equilibrium of the repeated game. It turns out then that the first part of the intuition is incorrect. Only if $M = \infty$ can the cartel agreement be noncooperatively enforced. If $M < \infty$, a familiar backward recursion argument yields the conclusion that the only possible equilibrium outcome is the repeated sequence of stationary Cournot productions. Thus, the coordination possibilities embodied in M come to naught. While the discontinuity at $M = \infty$ is rather disconcerting it is not at all clear that it is of economic importance since it crucially depends upon individual agents' sharp perception of a last period. Radner establishes that if we instead adopt as a solution concept his notion of ϵ (perfect) noncooperative equilibrium (which he has developed in the context of a wider research program), then the discontinuity disappears and, in a precise sense, the informal intuition given above holds true.

In Radner's approach, if $M = \infty$ then the cartel agreement can be enforced, whatever the number N of firms. This enforcement can be accomplished by the adoption by firms of the following reprisal strategy: Every firm will produce the cartel output as long as all other firms do, but if any deviates, each firm will increase production to the Cournot output and maintain it thereafter.

Green reexamines this conclusion when account is taken of a realistic characteristic of markets, namely, the imperfection of information. In particular: (i) markets are anonymous in the sense that only a summary statistic (for example, price) of the firms' strategies is publicly known, and (ii) markets are noisy in the sense that demand, at a given price, is random. Green exhibits an example where the cartel agreement of an infinitely repeated anonymous market is still enforceable for any finite number of firms (if there were a continuum of firms, then anonymity suffices for the collapse of the cartel). The equilibrium strategies are of the following form: If any departure of market prices from cartel prices is observed, then cooperation stops. These are rather farfetched strategies. They require that agents have the ability to discern prices perfectly and that they react discontinuously. Green proceeds to show that if in addition demand is noisy a different result emerges. When the number of firms is large, the noncooperative equilibria of the infinitely repeated noisy markets he considers yield production levels which are close to the stationary Cournot ones (and are, therefore, almost Walrasian). Strictly speaking, this result is established for noncooperative equilibria with stationary strategies, but it seems plausible that the result is true more generally. Also, discounting is important here. If, as in Radner, the payoff criterion were the long range average profit, then it would appear that the cartel outcome would be enforceable even with noise.

3. Noncooperative Equilibria in Economies with a Large Number of Agents

Consider a noncooperative game superimposed upon a given market economy. If the game is intended to model market transactions, then it should be expected that, with a relatively small number of economic agents (consumers and firms), the Walrasian solution will not generally emerge as a noncooperative equilibrium of the game. Indeed, at such solutions agents will have incentives to exploit monopoly power. Even more, if a noncooperative equilibrium exists, we will not expect it to be Pareto Optimal at all. In order to properly relate a specific noncooperative theory to Walrasian economics and the Hypothesis of Perfect Competition, we should ask if the noncooperative equilibria are Walrasian (or almost so), and therefore Pareto Optimal, when agents have no monopoly power. If this is not the case then we have a market failure (which, for reasons to be made clear later on, we shall designate Type I). A classical embodiment of the notion that monopoly power is absent is the hypothesis that individual agents are negligible or, more specifically, that a very large number of them, in the limit of a continuum, are present in the marketplace.

Two broad lines can be distinguished in the current research in Cournotian general equilibrium theory:

(i) the first, inagurated by the quantity setting model of Shubik [18] (see also Shapley [17], Jaynes *et al.* [12], and Dubey and Shapley [3]), emphasizes trade and treats all agents (buyers or sellers) symmetrically. In this Symposium it is represented by the Dubey, Mas-Colell and Shubik and Dubey papers.

(ii) the second, inagurated by the quantity setting model of Gabszewicz and Vial [5], stays closer to Cournot's original partial-equilibrium example. It maintains the distinction between firms and consumers and views the noncooperative game as being played among firms, the consumers adapting passively (i.e., as price takers) along an endogenously determined demand curve. The papers of Hart, Gabszewicz and Thisse, Novshek and Sonnenschein, Novshek, and Roberts fall broadly into this category. The models of Hart, Roberts, and Novshek and Sonnenschein have quantities as strategies while the model of Gabszewicz and Thisse has prices and that of Novshek has location and prices.

The approach taken in the Dubey *et al.* paper is axiomatic and it is developed primarily within the framework of a continuum of agents. It deals with a class of abstractly given market allocation mechanisms which satisfy a number of axioms (convexity of the strategy set, anonymity, aggregation of strategies, continuity of payoffs) intended to be characteristic of well-functioning markets. The conclusion can be phrased as asserting that, under the axioms, every noncooperative equilibrium is Walrasian relative to the set of "open" markets, where "open" means that, as far as the market is concerned, it is possible for individual agents to change slightly their trade. This set of open markets is endogenously determined. In fact, in some of the prototypical examples, the set of open and active (i.e., those where transactions take place) markets coincide, and it is possible (for somewhat degenerate reasons) to obtain equilibria for any a priori specification of nonactive markets. Thus, in those examples market failure (of Type I) is not only possible but even typical.

It is also shown in the Dubey *et al.* paper that (under the axioms), the noncooperative equilibria (with all markets open) of market games with a finite number of agents may fail to be Pareto Optimal for some specification of agents' characteristics. One may feel that it should be possible to go much further, i.e., to assert that except for coincidental cases, they never will be Pareto Optimal. This is accomplished in Dubey's paper for a particular quantity-setting example. But note that the issue is more subtle than it appears at first sight. Indeed, the incentive compatibility literature (see the recent *Review of Economic Studies* [13] Symposium) has taught us that it is possible to design mechanisms yielding Pareto Optimal noncooperative equilibria. In essence, Dubey establishes that, if to the axioms we add a key dimensionality condition on the set of strategies, then generic Pareto inefficiency obtains.

The Symposium contribution of Novshek and Sonnenschein is a continuing step in the research initiated in their previous paper [11]. Here they work out the Walrasian Equilibrium Theory and the Welfare-theoretic propositions of the limit continuum model whose finite number of traders approximations are the basic models of their noncooperative theory. The economy they consider has a continuum of firms, each with bounded (but "nonzero") nonconvexities in their production sets (i.e., relatively small efficiency scale). From the Novshek–Sonnenschein point of view, small nonzero efficiency scale is the cornerstone of the theory of perfect competition. They pay special attention to the existence problem and to the two fundamental propositions of Welfare economics. They emphasize that the validity of the second (on the sustainability of Pareto Optimal states as equilibria, modulo an appropriate redistribution of wealth) is not affected by the presence of externalities and is therefore unrelated to the convexity or not of the aggregate production set (individual production sets are always nonconvex but because the nonconvexities are bounded and there is a continuum of firms, the aggregate production set will be nonconvex only if externalities are present). A complete perspective on the status of the two fundamental propositions in the Novshek and Sonnenschein noncooperative theory of competition will be obtained by combining the results of this paper (on the relation between Pareto Optimality and Walrasian Equilibrium) with the conclusions of the earlier one (on the relation between Walrasian Equilibrium and Noncooperative Equilibrium).

The papers by Hart and Roberts can be regarded as studies in market failure for related quantity setting models. Suppose there is a finite number of firms and a consumption sector. The actions or strategies of a firm consist in choosing a feasible input–output vector. Equilibrium prices are determined so that the aggregate input–output vector is absorbed by consumers acting as price takers (there is a well-defined profit distribution rule). For matters to be well defined, there should be available a priori a selection from the correspondence which assigns equilibrium prices to aggregate input–output vectors. Once actions have been taken, the profits of firms are determined. Under the hypothesis that firms are aware of the dependence of price on actions and that they maximize profits (see Hart [8] for a justification in a similar model) we have a notion of noncooperative equilibrium and we can analyze its properties. It is then relevant to ask if there is an absence of (Type I) market failure, i.e., if the noncooperative equilibria tend to become Walrasian as the size of the economy relative to individual firms increases. The technique used by Hart and Roberts to expand the economy is replication of the number of firms *and* consumers without limit.

Roberts proves that there will not be market failure if (under other standard conditions) the price equilibrium selected depends continuously on the (mean) aggregate input–output vector (Gabszewicz and Vial [5] and Novshek and Sonnenschein [11] also have results of this type). He exhibits examples where price discontinuity leads to market failure. It is possible to give an intuitive justification of his conclusions. Absence of market failure is tantamount to every agent (firms as well as consumers) becoming a price taker as the size of the economy increases. Now, it is reasonably clear that this will happen if individual production sets are suitably bounded and prices depend continuously on the mean aggregate input–output vector. On the contrary, at a discontinuity point of the price function it is very likely that the isoprofit surfaces of individual firms will not become hyperplanes and so the economy may remain stable at one such point even if it is very far from being Walrasian. This is a significant case of market failure because the price continuity hypothesis is by no means a mild one. It essentially imposes two strong requirements: (i) a price equilibrium exists for every feasible aggregate input–output vector, (ii) it is unique.

An important instance of this variety of market failure appears in the paper by Hart. He shows that, unless we resort to economically quite strong smoothness and convexity hypotheses (which imply a form of substitutability among commodities), it is possible that no continuous selection of equilibrium prices exists at points with zero production of *several* goods (the existence of such a selection is an implication of his Simultaneous Reservation Price Property). For example, homogeneous production and utility functions which are not linear have discontinuous gradients at the origin. The economically significant reason for this lack of continuity is the presence of complementarities. Thus, think of goods that should be consumed (or used as inputs) in fixed proportions or, more generally, of goods which are indispensable in the sense that a positive amount is required in order get any output (or utility). The consequences are quite damaging. For example, if there are several indispensable goods, there is no hope of guaranteeing an efficient outcome in a completely decentralized manner, since any of them, produced alone, will command a zero price. Matters should be so coordinated that all goods are produced at once. Otherwise, it may well happen that the economy gets locked up in a situation with the "wrong" set of active markets. (Interestingly, the market failures in the Dubey *et al.* examples are also of this sort but the failure here is less degenerate.) Hart discusses a number of instructive and quite unsuspected examples. It should be emphasized that these market failures do not arise because of divergence of private and social incentives. In Hart's model, the cost–benefit analysis associated with a *single* firm is (asymptotically) identical whether we take the private or the social point of view.

The message of Hart's paper is to emphasize a crucial qualitative difference between active and nonactive markets, which does not come through in conventional Walrasian economics. What we have called the Hypothesis of Perfect Competition has two parts: price quoting and price taking. For active markets prices are embodied in transactions and so, there is no particular mystery about their origins. But for nonactive markets, Walrasian prices are more in the nature of a theoretical construct. It is indeed a very strong hypothesis to postulate that prices are universally quoted even for nonactive markets. It implies, for example, that every agent is perfectly informed about the set of possible commodities. If, as Hart does, we take the limited point of view that quoted prices are available only in active markets, then the sort of decentralized coordination that Walrasian prices are supposed to achieve will come about only if the theoretical clearing prices are well approximated by the prices obtained in a decentralized manner. Or, in other words, only if the Simultaneous Reservation Price Property (i.e., the possibility of continuous extension of the price function to multiple zero-production levels) holds. Otherwise, the usual Walrasian picture may be quite misleading. The Invisible Hand may have to work hard and coordinate extensively if the right set of commodities is to be made available. It is interesting to observe how entirely parallel are Hart's conclusions to the ones obtained by Makowski in his Symposium paper on innovation, itself based on a different approach to perfect competition.

Up to now, market failure has meant that noncooperative equilibrium does not yield full Walrasian equilibrium. There is a second type (Type II) of market failure, namely, when a Walrasian equilibrium of a limit continuum economy fails to be the limit of a sequence of noncooperative equilibria for approximating sequences of economies with a finite number of agents (or, more generally, when a Walrasian equilibrium is not a noncooperative equilibrium in some appropriate sense). The interpretation of such failure is clear: that particular Walrasian equilibrium should not properly be regarded as a decentralized equilibrium.

Type II market failures are also studied by Roberts. Under smoothness and convexity hypotheses on preferences and production sets, he is able to rule them out for Walrasian equilibria which are regular in a strong sense. By regular he means that some relevant Jacobian determinants do not vanish.

A crucial implication of regularity is the existence of a locally continuous price equilibrium selection function (a property which was already exploited with a similar objective in Roberts and Postlewaite [14]). In the context of his model, the standard result in the theory of regular economies holds, i.e., regular economies are generic (in other words, nonregularity corresponds to pathology). This is a satisfactory and reasonably general result. It would be hasty, however, to dismiss the significance of Type II failures. There are important directions in which Roberts result does not extend. Suppose there are some purely intermediate goods. Then, market failure seems to occur generically. Indeed, if demand equals supply it will always pay for a demander of the intermediate good to understate his demand slightly, thus creating excess supply and bringing the price to zero. Note that no locally continuous selection of equilibrium prices exists in this case. In fact, the presence of purely intermediate goods seems to present an as yet untackled modeling problem. In another direction Novshek and Sonnenschein [11] have established that in the presence of setup cost (even if very small), the availability of a locally continuous selection of equilibrium prices does not even generically suffice to rule out Type II failures. One also needs a multidimensional analog of the downward sloping demand curve condition.

As formulated in the previous paragraph, the absence of Type II failure implies the existence of noncooperative equilibria for all large number of agents' economies near the considered limit. It is, of course, well known that existence (i.e., consistency) failures are a major difficulty for the use of the noncooperative equilibrium concept in the analysis of market situations with a fixed finite number of traders (see, for example, Roberts and Sonnenschein [15]). The results of Roberts and Novshek and Sonnenschein [11] indicate that the problem becomes more tractable as the economy nears its continuum limit, but even then it is quite subtle. Thus it may be worthwhile to explore the usefulness of approximate noncooperative equilibrium concepts (the plural is important—there is more than one and which one is picked may make a difference). A beginning in this direction is to be found in Hart's paper. This may be a good point to remark that the existence question also obscures somewhat the analysis of Type I failures. Indeed, a given model may be "free" of them simply because the noncooperative equilibria fail to exist!

The paper by Novshek carries out a careful and penetrating analysis of a prototypical simple differentiated commodity model in the hereditary line of Hotelling [10]. No useful service would be performed here by a detailed description of the model and results. The Abstract and first pages of his paper are quite self-explanatory. It should be emphasized however that it contains a full treatment of the existence question (so, narrowing down the analysis to a simple, but still rich, model pays off in this case) and that a number of interesting and instructive points arise: (i) in order to get existence of noncooperative equilibrium (in location and price strategies) the Cournot stationary conjectures must be modified in a most sensible way, firms will no longer expect others to remain put if an effect of their strategies is to take away all the demand of a competitor; (ii) with no set-up cost for firms (and, of course, a number of other assumptions) a suitably defined noncooperative equilibrium will exist; (iii) with setup costs and the possibility of exit and entry there may be no equilibrium, but if the setup cost is small and an unlimited number of firms can, in principle, enter, then a noncooperative equilibrium will exist and, moreover, will closely approximate the Walrasian equilibrium. The Novshek and Sonnenschein [11] paper provides a far reaching generalization of this latter feature.

In their contribution Gabszewicz and Thisse analyze a numerically specified example of *price* (rather than quantity) competition among firms offering a spectrum of differentiated products. In the example there are two free parameters: the number of firms and the degree of substitutability between commodities. Roughly described, the result states that, for a fixed degree of substitutability, the noncooperative equilibrium approaches the Walrasian equilibrium as the number of (potential) firms increases. But this also happens if the number of firms stays fixed (but is larger than one) and the degree of substitutability increases. Of course, this is in line with Bertrand's classic counterexample [1], showing that if strategies are prices, then the perfectly competitive duopoly is a possible noncooperative outcome. Does this mean that the role of the number of agents as a fundamental explanatory variable of perfect competition is limited to quantity setting models? The answer is no to the extent that the number of agents may explain the prevalence of non-cooperation over cooperation.

A final but basic observation is that, ideally, the choice of strategy space (price, quantities, supply functions,...) or conjectures should not be exogenously given but should be determined from economic considerations. This appears to be a wide open field of research. Intuitively, it seems clear that factors such as the timing and the irreversibility of decisions regarding location, choice of technique, or scale of production are relevant as is, more generally, any factor which affects the strategic precommitment possibilities of firms. It may be that a static timeless approach is too limited for this analysis and that a multistage specification is required if conceptual fuzziness is to be avoided.

4. Perfect Competition as the Absence of Monopoly Power

Until now the emphasis has been on justifying the Perfect Competition Hypothesis. The contributions of Ostroy and Makowski can be viewed as analyses of its inner structure. Ostroy's paper concentrates on the exchange case, while the first by Makowski extends the theory to a production, firm-oriented setting.

Ostroy and Makowski both begin by defining a Walrasian equilibrium as perfectly competitive if agents are justified in treating prices as given in the specific sense that the Walrasian prices are still equilibrium prices if the individual agent is dropped from the economy. This test is devised to capture the notion of individual agents facing an infinitely elastic demand curve and therefore enjoying no monopoly power. Observe that, under the standard general equilibrium hypotheses on preferences and production sets, perfectly competitive Walrasian allocations have these two properties: (i) they are Pareto Optimal or, in their words, every consumer obtains maximum utility given the utility level of the other consumers, (ii) every group formed by all agents but one is able to protect their utility levels in the sense that no loss of utility need occur for any remaining agent as a result of dropping a single agent from the economy. In other words, at the given allocation no single agent can possibly succeed in bargaining for a higher level of utility with the rest of the economy since he has already succeeded in extracting all "surplus" accruing to the other agents as a result of his participation in trade. Ostroy defines allocations satisfying properties (i) and (ii) as no-surplus allocations and proves a simple but basic result, namely that an allocation is a no-surplus one if and only if it is Walrasian and perfectly competitive. Thus, a price-free characterization of the latter concept is obtained.

Ostroy's theory provides a general equilibrium and purely ordinal extension of the classical characterization of competitive equilibrium in terms of "marginal productivities." Indeed, an allocation is perfectly competitive (i.e., no-surplus) if and only if every agent receives exactly its "marginal contribution." It might also be pointed out that there are interesting relationships between the no-surplus concept and some of the cooperative game theoretic notions that have been used to analyze perfect competition (i.e., Core, Shapley Value). But the theory remains very definitively a non-cooperative one. It is a basic hypothesis that every agent bargains for surplus in isolation and that no collusion for that purpose is possible. The idea of a no-surplus equilibrium does not require the explicit structure of a game for its formulation. Nevertheless, it makes some sense to say that the idea is not based on stationary conjectures. Rather the contrary, every agent expects that the rest of the economy can and will, as a group, do everything possible to protect their levels of utility.

In his first paper Makowski shows that this no-surplus theory includes a theory of profits. Indeed, he sets up a model of individual production where the role of agents as producers (i.e., entrepreneurs) and consumers can be separated, and he proves that, in a precise sense, at a perfectly competitive outcome, profits measure the entrepreneurial contribution to "total surplus." Thus, for example, zero profit is equivalent to the redundancy of the entrepreneur. One of the contributions of his second paper is an extension of the theory to the joint ownership case. It takes this form: At a perfectly competitive equilibrium, (i) every owner of the firm agrees on the profit maximization criterion, and (ii) profits measure the surplus contributed by the firm.

It is possible for no-surplus allocations to exist for economies with a finite number of agents. For example, if the initial endowments allocation is Pareto Optimal it is also no-surplus (and, one might add, there are no gains from trade). As another instance, presented by Makowski, suppose that at the Walrasian Equilibrium every active firm has an inactive double. Then firms have no surplus to extract and are, therefore, perfect competitors (thus, in a market with two identical firms and constant average cost no-surplus theory agrees with the Bertrand solution). But such situations are rare. Typically, if there is only a finite number of agents, no surplus allocations will fail to exist, a reflection of the all-pervasive presence of at least some extent of monopoly power. In contrast, it accords with general intuition that in a continuum of agents situation monopoly power vanishes and we should expect Walrasian allocations to be no-surplus ones. Thus, consider the exchange case and assume all the necessary differentiability. Then prices represent precisely the welfare contribution of the marginal unit of commodities brought and sold, but if individual agents are infinitesimally small, all their transactions take place at the infinitesimal margin, and so, they contribute no surplus. Ostroy investigates this issue rigorously in the context of a replicated economy. There it takes the form of determining the conditions under which the Walrasian allocations will become approximately no-surplus as the number of agents increases (i.e., asymptotically no-surplus). He shows that the key condition is the existence of a unique (normalized) vector of efficiency prices for the given Walrasian allocation. This is a very weak condition since it can be violated only with extreme forms of (what else?) complementarities. If these are present, then Walrasian allocations may not be asymptotically no-surplus (i.e., we have a kind of Type II failure). Examples can be found in Ostroy's paper.

The second paper by Makowski, which is also firm oriented, explores the ramifications of a sensible ammendation to the perfect-competition concept as it has been discussed so far. The latter captures well the notion of agents not being able to influence prices. But it says nothing about prices quotation. As Hart does in his paper, Makowski hypothesizes that prices are quoted only in active markets. Therefore, when a firm is considered unable to influence prices, this is in reference only to prices that would be quoted at the feasible production plans of the firm or, for short, the prices "faced" by the firm. Note that, since they are unobservable, nothing is said here about the possibility to affect prices faced by other firms. Thus, as Makowski notes, a type of pecunary externality is compatible with perfect competition.

For Makowski, an allocation is perfectly competitive if: (i) there are prices for marketed commodities which put the consumers in price taking equilibrium, (ii) firms cannot influence the prices they face. The precise definition of this is analogous to Ostroy's and to the first Makowski paper. Essentially, the economy can do as well without the particular firm and at the same prices. Makowski is able to show that, in a precise sense, profits, at a perfectly competitive allocation, measure the contribution to social welfare of the particular firm, firms profit maximize and there is unanimity among joint owners on the profit motive.

Perfect competition in the sense of Makowski provides a theory of innovation and endogenous determination of marketed commodities. Indeed, finding the "right" set of commodities becomes a real issue. In particular, complementarities (Makowski emphasizes the ones connected with chains of intermediate products) may lead to inefficient perfectly competitive equilibria where there is no private or social incentive (remember that here they coincide) for any *single* firm to change its production plan (offering a new product, for example). The analytical conclusions are entirely analogous to Hart's. In fact, Makowski's model, which is more general, provides a useful perspective on Hart's analysis. The role of a large number of agents in the latter is simply to make the noncooperative equilibrium approximately perfectly competitive in the sense of the former.

Acknowledgment

I would like to acknowledge the help I have received in the preparation of these pages from the Institute for Advanced Studies at the Hebrew University and from Mr. D. Wells.

References

1. J. Bertrand, Théorie mathématique de la richesse sociale, *J. Savants* (1883), 499–508.
2. A. Cournot, "Recherches sur les principes mathématiques de la théorie des richesse," M. Riviere, Paris, 1838.
3. P. Dubey and L. Shapley, Non-cooperative exchange with a continuum of traders, *Econometrica*, in press.
4. F. Edgeworth, "Mathematical Psychics," Kegan Paul, London, 1881.
5. J. Gabszewicz and J. P. Vial, Oligopoly 'à la Cournot' in a general equilibrium analysis, *J. Econ. Theory* **4** (1972), 381–400.
6. J. Harsanyi "Rational Behaviour and Bargaining Equilibrium in Games and Social Situations," Cambridge Univ. Press, Cambridge, 1977.
7. O. Hart, Monopolistic competition in a large economy with differentiated commodities, *Rev. Econ. Stud.* **46** (1979), 1–30.
8. O. Hart, On shareholder unanimity in large stock market economies, *Econometrica* **47**, No. 5 (1979), 1057–1085.
9. W. Hildenbrand, "Core and Equilibria of a Large Economy," Princeton Univ. Press, Princeton, 1974.

10. H. Hotelling, Stability in competition, *Econ. J.* **39** (1939), 41–57.
11. W. Novshek and H. Sonnenschein, Cournot and Walras Equilibrium, *J. Econ. Theory* **19**, No. 2 (1978), 223–266.
12. J. Jaynes, M. Okuno, and D. Schmeidler, Efficiency in an atomless economy with fiat money, *Internat. Econ. Rev.* **19** (1978), 149–157.
13. *Rev. Econ. Stud.*, Symposium on incentive compatibility, **46**, No. 2 (1979).
14. J. Roberts and A. Postlewaite, The incentives for price-taking behaviour in lar exchange economies, *Econometrica* **44** (1974), 115–127.
15. J. Roberts and H. Sonnenschein, On the foundations of the theory of monopolistic competition, *Econometrica* **45** (1977), 101–113.
16. M. Rothschild, Models of market organization with imperfect information: A survey, *J. Pol. Econ.* **81** (1973), 1283–1308.
17. L. Shapley, Non-cooperative general exchange, *in* "Theory and Measurement of Externalities" (A. Y. Lin, Ed.), Academic Press, New York, 1976.
18. M. Shubik, Commodity money, oligopoly, credit and bankruptcy in a general equilibrium model, *Western Econ. J.* **11** (1973), 24–28.
19. G. Stigler, Perfect competition, historically contemplated, *in* "Essays in the History of Economics" Chap. 8, Univ. of Chicago Press, Chicago, 1965.
20. P. Dubey, A. Mas-Colell, and M. Shubik, Efficiency properties of strategic market games: an axiomatic approach, *J. Econ. Theory* **22** (1980), 339–362.
21. P. Dubey, Nash equilibria of market games: finiteness and inefficiency, *J. Econ. Theory* **22** (1980), 363–376.

Collusive Behavior in Noncooperative Epsilon-Equilibria of Oligopolies with Long but Finite Lives

Roy Radner

Bell Laboratories, Murray Hill, New Jersey 07974

Received March 9, 1979

In a game of a finite number of repetitions of a Cournot-type model of an industry, if firms are satisfied to get close to (but not necessarily achieve) their optimal responses to other firms' sequential strategies, then in the resulting non-cooperative "equilibria" of the sequential market game, (1) if the lifetime of the industry is large compared to the number of firms, there are equilibria corresponding to any given duration of the cartel, whereas (2) if the number of firms is large compared to the industry's lifetime, all equilibria will be close (in some sense) to the competitive equilibrium.

1. Introduction

In 1838 Augustin Cournot introduced his model of market equilibrium, which has become known in modern game theory as a noncooperative (or Nash) equilibrium [1]. Cournot's model was intended to describe an industry with a fixed number of firms with convex cost functions, producing a homogeneous product, in which each firm's action was to choose an output (or rate of output), and in which the market price was determined by the total industry output and the market demand function. A Cournot–Nash equilibrium is a combination of outputs, one for each firm, such that no firm can increase its profit by changing its output alone.

Cournot thought of his model as describing "competition" among firms; this corresponds to what we call today the "noncooperative" character of the equilibrium. He showed that, if the number of firms is regarded as a parameter of the market, a larger number of firms would lead to a larger industry output and a lower price (in equilibrium), and that as the number of firms increased without limit, the corresponding equilibria would converge to the situation he called "unlimited competition," in which marginal cost equaled price.

If there are at least two firms, then they can make more profit than in the Cournot–Nash equilibrium (CNE) by forming a cartel in which the total industry output is chosen to maximize total industry profit, and this profit

Reprinted from *Journal of Economic Theory* **22,** No. 2, 136–154 (April 1980)
ISBN 0-12-476750-8

is shared equally among the firms. This corresponds to what would be called a cooperative solution of the game.

What determines whether there will be a cooperative rather than a non-cooperative outcome in the market situation? If the market situation were repeated a number of periods, then, even in the absence of some institution (such as regulation) to enforce cooperation, it would seem that the firms would have opportunities to signal their willingness to cooperate. Furthermore, the larger the number of periods, the greater would be the relative loss due to defection from the cartel and a reversion to the CNE outputs and profits. On the other hand, the larger the number of firms, the greater would be the difficulty of holding the cartel together, at least according to conventional wisdom.

If the market situation is repeated, say T times, then this gives rise to a game in which the strategies available to the players (firms) are sequential. A sequential strategy is a sequence of functions, one for each period, each of which determines the output in that period as a function of the outputs of all firms in the previous periods. One can show that every perfect Cournot–Nash equilibrium of the T-period game results in each firm producing its one-period CNE output in each period.[1] (For this result, one assumes that each firm's objective is to maximize its average, or total discounted, profit over the T periods.) I should emphasize that this property of T-period perfect CNE's is satisfied for any finite T, no matter how large. On the other hand, one can show that if T is infinite, and each firm's objective is to maximize its long-run-average profit, then there is a perfect CNE of the (infinite-period) game that results in indefinite survival of the cartel.[2] The result for infinite T goes part of the way towards confirming our intuition about the determinants of cooperation, but has the unsatisfactory feature that the infinite case is not well approximated by the case of large but finite T. Another unsatisfactory feature of the result is that it holds for any number of firms, no matter how large.

In this paper I explore the consequences of weakening the strict rationality of the Cournot–Nash equilibrium concept, so that each player is satisfied to get close to (but not necessarily achieve) his best response to the other players' strategies. Formally, an *epsilon-equilibrium* is a combination of strategies, one for each player, such that each player's strategy is within epsilon in utility (e.g., average profit) of the maximum possible against the other players' strategies. I shall show that, for any fixed positive epsilon,

[1] A perfect equilibrium of a sequential game is defined in Section 3. As will be seen there, the restriction that the equilibrium be perfect excludes equilibria based on unconvincing threats. The statement in the text is no longer correct if one eliminates the condition that equilibria be perfect.

[2] This is a special case of a more general theorem on perfect equilibria of infinite supergames, due to Aumann and Shapley (unpublished) and Rubinstein [5, 6].

any given number of firms, and any integer k, there is an integer T_0 such that, for all T exceeding T_0, there is a perfect epsilon-equilibrium of the T-period game in which the cartel lasts exactly k periods. In choosing T_0, it is sufficient to make $(T_0 - k)$ larger than some number that depends on epsilon and the number of firms. In particular, one can (approximately) achieve any desired fraction, k/T, by taking T large enough.

The effect on perfect epsilon-equilibria of varying the number of firms depends on the relationship between the industry demand function and the number of firms. (The latter is a parameter of the game.) Suppose first that, as we compare markets with different numbers of firms, the demand price is the same function of the *average* industry output *per firm*; call this the *replication case*. This would be the situation that would obtain if, when we doubled the number of firms, we also duplicated the population of consumers. In the replication case, one can show that, for every fixed positive epsilon and T, as the number of firms increases without limit all perfect epsilon-equilibria approach competitive equilibrium (Cournot's "unlimited competition") in the following sense. For every positive ϵ, T, and N (>1), there is a number $B(\epsilon, T, N)$ such that, in every perfect ϵ-equilibrium of the T-period game, each firm's output and total industry output at each date are all within $B(\epsilon, T, N)$ of their corresponding one-period CNE values. The bounds $B(\epsilon, T, N)$ can be chosen so that, (1) for every ϵ and T, the ratios $B(\epsilon, T, N)/N^{1/2}$ are uniformly bounded in N, and (2) for every T and N, $B(\epsilon, T, N)$ approaches zero as ϵ approaches zero. One can further show that, for fixed ϵ and T, as N increases without limit, at every date (1) average output per firm approaches the competitive equilibrium output per firm, (2) market price approaches marginal cost, and (3) every firm's relative share of total industry output approaches zero. Finally, under the same conditions, the difference between each firm's profit and its one-period CNE profit is uniformly bounded in N, and approaches zero as ϵ approaches zero.

Leaving the replication case, suppose now that the industry demand function is fixed as we compare markets with different numbers of firms; call this the *fixed-demand* case. In this case, one can show that, for any fixed number of periods, T, there is a number B (depending on epsilon and T) such that, in all perfect epsilon-equilibria of the T-period game, the outputs and profits of all firms, total industry output and profit, and market price are all within B of their corresponding one-period CNE values, *uniformly in the number of firms*. Furthermore, the bound B tends to zero as epsilon tends to zero, with T fixed. This implies that, in the fixed-demand case, for any fixed number of periods and *small* epsilon, all perfect epsilon-equilibria are "close" to competitive equilibrium in terms of outputs, profits, and prices, for a sufficiently large number of firms.

Note that the effect of increasing the number of firms on reducing the possibilities for cooperation is observed in the replication case, but not in the fixed-demand case. In both cases, reducing epsilon reduces the possibilities for cooperation (i.e., keeps all perfect epsilon-equilibria closer to the CNE), and increasing the number of firms brings the CNE closer, of course, to the competitive equilibrium. Thus, for the replication case, one can paraphrase the results of this paper as follows: if firms are satisfied to get close to (but not necessarily achieve) their optimal responses to other firms' strategies, then in the resulting noncooperative "equilibria" of the sequential market game, (1) if the lifetime of the industry is large compared to the number of firms, there are equilibria corresponding to any given duration of the cartel, whereas (2) if the number of firms is large compared to the lifetime of the industry, all equilibria will be close (in some sense) to the competitive equilibrium.

Although the replication case is the one of central interest here, I shall use the fixed demand case (Section 5) as a stepping-stone in the analysis of the replication case (Section 6).

As will be seen below, several alternative definitions of perfect epsilon-equilibria may be reasonably considered. I shall begin the analysis with the simplest one (Section 4). A more satisfactory definition, is introduced in Section 7. An important behavioral implication of this second definition is that cooperation will tend to break down as the industry approaches the horizon T. In Section 8, I discuss some alternative interpretations of epsilon.

The entire analysis in the present paper is carried out only for a special model, in which the market demand function is linear, and all firms have the same linear homogeneous cost function (average and marginal costs are equal and constant). However, the analysis can be extended easily to the case in which each firm has a fixed (setup) cost of production, and in which there is free entry. In this case, the number of firms in the industry is endogenous.[3] This extension will be discussed in a forthcoming paper.

2. The One-Period Cournot Game

Consider an industry producing a single homogeneous product, with N firms. The cost to a single firm of producing a quantity Q is γQ. If firm j produces quantity Q_j, the market-clearing price P is determined by the industry demand function

$$P = \alpha - \beta \sum_{j=1}^{N} Q_j , \qquad (2.1)$$

[3] For this situation, Cournot–Nash equilibria in the one-period game have been studied by Novshek [2] and by Novshek and Sonnenschein [3].

if this is positive; otherwise it is zero. The profit to firm i is therefore

$$PQ_i - \gamma Q_i = \left(\alpha - \beta \sum_{j=1}^{N} Q_j\right) Q_i - \gamma Q_i$$

$$= \left(\alpha - \gamma - \beta \sum_{j\neq i} Q_j\right) Q_i - \beta Q_i^2.$$

Assume that $\alpha > \gamma$, and define

$$Q_i' \equiv \sum_{j\neq i} Q_j , \qquad \delta \equiv \alpha - \gamma; \tag{2.2}$$

then firm i's profit can be expressed as

$$p(Q_i , Q_i') \equiv (\delta - \beta Q_i') Q_i - \beta Q_i^2. \tag{2.3}$$

Equations (2) and (3) define a game with N players, in which the pure strategy of player i is a nonnegative number Q_i, and his utility is $p(Q_i , Q_i')$.

It is easily verified that, given Q_i', the Q_i that maximizes i's profit is

$$r(Q_i') \begin{cases} \equiv \dfrac{\delta - \beta Q_i'}{2\beta}, & \text{if } \textit{this is nonnegative}, \\ \equiv 0, & \textit{otherwise}. \end{cases} \tag{2.4}$$

I shall call $r(Q_i')$ firm i's *best response* to Q_i'. If the best response is positive, firm i's corresponding maximum profit is

$$g(Q_i') = \frac{(\delta - \beta Q_i')^2}{4\beta}; \tag{2.5}$$

otherwise it is zero. A *Cournot–Nash equilibrium* (CNE) is an N-tuple (Q_i) of outputs such that, for each i, Q_i is the best response to $\sum_{j\neq i} Q_j$. In other words, a CNE is a solution (Q_i) of

$$r\left(\sum_{j\neq i} Q_j\right) = Q_i , \qquad i = i,..., N.$$

It is easily verified that the unique CNE is given by

$$Q_i = Q_N^* \equiv \frac{\delta}{(N+1)\beta}, \qquad i = 1,...., N, \tag{2.6}$$

and the corresponding CNE profit per firm is

$$\frac{\delta^2}{\beta(N+1)^2}. \tag{2.7}$$

Note that the total industry CNE output is

$$\frac{N\delta}{(N+1)\,\beta}, \tag{2.8}$$

and the total industry CNE profit is

$$\frac{N\delta^2}{(N+1)^2\,\beta}. \tag{2.9}$$

Therefore, as N increases without bound, total CNE industry output approaches δ/β, total industry CNE profit approaches zero, and CNE price approaches $\alpha - \delta = \gamma$ (i.e., marginal cost), all of which conditions characterize a competitive equilibrium.

If the industry acts as a cartel to maximize total industry profit then the cartel output is $(\delta/2\beta)$, and the corresponding cartel profit is $(\delta^2/4\beta)$. If the cartel output and profit were divided equally among the firms, then the corresponding cartel output per firm would be

$$\hat{Q}_N = \frac{\delta}{2\beta N}, \tag{2.10}$$

and the cartel profit per firm would be

$$\frac{\delta^2}{4\beta N}. \tag{2.11}$$

Note that if $N > 1$, then the cartel profit per firm is strictly greater than the CNE profit per firm, so that (from the point of view of the firms) the CNE is not Pareto optimal.

If the capacities of the firms are sufficiently large, then no coalition of fewer than N firms can guarantee itself more than a zero profit. That is to say, for any output of the coalition, there is an output of the other firms such that the coalition's profit is not greater than zero. Hence in this case, the core is the set of all nonnegative allocations of the cartel profit among the firms.[4] Given the symmetry among the firms, the equal division of the cartel profits is a "reasonable" target for cooperation, and in any case is the one to which attention will be given in this paper.

In what follows, I shall simplify the formulas by taking $\beta = 1$ and $\delta = 1$, unless notice is given to the contrary. This normalization will not entail any essential loss of generality.

[4] For a characterization of the core with arbitrary capacities, see Radner [4].

3. The Several-Period Cournot Game

Consider now a sequential, *T-period*, game in which the one-period game is repeated T times (T finite). The resulting utility to a firm is assumed to be the average of the T one-period profits. Let Q_{it} denote the output of firm i at date $t (1 \leqslant t \leqslant T)$, i.e., during the ith one-period game. A pure strategy for firm i is a sequence of functions, σ_{it}, one for each date t; the function for date t determines i's output at t as a function of the outputs of all firms at all previous dates. A Cournot–Nash equilibrium of the T-period game is a combination of strategies, one for each firm, such that each firm's strategy is a best response to the combination of the other firms' strategies.

The concept of *perfect* equilibrium of the T-period game has been introduced by Selten (1975) to rule out equilibria in which players use threats that are not credible. For every date t, let H_t denote the *history* of all the firms' outputs through t, i.e., the array of outputs Q_{ik}, $i = 1,..., N$, $k = 1,..., t$. For any sequential strategy σ_i for firm i, any date t and any history H_{t-1} let $\sigma_i[t, H_{t-1}]$ denote the *continuation* of σ_i from date t on, given the history H_{t-1}. A strategy combination (σ_i) is a *perfect* CNE if, for every date t and history H_{t-1}, the strategy combination $(\sigma_i[t, H_{t-1}])$ is a CNE of the sequential game corresponding to the remaining dates $t,..., T$. Note that in the definition of a perfect CNE one must test, for each t, whether the combination of continuations is a CNE for *all* possible histories H_{t-1}, not just the history that would be produced by the strategy combination (σ_i).

It is easy to verify that in every perfect CNE of the T-period game, each firm produces output Q^* at each date, where Q^* is given by (2.6). This can be seen by "working backwards," since at the end of period t the firms face a $(T - t)$- period game. The resulting utility to each firm is, from (2.7), $1/(N + 1)^2$. (Recall that $\beta = \delta = 1$.)

On the other hand, if each firm were to produce its cartel output $\hat{Q}$ at each date (see (2.10)), then the resulting utility to each player would be $1/4N$. Since there are several periods, the firms have the opportunity to react differently to cooperative and noncooperative moves by the other firms. For example, consider the following strategy: firm i produces output $\hat{Q}$ in each period as long as every other firm has been doing the same; thereafter firm i produces Q^* in each period. Call this strategy C_T. Formally, define D_i as follows:

$$D_i \begin{cases} = \infty, & \text{if } Q_{jt} = \hat{Q} \text{ for all } t \text{ and all } j \neq i, \\ = \min\{t: Q_{jt} \neq \hat{Q} \text{ for some } j \neq i\}, & \text{otherwise.} \end{cases} \tag{3.1}$$

The pure strategy C_T is defined by:

$$Q_{it} \begin{cases} = \hat{Q} & \text{if } t \leqslant D_i, \\ = Q^* & \text{if } t > D_i. \end{cases} \tag{3.2}$$

More generally, for any integer k between 0 and T define the pure strategy C_k by:

$$Q_{it} \begin{array}{ll} = \hat{Q} & \text{if} \quad t \leqslant \min(D_i, k), \\ = Q^* & \text{if} \quad t > \min(D_i, k). \end{array} \tag{3.3}$$

Note that if i uses the strategy C_0, then he always produces the CNE output Q^*.

The strategy C_k is a special case of a slightly more general class, which I shall call *trigger strategies of order k*. Let D_i be defined again as in (3.1) and let Q^D be some output. If $D_i \geqslant k$, then

$$\begin{array}{rll} & = \hat{Q} & \text{if} \quad t \leqslant k, \\ Q_{it} & = Q^D & \text{if} \quad t = k+1, \\ & = Q^* & \text{if} \quad t \geqslant k+2. \end{array} \tag{3.4}$$

If $D_i \leqslant k$, then

$$Q_{it} \begin{array}{ll} = \hat{Q} & \text{if} \quad t \leqslant D_i, \\ = Q^* & \text{if} \quad t > D_i. \end{array} \tag{3.5}$$

One might call Q^D the *defection output*, which i uses once only if all other firms have stayed with the cartel for (at least) k periods.

Suppose now that all firms other than i use the same trigger strategy of order $k > 0$, with defection output equal to Q^*. I shall show that i's best response is a trigger strategy of order $(k - 1)$, with a defection output equal to

$$\tilde{Q} \equiv r[(N-1)\,\hat{Q}] = \frac{N+1}{4N}. \tag{3.6}$$

Note that $\tilde{Q}$ is the best *one-period* response to a total output of $(N-1)\hat{Q}$ by all the other firms, and yields a one-period profit of

$$\frac{(N+1)^2}{16N^2}. \tag{3.7}$$

To prove this, first observe that if at some date t any firm i produces an output different from $\hat{Q}$, then at all subsequent dates all firms other than i will produce Q^*, and it will be optimal for firm i to do the same. Hence firm i's best response has the property that

$$\begin{array}{ll} Q_{jt} \neq \hat{Q} & \textit{for some } j \textit{ implies} \\ Q_{it'} = Q^* & \textit{for all } t' > t. \end{array} \tag{3.8}$$

It follows that firm i's best response to the given trigger strategies of order k is a trigger strategy of some order n. It is straightforward to verify that if $n < k$ then the optimal defection output is $\tilde{Q}$, with resulting *total* profit

$$\frac{n}{4N} + \frac{(N+1)^2}{16N^2} + \frac{T-n-1}{(N+1)^2}. \tag{3.9}$$

If $n = k$, then the optimal defection output is $r[(N-1)Q^*] = Q^*$, and the corresponding total profit is

$$\frac{k}{4N} + \frac{1}{(N+1)^2} + \frac{T-k-1}{(N+1)^2}. \tag{3.10}$$

Finally, if $n > k$, then i's defection output is irrelevant and the corresponding profit is

$$\frac{k}{4N} + p[\hat{Q}, (N-1)\, Q^*] + \frac{T-k-1}{(N+1)^2}. \tag{3.11}$$

In (3.10) and (3.11), if $k = T$, then it is to be understood that the final term in the equation is zero. Since

$$\left(\frac{N+1}{4N}\right)^2 > \frac{1}{4N} = g[(N-1)\, Q^*] > p[\hat{Q}, (N-1)\, Q^*],$$

and since (3.9) is increasing in n, it follows that i's optimal response has $n = (k-1)$. This completes the proof that i's *optimal response to a trigger strategy of order* $k > 0$ *with defection output* $Q^* > \hat{Q}$ *is a trigger strategy of order* $k-1$ *with defection output* $\tilde{Q}$. *The resulting average* profit for i is

$$\left(\frac{1}{T}\right)\left[\frac{k-1}{4N} + \left(\frac{N+1}{4N}\right)^2 + \frac{T-k}{(N+1)^2}\right]. \tag{3.12}$$

Note that neither i's optimal response nor his resulting average profit depend on the other firms' defection output.

In particular, if all firms $j(\neq i)$ use the trigger strategy C_T, then i's best response gives him an average profit of

$$\frac{1}{T}\left[\frac{T-1}{4N} + \left(\frac{N+1}{4N}\right)^2\right], \tag{3.13}$$

whereas if *all* firms use C_T, then every firm's average profit is $(1/4N)$, which is the cartel profit (per firm). The difference between (3.13) and the cartel profit per firm is

$$\left(\frac{1}{T}\right)\left(\frac{N-1}{4N}\right)^2. \tag{3.14}$$

Hence, as T increases without limit, the advantage to any one firm of defecting from the cartel one period before the end of the game approaches zero.

4. Epsilon-Equilibria

In the previous section it was noted that, in the T-period game, all perfect Cournot–Nash equilibria have the property that each firm produces the one-period CNE output in each period. On the other hand, the advantage to any one firm of defecting from the cartel approaches zero as T gets large, provided the other firms use trigger strategies of order T.

These considerations suggest a weakened form of the Cournot–Nash equilibrium concept. For any positive number ϵ, an *ϵ-equilibrium* is an N-tuple of strategies, one for each firm, such that each fiirm's average profit is within ϵ of the maximum average profit it could obtain against the other firms' strategies. In this and the following sections I shall explore some of the properties of epsilon-equilibria in the T-period Cournot game. I do not, however, have a complete characterization of epsilon-equilibria in this game.

The first candidate for an epsilon-equilibrium is the situation in which each firm uses the trigger strategy C_k (with defection output Q^*). From (3.10) and (3.12) we see that the difference in average profit between the best response and C_k, for an individual firm, is

$$\left(\frac{1}{T}\right)\left[\left(\frac{N+1}{4N}\right)^2 - \frac{1}{4N}\right] = \left(\frac{1}{T}\right)\left(\frac{N-1}{4N}\right)^2. \tag{4.1}$$

Hence the N-tuple (C_k) is an ϵ-equilibrium with $k > 0$ if and only if

$$\left(\frac{1}{T}\right)\left(\frac{N-1}{4N}\right)^2 \leqslant \epsilon \quad \text{or} \quad T \geqslant \left(\frac{1}{\epsilon}\right)\left(\frac{N-1}{4N}\right)^2. \tag{4.2}$$

Note that (4.2) is independent of k, so that either (C_k) is an ϵ-equilibrium for all $k = 1,..., T$, or for none. Note, too, that for fixed ϵ, (4.2) is satisfied uniformly in N for sufficiently large T. Of course, (C_0) is a Cournot–Nash equilibrium, so it is an ϵ-equilibrium for all ϵ.

The concept of perfect CNE can be extended to epsilon-equilibria as follows. A strategy combination (σ_j) is a *perfect* ϵ-equilibrium if for every date t, every history H_{t-1}, and every firm i, the continuation of i's strategy from date t on, given the history H_{t-1}, is within ϵ of being the best response to the corresponding continuations of the other firms' strategies. In this definition, the utility of a continuation of a strategy is the average of the profits in *all* T periods. (For an alternative definition, see Section 7.)

It is easy to verify that (4.2) is a necessary and sufficient condition for the combination (C_k) of trigger strategies to be a perfect ϵ-equilibrium. Hence, *for any $\epsilon > 0$ there is a T_ϵ such that, for all $T \geqslant T_\epsilon$ and all $k = 0,..., T$, there is a perfect ϵ-equilibrium in which each firm produces its cartel output for* *exactly k periods*. Furthermore, one can take T_ϵ to be independent of the number of firms.

An examination of (3.8)–(3.11) shows that one can get similar results for N-tuples of trigger strategies that use defection outputs other than Q^*, and even for N-tuples of trigger strategies that differ among firms in both the orders of the trigger strategies and the defection outputs. No attempt will be made here to characterize all such perfect epsilon-equilibria, but it is clear that for fixed ϵ, the larger T is the larger, in some sense, is the set of perfect ϵ-equilibria.

In the rest of this paper, all epsilon-equilibria are to be understood as perfect, unless specific notice is given to the contrary.

5. Large Number of Firms: The Fixed-Demand Case

In the last section I considered how the set of (perfect) ϵ-equilibria varied with T, the number of periods, with the number of firms fixed. In this section I consider the effect of increasing N, the number of firms, with the horizon, T, fixed. I first analyze the case in which the total industry demand function remains fixed as the number of firms varies. The results for this case will be used to analyze the more interesting, but slightly more complicated, replication case (Section 6).

To begin the analysis of the fixed-demand case, first observe that, by (4.2), for fixed T, there is no (C_k) ϵ-equilibrium ($k \geqslant 1$) for ϵ sufficiently small.

I shall prove, in addition, a result that is in some ways stronger. Roughly speaking, I shall show that if ϵ is small then all ϵ-equilibria are close to the CNE, *uniformly in N*. To be precise I shall show: for every $\epsilon > 0$ and $T \geqslant 1$ there is a number $B(\epsilon, T)$ such that for every $N > 1$ and every ϵ-equilibrium the following are all bounded by $B(\epsilon, T)$:

$$\begin{gathered} | Q_{it} - Q_N^* |, \\ \left| \sum_{i=1}^{N} Q_{it} - NQ_N^* \right|, \\ \left| p\left(Q_{it}, \sum_{j\neq i} Q_{jt}\right) - \frac{1}{(N+1)^2} \right|, \end{gathered} \tag{5.1}$$

for $i = 1,..., N$, $t = 1,..., T$. In addition, for every T

$$\lim_{\epsilon\to 0} B(\epsilon, T) = 0. \tag{5.2}$$

The first line of (5.1) is the difference between firm i's output in period t and CNE output; the second line is the difference between total industry output in period t and industry CNE output; and the third line is the difference between firm i's profit in period t and CNE profit per firm. It follows that, for any positive number d, and any horizon T, there is a positive ϵ such that, for all N and all ϵ-equilibria of the T-period game with N firms, industry outputs and market prices in all periods $t = 1,\dots, T$ will be within d of their corresponding one-period CNE values (note that ϵ does not depend on N). In particular, as N increases without limit, the corresponding one-period CNE values will converge to their respective competitive equilibrium values, and hence any corresponding sequence of ϵ-equilibria will approach the "neighborhood" of competitive equilibrium defined by the distance d, with respect to total industry output and price.

To prove (5.1) and (5.2), I shall first do the one-period case, and then make an induction on T. For the one-period case, an ϵ-equilibrium is an N-tuple $(Q_1, \dots, Q_N)$ satisfying

$$p\left(Q_i, \sum_{j \neq i} Q_j\right) \geqslant g\left(\sum_{j \neq i} Q_j\right) - \epsilon, \qquad i = 1,\dots, N. \tag{5.3}$$

Define new variables x_i and x_i' by

$$\begin{aligned} x_i &\equiv Q_i - Q_N^* = Q_i - \frac{1}{N+1}, \\ x_i' &\equiv \sum_{j \neq i} x_j . \end{aligned} \tag{5.4}$$

Using (2.3) and (2.5) one easily verifies that (5.3) is equivalent to

$$(x_i + (x_i'/2))^2 \leqslant \epsilon, \qquad i = 1,\dots, N,$$

or to

$$| x_i + x_. | \leqslant 2h, \qquad i = 1,\dots, N,$$

where

$$x_. \equiv \sum_{j=1}^{N} x_j , \qquad h \equiv (\epsilon)^{1/2}. \tag{5.5}$$

Summing the inequalities (5.5) one gets

$$| x_. | \leqslant \frac{2Nh}{N+1} ; \tag{5.6}$$

this and (5.5) imply

$$| x_i | \leqslant \frac{2(2N+1)\,h}{N+1} , \tag{5.7}$$

$$| x_i' | \leqslant \frac{2(3N+1)\,h}{N+1} . \tag{5.8}$$

LEMMA. *If* $|x| \leqslant b$ and $|x'| \leqslant b$, then

$$p[Q_N^* + x, (N-1)\, Q_N^* + x'] - p[Q_N^*, (N-1)\, Q_N^*]| \leqslant \frac{b}{N+1} + 2b^2. \tag{5.9}$$

Proof. The inequality can be verified using (2.3), (2.6), and (2.7).

Note that the right-hand sides of inequalities (5.6)–(5.8) are all dominated by $6h$. Hence, by the lemma, one can take

$$B(\epsilon, 1) = \max\left[6h, \frac{6h}{N+1} + 2(6h)^2\right]. \tag{5.10}$$

For ϵ sufficiently small $((\epsilon)^{1/2} \leqslant 1/18)$, the right side of (5.10) is $6h = 6(\epsilon)^{1/2}$.

Now make the induction hypothesis that the main result is true for any number of periods up to and including T. Fix ϵ, and consider any $(T+1)$-period ϵ-equilibrium. Given the initial outputs Q_{i1}, $i = 1,\dots, N$, the remaining T-period strategies constitute, *a fortiori*, a T-period, ϵ'-equilibrium, where

$$\epsilon' = \frac{(T+1)\,\epsilon}{T}. \tag{5.11}$$

Let i be any particular firm, which will remain fixed for the time being, let $Q = Q_{i1}$ be i's output in period 1, and let S denote the strategy that i follows during periods 2 through $(T+1)$. Given the strategies of the other firms, one may denote i's average profit as

$$\frac{p(Q, Q')}{T+1} + V(Q, S) \equiv \pi(Q, S), \tag{5.12}$$

where Q' is the total output in period one of all the firms other than i.

The induction hypothesis is that all of the quantities in (5.1), for $i = 1,\dots, N$ and $t = 2,\dots, T+1$, are bounded by $b \equiv B(\epsilon', T)$. Actually, I shall strengthen the induction hypothesis to add the following inequalities:

$$\left|\sum_{j\neq i} Q_{jt} - (N-1)\, Q_N^*\right| \leqslant b, \qquad i = 1,\dots, N, \quad t = 2,\dots, T+1. \tag{5.13}$$

The definition of epsilon-equilibrium implies that

$$\pi(Q, S) \geqslant M - \epsilon,$$

where (5.14)

$$M \equiv \max_{q,s} \pi(q, s).$$

(In the definition of M, (q, s) ranges over all $(T+1)$-period strategies for firm i, holding constant the ϵ-equilibrium strategies of the other firms.) This last is equivalent to

$$\frac{p(Q, Q')}{T+1} + V(Q, S) \geqslant M - \epsilon,$$

or

$$p(Q, Q') \geqslant (T+1)[M - \epsilon - V(Q, S)]. \tag{5.15}$$

By the induction hypothesis,

$$\frac{(T+1)\, V(Q, S)}{T} - \frac{1}{(N+1)^2} \leqslant b. \tag{5.16}$$

To get a bound on M, note that

$$(T+1)M \geqslant g(Q') + Tm,$$

where

$$m = \max_X \min_Y \{p(X, Y): |\, Y - (N-1)\, Q_N^* \,| \leqslant b\}. \tag{5.17}$$

One easily verifies that

$$m = g[(N-1)\, Q_N^* + b] = \frac{1}{(N+1)^2} - \frac{b}{(N+1)} + \frac{b^2}{4}. \tag{5.18}$$

Putting together (5.15)–(5.18), one has

$$p(Q, Q') \geqslant g(Q') - \epsilon'',$$

where

$$\epsilon'' = \frac{T(N+2)\, b}{(N+1)} + (T+1)\, \epsilon. \tag{5.19}$$

The inequality (5.19) holds for all firms i. In other words, in a $(T+1)$-period ϵ-equilibrium, the first-period outputs constitute a one-period ϵ''-equilibrium, where ϵ'' is given by (5.19) and

$$b = B\left[\frac{(T+1)}{T}\, \epsilon, T\right]. \tag{5.20}$$

Hence, by the one-period case, the quantities in (5.1) and (5.13), with $t = 1$, are all bounded by

$$b' = 6(\epsilon'')^{1/2} = 6\left[\frac{T(N+2)\, b}{(N+1)} + (T+1)\, \epsilon\right]^{1/2}, \tag{5.21}$$

provided that $\epsilon''^{1/2} \leqslant 1/18$. If we take

$$B(\epsilon, T+1) = \max\{b', B(\epsilon, T)\}, \qquad (5.22).$$

then the induction step is completed, as far as the inequalities (5.1) and (5.13) are concerned. Furthermore, (5.20)–(5.22) determine a recursion formula for the bounds $B(\epsilon, T)$, which with the formulas (5.5) and (5.10) for $B(\epsilon, 1)$ prove (5.2), i.e., that $B(\epsilon, T)$ tends to zero as ϵ tends to zero, for fixed T.

6. Large Numbers of Firms: The Replication Case

In the replication case, the demand function depends on the number of firms, so that corresponding to (2.1) we have

$$P = \alpha - \frac{\beta_1 Q}{N}, \qquad (6.1)$$

where Q is the total industry output, P is the demand price, and β_1 is a parameter that is independent of N, the number of firms. One may motivate this formulation in terms of replicating an industry. Consider an industry with 1 firm and a given population of M potential buyers, whose demand function is given by

$$Q = \frac{\alpha - P}{\beta_1}. \qquad (6.2)$$

The N-fold replication of this industry is made up of N firms, together with a population of NM potential buyers with the same per capita demand at any price as the original population. The resulting demand function is then

$$\frac{Q}{N} = \frac{\alpha - P}{\beta_1},$$

which is equivalent to (6.1). Without essential loss of generality, I shall take $\beta_1 = 1$ and $\delta = \alpha - \gamma = 1$.

Corresponding to the formulas of Section 2, one has the following formulas, obtained by everywhere replacing β by $1/N$. Firm i's profit function is

$$p(Q_i, Q_i') = \left(1 - \frac{Q_i'}{N}\right) Q_i - \frac{Q_i^2}{N}. \qquad (6.3)$$

Its optimal response to Q_i' is

$$r(Q_i') \begin{cases} = \dfrac{N - Q_i'}{2N}, & \text{if } \textit{this is positive}, \\ = 0, & \textit{otherwise}, \end{cases} \qquad (6.4)$$

and its corresponding profit is

$$g(Q_i') = \frac{(N - Q_i')^2}{4N}, \tag{6.5}$$

if this is nonnegative, and zero otherwise.

The one-period CNE output and profit per firm are given by

$$Q_N^* = \frac{N}{N+1}, \tag{6.6}$$

$$g[(N-1)\,Q_N^*] = \frac{N}{(N+1)^2}. \tag{6.7}$$

The one-period cartel output and profit per firm are

$$\hat{Q}_N = \tfrac{1}{2}, \tag{6.8}$$

$$p[\hat{Q}_N, (N-1)\hat{Q}_N] = \tfrac{1}{4}. \tag{6.9}$$

Firm i's best response if each other firm produces the cartel output is

$$r[(N-1)\,\hat{Q}_N] = \frac{N+1}{4N}, \tag{6.10}$$

with corresponding profit

$$g[(N-1)\,\hat{Q}_N] = \frac{(N+1)^2}{16N}. \tag{6.11}$$

Turning to the T-period game, one easily verifies that the strategy combination in which each firm has the trigger strategy C_k (cf. Section 4) is an ϵ-equilibrium if and only if

$$T \geqslant \left(\frac{N}{\epsilon}\right)\left(\frac{N-1}{4N}\right)^2; \tag{6.12}$$

compare this with (4.2). Hence, as in the fixed-demand case, for every ϵ and N, every (C_k) strategy combination is an ϵ-equilibrium for all sufficiently large T. However, in this case one gets the result that, for fixed ϵ and T, no (C_k) strategy combination ($k > 0$) is an ϵ-equilibrium for sufficiently large N. In other words, *for any fixed ϵ and number of periods, the cartel cannot survive at all if the number of firms is large enough.*

Corresponding to the rest of the analysis in Section 5, one has the following results. For every ϵ, T, and $N(>1)$, there is a number $B(\epsilon, T, N)$ such that, in every ϵ-equilibrium, the following quantities are bounded by $B(\epsilon, T, N)$:

$$\begin{gathered} | Q_{it} - Q_N^* |, \\ \left| \sum_j Q_{it} - NQ_N^* \right|, \end{gathered} \tag{6.13}$$

for $i = 1, \ldots, N$ and $t = 1, \ldots, T$; the bounds $B(\epsilon, T, N)$ may be chosen so that, for every ϵ and T,

$$\frac{B(\epsilon, T, N)}{N^{1/2}} \text{ is uniformly bounded in } N, \tag{6.14}$$

and for every T and N,

$$\lim_{\epsilon \to 0} B(\epsilon, T, N) = 0. \tag{6.15}$$

It follows from (6.6) that average output per firm approaches 1, and market price approaches $1 - \alpha = \gamma$ (marginal cost) as N increases without limit. In addition, in every period every firm i's *relative* share of total industry output, which is

$$\frac{Q_{it}}{\sum_j Q_{jt}} = \frac{(1/N)\, Q_{it}}{(1/N) \sum_j Q_{jt}},$$

converges to zero as N gets large. Finally, one can show that, in every period, every firm i's profit is within

$$\frac{B(\epsilon, T, N)}{N+1} + \frac{2[B(\epsilon, T, N)]^2}{N} \tag{6.16}$$

of the one-period CNE profit, which is $N/(N+1)^2$, and this bound is uniformly bounded in N, and goes to zero with ϵ.

Thus, in these various ways, for large N, ϵ-equilibria are close to competitive equilibrium.

I shall omit the proof of these results, which parallels the argument in Section 5. The key facts are that, for the one-period case, Eqs. (5.5)–(5.8) are still valid, but with

$$h = (N\epsilon)^{1/2}, \tag{6.17}$$

and in the Lemma of Section 5, the right side of (5.9) must be replaced by

$$\frac{b}{N+1} + \frac{2b^2}{N}, \tag{6.18}$$

which is less than b for

$$b < \frac{N^2}{2(N+1)}. \tag{6.19}$$

In particular, for the one-period case one can take

$$B(\epsilon, 1, N) = (N\epsilon)^{1/2}, \tag{6.20}$$

provided that

$$(\epsilon)^{1/2} \leqslant \frac{N}{12(N+1)}. \tag{6.21}$$

7. An Alternative Definition of Perfect Epsilon-Equilibrium

As an alternative to the definition of perfect epsilon-equilibrium given in Section 4, one can take the utility of the continuation of a strategy to be the average of the profits in the remaining periods, rather than the average of the profits in all T periods.[5] This change leads to a definition of perfect epsilon-equilibrium that is more restrictive, in the sense that, for every positive epsilon, the set of perfect epsilon-equilibria is smaller. Results analogous to those of Sections 5 and 6 can be derived for this definition; I omit the details. However, the results in Section 4, on trigger strategies, are changed in an interesting way. For a fixed positive epsilon, and a fixed number of firms, the combination (C_k) of trigger strategies is a perfect epsilon-equilibrium for all sufficiently large horizons T and all k not too close to T, namely, if and only if

$$T - k \geqslant \left(\frac{1}{\epsilon}\right)\left(\frac{N-1}{4N}\right)^2 - 1.$$

Thus, for this alternative definition of epsilon-equilibrium, *a cartel held together by trigger strategies will break down as the industry approaches the horizon T.*

8. Interpretations of Epsilon

Why should a firm be satisfied with a less-than-optimal response to the strategies of other firms? One type of answer refers to the various costs of discovering and using alternative strategies, and alludes to the possibility that a truly optimal response might be more costly to discover and use than some alternative, "nearly optimal" strategy. In this interpretation, the "epsilon" for a particular firm represents a judgement of the firm that the additional benefits from improving its strategy would be outweighed by the additional costs. (In the present analysis, all firms were assumed to have the same epsilon, but this simplification is not strictly needed for the results.) It would be consistent with the spirit of the model for this judgement to be in part subjective, rather than necessarily based on some precise calculation of benefits and costs.

A second interpretation of epsilon might be based on the supposition that the firms realize that strict optimization of each firm's response to the other firms' strategies would lead to a breakdown of the cartel. This approach is intuitively appealing, but I am not aware of any satisfactory formal model of rational behavior on which it could be based.

Recall that, in the model of the present paper, it is assumed that each firm uses the criterion of average profit per period to compare strategies; thus

[5] This alternative was suggested to me by Sanford Grossman and Robert Rosenthal.

epsilon is measured in "dollars per period." This scale of measurement would be consistent with the cost-of-decision interpretation of epsilon-equilibrium. In a more general treatment, epsilon would be measured in units of utility. However, epsilon-equilibria would not be invariant under transformations of the utility functions of the firms that change the unit of measurement of utility. For example, if the preferences of a firm were scaled in terms of a von Neumann–Morgenstern utility function, then epsilon-equilibria would not be invariant under all transformations of the utility function that leave the firm's preferences invariant. A solution to this last problem would be to adopt a "canonical" utility representation for each firm, and then to interpret epsilon with reference to those canonical utility functions. This would be equivalent, for each firm, to interpreting epsilon as a given *percentage* of the difference in utility between two reference profits. Within this framework, the interpretation of the results of the present paper is straightforward, with the proviso that, for those situations in which the number of firms increases without limit, some condition of "similarity" of the epsilons of the different firms would have to be satisfied (as would naturally occur in the replication case).

Acknowledgments

I am grateful to R. Rosenthal, C. Futia, and A. Mas-Colell for helpful discussions of this problem. Preliminary versions of this paper were presented at the North American regional meeting of the Econometric Society, Boulder, Colo., June 1978, and at the IMSSS, Stanford University, July 1978. I thank J. Fraysse and M. Moreaux for pointing out an error in the previous published version. The views expressed here are those of the author and do not necessarily reflect those of Bell Laboratories or the Bell System.

References

1. A. Cournot, "Researches into the Mathematical Principles of the Theory of Wealth," Nathaniel T. Bacon, trans., Macmillan, New York/London, 1897; reprinted with notes by Irving Fisher, Macmillan, 1927; reprinted, Richard D. Irwin, Inc., Homewood, Ill., 1963; originally published as "Recherches sur les principes mathématiques de la théorie des Richesses," Hachette, Paris, 1838.
2. W. Novshek, "Nash–Cournot Equilibrium with Entry," Discussion Paper No. 303, Center for Math. Studies in Econ. and Man. Sci., Northwestern University, August 1977.
3. W. Novshek and H. Sonnenschein, Cournot and Walras equilibrium, *J. Econ. Theory* **19** (1978), 223–266.
4. R. Radner, Notes on the core of a cartel, unpublished lecture notes, Dept. of Econ., University of California, Berkeley, 1977.
5. A. Rubinstein, "Equilibrium in Supergames," Research Memorandum No. 25, Center for Research in Math. Economics and Game Theory, The Hebrew University, Jerusalem, May 1977.
6. A. Rubinstein, Equilibrium in supergames with the overtaking criterion, *J. Econ. Theory* **21** (1979), 1–9.
7. R. Selten, Re-examination of the perfectness concept for equilibrium points in extensive games, *Int. J. Game Theory* **4** (1975), 25–55.

Noncooperative Price Taking in Large Dynamic Markets

EDWARD J. GREEN*

California Institute of Technology, Pasadena, California 91125

Received March 21, 1979

1. INTRODUCTION

In "Researches into the Mathematical Principles of the Theory of Wealth" [1], Cournot founded the theory of oligopoly. His contribution can be divided into two parts. First, he proposed a static noncooperative equilibrium concept for a situation of dynamic inter-firm conflict. Second, he showed that this equilibrium solution coincides with perfect competition in markets where there are many agents.

Cournot's solution for oligopoly has come under heavy criticism for its static nature. Is it really plausible, the critics ask, that the commitment of each firm to a long-term level of production brings an end to strategic interaction in a market? A strongly opposing view has been put forth by Stigler, who suggests (in [9]) that firms in an oligopoly maintain a monopolistic price by threatening defectors with retaliatory actions. Such retaliation presupposes a dynamic equilibrium in which each firm observes the ongoing behavior of its rivals and makes decisions over time contingent on that behavior. The prerequisite for collusive equilibrium of this type is not necessarily that each individual firm should be capable of significantly affecting aggregate output, but only that each firm's action (whatever its scale relative to the industry) should be visible to its competitors. On this account, it has been suggested that even some very large markets may fail to be competitive.[1]

* Financial support for this research was provided through a grant from the Sloan Foundation to the Princeton University Economics Department. I would like to express my appreciation to Edward Prescott, who drew my attention to the problem studied here. I am grateful to Robert Anderson and Hugo Sonnenschein for discussions and suggestions which have greatly improved the paper.

[1] For instance, it has been suggested that markets for the services of doctors and other professionals are not competitive, despite the presence (at least in large cities) of many sellers. The presence of legal barriers to entry in these markets may explain why professionals earn more than they would in alternative employment, but it would not by itself account for the observation of price discrimination by professionals. An equal-profit condition would be satisfied in static equilibrium, because professionals would bid away from their colleagues those types of client whom it was particularly profitable to serve.

Reprinted from *Journal of Economic Theory* **22**, No. 2, 155–182 (April 1980)
ISBN 0-12-476750-8

In the present paper, Cournot's proposition that large markets are competitive will be reconciled with the possibility of equilibrium involving strategic interaction among firms. It will be shown that, except when extraordinarily precise information is available, firms in a market with many agents are not visible enough for the equilibrium described by Stigler to be sustained. This result will be proved by studying two formal representations of markets with many agents.

One of these representations involves initially choosing a particular market (with finitely many participants), and then forming a sequence of increasingly large markets by adjoining at each stage a new copy of the original one. The result of this procedure is called a *sequence of replica markets*. All of the markets in the sequence have the same statistical characteristics (e.g., the ratio of firms to consumers is constant), and they all share the same competitive market-clearing prices. Thus, it makes sense to ask whether the noncooperative equilibria of the markets in the sequence converge to competition. We will say that the *limit principle* is satisfied in situations where this convergence takes place.

The other representation of markets with many agents exploits the fact that, if counting measure on the set of agents in a market is normalized to make the set into a probability space, then a description of agents' characteristics and actions is mathematically a random vector defined on the sample space of agents. An analogous random vector defined on a nonatomic sample space may be substituted for a large finite market as an object of investigation. Such a random vector, called a *nonatomic market*, is natural to study because one occurs as the limit of a replica sequence of markets. We will say that the *inclusion principle* is satisfied in a situation where every noncooperative equilibrium of a nonatomic market is competitive.[2]

The outline of the paper is as follows. A dynamic noncooperative equilibrium concept will be developed in the next section. Then, in Section 3, a sequence of replica markets will be defined, each of which has a noncooperative equilibrium which supports the monopoly allocation at every time. This example refutes the limit principle for dynamic equilibrium. An example is also given in which, if each firm can observe the output level of every other firm, then a collusive noncooperative equilibrium exists for a market with a continuum of firms. Thus the most general form of the inclusion principle is refuted as well. Together these examples suggest that, even when there are

[2] Representations of markets with many agents have been used extensively to study the core of an economy. A standard reference for this work is [5]. Although results for the core are not very sensitive to which representation is used, there are substantial differences between the conditions which are sufficient to ensure the limit principle and the inclusion principle for noncooperative equilibrium. This matter is discussed in [2]. The term "inclusion principle," rather than "equivalence principle," is used here because of the issues raised in [6].

many firms, the potential for collusion envisioned by Stigler may still exist. In the remaining sections of the paper, the special nature of such potentially collusive markets will be shown.

In the counterexample to the inclusion principle, firms are required to have exhaustive non-price information about their competitors. In Section 4, it is proved that all equilibria which violate the principle require such information. This is done by interpreting dynamic markets within an abstract theory of repeated games, and providing a sufficient condition for all Nash equilibria of a repeated game to be constructible from Nash equilibria of the static game on which it is based. This condition yields an inclusion theorem for dynamic markets in which agents have information only about price and other market aggregates.

The inclusion principle derived in Section 4 sheds light on the failure of the limit principle. The principle must fail because there is information about individual producers which the price mechanism conveys in every finite market, but not in a nonatomic one. In fact, in a finite market, price information can reveal to a firm that a competitor has disregarded its strategic threat, although the identity of the violator is not revealed. If the price varies because of random demand, its informativeness about the supply side of the market should be reduced. As the scale of an individual producer becomes arbitrarily small relative to market demand in a sequence of replica dynamic markets, any stochastic demand disturbance should make strategic threats unenforceable in the limit. This is proved in Section 5, again in an abstract game-theoretic context. It yields a limit theorem for dynamic markets with demand uncertainty.

In Section 6 some concluding remarks are made concerning the relevance of the present results to industrial organization.

2. Noncooperative Equilibria Which Support the Monopoly Allocation

The first inclusion and limit theorems were derived by Cournot in a static partial equilibrium setting. These will be reviewed in this section, and counterexamples to their dynamic versions will be given in the next. These results may be reformulated in a general equilibrium setting. The positive results of this paper are immediate consequences of game theoretic results which apply straightforwardly to the general equilibrium version.

First, static and dynamic markets are defined. Intuitively, a static market consists of a set of firms, each of which supplies the market good at a total cost which depends on the quantity it produces, and an inverse demand function which determines the price as a function of mean supply. Implicitly, this inverse demand function is determined by the actions of price-taking consumers. The question to be investigated is: are profit-maximizing firms also price-takers when there are many firms?

A (stationary) dynamic market is a static market which operates repeatedly, its times of operation being indexed by the natural numbers. Firms maximize the discounted present value of their profits.[3] These definitions are now presented formally:

DEFINITION. A *cost function* is an element of the set $Y = \{f \mid f: R_+ \to R_+ \cup \{\infty\}, f \text{ is continuous}\}$. A *normal inverse demand function* is a continuous function $D: R_+ \cup \{\infty\} \to R_+$ with $D(\infty) = 0$. A *static market* is an ordered 4-tuple $\langle K, \mu, y, D\rangle$ where K is an abstract set of firms, μ is a probability measure on K, $y: K \to Y$ is a measurable function (Y may be considered discrete) which specified the cost function of each firm, and D is a normal inverse demand function. A (stationary) *dynamic market* is an ordered 5-tuple $\langle K, \mu, y, D, \beta\rangle$, of which the first four components specify a static market and $\beta \in (0, 1)$ is the market discount factor. Let M be a market (static or dynamic) with measure space $\langle K, \mu\rangle$ of firms. A *supply vector* for M is a bounded μ-measurable function $q: K \to R_+$.

Given a supply vector q for M, mean supply will be $\int_K q(k)\, d\mu$ and the market price will $D(\int_K q(k)\, d\mu)$. If a firm $k \in K$ has cost function $y(k) = f$, then a supply vector determines a net profit level for k. This net profit will be denoted by $\pi_k(q)$, and satisfies the equation

$$\pi_k(q) = q(k)\, D\left(\int_K q(i)\, d\mu\right) - f(q(k)). \tag{1}$$

In selecting its output level, either a firm may accept the market price as an exogenous parameter of its decision problem, or it may recognize its own influence on the market price. A price-taking equilibrium results when all firms act in the former way, and a noncooperative equilibrium results when they act in the latter way.

DEFINITION. A *price-taking equilibrium* of the static market $\langle K, \mu, y, D\rangle$ is a supply vector q such that, for almost all (w.r.t. μ) $k \in K$,

$$\pi_k(q) = \max_{r \in R_+} \left[rD\left(\int_K q(i)\, d\mu\right) - (y(k))(r)\right]. \tag{2}$$

[3] The present formulation of dynamic markets is restrictive. For instance, it does not allow for the holding of inventories. The inclusion theorem (Theorem 5) to be proved here generalizes straightforwardly to apply to richer models. I am confident that the limit theorem (Theorem 6) is also robust.

A *price-taking equilibrium* of the dynamic market $\langle K, \mu, y, D, \beta\rangle$ is a sequence $\langle q_t\rangle_{t\in N}$ of supply vectors such that, for almost all $k \in K$,

$$\sum_{t\in N} \beta^t \pi_k(q_t) = \max \left\{ \sum_{t\in N} \beta^t \left[r_t D \left(\int_K q_t(i)\, d\mu \right) - (y(k))(r_t) \right) \Big| \langle r_t\rangle_{t\in N} \in R_+{}^N \right\}. \tag{3}$$

A *noncooperative equilibrium* of the static market $\langle K, \mu, y, D\rangle$ is a supply vector q^* juch that, for almost all $k \in K$,

$$\pi_k(q^*) = \max_{q\in Q} \left[q(k)\, D \left(\int_K q(i)\, d\mu \right) - (y(k))(q(k)) \right], \tag{4}$$

where $Q = \{q \mid q \text{ is a supply vector and } q(i) = q^*(i) \text{ for all } i \neq k\}$.

To define noncooperative equilibrium for a dynamic market, the notion of a strategy must be introduced. A strategy of a firm is a rule which, at each time, determines an output level for the firm as a function of information which is available to the firm at that time. A strategy vector is an assignment of strategies to firms. Thus, if S is the space of strategies, a strategy vector is a measurable function f: $X \rightarrow S$. A noncooperative equilibrium of a dynamic market is a strategy vector f such that

(a) for almost all $k \in K$, $f(k)$ yields as high a discounted present value of returns (given that the other firms are using the strategies assigned to them by f) as would any other strategy $s \in S$, and

(b) Clause (a) will continue to hold at every future time for almost all $k \in K$, regardless of firms' information at that time.[4]

This rather informal definition of dynamic noncooperative equilibrium will be adequate to verify that the strategy vectors to be discussed in this section are equilibria. A more explicit definition will be given in Section 4. In the remainder of this section, straightforward generalizations of Cournot's theorems for static markets will be stated. The statement of the inclusion theorem requires no further preparation.

[4] Clause (b) ensures that a firm will not base its initial output decision on an expectation that, at a later time, it will produce at a level which from the perspective of that time will seem suboptimal. In the next section, equilibria will be studied in which firms in a market maintain collusion by means of mutual strategic threats. Although these threats will not be exercised in equilibrium, they will not have a deterrent effect unless it would be in the firms' interest to exercise them in the event that deviation from the cartel did occur. This explains why (a) must hold even conditional on firms having received information which they in fact will not receive in equilibrium. Condition (b) was introduced (in [8]) by Selten, whose concept of perfect Nash equilibrium is equivalent to the dynamic NCE defined here.

THEOREM 1. *Every noncooperative equilibrium of a nonatomic static market is a price-taking equilibrium.*

To facilitate the statement of Cournot's limit theorem, the notion of a sequence of replica markets is introduced. Intuitively, such a series is formed by starting with a finite market, and at each stage adding a new "twin" of each of the original market agents (firms and consumers). This is done explicitly for firms, but must be done implicitly for consumers. Since there are n times as many consumers of each type in the nth market as in the first, aggregate demand in the nth market at any price is n times what it is in the first. However, since the inverse demand function is defined formally in terms of mean quantity rather than of aggregate quantity, and since there are n firms in the nth market for every one in the first, all markets in the sequence should share the same inverse demand function. As replication continues, the members of the sequence should resemble the nonatomic representation of the market in their equilibrium behavior. The sequences are now defined formally, after which Cournot's limit theorem is immediately stated.

DEFINITION. A *sequence of replica* (*static or dynamic*) *markets* is an infinite sequence $\langle M_n \rangle_{n \in N}$ of markets such that the following hold for some finite set K, $y\colon K \to Y$, $\beta \in (0, 1)$ and normal inverse demand function D. For all n, $M_n = \langle K_n, \mu_n, y_n, D, \beta \rangle$, where

$$K_n = K \times \{0 \cdots n\} \tag{5}$$

$$\mu_n(B) = \#B/\#K_n \qquad \text{for all } B \subseteq K_n . \tag{6}$$

(That is, μ_n is normalized counting measure.)

$$y_n(\langle k, m \rangle) = y(k) \qquad \text{for} \quad k \in K,\ m \leqslant n. \tag{7}$$

The market $M_\infty = \langle K \times [0, 1], \mu_\infty, y_\infty, D, \beta \rangle$ is the *nonatomic representation* of the sequence if

$$\mu_\infty(B) = \sum_{k \in K} \lambda(\{r \in [0, 1] \mid \langle k, r \rangle \in B\}) \qquad \text{for all} \quad B \subseteq K \times [0, 1]. \tag{8}$$

(That is, μ_∞ is Lebesgue measure on the copies of [0, 1] in K_∞.)

$$y_\infty(\langle k, r \rangle) = y(k) \qquad \text{for all} \quad \langle k, r \rangle \in K_\infty . \tag{9}$$

THEOREM 2. *Suppose that $\langle M_n \rangle_{n \in N}$ is a sequence of replica static markets, that the supply vector q_n is a noncooperative equilibrium of M_n for every n,* *and that some subsequence of* $\langle\langle q_n, y_n\rangle\rangle_{n\in N}$ converges in distribution:[5] Then the subsequence has a limit $\langle q_\infty, y_\infty\rangle$, and q_∞ is a price-taking equilibrium of the nonatomic representation M_∞.

3. Noncooperative Equilibria Which Support the Monopoly Allocation *(continued)*

Counterexamples to the analogs of Theorems 1 and 2 for dynamic markets are constructed by exhibiting noncooperative equilibria of large markets, in which the monopoly price is maintained by mutual strategic threats among the firms. The existence of these equilibria in markets with finitely many firms was first pointed out by Friedman [4]. A counterexample is provided to the analog of Theorem 2, simply by noting that such an equilibrium may exist for every market in a sequence of replica dynamic markets. Such a sequence is easy to construct. It requires only one type of firm (K is a singleton $\{k\}$) with a production function $y(k) = f$ described by

$$\begin{aligned} f(r) &= 0, && \text{if } r \leqslant \tfrac{2}{3} \\ &= r - \tfrac{2}{3}, && \text{if } r > \tfrac{2}{3}. \end{aligned} \tag{10}$$

Price is specified by the inverse demand function

$$\begin{aligned} D(r) &= 1 - r, && \text{if } r \leqslant 1 \\ &= 0, && \text{if } r > 1. \end{aligned} \tag{11}$$

The discount factor for the sequence is $\beta = 0.9$. The counterexample to the limit principle is now presented.

Theorem 3. *There exist a sequence of replica dynamic economies* $\langle M_n\rangle_{n\in N}$ *and a double sequence of supply vectors* $\langle q_{nt}\rangle_{n,t\in n}$ *such that*

(a) *For each* n, *the sequence of supply vectors* $\langle q_{nt}\rangle_{t\in N}$ *is determined (in the sense that* q_{nt} *specifies firms' output levels at time* t*) by a noncooperative equilibrium of* M_n, *and*

(b) *For each* t *there is a supply vector* $q_{\infty t}$ *such that* $\lim_{n\to\infty} q_{nt} = q_{\infty t}$ *in distribution, but*

(c) $\langle q_{\infty t}\rangle_{t\in N}$ *is not a price-taking equilibrium of the nonatomic representation* M_∞ *of the sequence.*

[5] Let Z be a metric space. A sequence $\langle \eta_n\rangle_{n\in N}$ of probability measures converges weakly to a probability measure η if, for every bounded continuous function $f\colon Z \to R$, $\lim_{n\to\infty} \int_Z f d\eta_n \to \int_Z f d\eta$. If $\langle \Omega_n, \mu_n\rangle_{n\in N}$ is a sequence of probability spaces and $\langle \Omega, \mu\rangle$ is a probability space, and if $z_n : \Omega_n \to Z$ for every n, then $\langle z_n\rangle_{n\in N} \to z : \Omega \to Z$ in distribution if, when the measures η_n are defined by $\eta_n(B) = \mu_n(\{z_n \in B\})$ for all Borel sets $B \subseteq Z$ (and η is defined analogously for z), then $\langle \eta_n\rangle \to \eta$ weakly.

Proof. Let $\langle M_n \rangle_{n \in N}$ be determined by the conditions that $K = \{k\}$, $y(k) = f$ defined by (10), D is determined by Eq. (11), and $\beta = 0.9$. Recall that a strategy for a firm in a dynamic market is a rule which, at each time, determines an output level on the basis of information then available to the firm. The double sequence $\langle q_{nt} \rangle_{n,t \in N}$ will specify the output decisions of firms which follow the strategy

(d) Produce at level $\frac{1}{2}$ (the monopoly level) at time 0.

(e) If $D(\int_{K_n} q_{n0}\, d\mu_n) = D(\int_{K_n} q_{nt-1)}\, d\mu_n) = \frac{1}{2}$. Then produce at level $\frac{1}{2}$ at time t.

(f) If the condition of (e) is not satisfied at t, then produce at level $\frac{2}{3}$ (the output level corresponding to the unique noncooperative equilibrium of the static market $\langle K_n, \mu_n, y_n, D \rangle$).

By induction on t, $g_{nt} \equiv \frac{1}{2}$ for all n and t. Therefore condition (b) is satisfied with $q_{\infty t} = \frac{1}{2}$ for all t. Condition (c) is also satisfied, since $D(\int_{K_\infty} q_{\infty t}\, d\mu_\infty) = \frac{1}{2}$ while firms have zero marginal cost. Condition (a) is equivalent to the statement, proved below as Lemma 1, that for all firms to follow the strategy defined by (d), (e), and (f) is a noncooperative equilibrium of M_n. Q.E.D.

LEMMA 1. *For all firms to employ the strategy defined by* (d), (e), *and* (f) *above is a noncooperative equilibrium of the dynamic market* M_n.

Proof. Intuitively, each firm makes a strategic threat to the others. It announces: "Initially, we will participate in a cartel in which all firms produce equal shares of the monopoly output $n/2$. We will do our part to maintain this cartel, as long as there is reciprocity. However, if at any time a lowering of the market price indicates that another firm is exceeding its production limit, we will thereafter protect ourselves by acting as static Cournot oligopolists."

Consider the prospects of a potential deviant firm, if all other firms make this threat. Suppose that it were to adopt a strategy which would lead it, in this environment, to select an output sequence $\langle r_t \rangle_{t \in N}$. It will be shown that $r_t = \frac{1}{2}$ for all t is optimal. Because the strategy (d), (e), (f) produces this sequence if all other firms follow (d), (e), (f), part (a) of the definition of noncooperative equilibrium for a dynamic market is satisfied.

To show this, consider first an output sequence $\langle r_t \rangle_{t \in N}$ with $r_t \neq \frac{1}{2}$ for some t. Let $t_0 = \min\{t \mid r_t \neq \frac{1}{2}\}$. If other firm's outputs are determined by (d), (e), and (f), then the market price at time t is

$$
\begin{aligned}
D\left(\int_{K_n} q_{nt}\, d\mu_n\right) &= \tfrac{1}{2} && \text{for} \quad t < t_0 \\
&= (n + 1 - 2r_t)/2n && \text{for} \quad t = t_0 \qquad (12) \\
&= (n + 2 - 3r_t)/3n && \text{for} \quad t_0 < t.
\end{aligned}
$$

Since the outputs of other firms are the same for all sequences $\langle r'_t \rangle_{t \in N}$ which satisfy $t_0 = \min\{t \mid r'_t \neq \frac{1}{2}\}$, r_t must be the output level which maximizes returns at time t for $t_0 \leqslant t$; i.e., by (12),

$$r_{t_0}(n + 1 - 2r_{t_0})/2n - f(r_{t_0}) = \max_{r \in R_+} r(n + 1 - 2r)/2n - f(r), \quad (13)$$

and

$$r_t(n + 2 - 3r_t)/3n - f(r_t) = \max_{r \in R_+} r(n + 2 - 3r)/3n - f(r) \quad \text{for} \quad t_0 < t. \quad (14)$$

Solving Eqs. (13) and (14) yields $r_t = \frac{2}{3}$ for all $t \geqslant t_0$. Thus discounted profits are

$$\begin{aligned} \sum_{t \in N} (0.9)^t \left[\mathrm{r}_t D \left(\int_{K_n} q_{nt}\, d\mu_t \right) - f(r_t) \right] &\leqslant \sum_{t<t_0} (0.9)^t \, [(1/2)(1/2) - 0] \\ &\quad + (0.9)^{t_0} \, [(2/3)(1/2) - 0] \\ &\quad + \sum_{t_0<t} (0.9)^t \, [(2/3)(1/3) - 0] \\ &= \Big(\sum_{t<t_0} (0.9)^t \Big) \Big/ 4 + (0.9)^{t_0} \, (7/3). \quad (15) \end{aligned}$$

On the other hand, if $r'_t = \frac{1}{2}$ for all t and if $\langle q'_{nt} \rangle_{t \in N}$ is the sequence of supply vectors which are realized when the firm in question supplies $\langle r'_t \rangle_{t \in N}$, then the firm's discounted profits are

$$\begin{aligned} \sum_{t \in N} (0.9)^t \left[r'_t D \left(\int_{K_n} q'_{nt}\, d\mu_n \right) - f(r'_t) \right] &= \sum_{t<t_0} (0.9)^t \, [(1/2)(1/2) - 0] \\ &\quad + \sum_{t_0<t} (0.9)^t \, (1/2)(1/2) - 0] \\ &= \Big(\sum_{t<t_0} (0.9)^t \Big) \Big/ 4 + (0.9)^{t_0} \, (5/2). \quad (16) \end{aligned}$$

Together, (15) and (16) establish the optimality of the supply sequence $\langle r'_t \rangle_{t \in N}$ for the firm. Thus part (a) of the definition of noncooperative equilibrium is established. To show that part (b) of the definition holds, two cases must be considered at any future time in question. One possibility is that the market price has always been $\frac{1}{2}$ previously. In this case, the firm faces the same decision problem as it did in the initial period, so the earlier part of the proof is still relevant. The other possibility is that the firm has received information that some previous price has been other than $\frac{1}{2}$ (N.B. Although this possibility will not be realized in equilibrium, it must be considered for the reason explained in footnote 4). Then, since other firms will have this information also, they will always produce the Cournot output $\frac{2}{3}$ in the future. Thus it is optimal for the firm under consideration to produce this output in response. Q.E.D.

In a nonatomic market, the output decision of a single firm does not affect the price. Thus a firm cannot threaten its competitors by making its future actions contingent on the present price, because each competitor takes the price to be exogenous to its decision. Another description of this situation is that, if enforcement of a cartel is based only on price information, any firm can be a free rider on the cartel without being discovered. However, firms may be capable of observing the output levels of their competitors directly. Even in a large market, this output information might be supplied by a trade association or by the government. If the information is available, the limit principle may not hold.

THEOREM 4. *There exists a nonatomic dynamic market in which, if firms observe the output levels of their competitors directly, there is a noncooperative equilibrium which is not a price taking equilibrium.*

Proof. Let the market be the non-atomic representation of the sequence in Theorem 3, and let each firm produce $\frac{1}{2}$ unit of output as long as no competitor exceeds that output, but $\frac{2}{3}$ unit if some competitor has produced more than $\frac{1}{2}$ unit at some previous time. The proofs of Theorem 3 and Lemma 1 extend straightforwardly to show that these strategies are in noncooperative equilibrium, but that each firm will produce $\frac{1}{2}$ unit in every period, while price-taking firms would produce $\frac{2}{3}$ unit. Q.E.D.

4. AN INCLUSION THEOREM FOR REPEATED GAMES

The examples presented in the last section show that some justification is needed for applying static inclusion and limit theorems to actual markets. The question of when those results may legitimately be applied is the topic of this section and of the next. In these two sections, conditions will be given which insure that the opportunities for repeated trade in a large dynamic economy will be irrelevant to the decisions taken by agents at any particular time. Under these conditions, all dynamic noncooperative equilibria will be sequences of static equilibria. Therefore, facts about a static market will be true of the corresponding dynamic market as well.

These conditions will be studied in an abstract game theoretic context. This approach has three virtues. First, it makes it easy to deal with issues about agent's information (which have already appeared in Theorem 4). Second, at no extra cost it yields results which extend most of the literature on static price taking behavior to dynamic situations. For instance, the condition under which the dynamic inclusion principle holds is one already imposed by Dubey, Mas-Colell, and Shapley. Third, because the issues raised here are relevant whenever agents repeatedly face situations with "prisoner's dilemma" characteristics, the game theoretic results are of general interest. The theory of repeated games to be used here will now be presented. Then, the interpretation of a dynamic market as a repeated game will be explained.

Intuitively, a *repeated game* is simply a game which is replayed countably many times. A repeated game is defined in terms of three underlying spaces. The *players* are specified by a measure space $\langle K, \mu \rangle$. The measure μ will always be normalized to be a probability measure. For economy of notation, the σ-algebra on which μ is defined will not be referred to explicitly.

The *actions* available to a player are elements of a set A. Although it is assumed here that all players have the same set of feasible actions, this restriction could easily be removed.

The possible *outcomes* of the game at any time form a set X. An element of X specifies the information shared by all players about the results of a play of the game. For instance, in an economy the elements of X might be price vectors. It is important to note that this use of the term "outcome" is slightly different from the usual one, which is that an outcome completely specifies the result of a play (e.g., in an economy, X would be the set of feasible allocations) including aspects which may be unobservable to some of the players (e.g., other players' components of the allocation vector).

Throughout the paper, A and X will be assumed to be complete separable metric spaces, and mappings into these spaces from measurable spaces will be assumed to be Borel measurable.

Each player k is characterized by a *return function* $u_k : A \times X \rightarrow R$, and a *discount factor* $\beta_k \in (0, 1)$. A player attempts to maximize the discounted value of his returns from repeated plays of the game.[6]

A *play* q of the game is a measurable assignment of actions to players.[7] A^K will denote the set of plays. The outcome of a play is determined by the *outcome function* F: $A^K \rightarrow X$.

A *strategy* s is a rule by which a player determines an action to take at

[6] It is assumed that the discounted sum of optimal returns converges. In applications, this assumption typically is satisfied in equilibrium. If necessary, the assumption could be avoided by using a discounted overtaking criterion.

[7] It might be suggested that all (not necessarily measurable) functions from K to A ought to be included in the set of plays and that an outcome of the game should be assigned to every such function. Such a change would not significantly affect the results of this paper. In the case of the limit theorem (Theorem 6), plays of the finite-player games are trivially measurable, and the measurability of the limiting play is proved in the theorem. The inclusion theorem (Theorem 5) would continue to hold as stated, if the definition of anonymity used there were replaced by: a game is anonymous if any two plays differing only in the action of a single player have the same outcome.

each time, based on his knowledge at that time of the outcomes of past plays, and of his own past actions. If each past action has been generated as a deterministic function of prior outcomes and actions, the player can recover the information about his past actions recursively from his memory of past outcomes (this is easily proved by recursion on t). If the successive plays of the game are indexed by the natural numbers, a player's information at time t about prior history is specified by an element of X^t. Thus, s may be represented by a sequence $\langle s_t \rangle_{t \in N}$, where $s_0 \in A$, and $s_t : X^t \to A$ for $t \in N_+$. The space of strategies is then $A \times \prod_{t \in N+} A^{X^t}$, which will be denoted by S.

A *strategy vector* is an assignment $\langle s^k \rangle_{k \in K}$ of strategies to players such that, if $s^k = \langle s_t^k \rangle_{t \in N}$, then

(a) s_0^k is a measurable function of k, and

(b) for $x_0 \cdots x_{t-1} \in X$, $s_t^k(x_0, \ldots, x_{t-1})$ is a measurable function of k.

These conditions ensure that players' strategies determine recursively a sequence of plays and outcomes. The initial play q_0 is the vector $\langle s_0^k \rangle_{k \in K}$ of initial actions specified by the strategies. The initial outcome is $x_0 = F(q_0)$. The next play is $q_1 = \langle s_1^k(x_0) \rangle_{k \in K}$, and $x_1 = F(q_1)$, and so forth. This process defines an infinite sequence $\langle\langle q_t, x_t \rangle\rangle_{t \in N}$ of plays and outcomes, called the *history* generated by the strategy vector. The sequence $\langle x_t \rangle_{t \in N}$ determined by the history is called the *path*.

The interpretation of dynamic markets as repeated games is straightforward. Outcomes are prices. The return function of firm k specifies its profit as a function of its output level and the price. That is, if f is the total cost function of firm k, $u_k(a, x) = xa - f(a)$. The market discount rate β is β_k for each firm. The outcome function is $F(q) = D(\int_K q \, d\mu)$.

Now it is possible to make precise the informal definition of noncooperative equilibrium which was given in Section 2. Let S denote the space of strategies of the game. That is, $S = A \times \prod_{t \in N+} A^{X^t}$. Also, let y: $K \to R^{(A \times X)} \times (0, 1)$ specify the characteristics of players. That is, $y(k) = \langle u_k, \beta_k \rangle$. Three related concepts will now be defined. A static noncooperative equilibrium is a play which is a Nash equilibrium of the simple (nonrepeated) game. A dynamic quasi-equilibrium is a strategy vector which satisfies the defining condition of Nash equilibrium with respect to discounted returns at the initial time. A dynamic noncooperative equilibrium is a perfect (in the sense of footnote 4) dynamic quasi-equilibrium.

DEFINITION. A *static noncooperative equilibrium* of the repeated game $\langle K, A, X, F, \mu, y \rangle$ is a play $q^* \in A^K$ such that, for any other $q \in A^K$, the following implication holds for almost all $k \in K$: If $y(k) = \langle u, \beta \rangle$ and $q(i) = q^*(i)$ for all $i \neq k$, then

$$u(q(k), F(q)) \leqslant u(q^*(k), F(q^*)). \tag{17}$$

A *dynamic quasi-equilibrium* is a strategy vector $v^* \in S^K$ such that, for almost all $k \in K$, the following implication holds for all $v \in S^K$: If $y(k) = \langle u, \beta \rangle$, $v(i) = v^*(i)$ for all $i \neq k$, and $\langle\langle q_t, x_t \rangle\rangle_{t \in N}$, $\langle\langle q_t^*, x_t^* \rangle\rangle_{t \in N}$ are the histories generated by v and v^*, respectively, then

$$\sum_{t \in N} \beta^t u(q_t(k), x_t) \leqslant \sum_{t \in N} \beta^t u(q_t^*(k), x_t^*). \tag{18}$$

A *dynamic noncooperative equilibrium* is a strategy vector v^* such that

(a) v^* is a dynamic quasi-equilibrium, and (b) if $t \in N_+$, and $x_0^*, \ldots, x_{t-1}^* \in K$, and for each player k a new strategy is defined by

$$s_0 = s_t^*(x_0^*, \ldots, x_{t-1}^*) \tag{19}$$

and, for $r \in N_+$,

$$s_r(x_0, \ldots, x_{r-1}) = s_{t+r}^*(x_0^*, \ldots, x_{t-1}^*, \ldots, x_0, \ldots, x_{r-1}), \tag{20}$$

then the vector of these new strategies is also a dynamic quasi-equilibrium.

It was asserted at the end of Section 3 that an inclusion theorem holds for dynamic markets in which firms cannot discern changes in the output level of individual competitors. For this condition to be realized in a non-atomic market it is sufficient for the publicly observable outcome of the operation of the market to depend only on the distribution of firm's output level. This property of the outcome function can be generalized to abstract games.

DEFINITION. Denote the set of probability measures on A by $M(A)$. Let $m: A^K \to M(A)$ map plays to the distribution of actions which they determine as random variables. I.e., for $q \in A^K$ and $B \subseteq A$, $(m(q))(B) = \mu(\{k \mid q(k) \in B\})$. A game with outcome function F is *anonymous* if $F(q)$ depends on q only through $m(q)$ (i.e., if there is a function $G: M(A) \to X$ which makes the diagram

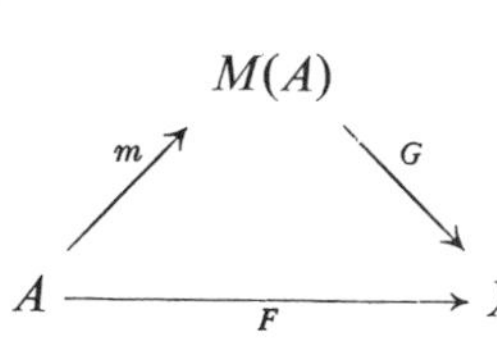

(21)

commute.

The preceding definitions make it easy to state and prove the result described at the beginning of this section, relating static and dynamic noncooperative equilibria. The inclusion theorem for dynamic markets with price information is an immediate corollary of this result.

THEOREM 5. *If* $v^* \in S^K$ *is a dynamic noncooperative equilibrium of the anonymous repeated game* $\langle K, A, X, F, \mu, y\rangle$, μ *is nonatomic, and* $\langle\langle g_t^*\ x_t^*\rangle\rangle_{t\in N}$ *is the history generated by* v^*, *then every* q_t^* *is a static noncooperative equilibrium of the game.*

Proof. It will be shown that, if some q_r^* is not a static NCE, then v^* is not a dynamic NCE. If q_r^* is not a static NCE, there is a subset $B \subseteq X$ with $\mu(B) > 0$, such that for every $k \in B$ (with $y(k) = \langle u, \beta\rangle$) there exists a play $q \in A^K$ with, $q(i) = q_r^*(i)$ for $i \neq k$, such that (17) fails to hold. That is, $u(q_r^*(k), F(q^*)) < u(q(k), F(q))$. Now, for some arbitrary player $k \in B$, define a new strategy as follows. Let his initial action s be the initial action $q_0^*(k)$ specified by $v^*(k)$, if $r \neq 0$, but let it be $q_0(k)$ if $r = 0$. For every $t > 0$, the function s_t will be a constant function. Everywhere on its domain X^t, the function will take the value $q_t^*(k)$ if $t \neq r$, or $q(k)$ if $t = r$. Define the strategy vector $v \in S^K$ by $v(k) = \langle s_t\rangle_{t\in N}$ and $v(i) = v^*(i)$ for $i \neq k$. It is claimed that (18) fails to hold for v and v^*, and that v^* is therefore not a dynamic NCE because this failure of (18) can be exhibited anywhere on the set B which has positive measure. This claim is substantiated by noting that, if $\langle x_t\rangle_{t\in N}$ is the path generated by v, $x_t = x_t^*$ (this fact is proved below as Lemma 2). By construction of $v(k)$, $q_t(k) = q_t^*(k)$ except for $t = r$. Therefore, for $t \neq r$, the tth summands of the left- and right-hand sides of (18) are identical. Consequently, (18) holds only if $u(q_r(k), x_r) \leqslant u(q_r^*(k), x_r^*)$. But this last inequality is equivalent to (17), which fails by assumption. Q.E.D.

LEMMA 2. *Let F be anonymous,* $v^* \in S^K$, $\langle x_t^*\rangle_{t\in N}$ *be the path generated by* v^*, $r \in N$, *and* $a \in A$. *For some* $k \in K$ *with* $\mu\{k\} = 0$, *define the strategy* $\langle s_t\rangle_{t\in N}$ *as follows: Define* $s_0 = q_0^*(k)$ *if* $0 \neq r$, *but* $s_0 = a$ *if* $0 = r$. *For* $t > 0$, *define* s_t *to be the constant function on* X^t *which is equal everywhere to* $q_t^*(k)$ *if* $t \neq r$, *but to* a *if* $t = r$. *Define* $v \in S^K$ *by* $v(k) = \langle s_t\rangle_{t\in N}$ *and* $v(i) = v^*(i)$ *for* $i \neq k$. *Let* $\langle x_t\rangle$ *be the path generated by* v. *Then for all* $t \in N$, $i \in K - \{k\}$, $q_t(i) = q_t^*(i)$ *and* $x_t = x_t^*$.

Proof. By induction on t. For $t = 0$, $q_t(i)$ is determined directly by $v^*(i)$ for all $i \neq k$. Since $\mu(\{k\}) = 0$, $m(q_0) = m(q^*)$, so $x_0 = s_0^*$ because F is anonymous. Now suppose that the lemma holds for $0,\ldots, t$. Then for $i \neq k$, if $v^*(i) = \langle s_t^*\rangle_{t\in N}$

$$q_{t+1}(i) = s_{t+1}^*(x_0,\ldots, x_t) = s_{t+1}^*(x_0^*,\ldots, x_t^*) = q_{t+1}^*(i).$$

As in the case $t = 0$, $m(q_{t+1}) = m(q_{t+1}^*)$, so $x_{t+1} = x_{t+1}^*$. This completes the induction. Q.E.D.

Theorem 5 is an inclusion theorem, if this term is interpreted broadly to mean a characterization of the equilibria of nonatomic games. It describes the dynamic noncooperative equilibria of a nonatomic anonymous iterated game in terms of the equilibria of the static game which is iterated. If the equilibria of the static game have some property, Theorem 5 entails that the equilibria of the iterated game inherit the property. Thus, the theorem proved in [2] extends immediately to dynamic economies. Theorem 1 of the present paper extends in a similar way.

Suppose that firms in a nonatomic dynamic market receive only price information about the operation of the market. Because price is a function of mean supply, the market is an anonymous game. By Theorem 5, if $\langle\langle q_t, x_t\rangle\rangle_{t\in N}$ is a dynamic NCE of the market, every q_t is a static NCE. By Theorem 1, then, every q_t is a price-taking equilibrium of the static market. It is evident from the definition of price-taking equilibrium that the sequence $\langle q_t\rangle_{t\in N}$ is therefore a price-taking equilibrium of the dynamic market. This proves the inclusion theorem for dynamic markets with price information only. In fact, the theorem continues to hold if firms receive other information about market aggregates (e.g., the variance of output levels in the market). The significance of this observation will be considered in Section 6.

5. A Limit Theorem for Anonymous Repeated Games with Random Outcomes

Although the inclusion principle is valid for dynamic markets under the hypothesis of anonymity, the limit principle remains invalid. This fact is evident from the counterexample given in the proof of Theorem 3. The reason why the implications of anonymity are different for the two principles is obvious. In a nonatomic market, anonymity guarantees that no firm can have any effect at all on the information which its competitors receive about the market. If inverse demand is strictly downward sloping, though, a unilateral change of output level by a firm in a finite market must have a perceptible effect on the market price. Although the magnitude of this price change becomes small in large replica markets, the change remains perceptible. The limit principle fails because the individual firm's effect on price information does not diminish in large markets, although its effect on the price level shrinks. In order for the limit principle to be valid for a dynamic market, a situation must occur in which price information about supply is unreliable.

One such situation is the existence of random fluctuations, not directly observed by firms, in consumers' demand schedules. Suppose that firms in this situation attempt to maintain a strategic noncooperative equilibrium like that described in Lemma 1. When the market price falls, each firm must decide whether the decline reflects a spontaneous downward shift of the inverse demand function, or whether it was caused by a competitor having exceeded his output quota. In a large market where the scale of an individual firm is insignificant relative to aggregate demand uncertainty, price information cannot provide evidence about the firm's level of output. Just as in the nonatomic market, the firm has incentive to break the cartel agreement.

In this section, a limit theorem will be proved which applies to the situation just discussed. The theorem applies only to equilibria of the type studied in Lemma 1, rather than to all dynamic noncooperative equilibria.

The limit theorem will be stated for anonymous repeated games with random outcomes. A game with random outcomes is one for which, at each play, the outcome is a random vector taking values in X, rather than a determinate value $x \in X$. The random vector which is the outcome depends only on the current play. Players' return functions are now interpreted as von Neumann–Morgenstern utility functions, and players are assumed to maximize expected discounted returns.

The definitions of a repeated game with random outcomes and of an anonymous game with random outcomes are the same as those given in the last section, except that now $F\colon A^K \to M(X)$ and $G\colon M(A) \to M(X)$. When plays have random outcomes, a strategy vector will not generate a unique path in X^N. Rather, it will determine a probability distribution over paths. If $B \subseteq X$, $x_0, \ldots, x_{t-1} \in X$, $\langle s^k \rangle_{k \in K}$ is a strategy vector, q is the play defined by $q(k) = s_t^k(x_0, \ldots, x_{t-1})$, and $\nu = F(q)$, then $\nu(B)$ is the probability that $x_t \in B$ conditional on the outcomes of the first t plays having been $x_0, \ldots, x_{t-1}$. In order for this conditional probability to be well defined, $\nu(B)$ must be a measurable function of $x_0, \ldots, x_{t-1}$. A sufficient condition for measurability of this function in the case of an anonymous game is that (a) G is continuous when $M(A)$ and $M(X)$ are endowed with the weak and total variation norm[8] topologies, respectively, and (b) $m(q)$ is measurable as a function of $x_0, \ldots, x_{t-1}$, when $M(A)$ has the weak topology. These conditions will be incorporated in the definitions of anonymity and of strategy vector.

DEFINITION. *A repeated game with random outcomes* $\langle K, A, X, F, \mu, y \rangle$ is defined exactly as was a repeated game in Section 4, except that $F\colon A^K \to M(X)$. The shorter term *repeated random game* will be used synonymously with this. A random game is *anonymous* if the diagram analogous to that which defines an anonymous deterministic game (but with $M(X)$ instead of X) commutes, and if G is a continuous function from $M(A)$ under the weak topology into $M(X)$ under the total variation norm topology. A *strategy* for a repeated random game is defined as in the deterministic case. An

[8] If $\mathscr{B}$ is a σ-field and $f\colon \mathscr{B} \to R$ is a countably additive set function, then the total variation norm of f is defined by $f \;= \sup\{\Sigma_{n \in N} \; f(B_n) \quad \langle B_n \rangle_{n \in N}$ is a sequence of disjoint elements of $\mathscr{B}\}$. If the range of G is any of the usual parametrized families of distribution (e.g., normal, if $X = R^n$) and does not contain any degenerate (e.g., singular covariance normal) distributions, then weak continuity of the parameter as a function of the distribution of actions is sufficient to guarantee continuity of G.

assignment $\langle s^k \rangle_{k \in K}$ of strategies to players is a *strategy vector* for a repeated random game if it satisfies the conditions specified in the deterministic case and if, in addition, when for $t \in N_+$ the function θ_t: $X^t \to M(A)$ is defined by

$$\theta_t(x_0, ..., x_{t-1}) = m(\langle s_t{}^k(x_0, ..., x_{t-1}) \rangle_{k \in K}), \tag{22}$$

each θ_t is measurable ($M(A)$ having the weak topology).

Let S^K denote the set of strategy vectors. To define the random path generated by a vector $v \in S^K$, let $\Omega = X^N$ and let $\mathscr{B}$ be the Borel σ-field generated by the product topology on Ω. Define the projection functions $\mathbf{x}_t$: $\Omega \to X$ for $t \in N$ by $\mathbf{x}_t(\langle x_0, x_1, ..., x_t, ... \rangle) = x_t$. Let $\mathscr{B}_t$ be the smallest σ-field with respect to which $\mathbf{x}_0, ..., \mathbf{x}_t$ are all measurable (N.B. $\mathscr{B}_t \subseteq \mathscr{B}$, and $\mathscr{R}_t$ is isomorphic as an algebra to the Borel σ-field on X^{t+1}, by [7, p. 6]).

Recall that, for a probability measure π defined on $\mathscr{B}$, a regular conditional probability relative to $\mathscr{B}_t$ is a function P_t: $\mathscr{B} x \Omega \to [0, 1]$ such that

(a) for fixed $\omega \in \Omega$, $P_t(\cdot \mid \tilde{y})$ is a probability measure defined on Ω,

(b) for fixed $B \subseteq \Omega$, $P_t(B \mid \cdot)$ is $\mathscr{B}_t$-measurable, and

(c) for all $B \in \mathscr{B}$ and $C \in \mathscr{B}_t$,

$$\pi(B \cap C) = \int_C P_t(B \mid \omega)\, d\pi(\omega). \tag{23}$$

For every probability measure π defined on $\mathscr{B}$, and every $t \in N$, a regular conditional probability relative to $\mathscr{B}_t$ exists, and any two of these differ only on a set of π measure zero (i.e., if P and P' are regular conditional probabilities relative to $\mathscr{B}_t$, then $\pi(\{\omega \mid \exists B \in \mathscr{B}(P(B \mid \omega) \neq P'(B \mid \omega)\}) = 0)$ [7, p. 147]. Thus, regular conditional probabilities may be used unambiguously to define random paths.

Definition. Let Ω, $\mathscr{B}$, $\mathbf{x}_t$, $\mathscr{B}_t$, and P_t be as above. Let $v \in S^k$, where $v = \langle s^k \rangle_{k \in K}$ and $s^k = \langle s_t{}^k \rangle_{t \in N}$. The *random path* generated by v is the probability space $\langle \Omega, \mathscr{B}, \pi \rangle$, which satisfies, for every Borel subset B of X,

$$\pi(\mathbf{x}_0(\omega) \in B) = \nu(B), \tag{24}$$

where $\nu = F(\langle s_0{}^k \rangle_{k \in K})$, and for $t \in N_+$,

$$P_t(\mathbf{x}_t(\omega) \in B \mid \omega) = \nu(B), \tag{25}$$

where $\nu = F(\langle s_t{}^k(\mathbf{x}_0(\omega), ..., \mathbf{x}_{t-1}(\omega)) \rangle_{k \in K})$, for all ω belonging to some $C_t \in B_{t-1}$ where $\pi(C_t) = 1$.

It is proved in the Appendix that the random path generated by a strategy vector exists and is unique. Definitions of static and dynamic NCE for a random game differ from the definitions in the deterministic case only in that expectations must be taken with respect to distributions of random outcomes and paths.

DEFINITION. *A static noncooperative equilibrium* of the repeated game $\langle K, A, X, F, \mu, y\rangle$ with random outcomes is defined as for a deterministic game, except that (17) becomes[9]

$$E_{F(q)}u(q(k), x) \leqslant E_{F(q^*)}u(q^*(k), x). \tag{26}$$

The definition of a *dynamic quasi-equilibrium* is the same as in the deterministic case, except that now the random paths $\langle \Omega, \mathscr{B}, \pi\rangle$ and $\langle \Omega, \mathscr{B}, \pi^*\rangle$ of v and v^*, respectively, are treated rather than histories in the deterministic case. Equation (18) is changed to

$$E_\pi(u(s_0{}^k, \mathbf{x}_0) + \sum_{t\in N_+} \beta^t u(s_t{}^k(\mathbf{x}_0, ..., \mathbf{x}_{t-1}), \mathbf{x}_t))$$
$$\leqslant E_{\pi^*}\left(u(s_0^{*k}, \mathbf{x}_0) + \sum_{t\in N_+} \beta^t u(s_t^{*k}(\mathbf{x}_0, ..., \mathbf{x}_{t-1}), \mathbf{x}_t)\right). \tag{27}$$

The definition of a *dynamic noncooperative equilibrium* is exactly the same as in the deterministic case.

An explicit definition is now given of the type of dynamic noncooperative equilibrium which was studied in Lemma 1. Recall that in that type of equilibrium, there is a play q_0 to which players are committed at each repetition of the game. This commitment is enforced by mutual threats that, if there is evidence that some player k has not taken action $q_0(k)$, then the other players will thereafter take the actions prescribed by another play q_1. This threat is self-enforcing, because q_1 is a static noncooperative equilibrium. Evidence that a player has departed from q_0 consists of an outcome which lies outside some subset $B \subseteq X$. That is, the players agree to play q_0 as long as outcomes in B have been observed in the past, but always to play q_1 if some outcome outside of B has occurred in the past.

DEFINITION. A *strategic noncooperative equilibrium* of the game $\langle K, A, X, F, \mu, y\rangle$ with random outcomes is a dynamic NCE $v \in S^K$ such that. for some triple $\langle q_0, q_1, B\rangle \in A^K \times A^K \times 2^X$, the following conditions are satisfied for every $k \in K$ (with $v(k) = \langle s_t\rangle_{t\in N}$):

(a) q_1 is a static NCE.

(b) $s_0(k) = q_0(k)$.

[9] The functions $u(q(k), x)$ and $u(s_t{}^k(\mathbf{x}_0, ..., \mathbf{x}_{t-1}, \mathbf{x}_t)$ are random variables on X and Ω in Eqs. (26) and (27), respectively.

(c) If, for any $t \in N_+$, $x_0, \ldots, x_{t-1} \in B$, then $s_t(x_0, \ldots, x_{t-1}) = q_0(k)$ and

(d) If, for any $t \in N_+$ and $r < t$, $x_r \notin B$, then $s_t(x_0, \ldots, x_r, \ldots, x_{t-1}) = q_1(k)$ for all $x_0, \ldots, x_{r-1}, x_{r+1}, \ldots, x_{t-1} \in X$.

By abuse of notation, the strategy vector defined by (b)–(d) above will also be referred to as $\langle q_0, q_1, B \rangle$.

There is a condition which, if the expectations referred to in its statement are well defined, is necessary and sufficient for a strategy vector $\langle q_0, q_1, B \rangle$ to be a strategic NCE. Some notation is introduced now to facilitate the statement of this condition. Let $k \in K$ be fixed. For $a \in A$, define q_a to be the play which results from q_0 when the action of k is changed to a. That is, $q_a(k) = a$, and $q_a(i) = q_0(i)$ for $i \neq k$. Define $\nu_j = F(q_j)$ for $j = 0$, 1, and $\nu_a = F(q_a)$ for all $a \in A$, and let E_j and E_a be the expectation operators (on functions defined over X) with respect to ν_j and ν_a, respectively.

LEMMA 3. *Let $q_0, q_1 \in A^K$, let q_1 be a static NCE, and suppose that for all $k \in K$ (with $y(k) = \langle u, \beta \rangle$), $E_1 u(q_1(k), x)$ is finite and $E_a u(a, x)$ is finite for every $a \in A$. Let $B \subseteq X$, and define*

$$V_k(a) = [E_a u(a, x) + \beta(1 - \beta)^{-1}(1 - \nu_a(B))\, E_1 u(q_1(k), x)]/[1 - \beta \nu_a(B)], \tag{28}$$

for all $a \in A$. Then $\langle q_0, q_1, B \rangle$ is a strategic NCE if and only if, for almost all $k \in K$,

$$V_k(q_0(k)) = \max_{a \in A} V_k(a). \tag{29}$$

Proof. By definition, $\langle q_0, q_1, B \rangle$ is a strategic NCE if and only if it is a dynamic NCE. Furthermore, by the reasoning explained in Lemma 1, the fact that q_1 is a static NCE entails that $\langle q_0, q_1, B \rangle$ is a dynamic NCE if and only if it is a dynamic quasi-equilibrium. Thus, it is sufficient to prove that (27) holds with $v^* = \langle q_0, q_1, B \rangle$ for all other $v \in S^K$ with $v(i) = v^*(i)$ for $i \neq k$, if and only if (29) holds. This proof consists of two parts. First, it is argued that one need only consider (27) with respect to v^* and strategy vectors $v = \langle q_a, q_1, B \rangle$ for $a \in A$. Second, a dynamic programming argument is used to evaluate the expected discounted returns in (27) for paths generated by these strategy vectors.

Both of these arguments are transparent when it is realized that the decision problem of player k is equivalent to a very simple Markov dynamic programming problem. In this equivalent problem there are two states: either all previous outcomes of the game have been in B (state 0), or some outcome has not been in B (state 1). In state 0, taking an action $a \in A$ yields a present return (the expected return $E_a u(a, x)$ from the play q_a) and incurs a risk (the probability $1 - \nu_a(B)$ of producing an outcome not in (B) of causing a change to state 1 in the next period. State 1 is an absorbing state, and in that state the player's best action is $q_1(k)$ which yields return $E_1u(q_1(k), x)$. A basic theorem of dynamic programming states that, if any optimal control rule exists for this problem, there is an optimal rule which specifies a fixed action $a \in A$ to be taken as long as state 0 persists. If player k follows this rule while other players use the strategies assigned by $\langle q_0, q_1, B\rangle$ the strategy vector $\langle q_a, q_1, B\rangle$ results. Thus, if any strategy of k leads to a violation of (27) the equation fails to hold for some strategy vector of this special form.

It remains to calculate the expected discounted returns to player k from paths of strategy vectors $\langle q_a, q_1, B\rangle$. (N.B. If $a = q_0(k)$, then $\langle q_a, q_1, B\rangle = \langle q_0, q_1, B\rangle$.) Denote his expected discounted return from the path of $\langle q_a, q_1, B\rangle$ by $V_k(a)$. With this interpretation of $V_k(a)$, (29) holds if and only if $\langle q_0, q_1, B\rangle$ is a dynamic quasi-equilibrium. Thus it is only necessary to verify that (28) is true under this interpretation, in order to complete the proof.

To do this, note that $V_k(a)$ must equal the expected discounted return in the equivalent dynamic program under the control rule: perform action a in state 0, and action $q_1(k)$ in state 1. From the first time that state 1 occurs, the expected discounted return is $(1 - \beta)^{-1}E_1u(q_1(k), x)$. Thus, if $W:\{0, 1\} \to R$ is the value function of the control rule, $V_k(a) = W(0)$ and $(1 - \beta)^{-1}E_1u(q_1(k), x) = W(1)$. $W(0)$ is defined by the functional equation

$$\begin{aligned} W(0) &= E_a u(a, x) + \beta[P(\text{the state next period will again be } 0) \cdot \\ &\quad W(0) + P(\text{the state next period will change to } 1) \cdot W(1)]. \end{aligned} \tag{30}$$

Given that the transition probabilities are $\nu_a(B)$ and $(1 - \nu_a(B))$, respectively, (30) is equivalent to (28). Q.E.D.

Lemma 3 will be used to prove a limit theorem for anonymous repeated games with random outcomes. To state this theorem, a sequence of replica repeated games must be defined. This definition is a straightforward generalization of that of a sequence of replica dynamic markets.

DEFINITION. Let $H = \langle K, A, X, F, \mu, y\rangle$ be an anonymous repeated game with random outcomes. In particular, let the diagram

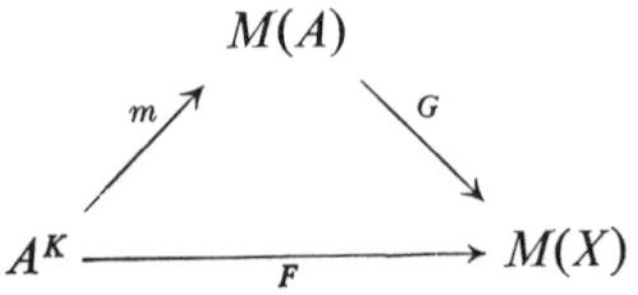

(31)

commute. Suppose that K is a finite set. Then, a *sequence of replica repeated games* $\langle H_n\rangle_{n\in N}$ with random outcomes is defined as follows: For every $n \in N$, $H_n = \langle K_n, A, X, F_n, \mu_n, y_n\rangle$, where $K_n = K \times \{0,\ldots, n\}$, μ_n is determined by $\mu_n(\{\langle k, r\rangle\}) = \mu(\{k\})/(n+1)$ for all $\langle k, r\rangle \in K_n$, and $y_n(\langle k, r\rangle) = y(k)$ for all $\langle k, r\rangle \in K_n$. It remains to define the outcome function F_n. Let $m_n\colon A^{K_n} \to M(A)$ map plays of H_n to the distributions of actions which they determine as random variables on $\langle K_n, \mu_n\rangle$. Then define $F_n : A^{K_n} \to M(X)$ by $F_n(q) = G(m_n(q))$ for all $q \in A^{K_n}$. Define the *nonatomic representation* H_∞ of the sequence analogously, where $K_\infty = K \times [0, 1]$, and, for $B \subseteq K_\infty$, $\mu_\infty(B) = \sum_{k\in K} \mu(\{k\}) \cdot \lambda(\{r \in [0, 1] \mid \langle k, r\rangle \in B\})$.

The limit theorem to be proved here states that, under appropriate hypotheses, the limit of strategic noncooperative equilibria is trivial in the sense that the "collusive" play supported in the limit must itself be a static noncooperative equilibrium. Formally, if $\langle H_n\rangle_{n\in N}$ is a sequence of replica repeated games with random outcomes, if $\langle q_0{}^n, q_1{}^n, B_n\rangle$ is a strategic NCE of H_n for each n, and if $\langle\!\langle y_n, q_0{}^n, q_1{}^n\rangle\!\rangle_{n\in N} \to \langle y_\infty, q_0{}^\infty, q_1{}^\infty\rangle$ in distribution, then $q_0{}^\infty$ is a static NCE of H_∞.

The statement and proof of the limit theorem are now given.

THEOREM 6 (limit theorem for anonymous repeated games with random outcomes). *Suppose that* $\langle H_n\rangle_{n\in N}$ *is a sequence of replica repeated games with random outcomes, having* H_∞ *as nonatomic representation. Let* $H = \langle K, A, X, F, \mu, y\rangle$, *and let* G *make* (31) *commute.*[10] *Suppose that* $\langle q_0{}^n, q_1{}^n, B_n\rangle$ *is a strategic NCE of* H_n *for every* $n \in N$, *and that the following hypotheses are satisfied.*

(a) *The countable subset* $D \subseteq A$ *is dense in* A.

(b) *If* $y(k) = \langle u, \beta\rangle$ *for some* $k \in K$, *then* $E_{G(\eta)}u(a, x)$ *is a finite-valued, continuous function on* $A \times M(A)$, *where* $M(A)$ *has the weak topology.*

(c) *The sequence* $\langle\!\langle y_n, q_0{}^n, q_1{}^n\rangle\!\rangle_{n\in N}$ *converges in distribution.*

Then there is a random vector $\langle y_\infty, q_0{}^\infty, q_1{}^\infty\rangle$ *defined on* K_∞ *such that*

$$\langle\!\langle y_n, q_0{}^n, q_1{}^n\rangle\!\rangle_{n\in N} \to \langle y_\infty, q_0{}^\infty, q_1{}^\infty\rangle \tag{32}$$

in distribution, and $q_0{}^\infty$ *is a static NCE of* H_∞.

[10] In particular, it is assumed that G is continuous when $M(X)$ is endowed with the total variation norm topology. This assumption restricts the amount of information that outcomes of the game can carry. For instance, if a deterministic outcome is interpreted as a probability measure concentrated on a single point, then the example constructed to refute the limit principle for repeated deterministic games may be considered as a sequence of replica repeated games with random outcomes. In that example, G is continuous when $M(X)$ is given the weak topology, but not when it is given the total variation norm topology (although the conditional probabilities needed to define the random path are well defined (they are all 1 or 0)). Thus the continuity requirement on G in the theorem cannot be relaxed. An example in which very accurate information is revealed in a large market, so that a strong continuity requirement might be presumed not to hold, is the enforcement by professional associations of prohibitions on advertising by members. At essentially no cost, an association can monitor perfectly whether the prohibition is being observed.

Proof. The two ideas behind this proof are that the analog (with expected utilities) of Theorem 5 must be true for nonatomic games with random outcomes, and that the functions V_k defined by (28) are continuous in the actions and measures involved in their definition. If q_0^∞ is not a static NCE of H_∞, the first assertion entails that $\langle q_0^\infty, q_1^\infty, B_\infty \rangle$ cannot be a dynamic quasi-equilibrium for any $B_\infty \subseteq X$. Therefore (29) cannot be satisfied almost everywhere for H_∞ by any $\langle q_0^\infty, q_1^\infty, B_\infty \rangle$. By the second assertion, neither can (29) hold almost everywhere on K_n, for the nearby games H_n and strategy vectors $\langle q_0^n, q_1^n, B_n \rangle$ when n is large.

Formally, the limiting random vector $\langle y_\infty, q_0^\infty, q_1^\infty \rangle$ exists by Skorokhod's theorem [5, p. 50]. Suppose that q_0^∞ is not a static NCE. Then there is a set $J \subseteq K_\infty$, with $\mu_\infty(J) > 0$, on which (26) does not hold for all necessary q when $q^* = q_0^\infty$. Because K is finite, for some $k \in K$ (N.B. k will refer throughout the proof to this fixed element of K), $\mu_\infty(J \cap (\{k\} \times [0, 1])) > 0$. Without loss of generality, it may be assumed that $J \subseteq \{k\} \times [0, 1]$.

Because H_∞ is nonatomic and anonymous, and because D is dense in A, the failure of (26) is equivalent by (b) to the existence of some $d \in D$ such that

$$E_{F_\infty(q_0^\infty)} u(q_0^\infty(\langle k, r \rangle), x) < E_{F_\infty(q_0^\infty)} u(d, x). \tag{33}$$

As above, the countability of D permits (33) to be assumed without loss of generality to hold everywhere on J for some fixed action d of D (N.B. d also to be held fixed throughout the proof). Similarly, by the separability of R_+, it may be assumed that a stronger version

$$E_{F_\infty(q_0^\infty)} u(d, x) - E_{F_\infty(q_0^\infty)} u(q_0^\infty(\langle k, r \rangle), x) > \delta \tag{34}$$

of (33) holds uniformly on J for some $\delta > 0$, and that by (b),

$$| E_{F(q_1^\infty)} u(q_1^\infty(\langle k, r \rangle), x)| < \epsilon. \tag{35}$$

holds uniformly on J for some $\epsilon > 0$.

By (b), (34), and (35), for each r with $\langle k, r \rangle \in J$, there exist open sets U_{0r}^*, $U_{1r}^* \subseteq A$ and W_{0r}, $W_{1r} \subseteq M(A)$ with $q_j^\infty(\langle k, r \rangle) \in U_{jr}^*$ and $m_\infty(q_j^\infty) \in W_{jr}$ for $j = 0, 1$, which satisfy

$$E_{G(\eta)} u(d, x) - E_{G(\theta)} u(a, x) > \delta \tag{36}$$

for η, $\theta \in W_{0r}$ and $a \in U_{0r}^*$ and

$$| E_{G(\eta)} u(a, x)| < \epsilon \tag{37}$$

for $\eta \in W_{1r}$ and $a \in U_{1r}^*$.

There are open U_{jr} for $j = 0, 1$ and $\langle k, r\rangle \in J$, such that $q_j^\infty(\langle k, r\rangle) \in U_j$. and $\bar{U}_{jr} \subseteq U_{jr}^*$ (N.B. $\bar{U}$ is the closure of U). Let $\Gamma = \bigcup_{\langle k,r\rangle \in J} (U_{0r} \times U_{1r})$. By (a) and Lindelöf's theorem [3, p. 12] there is a countable subset $Y \subseteq [0, 1]$ such that $\{U_{0r} \times U_{1r} \mid r \in Y\}$ is a cover of Γ. Since $\mu_\infty(J) > 0$ and $J \subseteq \{\langle k, r\rangle \mid \langle q_0^\infty(\langle k, r\rangle), q_1^\infty(\langle k, r\rangle)\rangle \in \Gamma\}$, and since Y is countable, there is some $U = U_{0r} \times U_{1r}$ such that

$$\mu_\infty(\{\langle k, r\rangle \mid \langle q_0^\infty(\langle k, r\rangle), q_1^\infty(\langle k, r\rangle)\rangle \in U\}) > 0. \tag{38}$$

By [7, p. 4] there is a continuous function $f: A \times A \to [0, 1]$ having support in $\bar{U}^*$ (where $U^* = U_{0r}^* \times U_{1r}^*$ for the same r which defines U) juch that $f = 1$ on $\bar{U}$. By (38),

$$\int_{[0,1]} f(\langle q_0^\infty(\langle k, r\rangle), q_1^\infty(\langle k, r\rangle)\rangle)\, d\lambda(r) > 0. \tag{39}$$

It is evident from (c) and the definition of convergence in distribution that asymptotically (i.e., for all sufficiently large $n \in N$) there exist $r_n \leqslant n$ for which

$$\langle q_0^n(\langle k, r_n\rangle), q_1^n(\langle k, r_n\rangle)\rangle \in U. \tag{40}$$

For $n \in N$, define $a_j^n = q_j^n(\langle k, r_n\rangle)$ for $j = 0, 1$. Also define (as in Lemma 4) q_d^n to be the play of H_n which results when $\langle k, r_n\rangle$ deviates from q_0^n by taking action d. I.e., $q_d^n(\langle k, r_n\rangle) = d$ and $q_d^n(\langle k', r'\rangle) = q_0^n(\langle k', r'\rangle)$ if $k' \neq k$ or $r' \neq r_n$. Define $\eta_j^n = m_n(q_j^n)$ for $j = 0, 1, d$. By (c),

$$\langle \eta_j^n\rangle_{n\in N} \to m_\infty(q_j^\infty) \tag{41}$$

for $j = 0, 1$, and

$$\langle \eta_d^n\rangle_{n\in N} \to m_\infty(q_0^\infty). \tag{42}$$

Thus asymptotically $\eta_0^n, \eta_d^n \in W_{0r}$ and $\eta_1^n \in W_{1r}$, so that (36), (37) and (40) imply that for sufficiently large n,

$$E_{G(\eta_d^n)} u(d, x) - E_{G(\eta_0^n)} u(a_0^n, x) > \delta \tag{43}$$

and

$$| E_{G(\eta_1^n)} u(a_1^n, x)| < \epsilon. \tag{44}$$

Equations (43) and (45) will be used now to establish that (29) fails asymptotically for $q_0 = q_0^n$, so that $\langle q_0^n, q_1^n, B_n\rangle$ cannot be a strategic NCE of H_n. Define $\nu_j^n = G(\eta_j^n)$ and let E_j^n be expectation with respect to ν_j^n for $j = 0, 1, d$. It will be shown that asymptotically

$$\begin{aligned}&[E_0^n u(a_0^n, x) + \beta(1-\beta)^{-1}(1 - \nu_0^n(B_n))\, E_1^n u(a_1^n, x)]/[1 - \beta\nu_0^n(B_n)]\\ &\quad< [E_d^n u(d, x) + \beta(1-\beta)^{-1}(1 - \nu_d^n(B_n))\, E_1^n u(a_1^n, x)]/[1 - \beta\nu_d^n(B_n)).\end{aligned} \tag{45}$$

By (28), (45) is equivalent for H_n to $V_{\langle k,r_n\rangle}(q_0{}^n(\langle k, r_n\rangle)) < V_{\langle k,r_n\rangle}(d)$, so that (45) contradicts (29) for H_n. Thus the theorem will hold by Lemma 3.

Multiplying both sides of (45) by $[1 - \nu_0{}^n(B_n)]$ yields

$$\begin{aligned} &E_0{}^n u(a_0{}^n, x) + \beta(1-\beta)^{-1}(1 - \nu_0{}^n(B_n))\, E_1{}^n u(a_1{}^n, x) \\ &\quad < [(1 - \beta\nu_0{}^n(B_n))/(1 - \beta\nu_d{}^n(B_n))][E_d{}^n u(d, x) + \beta(1-\beta)^{-1} \\ &\quad \times (1 - \nu_d{}^n(B_n))\, E_1{}^n u(a_1{}^n, x)]. \end{aligned} \tag{46}$$

For each $\xi > 0$ there is an open $W_\xi \subseteq M(A)$, with $m_\infty(q_0{}^\infty) \in W_\xi$, which satisfies

$$\sup_{B \subseteq X} |\, 1 - [[1 - \beta(G(\eta))(B)]/[1 - \beta(G(\theta))(B)]]| < \xi \tag{47}$$

for $\eta, \theta \in W_\xi$. By (41), (42), and (47), (46) holds asymptotically if

$$E_0{}^n u(a_0{}^n, x) - E_d{}^n u(d, x) + \beta(1-\beta)^{-1}[\nu_d{}^n(B_n) - \nu_0{}^n(B_n)]\, E_1{}^n u(a_1{}^n, x) < 0 \tag{48}$$

asymptotically. By (d), (41), and (42), $\lim_{n\to\infty} [\nu_d{}^n(B_n) - \nu_0{}^n(B_n)] = 0$, so by (44), (48) holds asymptotically if

$$\overline{\lim_{n\to\infty}}\, [E_0{}^n u(a_0{}^n, x) - E_d{}^n u(d, x)] < 0. \tag{49}$$

This completes the proof, because (43) implies (49). Q.E.D.

From Theorems 2 and 6, it is evident that the paths of strategic noncooperative equilibria of a sequence of replica dynamic markets with unobserved random demand fluctuations converge to a price-taking equilibrium of the nonatomic representation of the sequence. One difficulty arises in the application of Theorem 6 here. That is, G will not be continuous if firms have unbounded production sets. However, if marginal costs become sufficiently high as output levels rise, this difficulty may be handled by imposing prior bounds, uniform in n, on the output levels which firms would consider. Hypothesis (d) is satisfied in the resulting sequence of replica markets because inverse demand is continuous and production sets are compact.

6. Concluding Remarks

The results which have been presented here concern the extent to which price-taking behavior characterizes the noncooperative equilibria of large economies. Theorems 1 and 2 of the present paper exemplify the positive results for this question which hold under the simplifying assumption that trade in each market occurs only once, during a single, initial trading period in which all markets clear simultaneously. Theorems 3 and 4 show that the validity of these results for actual markets, which continue to be active over time cannot be taken for granted. Finally, Theorems 5 and 6 describe the extent to which results for static markets can legitimately be applied to temporal trade. In this section, the practical significance of these results will be examined.

Most economists are in rough agreement about which actual markets are paradigm cases which corroborate the static theory of competitive behavior in large markets, and which markets are accounted for less successfully by the theory. Theorems 5 and 6 justify the application of the static theory to the paradigm cases, and they also clarify the status of some of the marginal cases. Theorem 5 asserts (in conjunction with Theorem 3) that, if firms in a market literally have no effect on the price, then the market must be competitive unless firms have access to extremely disaggregated information about their competitors. Theorem 6 states that, in the presence of imperfections which may reasonably be thought to exist in the price system, the assumption in Theorem 5 that individual firms do not influence the price may be taken as a good approximation of the situation in large finite markets. Thus, when a market contains many uncoordinated sellers, the static theory may legitimately be used to predict that the market will be competitive.

Problems typically arise in deciding what the words "many" and "uncoordinated" mean, when the applicability of the theory of large markets to a particular market is in question. Thus one class of marginal cases for the static theory consists of moderately concentrated industries (typically having fewer than a dozen major suppliers), and another class consists of markets in which the actions of a trade or professional association might affect the behavior of sellers. One school of thought in the economics profession holds that collusive agreements of even the smallest size are very unstable and that noncooperative equilibria converge rapidly to price-taking as the number of sellers is increased, so that there is a strong presumption that markets in both of these classes are competitive. An apparently conflicting view is held by a number of economists who have been persuaded of the monopolistic effects of professional associations in medicine, law, and so forth, on the basis of evidence which for the most part has been rather impressionistic.

Each of these views presupposes a set of beliefs about what determines whether firms in an industry would be able to detect and punish a competitor which attempted to violate a cartel agreement. It has long been recognized in the informal literature on industrial organization that this question, more than the question of how concentrated the industry is according to the usual quantitative measures, is important in assessing the competitiveness of an industry with restricted entry. By stating precise, formal criteria for cartel organization in an industry to be enforceable, Theorems 5 and 6 point the way toward an embodiment of this informal tradition in a rigorous, empirically satisfactory theory.[11] Industry studies based on such a theory would help to resolve long-standing empirical disputes about the extent of cartel organization, and might contribute to the determination of antitrust policy on a more rational basis.

APPENDIX: Existence and Uniqueness of a Random Path

Let $v = \langle s^k \rangle_{k \in K} \in S^K$, where $s^k = \langle s_t{}^k \rangle_{t \in N}$ for each t. It will be proved that there is a unique Borel measure on $\Omega = X^N$ which satisfies definition of a random path of v of an anonymous repeated random game.

Lemma 4. *To prove the existence and uniqueness of a random path, it is sufficient to prove that there is a unique sequence $\langle \pi_t \rangle_{t \in N}$ such that*

(a) *π_t is a measure defined on $\mathscr{B}_t$ for each t,*

(b) *if $t < t'$, then π_t is the restriction of $\pi_{t'}$ to $\mathscr{B}_t$,*

(c) *the equation*

$$\pi_0 = F(\langle s_0{}^k \rangle_{k \in K}) \tag{50}$$

holds, and

(d) *if $t \in N_+$ and P_t^* is regular conditional probability for π_t relative to $\mathscr{B}_{t-1}$, then for every Borel subset B of X,*

$$P_t^*(\mathbf{x}_t(\omega) \in B \mid \omega) = \nu(B), \tag{51}$$

where $\nu = F(\langle s_t{}^k(\mathbf{x}_0(\omega),\ldots, \mathbf{x}_{t-1}(\omega)) \rangle_{k \in K})$, for all ω belonging to some $C_t \in \mathscr{B}_{t-1}$ where $\pi_t(C_t) = 1$.

Proof. By the Kolmogorov consistency theorem [7, p. 139], for any sequence satisfying (a)–(d) there is a unique Borel measure π on Ω such that π_t is the restriction of π to $\mathscr{B}_t$, for every t. Thus (50) and (51) are equivalent to (24) and (25), so $\langle \Omega, \mathscr{B}, \pi \rangle$ is a random path generated by v. If $\langle \Omega, \mathscr{B}, \pi' \rangle$ is any random path generated by v, and if π_t' is the restriction of π' to $\mathscr{B}_{t'}$ then $\langle \pi_t' \rangle_{t \in N}$ satisfies (a)–(d). By the uniqueness of the Kolmogorov extension, $\langle \pi_t \rangle_{t \in N} \neq \langle \pi_t' \rangle_{t \in N}$ if $\pi \neq \pi'$. Thus, uniqueness of the sequence satisfying (a)–(d) is sufficient for the uniqueness of the random path. Q.E.D.

Lemma 5. *A unique sequence $\langle \pi_t \rangle_{t \in N}$ exists which satisfies* (a)–(d) *of Lemma* 4.

[11] In particular, Eq. (29) suggests how the hypothesis that there is collusion in a particular industry might be tested on the basis of a time series of prices and market shares for that industry. Evidence from such a test would be more persuasive than that from cross-industry comparisons on which current attempts to measure the extent of collusion are based.

Proof. A sequence satisfying (a)–(d) will be constructed recursively. At each stage the measure chosen will be determined uniquely. To begin with, (50) defines π_0. Supposing that π_t has been chosen, condition (d) will be used to uniquely define π_{t+1} on $\mathscr{B}_{t+1}$. Define a *block* in X^{t+2} to be a product set $C \times B$, where $C \in \mathscr{B}_t$[12] and B is a Borel subset of X. Define π^*: $\mathscr{B}_t \times \mathscr{B}_0 \to [0, 1]$ by

$$\pi^*(C \times B) = \int_C P^*_{t+1}(\mathbf{x}_{t+1}(\omega) \in B \mid \omega)\, d\pi_t(\omega), \tag{52}$$

where Eq. (51) is taken as the *definition* of P^*_t. (N.B. The measurability of $P^*_{t+1}(\mathbf{x}_{t+1} \in B \mid \cdot)$ with respect to $\mathscr{B}_t$ is guaranteed by the definitions of strategy vector and anonymous game.) Now define $\mathscr{B}^* \subseteq \mathscr{B}_{t+1}$ to be the class of finite unions of disjoint blocks. $\mathscr{B}^*$ is a Boolean algebra [3, p. 185], and π^* determines a finitely additive measure on $\mathscr{B}^*$. In fact, it is evident from Lebesque's monotone convergence theorem that π^* is countably additive on $\mathscr{B}^*$. By the Caratheodory–Hahn extension theorem [3, p. 136], π^* extends uniquely to a measure on the smallest σ-field containing $\mathscr{B}^*$. By [7, p. 6], this σ-field is $\mathscr{B}_{t+1}$. Let the extension measure be π_{t+1}. Conditions (a) and (b) are trivially verified, and it follows from (23) that p^*_{t+1} defined by (51) are trivially verified, and it follows from (23) that p^*_{t+1} defined by (51) agrees almost surely with regular conditional probability for $B \in \mathscr{B}^*$, so that π_{t+1} satisfies (d) and is the unique extension of π_t which does so. This completes the induction. Q.E.D.

The existence and uniqueness of the random path of v are an immediate consequence of Lemmas 4 and 5:

THEOREM 7. *If H is an anonymous repeated game with random oucomes and v is a strategy vector for H, then v generates a unique random path $\langle \Omega, \mathscr{B}, \pi \rangle$.*

REFERENCES

1. A. A. COURNOT [1838], "Researches into the Mathematical Principles of the Theory of Wealth," Irwin, Homewood, Ill., 1963.
2. P. DUBEY, A. MAS-COLELL, AND M. SHUBIK, Efficiency properties of strategic market games: an axiomatic approach, *J. Econ. Theory* **22** (1980), 339–362.
3. N. DUNFORD AND J. SCHWARTZ, "Linear Operators," Vol. I, Interscience, New York, 1958.
4. J. W. FRIEDMAN, A non-cooperative equilibrium for supergames, *Rev. Econ. Stud.* **28** (1971), 1–12.

[12] In this proof, $\mathscr{B}_t$ will indicate both the Borel subsets of X^{t+1} and the smallest subfield of X^N with respect to which $\mathbf{x}_0, \ldots, \mathbf{x}_t$ are Borel measurable. The intended reference will be clear from context.

5. W. Hildenbrand, "Core and Equilibria of a Large Economy," Princeton Univ. Press, Princeton, N. J., 1974.
6. W. Novshek and H. Sonnenschein, Cournot and Walras equilibrium, *J. Econ. Theory* **19** (1978), 223–266.
7. K. R. Parthasarathy, "Probability Measures on Metric Spaces," Academic Press, New York, 1967.
8. R. Selten, A re-examination of the perfectness concept for equilibrium points in extensive games, *Internat. J. Game Theory* **4** (1975), 25–55.
9. G. J. Stigler, A theory of oligopoly, *J. Pol. Econ.* **72** (1964), 44–61.

The No-Surplus Condition as a Characterization of Perfectly Competitive Equilibrium*

Joseph M. Ostroy

Department of Economics, University of California, Los Angeles, California 90024

Received January 5, 1979

In the Walrasian definition of competitive equilibrium, attention is confined to the consistency of individuals' plans on the presumption that each agent regards itself as a price-taker. Thus, Walrasian equilibrium may exist where there is no supporting evidence for that presumption—e.g., in an economy with a small number of agents. The self-imposed limitations of the definition imply that it describes necessary but not sufficient conditions for perfectly competitive equilibrium—i.e., an equilibrium for which the presumption of price-taking is justified. In this paper we propose an alternative definition that brings out the perfectly competitive character of the equilibrium that is implicitly behind the usual interpretation.

The approach adopted here has as a basic premise that the description of perfect competition should be invariant to the number of agents. Contrary to what appears to be the typical view that it is logically tied to the study of economies with large numbers of agents, we find that an analysis of the conditions for perfectly competitive equilibrium with small numbers yields a characterization that is essentially the same as it is for large. What differs between economies with small and large numbers is simply the likelihood of its occurrence.

Consider a group of agents and an allocation that maximizes the utility of one of them, say j, subject to requirement that the others are made no worse off than they would be by reallocating resources among themselves, without j. At such an allocation, j is extracting all the gains from trade he might reasonably expect by, as it were, joining the economy; and, the others may be receiving absolutely no surplus from the presence of j. Suppose an economy exhibits an allocation that simultaneously fulfills this condition for all agents taken one at a time. Such a situation is a special case of what will be called a *no-surplus allocation* that we propose as an alternative to the Walrasian definition of competitive equilibrium.

* This work was supported by NSF Grant SOC77-18086.

Reprinted from *Journal of Economic Theory* **22,** No. 2, 183–207 (April 1980)
ISBN 0-12-476750-8

Some justifications for the proposed definition are the following:

(1) Whether the number of agents is large or small, a no-surplus allocation is a Walrasian equilibrium.

(2) A no-surplus allocation is equivalent to the condition that each agent faces perfectly elastic demand schedules, at Walrasian prices, for the goods it sells.

(3) Although almost all Walrasian allocations in economies with small numbers are not no-surplus, in economies with large numbers and a finite number of commodities almost all Walrasian allocations are.

In this paper we shall demonstrate (1)–(3) for the most elementary but nevertheless representative case of finite exchange economies and for sequences of exchange economies consisting of replicas of a fixed finite economy. A novelty of the demonstration is that for large economies we shall permit the presence of external effects. More general sequences of economies exhibit similar conclusions (see Ostroy [14]). Related results have been established by Makowski [10] for economies with production by firms.

The concept of no-surplus is reminiscent of the marginal productivity theory of distribution. With such an allocation each agent may be said to be obtaining its marginal product and since this is true for all agents simultaneously, the total product (allocation) may be said to be entirely exhausted by the sum of the marginal products (see Theorem 2, below). The analogy is further exploited by Makowski and it is shown in Ostroy [15] that the marginal-productivity-product-exhaustion and no-surplus descriptions of perfect competition are essentially equivalent for economies with a continuum of traders.

In the final section, the no-surplus and core characterizations of perfectly competitive equilibrium are compared. Elsewhere, we shall exhibit the connections with the Shapley value (Shapley [18]), and the concept of incentive-compatibility of Walrasian equilibria (Roberts and Postlewaite [16]). Mas-Colell [12] has shown that the no-surplus condition can be used to abstract some of the common elements of the Core and Value Convergence Theorems. In the context of economies regarded as games with transferable utility, Geanakoplos [7] has independently demonstrated that the marginal-productivity-product-exhaustion condition can be used to derive the equivalence of the core, Shapley value, bargaining set, and Walrasian equilibria.

I. Notation and Preliminary Definitions

The concepts and results below are formulated for an exchange economy $\mathscr{E} = \{(S_i, w_i)\}_{i=1}^{i=n}$, where S_i describes the preferences and w_i the initial endowments of a typical agent i. It is assumed throughout that the relevant commodity space is R_+^ℓ so that $w_i \in R_+^\ell$. An *allocation* is denoted by $X = (x_i)$, $x_i \in R_+^\ell$; and, unless otherwise noted, X will also be assumed to satisfy the feasibility condition, $\sum(x_i - w_i) = 0$.

For an allocation X, $S_i(X)$ is a subset of R_+^ℓ. If $y \in S_i(X)$, then i would prefer y to x_i given the allocations x_j in X for $j \neq i$. Let $\partial S_i(X)$ be the R_+^ℓ-boundary of $S_i(X)$, the set of points in the closure of $S_i(X)$ that does not belong to its R_+^ℓ-interior. For each $i = 1,..., n$ and $X = (x_i)$, assumptions on preferences will include (some of) the following:

A_1: $S_i(X)$ is open in R_+^ℓ;

A_2: $x_i \in \partial S_i(X)$;

A_3: $p \in R^\ell$, $p \neq 0$, $\inf p[S_i(X) - w_i] = 0$, and $y \in S_i(X)$ implies $p(y - w_i) > 0$;

A_4: $S_i(X)$ is convex;

A_5: $X' = (x_i')$ and $x_j' = x_j$ implies $S_j(X') = S_j(X)$;

A_6: $\{(y, X): y \in S_i(X)\}$ is open in $R_+^\ell \times \underbrace{(R_+^\ell \times \cdots \times R_+^\ell)}_{n}$

Consistent with the interpretation of $S_i(X)$ as indicating strictly preferred elements, A_1 and A_2 imply that the underlying preference ordering is irreflexive since $S_i(X)$ does not contain its boundary and $x_i \in \partial S_i(X)$. A_2 is a version of local nonsatiation that also implies $S_i(X)$ is not empty. A_3 rules out the possible difficulties that arise from the fact that $S_i(X)$ is merely R_+^ℓ-open. If $\inf p[S_i(X) - w_i] = 0$ and $pw_i \neq 0$, it is well known that A_3 is superfluous. However, since the conditions that would guarantee $pw_i \neq 0$ are not otherwise needed for the results below, we simply impose A_3. Note that A_3 obviates the need for any assumptions on w_i or $\sum w_i$ being in the interior of R_+^ℓ. A_4 is essential for a linear price description of perfectly competitive, Walrasian equilibrium. A_5 says that an agent's preferences are unaffected by any part of the allocation that is not assigned to the agent—i.e., there are no external effects. The continuity condition, A_6, will not be used in any of the formal results but it will be called upon, informally, to extend some conclusions.

In the following we shall be concerned with the influence of any single agent j on the rest of the economy and it will be convenient to adopt the convention in which $(\cdot)^j$ indicates the corresponding sum excluding j. Thus, $S^j(X) = \sum_{i \neq j} S_i(X)$, $w^j = \sum_{i \neq j} w_i$, and $x^j = \sum_{i \neq j} x_i$. Similarly, we shall use $(\cdot)^0$ to indicate that the sum excludes no agent. Thus, $S^0(X) = \sum S_i(X)$, $w^0 = \sum w_i$, and $x^0 = \sum x_i$.

Remark 1. Since $\sum x_i = w^0$, A_1 and A_2 imply that the condition $w^0 \notin S^0(X)$ is equivalent to $w^0 \in \partial S^0(X)$. With A_5, $w^0 \in \partial S^0(X)$ has the usual interpretation that X is Pareto-optimal—there is no other feasible allocation that would be preferred by all agents. However, without A_5, if $w^0 \in \partial S^0(X)$ no such conclusion is warranted. We can only maintain the rather trivial implication that if any agent is to reach a more preferred allocation *without relying on trade with others*, total resources must be other than w^0.

II. The No-Surplus Condition and Its Dual in $\mathscr{E}$

For the following definitions and throughout the remainder of the paper A_1 and A_2 are assumed.

Trade is productive for all the members of $\mathscr{E}$ whenever there exists an allocation $X = (x_i)$ such that each agent can achieve a surplus through trade —i.e., $x_i \in S_i(W)$, where $W = (w_i)$ is the initial allocation. We may say that the surplus produced through trade is maximal when X is *Pareto-optimal* (PO).

$$\text{PO:} \qquad w^0 \in \partial S^0(X).$$

Following the logic of marginal productivity theory, can an allocation be found that uniquely imputes the total surplus produced through trade to the separate contributions of the participating agents? To formulate this condition we require that each agent receive neither more nor less than its marginal product.

For an exchange economy, we shall say that at the allocation X no agent is receiving more than it is worth if it satisfies the *nonnegative surplus* (NNS) condition.

$$\text{NNS:} \qquad w^j \notin S^j(X), \qquad j = 1, \ldots, n.$$

NNS places an upper bound on the extent to which an agent can exploit its monopoly power by saying, in effect, that no seller j can enforce an outcome in which its customers would do better by refusing to deal with j and going elsewhere.

At an allocation X no agent is receiving less than it is worth if it satisfies the *nonpositive surplus* (NPS) condition.

$$\text{NPS:} \qquad w^j \in \text{cl } S^j(X), \qquad j = 1, \ldots, n \qquad (\text{cl} = \text{closure}).$$

Otherwise, if $w^j \notin \text{cl } S^j(X)$, j is contributing a positive surplus and can therefore claim to be receiving less than it is worth to the rest of the economy. (Unless there are no external effects, A_5, the NNS and NPS conditions may not reflect their marginal productivity interpretations in finite economies. See Remark 2, below.)

An allocation X satisfies NNS and NPS if and only if $w^j \in \partial S^j(X)$, $j = 1,..., n$, where $\partial S^j(X)$ the $R_+{}^l$-boundary of $S^j(X)$. To continue the analogy with marginal productivity theory, if each agent is paid its marginal product, will the sum of the payments just exhaust the total product? For an exchange economy, the question is whether there exists a *no-surplus* (NS) allocation —i.e., an X such that

$$\text{NS:} \qquad w^m \in \partial S^m(X), \qquad m = 0, 1,..., n.$$

The geometrical properties that flow from the convexity hypothesis, A_4, can be exploited to give additional perspective on the concept of NS, especially its relation to Walrasian equilibrium.

Let $P = \{p \in R^l: \| p \| = 1\}$, where $\| \cdot \|$ denotes the Euclidean norm, be the set of vectors on the surface of the unit ball of R^l. Define

$$Q^m(X) = \{ p \in P: \inf p[S^m(X) - w^m] \geqslant 0\}, \qquad m = 0, 1,..., n.$$

If $w^m \notin S^m(X)$, then $Q^m(X) \neq \varnothing$ and conversely, if A_3 is assumed, $Q^m(X) \neq \varnothing$ will be shown to imply $w^m \notin S^m(X)$. This will be used to give a description of X as an NS allocation in terms of the sets $Q^m(X)$.

THEOREM 1. *Let $\mathscr{E}$ satisfy* A_1–A_4. *Then X is an* NS *allocation if and only if* $Q^m(X) \neq \varnothing$, $m = 0, 1,..., n$, *and*

(i) $Q^0(X) \subset Q^j(X)$, $j = 1,..., n$,

(ii) $p \in Q^m(X)$ *implies* $\inf p[S^m(X) - w^m] = 0$, $m = 0, 1,..., n$.

Proof. If $Q^m(X)$, $m = 0, 1,..., n$, satisfy (i) and (ii) and $p \in Q^0(X)$, then $\inf p[S^0(X) - w^0] = \inf p[S^j(X) - w^j]$, $j = 1,..., n$. By construction,

$$\inf p[S^0(X) - w^0] = \inf p[S^j(X) - w^j] + \inf p[S_j(X) - w_j]. \tag{1}$$

Therefore, $\inf p[S_j(X) - w_j] = 0$ and by A_3 if $y \in S_j(X)$, $p(y - w_j) > 0$. Thus, for any $p \in Q^0(X)$, if $y \in S^m(X)$, $p(y - w^m) > 0$, $m = 0, 1,..., n$. This and (ii) imply that $w^m \notin S^m(X)$, all m.

To show that $w^m \in \partial S^m(X)$ it suffices to show that $w^m \in \text{cl}\, S^m(X)$. Suppose the contrary and let $0 \neq \| z^m \| = \inf \| \text{cl}\, S^m(X) - w^m \|$. By A_4 and a standard argument used in the proof of the Separation Theorem, we may set $p = (\| z^m \|)^{-1} z^m \in P$ and obtain the conclusion that $p \in Q^m(X)$. But $0 \neq pz^m = \| z^m \| \leqslant \inf p[S^m(X) - w^m]$, contradicting (ii).

If X is NS, the Separation Theorem implies that $Q^m(X) \neq \varnothing$, $m = 0, 1,..., n$. Let $p \in Q^0(X)$. Since $w^m \in \text{cl}\, S^m(X)$, $\inf p[S^m(X) - w^m] \leqslant 0$. Again by A_4 and (1), above, we may conclude that $\inf p[S^j(X) - w^j] = 0$, $j = 1,..., m$. This establishes (i).

If $p \in Q^m(X)$ and $\inf p[S^m(X) - w^m] > 0$, then $S^m(X)$ can be strictly separated from w^m, which contradicts the fact that $w^m \in \partial S^m(X)$. This establishes (ii).

The following gives a sufficient condition for X to be an NS allocation.

COROLLARY 1.1. *Let* $\mathscr{E}$ *satisfy* A_1–A_4. *If* X *is such that* $Q^0(X) = Q^j(X) \neq \varnothing$, $j = 1,\ldots, n$, *then* X *is* NS.

Proof. It suffices to show condition (ii) of Theorem 1. Since $\bigcap_j Q^j(X) = Q^j(X) = Q^0(X)$ and $p \in \bigcap Q^j(X)$, we have $p(x^j - w^j) \geqslant \inf p[S^j(X) - w^j] \geqslant 0$. This implies $p(x^m - w^m) = 0$, $m = 0, 1,\ldots, n$ and therefore, $\inf p[S^m(X) - w^m] = 0$, $m = 0, 1,\ldots, n$.

To show that the above sufficient condition is practically necessary for NS, we demonstrate

COROLLARY 1.2. *Let* $\mathscr{E}$ *satisfy* A_1–A_4 *and let* X *be an allocation such that the set of net trade vectors* $\{(x_i - w_i)\}$ *is not contained in a subspace of dimension less than* $(l - 1)$. *Then* X *is* NS *if and only if there is a* $p \in P$ *such that* $Q^0(X) = Q^j(X) = \{p\}$, $j = 1,\ldots, n$.

Proof. By Corollary 1.1, if $Q^0(X) = Q^j(X)$, X is NS.

If X is NS, by the argument in Corollary 1.1, there is at least one $p \in P$ such that $p(x_i - w_i) = 0$, $i = 1,\ldots, n$. Since the dimension of the span of $\{(x_i - w_i)\}$ is not less than $(l - 1)$ and $p \in P$ is in its orthogonal complement the dimension is not more than $(l - 1)$ and the dimension of the orthogonal complement is therefore 1.

It has been demonstrated by Mas-Colell [11] and Shafer and Sonnenschein [17] that only those properties of preferences embodied in A_1–A_4 and A_6 are required for the existence of Walrasian equilibrium. Following this lead, as well as a similar framework used by Vind [22], the concept of NS is also formulated so as to depend only on the geometrical character of the preference mapping $S_i(X)$. Since these restrictions do not necessarily include completeness or transitivity, preferences need not be numerically representable. However, additional confirmation of the links between the NS concept and the marginal productivity theory of distribution is gained by assuming that $S_i(X)$ may be derived from a function $u_i : R_+{}^l \to R$ as $\{y\colon u_i(y) > u_i(x_i)\}$.

Let $\mathscr{E}_u = \{(u_i, w_i)\}$ be a numerical representation of $\mathscr{E} = \{(S_i, w_i)\}$. An allocation $X = (x_i)$ produces the utility vector $u(X) = (u_1(x_1),\ldots, u_n(x_n))$. Assuming each u_i is continuous, define

$$v_u{}^0 = \max_{\substack{y_i \in R_+{}^\ell \\ \Sigma y_i = w^0}} \sum u_i(y_i),$$

$$v_u{}^j = \max_{\substack{y_i \in R_+{}^\ell \\ \Sigma_{i\neq j} y_i = w^j}} \sum_{i \neq j} u_i(y_i).$$

Regarding v_u^0 as the maximum total product from $\mathscr{E}_u$ and v_u^j as the maximum when j does not participate, the marginal product of j in $\mathscr{E}_u$ is $(v_u^0 - v_u^j)$. We shall say that $\mathscr{E}_u$ exhibits *product-exhaustion* (PE) if there is an allocation $X = (x_i)$ such that all agents receive their marginal products, i.e., for each $j = 1,\ldots, n$,

$$\text{PE:} \qquad u_j(x_j) = v_u^0 - v_u^j.$$

While the NS concept of marginal productivity is entirely ordinal, the definition of PE depends upon the particular numerical scaling used to represent preferences. To remove some spurious differences let $U(\bar{u}_i) = \{u_i : u_i = \alpha_i \bar{u}_i, \alpha_i > 0\}$ be the set of positive scalar multiples of the function $\bar{u}_i$ and let $\mathscr{E}_U = \{(U(\bar{u}_i), w_i)\}$ describe an equivalence class of numerical representations for $\mathscr{E} = \{(S_i, w_i)\}$. $\mathscr{E}_U$ will be said to satisfy PE if there is an $\mathscr{E}_u \in \mathscr{E}_U$ exhibiting PE.

THEOREM 2. *Let* $\mathscr{E} = \{(S_i, w_i)\}$ *be representable by* $\mathscr{E}_U = \{(\bar{u}_i), w_i)\}$, *where each* $\bar{u}_i$ *is continuous, concave and increasing on* R_+^ℓ. *Then* $X = (x_i)$ *is an* NS *allocation for* $\mathscr{E}$ *if and only if* $\mathscr{E}_U$ *satisfies* PE.

The proof depends on the following property of exchange economies with concave utilities. It is one of the derivable implications of the fact that such an economy can be regarded as a balanced game. (See Shapley and Shubik [19] and Billera and Bixby [3].)

LEMMA 1. *If each* u_i *is continuous and concave on* R_+^ℓ, *then* $\mathscr{E}_u = \{(u_i, w_i)\}_{i=1}^{i=n}$ *satisfies*

$$v_u^0 \geqslant (n-1)^{-1} \sum_{j=1}^{j=n} v_u^j.$$

Proof. Let $\sum_{i \neq j} u_i(x_i^j) = v_u^j$, $j = 1,\ldots, n$. Such an allocation exists by virtue of the continuity of each u_i and the compactness of the domain over which the maximum is to be achieved. For each $i = 1,\ldots, n$, put

$$x_i = (n-1)^{-1} \sum_{j \neq i} x_i^j.$$

Then,

$$(n-1)^{-1} \sum_{j=1}^{j=n} v_u^j = (n-1)^{-1} \sum_{j=1}^{j=n} \sum_{i \neq j} u_i(x_i^j) = \sum_{i=1}^{i=n} (n-1)^{-1} \sum_{j \neq i} u_i(x_i^j)$$

$$\leqslant \sum u_i \left((n-1)^{-1} \sum_{j \neq i} x_i^j\right) = \sum u_i(x_i),$$

where the inequality follows from concavity.

Since $\sum_{i\neq j} x_i^j = w^j$ and $(n-1)^{-1} \sum w^j = w^0$,

$$\sum x_i = (n-1)^{-1} \sum_i \sum_{j\neq i} x_i^j = (n-1)^{-1} \sum_j \sum_{i\neq j} x_i^j$$

$$= (n-1)^{-1} \sum w^j = w^0,$$

and therefore $X = (x_i)$ is an allocation for $\mathscr{E}_u$. Thus, $v_u^0 \geqslant \sum u_i(x_i)$ which, with the above inequality, establishes the desired conclusion.

Proof of Theorem 2. If $X = (x_i)$ satisfies PE for $\mathscr{E}_u$ then $u_j(x_j) = v_u^0 - v_u^j$ and

$$\sum u_j(x_j) = \sum (v_u^0 - v_u^j) = nv_u^0 - \sum v_u^j \geqslant v_u^0,$$

where the inequality follows from Lemma 1. Since $X = (x_i)$ is an allocation for $\mathscr{E}_u$, $\sum u_j(x_j) = v_u^0$ and therefore $w^0 \in \partial S^0(X)$. From PE,

$$\sum_{i\neq j} u_i(x_i) = \sum_{i=1}^{i=n} u_i(x_i) - u_j(x_j) = v_u^0 - (v_u^0 - v_u^j) = v_u^j,$$

and therefore $w^j \in \partial S^j(X)$, $j = 1,..., n$.

For the converse, let

$$V^0 = \left\{ v = (v_1 ,..., v_n) \colon v_i \leqslant \bar{u}_i(y_i), \sum y_i = w^0, y_i \in R_+^\ell \right\}.$$

By the concavity and continuity of each $\bar{u}_i$, V^0 is known to be closed and convex. When X is NS, $w^0 \in \partial S^0(X)$, and therefore $\bar{u}(X) \in \partial V^0$. The fact that each $\bar{u}_i$ is increasing is well known to imply that if $v \in V^0$, then $[v - \bar{u}(X)] \notin R_+^n \backslash \{0\}$. Thus, by the Support Theorem for convex sets, there is an $\alpha = (\alpha_1 ,..., \alpha_n)$, $\alpha_i \geqslant 0$, $\sum \alpha_i = 1$ such that $\sup_{v\in V^0} \alpha v = \alpha \bar{u}(X)$.

Further, the hypothesis that X is NS and each $\bar{u}_i$ is increasing implies that $\alpha_j > 0$ whenever $w_j \neq 0$. Otherwise, if $\alpha_j = 0$ and $w_j \neq 0$

$$\sum_{i\neq j} \alpha_i \bar{u}_i(x_i) = \sum_{i=1}^{i=n} \alpha_i \bar{u}(x_i) = \max_{\substack{y_i \in R_+^\ell \\ \sum_{i\neq j} y_i = w^0}} \sum_{i\neq j} \alpha_i \bar{u}_i(y_i) > \max_{\substack{y_i \in R_+^\ell \\ \sum_{i\neq j} y_i = w^j}} \sum_{i\neq j} \alpha_i \bar{u}_i(y_i).$$

But the inequality contradicts the assumption that $w^j \in \partial S^j(X)$.

Without loss of generality assume each $w_i \neq 0$, and therefore each $\alpha_i > 0$. Putting $u_i = \alpha_i \bar{u}_i$, $i = 1,..., n$, we have for the economy $\mathscr{E}_u$,

$$\sum u_i(x_i) = v_u^0 = \max_{\substack{y_i \in R_+^\ell \\ \sum y_i = w^0}} \sum \alpha_i \bar{u}_i(y_i).$$

Since $w^j \in \partial S^j(X)$ and u_i is increasing, $v_u^j \geqslant \sum_{i \neq j} u_i(x_i)$. If $v_u^j > \sum_{i \neq j} u_i(x_i)$ for some j, then

$$\sum_j v_u^j > \sum_j \sum_{i \neq j} u_i(x_i) = (n - 1)\, v_u^0,$$

contradicting Lemma 1. Therefore, for each j, $\sum_{i \neq j} u_i(x_i) = v_u^j$, and we have the desired conclusion that $u_j(x_j) = v_u^0 - v_u^j$.

III. Walrasian and Perfectly Competitive Equilibrium

A Walrasian equilibrium (WE) for $\mathscr{E}$ is a pair (X, p), where X is an allocation and $p \in P$, such that for each i,

$$\text{WE:} \qquad p(x_i - w_i) = 0 \qquad \text{and} \qquad y \in S_i(X) \;\; \text{implies} \;\; p(y - w_i) > 0.$$

It is useful to give an alternative description.

Proposition 1. *Let $\mathscr{E}$ satisfy* A_1–A_3. *Then (X, p) is a* WE *if and only if* $p \in \bigcap_{j=1}^{j=n} Q^j(X)$.

Proof. If (X, p) is a WE, $\inf p[S_i(X) - w_i] \geqslant 0$. This yields by summation $\inf p[S^j(X) - w^j] \geqslant 0$ and therefore $p \in Q^j(X)$.

If $p \in \bigcap Q^j(X)$, $\inf p[S^j(X) - w^j] \geqslant 0$. By A_2, $px_i \geqslant \inf p\; S_i(X)$ and therefore $px^j \geqslant \inf p\, S^j(X)$. Thus, $p(x^j - w^j) = p(w_j - x_j) \geqslant \inf p[S^j(X) - w^j] \geqslant 0$, for all $j = 1, \ldots, n$. This implies $p(x_j - w_j) = \inf p[S_j(X) - w_j] = 0$, all j. The remaining part of the definition of WE follows from A_3.

Inspection of Theorem 1 and Proposition 1 yields.

Proposition 2. *Let $\mathscr{E}$ satisfy* A_1–A_4. *If X is an* NS *allocation, there is a $p \in P$ such that (X, p) is a* WE.

Comparing the definition of X as a WE allocation to the definition of an NS allocation the former simply requires that $\bigcap_j Q^j(X) \neq \varnothing$ while the latter demands that, in "most" cases, $Q^j(X) = Q^0(X)$. (Compare Corollaries 1.1 and 1.2.) Assuming that $Q^0(X) = \{p\}$, if $Q^j(X) \neq \{p\}$, there are valuations of resources for the "one-fewer" sets of agents that are not common to the valuation of resources by the economy as a whole. The definition of WE resolves the issue of resource valuation by imposing the condition that only those elements of each $Q^j(X)$ that are common to $Q^0(X)$ are acceptable. This is nothing other than the well-known restriction that individual agents must take prices as given. However, with an NS allocation, we shall show that such a restriction is superfluous. This will be accomplished by constructing a definition of equilibrium in which competitive self-interest dictates price-taking behavior and that the definition is equivalent to the NS condition.

Informally, demands are perfectly elastic at the price vector p when the attempt by any agent to set prices for the goods it supplies at levels higher than p results in the loss of all sales *and* markets for the goods supplied by others clear without any adjustment in their prices. To make this experiment possible, each agent must have control over the prices of the goods it supplies.

Normally the commodity space, R_+^ℓ, would be chosen so that the number of goods, l, is as small as possible. It aggregates into one all those goods for which individuals have identical, constant marginal rates of substitution. The resulting interpretation is that each commodity represents a market with the presumption that on any market one and only one price will be charged. Upon such a foundation the concept of WE is applied to determine market-clearing prices. Here we do not take the market with its single price for granted. Rather, the purpose is to open up the model to price-setting by individual agents so as to allow "markets" to emerge as a conclusion.

We shall assume that commodities are disaggregated to bring the specification of initial endowments into the appropriate form of a *personalized commodity space* in which each agent is the unique supplier of its own goods. Formally, commodities are in personalized form if

$$w_i, w_j \in R_+^\ell, \qquad i \neq j, \text{ implies } w_i w_j = 0.$$

For any agent j, we may divide the l (disaggregated) commodities into those that could be supplied by j and those that could not. For $p \in R^\ell$, let p_j be the vector of prices of the former and p^j the prices of the latter. For any p and j, $p = (p^j, p_j)$, let $q(p; j)$ denote any vector $q = (q^j, q_j) \in R^\ell$ such that $q^j = p^j$ and $q_j \geqslant p_j$ and $q_j \neq p_j$. At $q(p; j)$ the price of at least one of j's goods is higher than at p while the prices of the remaining goods, that j cannot control, are the same as in p.

The pair (X, p) is a *perfectly determinate price equilibrium* (PD) for $\mathscr{E}$ if for each $j = 1, \ldots, n$ and any $i \neq j$, if y satisfies

$$\text{PD}_1: \quad q(p; j)(y - w_i) = 0, \; (q(p; j) - p)y \neq 0, \quad \text{then} \quad y \notin \text{cl } S_i(X)$$

and there exists y_i^j, $i \neq j$, such that

$$\text{PD}_2: \quad q(p; j)(y_i^j - w_i) = 0, \quad y_i^j \in \text{cl } S_i(X) \quad \text{and} \quad \sum_{i \neq j} y_i^j = w^j.$$

To interpret, the opportunities available to i are strictly smaller when they are defined by the price vector $q(p; j)$ rather than p since the price of all goods other than j's are the same but j's prices are higher. However, PD states that if i is a purchaser from j, $(q(p; j) - p)y \neq 0$, i has not made the best use of his smaller opportunity set since y is not in cl $S_i(X)$, while if i had refused to deal with j, then trading at the same prices, he could have found buyers and sellers willing to make exchange leading to y_i^j in cl $S_i(X)$. If preferences were transitive and continuous, y_i^j would be strictly preferred to y_i. We shall regard the existence of (X, p) satisfying PD as synonymous with a price equilibrium exhibiting perfectly elastic demands.

THEOREM 3. *Let $\mathscr{E}$ satisfy A_1–A_5 and assume initial endowments are personalized. Then X is an NS allocation if and only if there is a $p \in P$ such that (X, p) is* PD.

Proof. From Corollary 1.1, if X is NS, there is a $p \in P$ such that (X, p) is a WE. Thus, $pw_i = px_i = \inf pS_i(X)$. If $q(p; j)(y - w_i) = 0$ and $(q(p; j) - p)y \neq 0$, then $py < px_i$ and therefore $y \notin \text{cl}\, S_i(X)$ and PD_1 is satisfied. Since $p \in Q^0(X)$ may be chosen so that $p \in Q^j(X)$ and because X is NS, $pw^j = \inf pS^j(X) = px^j$. Also by NS there exists $y_i^j \in \text{cl}\, S_i(X)$ such that $\sum_{i \neq j} y_i^j = w^j$ and therefore for all i and j, $i \neq j$, $py_i^j \geqslant \inf pS_i(X)$, which implies $p(y_i^j - w_i) = 0$ or $q(p; j)(y_i^j - w_i) = 0$, and PD_2 is established.

For the converse it suffices to show that if (X, p) is PD, it is a WE, and therefore satisfies $p \in \bigcap_j Q^j(X)$. If (X, p) is a WE, PD_2 clearly implies NS.

From PD_2 we have $p(y_i^j - w_i) = 0$, and since $y_i^j \in \text{cl}\, S_i(X)$, $\inf pS_i(X) \leqslant py_i^j$. If $\inf pS(X) < py_i^j = pw_i$ for some i, then we may choose $q(p; j)$ close to p and y close to x_i such that $q(p; j)(y - w_i) = 0$ and $(q(p; j) - p)y \neq 0$ such that $y \in \text{cl}\, S_i(X)$, contradicting PD_1. Therefore, $pw_i = py_i^j = \inf pS_i(X) \leqslant px_i$ for all i and therefore $pw_i = px_i$. The remainder of the definition of WE follows from A_3.

An implication of Theorem 3 is that PD or NS may be regarded as the definition of perfectly competitive equilibrium. With it we have the conclusion that agents will rationally choose to set as prices for the commodities they supply the ones dictated by WE.

Remark 2. Without A_5, the absence of external effects, the definition of perfectly competitive equilibrium for finite exchange economies would be deficient. If j set a higher price and sells nothing because his customers go elsewhere, the resulting allocation could be substantially different and, with external effects, preferences could be substantially changed. Thus, even though WE satisfies NS, an agent can possess monopoly power by recognizing the possible adverse effects to customers who might otherwise go elsewhere. This is an added complication due to small numbers. With large numbers external effects do not create a separate problem because the possible disruption to others caused by refusing to deal with any one agent vanishes as the relative size of the agent vanishes.

A trivial illustration of an NS economy occurs whenever the initial endowments for $\mathscr{E}$ are PO. A nontrivial illustration is provided by the following:

EXAMPLE 1. Let the tastes of agent $i = 1, 2, 3$ be represented by the utility function $u_i(x_i) = u_i(x_{i1}, x_{i2}, x_{i3})$, initial endowments by the matrix W and final allocations by the matrices X_α, where

$$u_1(x_1) = [x_{11}(x_{12} + x_{13})]^{1/2},$$
$$u_2(x_2) = [x_{22}(x_{21} + x_{23})]^{1/2},$$
$$u_3(x_3) = [x_{33}(x_{31} + x_{32})]^{1/2};$$

$$W = \begin{array}{c|ccc} i \backslash c & & & \\ \hline & 2 & 0 & 0 \\ & 0 & 2 & 0 \\ & 0 & 0 & 2 \end{array}; \quad X_\alpha = \begin{array}{c|ccc} i \backslash c & & & \\ \hline & 1 & \alpha & 1-\alpha \\ & 1-\alpha & 1 & \alpha \\ & \alpha & 1-\alpha & 1 \end{array}$$

To show that $\mathscr{E}$ is an NS economy, it must be demonstrated that for any X such that $w^j \notin S^j(X)$, $j = 1, 2, 3$, $w^m \in \partial S^m(X)$, $m = 0, 1, 2, 3$. Taking $X = X_\alpha$, $0 \leqslant \alpha \leqslant 1$, this result is easily verified. Note that these allocations are at the opposite extreme from no-trade since their attainment requires that all agents participate in trade. Of course, because each X_α is an NS allocation and there are only three traders, any pair could also do as well by itself. Each agent's participation in an NS allocation is essential only to itself.

It may also be verified that each X_α is a WE (Proposition 2) at prices $p = (r, r, r)$, $r > 0$; and, if any agent j were to raise the price of its good above its value in p, j would sell nothing and excess demands among the other agents be zero without disturbing the other prices (Theorem 3). Further, for any X_α, each agent obtains its marginal product—i.e., $u_j(x_j) = 1 = v_u^0 - v_u^j = 3 - 2$ (Theorem 2).

Remark 3. Note that in Example 1 individual preferences are not strictly convex. (Strict convexity obtains if every line segment connecting two distinct points on $\partial S_i(X)$ lies in $S_i(X)$.) When the commodity space is put in personalized form strict convexity and NS imply that there can be no trade.

At an NS allocation each agent j must be faced with an $S^j(X)$, a portion of whose boundary coincides with the hyperplane $\{y: p(y - w^j) = 0\}$, where p is a WE price vector. If the hyperplane supported $S^j(X)$ but $S^j(X)$ were strictly convex, the only point of intersection would be at $x^j \in \partial S^j(X)$ and therefore $w^j \in \partial S^j(X)$ if and only if $x^j = w^j$.

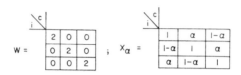

Since strict convexity is the rule even after commodities are put in personalized form, this observation shows that most finite economies will fail to admit an NS allocation. It also exhibits a geometric parallel with the apparently quite different conclusions for large economies. When the scale of each agent becomes very small, the quantities x^j and w^j will differ very little from w^0 and therefore from each other. In this case, $x^j \in \partial S^j(X)$ will imply $w^j \in \partial S^j(X)$ provided that the boundary of $S^j(X)$ in the neighborhood of x^j is, at least to a first approximation, linear—i.e., differentiable. Since differentiability of aggregate preferences will be the rule when preferences are convex, this explains why most large economies will exhibit NS.

IV. The No-Surplus Condition and Its Dual in $\mathscr{E}_\infty$

In this section the characterization of perfectly competitive equilibrium established for finite exchange economies is extended to a simple sequence of economies in which the number of agents is indefinitely increasing. The limit of this process of replication will describe an economy $\mathscr{E}_\infty$. Although not all will be given here, each result in Sections II and III for the economy $\mathscr{E}$ has an extension to $\mathscr{E}_\infty$. This will be emphasized by the notation Theorem 1_∞ or Proposition 2_∞, below, to denote the analogs of Theorem 1 and Proposition 2 for $\mathscr{E}$. Whereas for $\mathscr{E}$ an NS allocation is a WE but not conversely, for $\mathscr{E}_\infty$ the concepts of WE and NS are practically equivalent.

By dividing up the economy $\mathscr{E} = \{(S_i, w_i)\}_{i=1}^{i=n}$, another economy may be constructed with a larger number of agents each of whom operates on a smaller scale. Let $\mathscr{E}_k = \{(S_{i_h}, w_{i_h})\}$, $i = 1,\ldots, n$ and $h = 1,\ldots, k$, be such that for each i and h,

$$kw_{i_h} = w_i .$$

For an allocation $X = (x_i)$ for $\mathscr{E}$, define $[X]^k = (x_{i_h})$, $i = 1,\ldots, n$ and $h = 1,\ldots, k$ such that for each i and h,

$$kx_{i_h} = x_i .$$

Since X is a feasible allocation for $\mathscr{E}$ $(\sum x_i = \sum w_i)$, $[X]^k$ is a feasible allocation for $\mathscr{E}_k$—i.e.,

$$\sum_i \sum_h x_{i_h} = k \sum_i x_{i_h} = \sum x_i = \sum w_i = k \sum_i w_{i_h} = \sum_i \sum_h w_{i_h} .$$

Attention will be confined to allocations for $\mathscr{E}_k$ that can be written as $[X]^k$—all agents of the same type i receive the same allocation. Further, the sequences of allocations considered for the sequence of economies $\{\mathscr{E}_k\}$, $k = 1, 2,\ldots,$ will be restricted to $\{[X]^k\}$—variations in the allocation as k varies are based entirely on scalar multiplication of the fixed allocation X for $\mathscr{E}$.

To complete the description of $\mathscr{E}_k$, define $S_{i_h}([X]^k)$ such that for each i and h,

$$kS_{i_h}([X]^k) = S_i(X).$$

With A_5, $\{\mathscr{E}_k\}$ is a sequence of Edgeworth replica economies that approaches a special case of a continuum of traders economy (Aumann [1]). Without A_5, the above assumption on preferences preserves the replication hypothesis by requiring that the consequences of external effects vary in proportion to the size of the agents. Twice as many individuals each consuming half as much creates no change in aggregate external effects.

For $k = 1, 2,\ldots$, let $\{j(k)\}$ be a sequence that selects one of the agents of one of the types $j = 1,\ldots, n$ from each $\mathscr{E}_k$. With the above restrictions, $j(k)$ could be set equal to j_k, the last agent of type j in $\mathscr{E}_k$. The total resources of all agents in $\mathscr{E}_k$ except $j(k)$ is

$$w^{j(k)} = \sum_{i \neq j} \sum_{h} w_{i_h} + \sum_{h \neq k} w_{j_h} = k \sum_{i \neq j} w_{i_h} + (k-1)\, w_{j_h} = w^j + \frac{k-1}{k} w_j .$$

Analogously, define

$$S^{j(k)}([X]^k) = \sum_{i \neq j} \sum_{h} S_{i_h}([X]^k) + \sum_{h \neq k} S_{j_h}([X]^k)$$

$$= k \sum_{i \neq j} S_{i_h}([X]^k) + (k-1)\, S_{j_h}([X]^k) = S^j(X) + \frac{k-1}{k} S_j(X).$$

The last equality allows us to write $S^{j(k)}([X]^k)$ in the more compressed form $S^{j(k)}(X)$ without any ambiguity.

To extend the NS concept to $\mathscr{E}_\infty$, define

$$d(\partial S^{j(k)}(X), w^{j(k)}) = \inf \| \partial S^{j(k)}(X) - w^{j(k)} \|.$$

The distance is nonzero if and only if either (1) $w^{j(k)} \notin \text{cl}\, S^{j(k)}(X)$, in which case $j(k)$ is contributing a positive surplus to $[X]^k$, or (2) $w^{j(k)} \in S^{j(k)}(X)$ and $j(k)$ is contributing a negative surplus. We shall say that $\{[X]^k\}$ satisfies the NS condition for $\mathscr{E}_\infty$ (NS_∞) if for any $\{j(k)\}$, $k = 1, 2,\ldots,$

$$\text{NS}_\infty: \qquad \lim k\, d(\partial S^{j(k)}(X), w^{j(k)}) = 0.$$

NS_∞ requires not only that the surplus contributed by any one agent, positive or negative, go to zero as k increases, but it must go to zero sufficiently rapidly so that the surplus contributed by any agent to all other agents goes to zero faster than $(k)^{-1}$, a measure of the size of $j(k)$.

For the allocation $[X]^k$ for $\mathscr{E}_k$, define

$$Q^{j(k)}([X]^k) = \{ p \in P \colon \inf p[S^{j(k)}(X) - w^{j(k)}] \geqslant 0\}.$$

There is no ambiguity in writing $Q^{j(k)}([X]^k)$ as $Q^{j(k)}(X)$. For a sequence $\{j(k)\}$ in which $j(k) = j$, let

$$Q^{j(\infty)}(X) = \bigcap_{k=1}^{k=\infty} Q^{j(k)}(X).$$

For $\mathscr{E}$, Corollaries 1.1 and 1.2 showed that $Q^j(X) = Q^0(X)$, $j = 1,..., n$, is sufficient and practically necessary for X to be NS. In the following extension of Theorem 1 describing NS_∞ in terms of its dual, it is shown that for $\mathscr{E}_\infty$ there is complete equivalence.

THEOREM 1_∞. *Let $\mathscr{E}$ satisfy A_1–A_4. Then $\{[X]^k\}$ is NS_∞ for $\{\mathscr{E}_k\}$ if and only if $Q^{j(\infty)}(X) = Q^0(X), j = 1,..., n$.*

The Theorem is proved with the aid of the following.

LEMMA 2. *Let $\mathscr{E}$ satisfy A_1, A_2, and A_4 and let $\{[X]^k\}$ be a sequence of allocations for $\{\mathscr{E}_k\}$ such that $Q^{j(k)}(X) \neq \varnothing$. Then if $j(k) = j$, $k = 1, 2,...$,*

(i) *$\{Q^{j(k)}(X)\}$ is a decreasing sequence of closed subsets of P.*

(ii) *$Q^{j(\infty)}(X) \subset Q^0(X)$.*

Proof. To show that $Q^{j(k)}(X)$ is closed, let $p^r \in Q^{j(k)}(X)$ and $\lim p^r = p$. Thus, $\inf p^r[S^{j(k)}(X) - w^{j(k)}] \geqslant 0$, or $p \in Q^{j(k)}(X)$.

To establish that $\{Q^{j(k)}(X)\}$ is decreasing, it suffices to show that for any $k > 1$ and $j(k) = j(k-1)$, if $p \in Q^{j(k)}(X)$ then $p \in Q^{j(k-1)}(X)$. Letting $p \in Q^{j(k)}(X)$,

$$\begin{aligned}
&\inf p[S^{j(k)}(X) - w^{j(k)}] \\
&\quad = \inf p\left[S^j(X) + \frac{k-1}{k} S_j(X) - \left(w^j + \frac{k-1}{k} w_j\right)\right] \\
&\quad = \inf p[S^j(X) - w^j] + \frac{k-1}{k} \inf p[S_j(X) - w_j] \geqslant 0. \qquad (1)
\end{aligned}$$

By A_2, $\inf p[S^0(X) - w^0] \leqslant 0$ and since

$$\inf p[S^0(X) - w^0] = \inf p[S^{j(k)}(X) - w^{j(k)}] + (k)^{-1} \inf p[S_j(X) - w_j],$$

we must have

$$\inf p[S_j(X) - w_j] \leqslant 0. \qquad (2)$$

When $0 \geqslant \alpha = \inf p[S_j(X) - w_j]$, $((k-2)/(k-1))\alpha \geqslant ((k-1)/k)\alpha$. Thus, (1) and (2) yield

$$\inf p[S^j(X) - w^j] + \frac{k-2}{k-1} \inf p[S_j(x) - w_j] \geqslant 0. \qquad (3)$$

But (3) means that $p \in Q^{j(k-1)}(X)$, which demonstrates (i).

To establish (ii), first note that since $Q^{j(\infty)}(X)$ is the intersection of a decreasing sequence of nonempty compact sets, it is nonempty. If $p \in Q^{j(\infty)}(X)$, then the inequality in (1) is satisfied for all k which obviously implies that $\inf p[S^j(X) - w^j] + \inf p[S_j(X) - w_j] = \inf p[S^0(X) - w^0] \geqslant 0$, or $p \in Q^0(X)$.

Proof of Theorem 1_∞. If $\bigcap_k Q^{j(k)}(X) = Q^0(X)$, then since part (i) of Lemma 2 shows that $\{Q^{j(k)}(X)\}$ is decreasing we must have $Q^0(X) \subset Q^j(X)$, $j = 1,\ldots, n$. Therefore, Proposition 1 allows us to conclude that for any $p \in Q^0(X)$, $\inf p[S_j(X) - w_j] = p(x_j - w_j) = 0, j = 1,\ldots, n$.

Let $\| z^{j(k)} \| = \inf \| \text{cl } S^{j(k)}(X) - w^{j(k)}\|$. If for all $j(k)$, $\| z^{j(k)} \| = 0$, there is nothing more to prove—i.e., $\| z^{j(k)}\| = 0$, $Q^{j(k)}(X) \neq \varnothing$ and A_3 imply that $w^{j(k)} \in \partial S^{j(k)}(X)$. Therefore, assume $\| z^{j(k)}\| \neq 0$. Letting $p^{j(k)} = (\| z^{j(k)}\|)^{-1} z^{j(k)}$, we obtain as in the proof of Theorem 1 that $p^{j(k)} \in Q^{j(k)}(X)$. But

$$\begin{aligned} 0 < k \| z^{j(k)}\| = kp^{j(k)}z^{j(k)} &\leqslant k \inf p[S^{j(k)}(X) - w^{j(k)}] \\ &\leqslant kp^{j(k)}(x^{j(k)} - w^{j(k)}) = p^{j(k)}(w_j - x_j). \end{aligned}$$

The last equality follows from the identity

$$\begin{aligned} k(x^{j(k)} - w^{j(k)}) &= k \left[x^j + \frac{k-1}{k} x_j - \left(w^j + \frac{k-1}{k} w_j\right)\right] \\ &= k(x^j - w^j) + (k-1)(x_j - w_j) = (w_j - x_j). \qquad (1) \end{aligned}$$

Since $p \in Q^0(X)$ implies $p(w_j - x_j) = 0$ and by hypothesis $\inf \| Q^0(X) - p^{j(k)}\| \to 0$, we have the desired conclusion that $k \| z^{j(k)}\| \to 0$.

For the converse, we first show that NS_∞ implies $w^0 \notin S^0(X)$ and therefore $Q^0(X) \neq \varnothing$. Suppose the contrary that $w^0 \in S^0(X)$. Then since $w^{j(k)} \to w^0$, by A_1 we have for sufficiently large k that $w^{j(k)} \in S^0(X)$. Now, $S^0(X) = S^{j(k)}(X) + S_{j(k)}(X)$ and for k large, $S_{j(k)}(X)$ intersects any ϵ-neighborhood of the origin. Therefore, for all sufficiently large k, $w^{j(k)} \in S^{j(k)}(X)$, which contradicts the hypothesis that $\{[X^k]\}$ is NS_∞.

Let $p \in Q^0(X)$. Then A_2 implies

$$0 = \inf p[S^0(X) - w^0] = \inf p[S^{j(k)}(X) - w^{j(k)}] + (k)^{-1} \inf p[S_j(X) - w_j].$$

Multiplying by k, we obtain

$$0 = k \inf p[S^{j(k)}(X) - w^{j(k)}] + \inf p[S_j(X) - w_j].$$

Since $\{[X]^k\}$ is NS_∞,

$$\lim \sup\{k \inf p[S^{j(k)}(X) - w^{j(k)}]\} \leqslant 0.$$

Thus, $\inf p[S_j(X) - w_j] \geqslant 0, j = 1,\ldots, n$, which implies $\inf p[S_j(X) - w_j] = 0$, all j. Therefore,

$$\inf p[S^j(X) - w^j] + \frac{k-1}{k} \inf p[S_j(X) - w_j] \geqslant 0,$$

which means that for all k, $p \in Q^{j(k)}(X)$. This establishes $Q^0(X) \subseteq Q^{j(\infty)}(X)$. Part (ii) of Lemma 2 gives the opposite inclusion.

To exhibit the connections with WE, simply extend Proposition 1. Clearly, if (X, p) is a WE for $\mathscr{E}$, $([X]^k, p)$ is a WE for $\mathscr{E}_k$, $k = 1, 2, \ldots$; and, with A_4, the converse holds.

PROPOSITION 1_∞. *Let $\mathscr{E}$ satisfy A_1–A_4. Then (X, p) is a WE for $\mathscr{E}$ if and only if $p \in \bigcap_j Q^{j(\infty)}(X)$.*

The following extension of Proposition 2 is contained in the proof of Theorem 1_∞.

PROPOSITION 2_∞. *Let $\mathscr{E}$ satisfy A_1–A_4. If $\{[X]^k\}$ is NS_∞, there is a $p \in P$ such that $([X]^k, p)$ is a WE for $\mathscr{E}_k$.*

The relation between WE and NS_∞ is summarized by

COROLLARY $1_\infty \cdot 1$. *Let $\mathscr{E}$ satisfy A_1–A_4 and let X be an allocation for $\mathscr{E}$ such that $Q^0(X) = \{p\}$. Then (X, p) is a WE if and only if $\{[X]^k\}$ is NS_∞.*

Proof. If (X, p) is a WE for $\mathscr{E}$, then $Q^{j(k)}(X) \neq \varnothing$ and therefore by Lemma 2, $Q^{j(\infty)}(X) \subset Q^0(X)$. Since $Q^0(X) = \{p\}$, $Q^{j(\infty)}(X) = Q^0(X)$ and by Theorem 1_∞, $\{[X]^k\}$ is NS_∞.

The converse implication is Proposition 2_∞.

As is the case for $\mathscr{E}$ (see Corollary 1.2), the hypothesis in Corollary $1_\infty \cdot 1$ can, with a mild qualification, be derived as a conclusion.

COROLLARY $1_\infty \cdot 2$. *Let $\mathscr{E}$ satisfy A_1–A_4 and assume that for any X for which $Q^{j(k)}(X) \neq \varnothing$, $\{(x_i - w_i)\}$ does not lie in a subspace of dimension less than $(l - 1)$. Then $\{[X]^k\}$ is NS_∞ if and only if $Q^0(X) = \{p\}$.*

Proof. If $Q^0(X)$ is not a singleton, the dimensionality assumption on $\{(x_i - w_i)\}$ implies that there is at least one $p \in Q^0(X)$ and one j such that $p(w_j - x_j) < 0$. The identity (1) in the proof of Theorem 1_∞ means that $kp[x^{j(k)} - w^{j(k)}] < 0$. By A_2, $k \inf p[S^{j(k)}(X) - w^{j(k)}] \leqslant kp(x^{j(k)} - w^{j(k)})$. Thus, there is a $p \in Q^0(X)$ that does not belong to any $Q^{j(k)}(X)$. But this contradicts the condition $Q^0(X) = Q^{j(\infty)}(X)$ that is established in Theorem 1_∞ as necessary for NS_∞.

The converse implication follows from Lemma 2, part (ii), and Theorem 1_∞.

Remark 4. The principal mathematical distinction between $\mathscr{E}$ and $\mathscr{E}_\infty$ is the conclusion in part (ii) of Lemma 2. For $\mathscr{E}$, the analog of (ii)—$Q^j(X) \subset Q^0(X)$—does not hold even for a WE. This discrepancy accounts for the differences between Theorems 1 and 1_∞ and Corollaries $1 \cdot 1$ and $1_\infty \cdot 1$.

To complete the extension from $\mathscr{E}$ to $\mathscr{E}_\infty$, analogs of Theorems 2 and 3 should be given demonstrating that NS_∞ is equivalent, respectively, to product-exhaustion and to perfectly determinate prices for $\mathscr{E}_\infty$. Results similar to what would be called here Theorem 2_∞ are found in Mas-Colell [12] and Geanakoplos [7].

Because commodities are personalized in the statement of Theorem 3, a literal extension would require an infinite-dimensional commodity space. (This is the subject of Ostroy [15].) Here, however, such a construction is unnecessary. We need only consider a space of dimension $2l$ so as to distinguish the goods supplied by any one $j(k)$ and those supplied by others. Rather than proceed with the formal details, we shall outline an independent proof that suggests why NS_∞ would imply the perfect determinacy of prices. It also shows, by invoking the continuity assumption on preferences, A_6, that we shall be able to obtain a perfectly competitive equilibrium even in the presence of external effects. (Compare Remark 2.)

If X is an allocation for $\mathscr{E}$, let $Y^k = (y^k_{i_h})$ be an allocation for $\mathscr{E}_k$ defined by

$$\begin{aligned} y^k_{i_h} &= w_{i_h}, && \text{if} \quad i_h = j_k, \\ &= x_{i_h}, && \text{if} \quad i = j \quad \text{and} \quad i_h \neq j_k, \\ &= x_{i_h} - (k)^{-1}(x_{i_h} - w_{i_h}), && \text{if} \quad i \neq j. \end{aligned}$$

Y^k describes a reallocation away from $[X]^k$ in which everyone refuses to trade with j_k. Those agents of the same type as $j(k)$ obtain the same outcome as in $[X]^k$ while the members of the other types cut back their excess demands by $(k)^{-1}$. Note that $\sum_i \sum_h y_{i_h} = w^0$, so Y^k is in fact a feasible allocation for $\mathscr{E}_k$.

The total disruption caused by refusing to trade with j_k may be measured by

$$\| Y^k - [X]^k \| = \sum_i \sum_h \| y^k_{i_h} - x_{i_h} \|.$$

Substituting the definition of Y^k, this equals

$$\sum_{i \neq j} \sum_h \|(x_{i_h} - (k)^{-1}(x_{i_h} - w_{i_h}) - x_{i_h})\| + \|(w_{j_k} - x_{j_k})\|$$

$$= \sum_{i \neq j} \|(w_{i_h} - x_{i_h})\| + \|(w_{j_k} - x_{j_k})\| = (k)^{-1} \sum_i \|(w_i - x_i)\|.$$

Therefore, $\lim \| Y^k - [X]^k \| = 0$.

If (X, p) is a WE for $\mathscr{E}$ and $Q^0(X) = \{p\}$, then even if there are external effects, $[X]^k$ is a stable, noncooperative equilibrium for $\mathscr{E}_k$ when k is large because if any agent were to raise the prices of its commodities, the others could, with impunity, go elsewhere.

More precisely, when $[X]^k$ is a WE allocation for $\mathscr{E}_k$, $w^{j(k)} \notin S^{j(k)}(X)$. By invoking A_6 and $\lim \| Y^k - [X]^k \| = 0$, we have for all k sufficiently large, $w^{j(k)} \notin S^{j(k)}(Y^k)$, and therefore $Q^{j(k)}(Y^k) \neq \varnothing$. Lemma 2 may be extended, using A_6 and $\lim \| Y^k - [X]^k \|$, to show that for some k', $\bigcap_{k>k'} Q^{j(k)}(Y^k) \subset Q^0(X)$. Similarly, if $Q^0(X) = \{p\}$ then $\bigcap_{k>k'} Q^{j(k)}(Y_k) = Q^0(X)$ for every $\{j(k)\}$ and the arguments used in the proof of Theorem 1_∞ may be generalized to yield

$$\lim\{k \inf \| \partial S^{j(k)}(Y^k) - w^{j(k)} \|\} = 0.$$

We conclude this section with an example illustrating that the condition $Q^{j(\infty)}(X) = Q^0(X)$ in Theorem 1_∞ is necessary for ANS by showing that without it there is nonvanishing monopoly power to small-scale agents. To avoid complications, A_5 is assumed.

EXAMPLE 2. Consider the economy of equal numbers of type 1 and type 2 traders illustrated by the Edgeworth–Bowley box of Fig. 1.

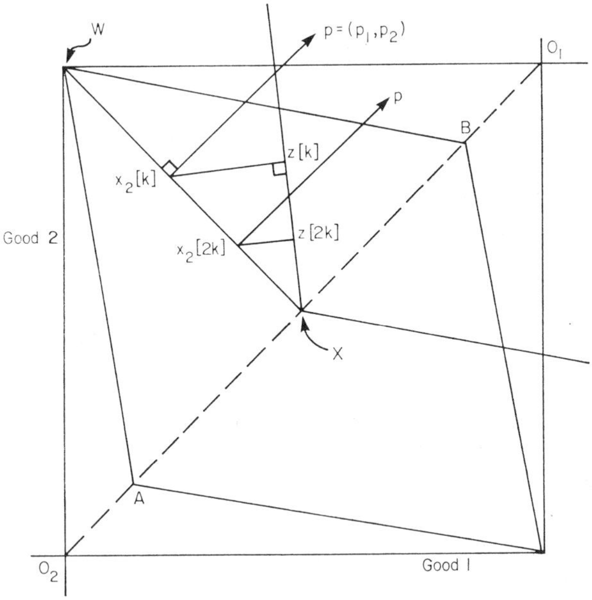

FIGURE 1

Let $\mathscr{E}_k^{j(k)}$ denote the economy consisting of all agents in $\mathscr{E}_k$ except $j(k)$, $j = 1, 2$. No matter what the value of k, the WE allocations for $\mathscr{E}_k$ include all points along the line AB, while the WE allocations for $\mathscr{E}_k^{1(k)}$ or $\mathscr{E}_k^{2(k)}$ include only the points A or B, respectively.

The example is of some historical interest because of its similarity to Edgeworth's master–servant example in which each master has need of only one servant and one servant cannot serve two masters. If the minimum wage at which servants would offer themselves is α and the maximum wage at which masters would accept is β, Edgeworth noted that as long as there is an equal number of masters and servants, then no matter how many there are, the equilibrium wage is indeterminate, lying somewhere between α and β ($\alpha < \beta$). If there is one more master than servant (or one more servant than master) indeterminacy disappears and the wage rate becomes β (or α). Edgeworth attributed the indeterminacy to the indivisibility of the good "domestic service" and on the basis of his example modified his proposition that large numbers of traders in a market lead to a determinate outcome only when goods are divisible. The self-evident similarity of the master–servant example to Example 2, in which goods are divisible, suggests that some other explanation is called for. What is common to Edgeworth's example and Example 2 is the failure of NS_∞.

To see this, consider the WE allocation $X = (x_1, x_2)$ in Fig. 1 replicated k times for $\mathscr{E}_k$ and consider how close the members of $\mathscr{E}_k^{1(k)}$ can come to doing as well. From the construction of Y^k, above, all of the type 1 traders can share x_1 and all of the type 2's may share $x_2[k] = x_2 - (1/k)(x_2 - w_2)$. It would then require $z[k] = (z_1[k], z_2[k])$ additional resources to minimize, with respect to Euclidean distance, the amounts of additional resources necessary for all the type 2 agents to be as satisfied as they are in $[X]^k$. If we double k, we may decrease the additional resources to make *each* type 2 agent as satisfied, but we cannot decrease the amounts by more than one-half, i.e., $2 \| z[2k] \| = \| z[k] \|$. Thus, the influence of any type 1 agent, measured in this way, does not decrease as k increases, and $\{[X]^k\}$ does not satisfy NS_∞.

To exhibit the consequences for the elasticity of demand, assume that other traders are transacting at the WE prices p. Then, the maximum exchange rate a seller of type 1 can set, without losing all his business, does not go to p as k increases. After the type 2 traders have purchased all that the $(k - 1)$ type 1 traders are willing to supply at p, the remaining type 1 trader can offer any exchange rate ρ such that $p_1/p_2 < \rho < z_1[k]/z_2[k]$ and sell, when k is large, as much of commodity 1 as it likes.

If the preferences of the type 2 traders were differentiable at the WE allocation X, and therefore there were a unique supporting hyperplane to $S^0(X) = S_1(X) + S_2(X)$ at w^0, $\{[X^k]\}$ would, by Corollary $1_\infty \cdot 1$, satisfy NS_∞. In this case (not illustrated), the angle between p and $z[k]$ would tend to zero as k increased and the sequence $\{[X^k]\}$ would be approaching one in which WE prices p became PD.

Remark 5. Let $\delta(A, B)$ denote the Hausdorff distance between two nonempty closed sets in R^l. The condition (a) $\bigcap_{k=1}^{k=\infty} Q^{j(k)}(X) = Q^0(X)$ used to characterize NS_∞ in Theorem 1_∞ is equivalent to (b) $\lim \delta(Q^{j(k)}(X), Q^0(X)) = 0$. Condition (b) is shown in [15] to replace (a) in economies that do not have a finite number of types of agents.

Let $W(\mathscr{E}_k)$ and $W(\mathscr{E}_k^{j(k)})$ be subsets of P denoting the (closed) sets of price vectors corresponding to WE allocations in $\mathscr{E}_k$ and $\mathscr{E}_k^{j(k)}$. Since $\lim \delta(W(\mathscr{E}_k^{j(k)}), W(\mathscr{E}_k))$ does not exist in Example 2, it might be conjectured that this is the source of nonvanishing monopoly power of individual agents and that (c) $\lim \delta(W(\mathscr{E}_k^{j(k)}), W(\mathscr{E}_k)) = 0$ is an alternative to $\lim \delta(Q^{j(k)}(X), Q^0(X)) = 0$ as a characterization of NS_∞. This conjecture is false in both directions—(b) neither implies nor is implied by (c).

To show that (c) does not suffice for (b), simply perturb the initial endowments in Example 2 so that $W(\mathscr{E}_k) = \{p\}$ for all k but the WE allocation remains at the point where preferences are kinked. It may then be demonstrated that (c) holds. However, as long as preferences are not differentiable at the WE allocation, the same argument exhibiting the failure of NS_∞ in Example 2 leads to the same conclusion here.

To show that (c) is not necessary, consider an Edgeworth–Bowley box example where preferences are differentiable in the interior and there are a continuum of WE prices and allocations for each $\mathscr{E}_k$. Examples may be constructed to show that $W(\mathscr{E}_k^{j(k)})$ does not approach $W(\mathscr{E}_k)$—i.e., (c) fails. (For a graphical illustration see Bewley [2], Example 2].) Nevertheless, the smoothness of preferences implies that as k increases the total surplus attributable to any agent at any Walrasian allocation goes to zero. Even though the removal of any one would cause an abrupt change in WE prices, no agent can usefully exploit this. The failure of markets to clear when an agent threatens to withdraw his supplies if he does not receive a higher price may be essentially confined to the disappointed demands of the very trader who is asking for more.

V. No-Surplus and Core Equivalence as Alternative Characterizations of Perfectly Competitive Equilibrium

The presence of external effects vitiates any comparisons between the core, which is limited to allocations that are truly Pareto-optimal, and NS. (See Remark 1.) Thus, in the following discussion A_5 is assumed. It will be useful to separate the comparisons for $\mathscr{E}$ from those for $\mathscr{E}_\infty$.

$\mathscr{E}$: Let T be any nonempty subset of $I = \{1,..., n\}$, the index set of agents. Define $w_T = \sum_{i \in T} w_i$, $S_T(X) = \sum_{i \in T} S_i(X)$ and $Q_T(X) = \{p \in P\colon \inf p[S_T(X) - w_T] \geqslant 0\}$.

An allocation X is said to be in the core of $\mathscr{E}$ if for all T, $w_T \notin S_T(X)$. With A_1–A_5, it may be shown that X is in the core if and only if for all T, $Q_T(X) \neq \varnothing$.

Consider the following three conditions:

(i)	$Q^j(X) = Q^0(X) \neq \varnothing, \quad j = 1,..., n$	(NS)	Corollary 1.2
(ii)	$\bigcap_j Q^j(X) \neq \varnothing$	(WE)	Proposition 1
(iii)	$Q_T(X) \neq \varnothing, \quad \text{all} \quad T \subseteq I$	(CORE)	

Obviously, (i) $\Mapsto$ (ii), where $\Mapsto$ means "implies but is not implied by." Further, it is well known that (ii) $\Mapsto$ (iii).

The core criterion for $\mathscr{E}$ to be perfectly competitive is that (iii) $\Rightarrow$ (ii). The NS criterion is (i), assuming the linear independence hypothesis in Corollary 1.2. The relation between the two criteria is summarized by

PROPOSITION 3. *For* $\mathscr{E}$, (i) $\Mapsto$ [(iii) $\Rightarrow$ (ii)].

The implication $\Rightarrow$ follows from the fact that (i) implies all of the other conditions. The following example demonstrates $\Mapsto$.

EXAMPLE 3. Let tastes be defined by the utility functions $u_i(x_i) = u_i(x_{i1}, x_{i2}, x_{i3})$, $i = 1, 2, 3$, and 4, and let initial and final allocations be given by W and X^*, respectively, where

$$\begin{aligned} u_1(x_1) &= (x_{11}x_{12}x_{13})^{1/3}, \\ u_2(x_2) &= (x_{21}x_{22}x_{23})^{1/3}, \\ u_3(x_3) &= (x_{31}x_{32}x_{33})^{1/3}, \\ u_4(x_4) &= \frac{x_{41} + x_{42} + x_{43}}{3}; \end{aligned}$$

$$W = \begin{array}{c|c|c|c|} {}_{i}\diagdown^{c} & & & \\ \hline & 3 & 0 & 0 \\ \hline & 0 & 3 & 0 \\ \hline & 0 & 0 & 3 \\ \hline & 1 & 1 & 1 \\ \hline \end{array} ; \quad X^* = \begin{array}{c|c|c|c|} {}_{i}\diagdown^{c} & & & \\ \hline & 1 & 1 & 1 \\ \hline & 1 & 1 & 1 \\ \hline & 1 & 1 & 1 \\ \hline & 1 & 1 & 1 \\ \hline \end{array}$$

With little difficulty, the reader may verify that X^* is a WE allocation at the price vector $p^* = (r, r, r)$, $r > 0$, that yields the utility vector $u^* = (u_1^*, u_2^*, u_3^*, u_4^*) = (1, 1, 1, 1)$.

An outline of the argument that X^* is the only allocation in the core is as follows: The coalition $\overline{123}$ can achieve any (u_1, u_2, u_3) such that $u_1 + u_2 + u_3 = 3$, and 4 can achieve $u_4 = 1$ on its own. It follows that for any $u = (u_1, u_2, u_3, u_4)$ in the core, $u_1 + u_2 + u_3 = 3$ and $u_4 = 1$, and if $u_i < 1$, $i \neq 4$, then because $w_T \in \operatorname{cl} S_T(X^*)$, $T = \overline{i4}$, the coalition $\overline{i4}$ will upset u. This means that $u = (1, 1, 1, 1)$ and this is achievable only by the allocation X^*.

X^* does not satisfy NS—$w_T \notin \operatorname{cl} S_T(X^*)$ for $T \in \{\overline{124}, \overline{134}, \overline{234}\}$.

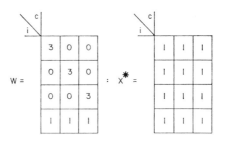

The core does not capture the monopoly power of individuals 1, 2, or 3. For example, without 1, the WE price vector for the economy $\mathscr{E}^1$, the economy without agent 1, is $p = (2r, r, r)$. In terms of prices, 1's contribution or marginal product may be measured by the decrease in the WE price of the commodity he supplies. From a noncooperative point of view, there does not appear to be any reason why 1 should surrender all of the surplus represented by this price decrease to the other traders.

Such a finding has already been reported for economies composed of a (nonatomic) continuum of agents and large or atomic agents. See Gabszewicz and Mertens [6] and Shitovitz [20]. They constructed classes of economies exhibiting Equivalence, i.e., [(iii) $\Rightarrow$ (ii)], but the presence of the large traders precludes (i). Example 3 shows that such results also occur in purely atomic economies.

$\mathscr{E}_\infty$: Let I_k be the index set of agents in $\mathscr{E}_k$. The analogous conditions are quite similar.

(i) $Q^{j(\infty)}(X) = Q^0(X) \neq \varnothing, \quad j = 1,\ldots, n$	(NS)	Theorem 1_∞
(ii) $\bigcap_j Q^{j(\infty)}(X) \neq \varnothing$	(WE)	Proposition 1_∞
(iii) $Q_T(X) \neq \varnothing$, all $T \subseteq I_k$, $k = 1, 2,\ldots$	(CORE)	

As in $\mathscr{E}$, (i) $\mapsto$ (ii), and (ii) $\mapsto$ (iii). Again, the core criterion for $\mathscr{E}_\infty$ to be perfectly competitive is [(iii) $\Rightarrow$ (ii)] and NS_∞ is (i). Example 2 demonstrates that [(iii) $\Rightarrow$ (ii)] $\not\Rightarrow$ (i) and therefore we have the analog of Proposition 3 for $\mathscr{E}_\infty$.

The result [(iii) $\Rightarrow$ (ii)], the core convergence theorem, was initiated by Edgeworth [5], revived by Shubik [21], and put into its current form by Debreu and Scarf [4]. (Hildenbrand [9] gives the considerable extensions of this result.) To establish the NS_∞ property requires a different method of proof than [(iii) $\Rightarrow$ (ii)] and it does not hold in quite the same generality. However, *when $Q^0(X) = \{p\}$, the core convergence theorem is an immediate implication of* Lemma 2 in Section IV. In this respect, our approach is closely related to the simplication of the Debreu–Scarf result obtained by Hansen [8].

Remark 6. In the demonstration of (i), allocations were restricted to those satisfying equal treatment—allocations of the form $[X]^k$. With the core approach, $[X]^k$ may be derived as a conclusion. This can also be demonstrated via the NNS condition of Section II. In fact, the NNS condition may be used to exhibit the analog of (i) for sequences of economies in which agents are not drawn from a fixed, finite set of types. This result, in Ostroy [14], parallels a core convergence theorem of Nishino [13].

If we adopt a generic point of view, distinctions between the core criterion and NS vanish. For $\mathscr{E}_\infty$, they coincide when $Q^0(X) = \{p\}$ and for $\mathscr{E}$, even though endless cases such as Example 3 may be constructed, the fact remains that within the entire class of finite economies each criterion says that the set of perfectly competitive economies is negligible.

It is only at the conceptual level that differences emerge. With the core criterion, perfectly competitive equilibrium is obtained as the residual outcome after all groups of agents cooperate in the interests of improving upon any given allocation but no group is able to hold together to use its potential monopoly power to extract a more favorable outcome. With NS, just the opposite occurs. Only small groups (individuals) are able to form but they are relied upon to bargain as monopolists for the maximum they can possibly extract. It is remarkable that these two seemingly contradictory approaches should "almost always" yield the same conclusion. It appears that the economic forces permitted and precluded by the one are almost always counterbalanced by what is precluded and permitted by the other. However, a closer look at the discrepancies, such as Example 3 for $\mathscr{E}$, Example 2 for $\mathscr{E}_\infty$ (due to Edgeworth!), or the results of Shitovitz [20] and Gabszewicz and Mertens [6] for so-called "mixed" economies show that what is permitted and precluded by the one is not always counterbalanced by the other. Which interpretation—the core or NS criterion—is the preferred description of what will frequently be equivalent mathematical conditions characterizing perfectly competitive equilibrium should be judged on its eventual connections to the theory of imperfect competition.

Acknowledgment

Much of this material was formulated in discussions with Louis Makowski. I have also benefited from many comments by Bryan Ellickson and Juan Urrutia. Fritz Grafe pointed out several inaccuracies in an earlier version.

References

1. R. J. Aumann, Markets with a continuum of traders, *Econometrica* **32** (1964), 39–50.
2. T. F. Bewley, Edgeworth's conjecture, *Econometrica* **41** (1973), 415–452.
3. L. Billera and R. Bixby, A characterization of polyhedral market games, *Internat. J. Game Theory* **2** (1973), 253–261.
4. G. Debreu and H. Scarf, A limit theorem on the core of an economy, *Internat. Econ. Rev.* **4** (1963), 235–246.
5. F. Y. Edgeworth, "Mathematical Phychics," Kegan Paul, London, 1881.
6. J. Gabszewicz and J. F. Mertens, An equivalence theorem for the core of an economy whose atoms are not "too" big, *Econometrica* **39** (1971), 713–721.
7. J. Geanakoplos, "The Bargaining Set and Nonstandard Analysis," Technical Report No. 1, Center on Decision and Conflict in Complex Organizations, Harvard University, June 1978.
8. T. Hansen, A note on the limit theorem of the core of an exchange economy, *Internat. Econ. Rev.* **19** (1969), 469–483.

9. W. HILDENBRAND, "Core and Equilibria of a Large Economy," Princeton Univ. Press, Princeton, N. J., 1974.
10. L. MAKOWSKI, A characterization of perfectly competitive economies with firms, *J. Econ. Theory* **22** (1980), 208–221.
11. A. MAS-COLELL, An equilibrium existence theorem without complete or transitive preferences, *J. Math. Econ.* **1** (1974), 237–246.
12. A. MAS-COLELL, Marginal contributions and Walrasian allocations, unpublished manuscript, 1978.
13. H. NISHINO, On the occurrence and the existence of competitive equilibria, *Keio Econ Stud.* **8** (1971), 33–67.
14. J. M. OSTROY, "Convergence to Perfectly Competitive Equilibria," UCLA Discussion Paper No. 112, March 1978.
15. J. M. OSTROY, The no-surplus condition and its dual in non-atomic exchange economies, unpublished manuscript, November 1979.
16. D. ROBERTS AND A. POSTLEWAITE, The incentives for price-taking behavior in large exchange economies, *Econometrica* **44** (1976), 115–128.
17. W. SHAFER AND H. SONNENSCHEIN, Some theorems on the existence of competitive equilibrium, *J. Econ. Theory* **11** (1975), 83–93.
18. L. S. SHAPLEY, A value for *n*-person gamel, *in* "Contributions to the Theory of Games II" (H. W. Kuhn and A. W. Tucker, Eds.), Princeton Univ. Press, Princeton, N. J., 1953.
19. L. S. SHAPLEY AND M. SHUBIK, On market games, *J. Econ. Theory* **1** (1969), 9–25.
20. B. SHITOVITZ, Oligopoly in markets with a continuum of traders, *Econometrica* **41** (1974), 467–501.
21. M. SHUBIK, Edgeworth market games, *in* "Contributions to the Theory of Games, IV" (A. W. Tucker and R. D. Luce, Eds.), Princeton Univ. Press, Princeton, N. J., 1959.
22. K. VIND, Edgeworth allocations in an exchange economy with many traders, *Internat. Econ. Rev.* **5** (1964), 165–177.

A Characterization of Perfectly Competitive Economies with Production*

LOUIS MAKOWSKI

Department of Applied Economics, University of Cambridge, Cambridge CB3 9DE, England

Received January 10, 1979

This paper answers the question, what do you need for perfect competition with production? The answer given is that you need to realize an allocation in which no individual contributes a surplus to anyone else. This essentially amounts to giving each individual his "marginal product." In the model of perfect competition, profits are competitively determined rents: they reflect the marginal product of entrepreneurs. And the competitive theory of value derives from the competitive theory of distribution.

It is well known that a Walrasian equilibrium will generally not be a perfectly competitive equilibrium: heuristically, an equilibrium in which no single economic agent can influence the level of equilibrium prices. When will a Walrasian equilibrium be perfectly competitive?

For exchange economies, Ostroy in [4] has formulated the no surplus condition as a test for verifying whether a Walrasian equilibrium is perfectly competitive. It has been observed by Ostroy in [5] that the no surplus theory is a generalized marginal productivity theory of distribution.

In this paper, some of Ostroy's results are extended to general economies with production. The extension occurs in an Arrow–Debreu type production model with one important difference: production possibilities belong to individuals ("entrepreneurs") rather than to firms.

The main results of the paper may now be summarized.

(1) Perfectly competitive allocations are no surplus allocations (Theorems 1 and 2 below).

(2) Perfectly competitive entrepreneurs fully appropriate their contribution to aggregate consumers' surplus in the form of profits. Alternatively expressed, profits measure surplus contributed by entrepreneurs (Proposition 1 below). Thus,

* This paper has grown out of conversations with Joseph Ostroy. He is virtually its co-author. Of course, any errors are solely my responsibility. Research for the paper was partly supported by NSF Grant SOC 74-17982, and partly by a grant from the (U.K.) Social Science Research Council. This support is gratefully acknowledged.

Reprinted from *Journal of Economic Theory* **22**, No. 2, 208–221 (April 1980)
ISBN 0-12-476750-8

(3) Under perfect competition profits are competitively determined rents to entrepreneurial ability (Proposition 2 below).

(4) In the "long-run" when entrepreneurial abilities are not scarce and hence essentially redundant, there is product exhaustion with zero profits whether or not there are constant returns to scale (Theorem 3 and, in particular, Lemma 4).

(5) In a special case of the model, so called "simple production economies,"

(a) No surplus allocations are equivalent to allocations that give each agent his marginal product. Alternatively expressed, no surplus is equivalent to product exhaustion or "adding up" (Lemmas 6, 7). Thus, in view of (1),

(b) There is perfect competition if and only if there is adding up.

(c) The fact that profits are rents, (3), is reflected in the simple formula that for each individual his profits equal the marginal productivity of his entrepreneurial abilities (Theorem 4). Thus,

(d) In the long-run there is product exhaustion or adding-up with zero profits since the marginal productivity of entrepreneurs equals zero (Lemma 8).

The results under (5) perhaps deserve some elaboration. They effectively say that the no surplus condition yields a modern solution to the classical adding-up problem. In particular, it is remarkable that adding up is not only implied by perfect competition (as neoclassical economists knew), but also implies perfect competition.

1. Competitive Allocations as No Surplus Allocations

1A. *The Basic Model*[1]

There is a finite set of individuals I. The economy is described by a triple $(X_i, Y_i, A_i)_{i \in I}$ consisting of a trading possibility set $X_i \subset R^n$ for each individual $i \in I$, a production possibility set $Y_i \subset R^n$ for each individual, and an "at least as good as" correspondence A_i from X_i to X_i for each individual. A_i completely preorders X_i; i.e., for any x_i, y_i, z_i in X_i $x_i \in A_i(x_i)$ (reflexivity), $x_i \in A_i(y_i)$ and $y_i \in A_i(z_i)$ implies $x_i \in A_i(z_i)$ (transitivity), and $x_i \in A_i(y_i)$ or $y_i \in A_i(x_i)$ (completeness).[2]

[1] Given sets A and B in R^n and points x and p in R^n, $px < pA$ means $px < py$ for all $y \in A$; conv A means the convex hull of A; ri A means the relative interior of A; and $A-B$ means the set of all points $y = y^1 - y^2$, where $y^1 \in A$ and $y^2 \in B$.

[2] Both the completeness and transitivity assumptions can be substantially weakened, at some cost in terms of complicating the exposition.

A pair $(x, y) \in \times_i X_i \times_i Y_i$ is a *feasible allocation* if $\sum_i x_i = \sum_i y_i$. Similarly, a pair

$$(x^i, y^i) \in \bigtimes_{\substack{h \in I \\ h \neq i}} X_h \bigtimes_{\substack{h \in I \\ h \neq I}} Y_h$$

is a *feasible allocation for the economy without individual i* if $\sum_{h \neq i} x_h{}^i = \sum_{h \neq i} y_h{}^i$. Henceforth, (x, y) and (x^i, y^i) will represent such feasible allocations respectively.

1B. *Competitive Equilibrium*

It will be convenient to define a "better than" correspondence B_i from X_i to X_i for each individual i: $B_i(x_i) \equiv \{ y_i \in X_i : y_i \in A_i(x_i) \text{ but } x_i \notin A_i(y_i)\}$.

Letting $p \in R^n$, (x, y, p) is a *Walrasian equilibrium* (written $(x, y, p) \in W$) if for each i, $px_i = py_i = \sup pY_i < pB_i(x_i)$. Similarly, (x^i, y^i, p) is a *Walrasian equilibrium for the economy without individual i* (written $(x^i, y^i, p) \in W^i$) if for each $h \neq i$, $px_h{}^i = py_h{}^i = \sup pY_h < pB_h(x_h{}^i)$.

Suppose $(x, y, p) \in W$. Individual *i has no monopoly power* in the equilibrium (written $(x, y, p) \in C^i$) if there exists an $(x^i, y^i, p) \in W^i$. That is, i has no monopoly power in (x, y, p) if the economy can, without i's supplies and demands, still achieve a Walrasian equilibrium *at the same prices p*. If i has no monopoly power in (x, y, p) then i cannot influence the level of Walrasian equilibrium prices, at least according to a basic test: If when all other individuals charge the prices in p, i tries to get higher prices than those in p for all the commodities he sells in the Walrasian equilibrium and tries to get lower prices than those in p for all the commodities he buys in the equilibrium he will be unsuccessful. Any individual h, $h \neq i$, will clearly prefer to buy (sell) all the commodities he wants to buy (sell) at the lower (higher) prices in p rather than at the higher (lower) prices offered by i. But if i has no monopoly power in (x, y, p) then all $h \neq i$ can buy (sell) all they want at p without i.

Aggregating over individuals, (x, y, p) is a *Competitive Equilibrium* (written $(x, y, p) \in C$) means $(x, y, p) \in W$ and for each i, i has no monopoly power in (x, y, p). Thus, if $(x, y, p) \in C$, then no one individual can influence the level of Competitive Equilibrium prices by withdrawing his supplies and demands from the market. Alternatively expressed, in a Competitive Equilibrium no one individual can influence the level of equilibrium prices by trying to sell all his goods at prices higher than p and buy all his goods at prices lower than p. Thus a Competitive Equilibrium satisfies a basic test for the existence of perfect competition in the heuristic sense.

Remark 1. It should be noted that there are other tests—perhaps second-order tests—for the existence of perfect competition in the heuristic sense that a Competitive Equilibrium may not satisfy. For example, if an individual tries to sell some—but not all—of his commodities for more than their equilibrium prices, he may be able to influence the level of prices, even in a Competitive Equilibrium. This objection will be overcome somewhat in the next section. Also, an individual may be able to influence the level of equilibrium prices by "cornering a market"—buying up all supplies of a commodity and then reselling the commodity as a monopolist.[3] In spite of these objections, I would argue that the relatively simple definition of a Competitive Equilibrium given above reflects a lot of what we intuitively mean by a competitive equilibrium.

1C. *The No Surplus Condition*

Let $A^i(x) \equiv \{(x^i, y^i)\text{: for each } h \neq i,\ x_h{}^i \in A_h(x_h)\}$. Individual *i contributes no surplus in* (x, y) (written $(x, y) \in NS^i$) means $A^i(x) \neq \varnothing$ but for any $(x^i, y^i) \in A^i(x)$ and any $h \neq i$ $x_h{}^i \notin B_h(x_h)$. If $(x, y) \in NS^i$ then the set of all individuals except i can on their own achieve an allocation in which every individual in the set is as well off as with x. Alternatively expressed, if $(x, y) \in NS^i$ then x imputes to i his entire contribution to aggregate consumers' surplus.

Let the aggregate production set be $Y \equiv \sum_i Y_i$; (x, y) is a *no surplus allocation* (written $(x, y) \in NS$) means $0 \notin \sum_i B_i(x_i) - Y$ and for each i, i contributes no surplus in (x, y). The first condition says that x is a Pareto optimum. The second says that every individual is inessential to the welfare of all others relative to the allocation x.

Note that the no surplus condition is purely technological; it does not depend on prices.

Let us assume

(A1) For each i and each $x_i \in X_i$: $x_i \in cl\ B_i(x_i)$ (local nonsatiation).

(A2) For each i and each $x_i \in X_i$: $px_i \leqslant pB_i(x_i)$, $p \neq 0$, implies $px_i < pB_i(x_i)$.

(A3) $0 \notin \sum_i B_i(x_i) - Y$ implies $0 \notin ri\ (\text{conv}(\sum_i B_i(x_i) - Y))$.

Assumptions (A1)–(A2) are standard. The economic literature contains a number of sets of sufficient conditions guaranteeing (A2). Assumption (A3) will be satisfied if $\sum_i B_i(x_i)$ and Y are convex. We use a generalization of the standard convexity assumptions to allow for the possibility of nonconvexities and indivisibilities. We now prove that

THEOREM 1. (characterization of competitive equilibria). *Assume* (A1)–(A3). *Then* (x, y, p) *is a Competitive Equilibrium iff* (x, y) *is a no surplus allocation.*

[3] I am indebted to Earl Thompson for pointing out to me the importance of "cornering the market" strategies.

Theorem 1 is an extension to economies with production of the basic characterisation result in Ostroy [4]. Since, given (A1), any Walrasian equilibrium is a Pareto optimum, the theorem is a direct consequence of the following two lemmas.

LEMMA 1. *Assume* (A1) *and suppose* $(x, y, p) \in W$. *Then for any individual* i, i *has no monopoly power in* (x, y, p) *iff* i *contributes no surplus in* (x, y).

Proof. If $(x, y, p) \in C^i$ then there exists $(x^i, y^i, p) \in W^i$. It is easy to verify that $(x^i, y^i) \in A^i(x)$. Hence, since (x, y) is in the core, $(x, y) \in NS^i$.

On the other hand, suppose $(x, y) \in NS^i$. We show that $(x^i, y^i, p) \in W^i$, where $(x^i, y^i) \in A^i(x)$. Since for all $h \neq i$, $px_h{}^i \geqslant px_h = py_h \geqslant py_h{}^i$, if there exists an h such that the above held with some inequalities then $\sum_h x_h{}^i = \sum_h y_h{}^i$ would be contradicted. So,

$$px_h{}^i = py_h{}^i = \sup pY_h < pB_h(x_h{}^i).$$

The last inequality follows from the fact that $x_h{}^i \in A_h(x_h)$ and $x_h \in A_h(x_h{}^i)$, so $B_h(x_h{}^i) = B_h(x_h)$. Q.E.D.

LEMMA 2 (existence of values). *Assume* (A1)–(A3). *Then if* (x, y) *is a no surplus allocation, there exists some* $p \neq 0$ *such that* $(x, y, p) \in W$.

Proof. $(x, y) \in NS$ implies $0 \notin \sum_i B_i(x_i) - Y$. So, in view of (A3), there exists $p \neq 0$ such that $p \sum_i B_i(x_i) - pY \geqslant 0 = \sum_i px_i - \sum_i py_i$. Or, in view of (A1), for each i

$$px_i \leqslant pB_i(x_i) \qquad \text{and} \qquad py_i \geqslant pY_i .$$

In view of (A2), it suffices to show that $px_i = py_i$. If not, for some i $\sum_{h \neq i} px_h > \sum_{h \neq i} py_h$. Consider $(x^i, y^i) \in A^i(x)$. $\sum_h px_h{}^i \geqslant \sum_h px_h > \sum_h py_h \geqslant \sum_h py_h{}^i$, contradicting $\sum_h x_h{}^i = \sum_h y_h{}^i$. Q.E.D.

2. PROFITS AS RENTS

In this section we want to characterize the nature of the profits in the model. To do so, we must isolate the contribution of an individual's production possibilities from that of his trading possibilities (which reflect his endowment); in general both will contribute to the individual's consumer surplus. To isolate these two contributions, we shall make the following, basically technical assumption:

(A4) For any $i \in I$ there exists an $\bar{i} \in I$ such that $X_{\bar{i}} = X_i$, $A_{\bar{i}} = A_i$, but $Y_{\bar{i}} = \{0\}$.

That is, if i has entrepreneurial abilities there is another individual with the same preferences and endowment but no entrepreneurial abilities.[4] Comparing i's equilibrium allocation with that of his double, $\bar{i}$, will allow us to isolate the contribution of Y_i *provided* i is a perfectly competitive entrepreneur, as well as a perfectly competitive consumer. To establish this proviso, we shall need a slightly stronger notion of competitive equilibrium and a corresponding, slightly stronger no surplus condition.

2A. *Perfectly Competitive Equilibrium*.

First, two preliminary definitions. A pair $(\bar{x}, \bar{y}^i) \in \times_i X_i \times_{h \neq i} Y_h$ is a *feasible allocation for the economy without i as an entrepreneur* if $\sum_i \bar{x}_i = \sum_{h \neq i} \bar{y}_h{}^i$. Henceforth $(\bar{x}, \bar{y}^i)$ will represent such a feasible allocation. $(\bar{x}, \bar{y}^i, p)$ is a *Walrasian equilibrium for the economy without individual i as an entrepreneur* (written $(\bar{x}, \bar{y}^i, p) \in W(Y_i)$) means that for each $h \neq i$, $p\bar{x}_h = p\bar{y}_h{}^i = \sup pY_h < pB_h(\bar{x}_h)$ and $p\bar{x}_i = 0 < pB_i(\bar{x}_i)$.

Now suppose $(x, y, p) \in W$. Individual *i is a perfectly competitive entrepreneur* in (x, y, p) (written $(x, y, p) \in C^i(Y_i)$) if there exists a $(\bar{x}, \bar{y}^i, p) \in W(Y_i)$. The idea behind the definition can be explained. Think of individual i as playing two roles, entrepreneur and consumer. As noted earlier, for the purpose of this section we are interested in isolating i's ability to influence prices as an entrepreneur. If i is a perfectly competitive entrepreneur in (x, y, p) then the economy can, without i's supplies and demands as entrepreneur, still achieve a Walrasian equilibrium *at the same prices p*. Thus i as entrepreneur *cannot* influence the level of Walrasian equilibrium prices, at least according to a basic test: If when all other individuals charge the prices in p, i as entrepreneur tries to get higher prices than those in p for all the commodities he sells in the Walrasian equilibrium and tries to get lower prices than those in p for all the commodities he buys in the equilibrium he will be unsuccessful. Any individual h, $h \neq i$, will clearly prefer to buy (sell) all the commodities he wants to buy (sell) at the lower (higher) prices in p rather than at the higher (lower) prices offered by i as entrepreneur. Similarly, i as consumer will want to buy and sell at the prices in p. But if i is a perfectly competitive entrepreneur in (x, y, p) then all $h \neq i$ can buy (sell) all they want to at the prices p without i acting as entrepreneur. Similarly, i as consumer can buy and sell all he wants to at p.

Aggregating over individuals, (x, y, p) is a *Perfectly Competitive Equilibrium* (written $(x, y, p) \in PC$) if $(x, y, p) \in W$, and for each individual i, i has no monopoly power in (x, y, p) and also, in particular, i is a perfectly competitive

[4] Note that we identify i's "production possibilities" with his "entrepreneurial abilities". The validity of this identification follows from an interpretation of the current model as one with endogenous firm formation (see the Supplement to [3]). Entrepreneurial abilities may be heuristically thought of as abilities to *organize* (organ-ize) factors into productive units.

entrepreneur in (x, y, p). Thus, if (x, y, p) is a Perfectly Competitive Equilibrium, no one individual or entrepreneur can influence the level of equilibrium prices by withdrawing his supplies and demands from the market. Alternatively expressed, in a Perfectly Competitive Equilibrium no one individual or entrepreneur can influence the level of equilibrium prices by trying to sell all his goods at prices higher than p and buy all his goods at prices lower than p.

2B. *The Strong No Surplus Condition*

Let $A^{\bar{i}}(x, Y_i) \equiv \{(\bar{x}, \bar{y}^i)$: for each $h \neq i$, $\bar{x}_h \in A_h(x_h)$ and $\bar{x}_i \in A_i(x_{\bar{i}})\}$. Individual *i contributes no surplus as an entrepreneur in* (x, y) (written $(x, y) \in NS(Y_i)$) means $A^{\bar{i}}(x, Y_i) \neq \varnothing$ but for any $(\bar{x}, \bar{y}^i) \in A^{\bar{i}}(x, Y_i)$ and any $h \neq i$ $\bar{x}_h \notin B_h(x_h)$ and $\bar{x}_i \notin B_i(x_{\bar{i}})$. That is, if i stops acting as an entrepreneur the economy can achieve an allocation in which everyone except i is as well off as with x and i is as well off as $\bar{i}$ is in x. The pair (x, y) is a *strong no surplus allocation* (written $(x, y) \in NS^*$) means $(x, y) \in NS$ and also in particular, for each individual i, i contributes no surplus as an entrepreneur in (x, y).

We now prove

THEOREM 2 (characterization of perfectly competitive equilibria). *Assume* (A1)–(A4). *Then* (x, y, p) *is a Perfectly Competitive Equilibrium iff* (x, y) *is a strong no surplus allocation.*

The theorem follows readily from Theorem 1 and the following lemma. The lemma is styled "full appropriation" for reasons explained in Remark 4 below.

LEMMA 3 (full appropriation). *Assume* (A1) *and* (A4), *and suppose* $(x, y, p) \in W$. *Then for any individual* $i \in I$, *i is perfectly competitive entrepreneur in* (x, y, p) *iff i contributes no surplus as an entrepreneur in* (x, y).

Proof. Suppose $(\bar{x}, \bar{y}^i, p) \in W(Y_i)$, then it is easy to verify that $(\bar{x}, \bar{y}^i) \in A^{\bar{i}}(x, Y_i)$. Also, $(\bar{x}, \bar{y}^i) \in A^{\bar{i}}(x, Y_i)$ and $\bar{x}_h \in B_h(x_h)$ for some $h \neq i$ or $\bar{x}_i \in B_i(x_{\bar{i}})$ would imply $\sum_i p\bar{x}_i > \sum_h p\bar{y}_h{}^i$, contradicting the feasibility of $(\bar{x}, \bar{y}^i)$. So $(x, y) \in NS(Y_i)$.

Suppose $(x, y) \in NS(Y_i)$, so $(\bar{x}, \bar{y}^i) \in A^{\bar{i}}(x, Y_i)$. Then for all $h \neq i$

$$p\bar{x}_h \geqslant px_h = \sup pY_h \geqslant p\bar{y}_h{}^i$$

and

$$p\bar{x}_i \geqslant p\bar{x}_{\bar{i}} = 0.$$

Since $\sum_i \bar{x}_i = \sum_h \bar{y}_h{}^i$, the above inequalities must all be equalities. So

$$p\bar{x}_h = \sup pY_h = p\bar{y}_h{}^i < pB_h(x_h) = pB_h(\bar{x}_h),$$
$$p\bar{x}_i = 0 < pB_i(x_i) = pB_i(\bar{x}_i).$$

Observe that $B_h(x_h) = B_h(\bar{x}_h)$ since $\bar{x}_h \in A_h(x_h)$ and $x_h \in A_h(\bar{x}_h)$. Similarly, $B_i(x_i) = B_i(\bar{x}_i)$. Q.E.D.

2C. *Perfect Competition, Free Entry, and the Long Run*

The triple (x, y, p) is a *perfectly competitive long-run equilibrium* (written $(x, y, p) \in LPC$) if $(x, y, p) \in PC$ and for each individual $i \in I$, $py_i = 0$ (i.e., profits are zero).

Let $A(x, Y_i) \equiv \{(\bar{x}, \bar{y}^i)$: for each $h \in I$ (including i), $\bar{x}_h \in A_h(x_h)\}$. Individual *i is a redundant entrepreneur in* (x, y) (written $(x, y) \in RE^i$) means $A(x, Y_i) \neq \varnothing$ but for any $(\bar{x}, \bar{y}^i) \in A(x, Y_i)$ and any $h \in I$ $\bar{x}_h \notin B_h(x_h)$. That is, everyone *including* i can do as well as in x if i stops being an entrepreneur. Aggregating over individuals, *(all) entrepreneurs are redundant in* (x, y) if for every $i \in I$, $(x, y) \in RE^i$.

Assume

(A5) for each individual $i \in I$, $0 \in Y_i$ (possibility of inaction).

We now prove

THEOREM 3 (characterization of perfectly competitive long-run equilibrium). *Assume* (A1)–(A5). *Then* $(x, y, p) \in LPC$ *iff* (x, y) *is a strong no surplus allocation and entrepreneurs are redundant in* (x, y).

The theorem follows readily from Theorem 2 and the following two lemmas, each of which has some interest in itself.

LEMMA 4 (sufficient condition for zero profits). *Assume* (A1) *and* (A5), *and suppose* $(x, y, p) \in W$. *Then if i is a redundant entrepreneur in* (x, y), *i earns zero profits in* (x, y, p) (i.e. $py_i = 0$).

Proof. By assumption there exists a $(\bar{x}, \bar{y}^i) \in A(x, Y_i)$. Therefore for all $h \neq i$,

$$p\bar{x}_h \geqslant px_h = py_h \geqslant p\bar{y}_h{}^i$$

and

$$p\bar{x}_i \geqslant px_i = py_i \geqslant 0.$$

Since $\sum_{h\in I} p\bar{x}_h = \sum_{h\neq i} p\bar{y}_h{}^i$, $py_i = 0$. Q.E.D.

LEMMA 5 (profits as surplus). *Assume* (A1), (A4), *and* (A5), *and suppose* $(x, y, p) \in PC$. *Then for any* $i \in I$, *individual i earns zero profits in* (x, y, p) (i.e., $py_i = 0$) *iff he is a redundant entrepreneur in* (x, y).

Proof. In view of Lemma 4 we need only show the "only if" part. So assume $py_i = 0$. Thus, since $(x, y, p) \in W$, $px_i = 0 < pB_i(x_i)$ and $px_{\bar{i}} = 0 < pB_{\bar{i}}(x_{\bar{i}})$. Or, given completeness of preferences, $x_{\bar{i}} \in A_i(x_i)$. Also, i is a perfectly competitive entrepreneur in (x, y, p) implies there exists $(\bar{x}, \bar{y}^i) \in A^{\bar{i}}(x, Y_i)$. So $\bar{x}_i \in A_i(x_{\bar{i}})$. But then $\bar{x}_i \in A_i(x_i)$, i.e., $(\bar{x}, \bar{y}^i) \in A(x, Y_i)$. To complete the proof observe that $(\bar{x}, \bar{y}^i) \in A(x, Y_i)$ and $\bar{x}_h \in B_h(x_h)$ for some $h \in I$ would imply $\sum_i p\bar{x}_i > \sum_h p\bar{y}_h{}^i$, contradicting the feasibility of $(\bar{x}, \bar{y}^i)$.
Q.E.D.

Remark 2. The import of Lemma 4 is that it provides an answer to the classical question, when will a perfectly competitive entrepreneur's payments to his factors exhaust his product? The answer being that these payments will exhaust his product if he is a redundant entrepreneur. Note that this answer, in contrast to the more popular constant returns to scale answer, is consistent with the possibility of U-shaped cost curves. (Lemma 4 does not depend on any convexity assumptions.) Also note that according to Lemma 5, that an entrepreneur is redundant is not only sufficient but also necessary for product exhaustion *if the entrepreneur is a perfect competitor.*

Remark 3. We wish to argue that the Redundant Entrepreneurs Condition characterizes not only the final allocation in a perfectly competitive economy that is in long run (i.e., zero profits) equilibrium—as proved in Theorem 3—but also characterizes the final allocation in a perfectly competitive economy in which free entry by competitor firms has fully run its course, exploiting all profit potentials. So those long-run perfectly competitive equilibria resulting from free entry, like the long-run equilibria described in principles texts, may be characterized as long-run equilibria in which all entrepreneurs are redundant. To see this, think of a perfectly competitive equilibrium in which free entry has fully run its course as being an equilibrium in which for each active entrepreneur in the economy there is an inactive, potential entrepreneur with essentially the same production possibilities. The latter individual is indifferent between operating and not operating because the former entrepreneur is just breaking even in the equilibrium. Now clearly any active entrepreneur is redundant because if any active entrepreneur were to stop being an entrepreneur, his inactive "double" could just take his place and the equilibrium allocation could be achieved without that active entrepreneur.

Remark 4. Lemma 5 may be equivalently expressed: a perfectly competitive entrepreneur earns positive profits iff he contributes a positive surplus to somebody. We wish to establish the stronger proposition that a perfectly competitive entrepreneur's profits *measure* his contribution to surplus. This is a generalized "adding-up" proposition.

To establish the proposition recall that if an individual i is a perfectly competitive entrepreneur then, by definition, whether or not he acts as an entrepreneur will not affect the level of equilibrium prices. So, for each individual $h \neq i$, whether or not i is an entrepreneur does not matter to h: he faces the same budget constraint with or without i as entrepreneur. Summarizing,

PROPOSITION 1A. *A perfectly competitive entrepreneur contributes nothing to the consumer surplus of anyone besides himself.*

This, of course, is the import of Lemma 3 above. It may be alternatively expressed by saying that a "full appropriation condition" characterizes any entrepreneur who is a perfect competitor: an entrepreneur who is a perfect competitor fully appropriates from all other individuals, *in the form of profits*, any contribution he may make to their consumer surplus. For a similar observation in a somewhat different context, see Hart [1].

On the other hand, if i acts as an entrepreneur he may earn entrepreneurial profits; if he stops acting as an entrepreneur he will lose these profits. And this potential wealth loss is the *only* effect that the cessation of i's entrepreneurial activities will have on i's budget line or welfare since he will face the same prices whether or not he acts as an entrepreneur: The wealth loss will result in a *parallel* shift downward in i's budget line, the magnitude of the shift being measured by i's profits. Since his new optimum will be on the new lower budget line, we have,

PROPOSITION 1B. *The contribution of a perfectly competitive entrepreneur to his consumer surplus (and aggregate consumer surplus) is measured by his entrepreneurial profits.*

To bring Proposition 1 into focus by way of contrast, we observe that in an arbitrary Walrasian equilibrium profits do *not* in general measure surplus. For example, an entrepreneur with a constant returns-to-scale technology will earn zero profits in any Walrasian equilibrium, but he may be the only individual in the economy with production possibilities (!) and thus be contributing a substantial surplus in any Walrasian equilibrium.

Remark 5. A second proposition is implicit in the first. Since a perfectly competitive entrepreneur cannot affect prices, he appropriates his entire contribution to consumers' surplus in the form of profits. Thus,

PROPOSITION 2. *For a perfectly competitive entrepreneur, his profits are really competitively determined rents on his entrepreneurial abilities. (Or, alternatively expressed, his profits are really rents that reflect the contribution to aggregate consumers' surplus of his production possibilities.)*

3. A Special Case of the Model: A Simple Production Economy

Following Ostroy [5], we observed that the no surplus theory may be viewed as a generalized marginal productivity theory of distribution. And it becomes exactly a marginal productivity theory of distribution in what he calls "simple production economies." This seminal result, which is discussed in detail in [5], is generalized below only insofar as we include the possibility of entrepreneurs and characterize entrepreneurs' marginal productivity.

The result may be alternatively expressed. Perfectly competitive economies, which we have shown earlier are characterized by a no surplus condition, are also characterized by the marginal productivity theory of distribution: There is perfect competition *if and only if* there is adding-up! And furthermore, this theory of distribution corresponds to an implicit theory of value in an appropriate dual price space (e.g., see Lemma 2 above). In this view, the competitive theory of value derives from the competitive theory of distribution. Indeed, the appropriate dual price space to support some (nonconvex) no surplus allocations may involve nonlinear—but perfectly competitive (!)—pricing. This is illustrated in [2].[5]

Suppose each individual i has an endowment of resources $r_i \in R_+^{n-1}$ which can be transformed into a single output q. And suppose individuals desire only q's. Specifically, for each i

$$X_i = \{x_i \in R^n \colon x^i = (-r_i, q_i), \text{ where } q_i \in R_+\},$$

and i's "utility function" is given by $U_i(-r_i, q_i) = q_i$. (It simplifies matters to not allow for free disposal in characterizing X_i. It is quite harmless.)

Also suppose that each individual i has a production function f_i from R_+^{n-1} to R_+. The aggregate production function is f from R_+^{n-1} to R_+, and the aggregate production function without i acting as an entrepreneur is f^i from R_+^{n-1} to R_+. (The functions f_i, f, and f^i are functional representations of Y_i, $\sum_i Y_i$, and $\sum_{h \neq i} Y_h$, respectively.) We assume that if $r^1 \geqslant r^2$, r^1 and r^2 in R_+^{n-1}, then $f_i(r^1) \geqslant f_i(r^2)$, and similarly $f(r^1) \geqslant f(r^2)$ and $f^i(r^1) \geqslant f^i(r^2)$, so that all resources can be utilized in production at no cost in terms of output forgone.

Since individuals always supply all their resources to production, there is a one-to-one correspondence between points $x_i \in X_i$ and points $q_i \in R_+$, namely $x_i = (-r_i, q_i)$. Thus we can, for simplicity, regard a (consumption) allocation in our simple production economy as a point $(q_i) \in R_+^{\#I}$. Using

[5] The equilibrium allocation in the firm-specific labor example in [2] is a no surplus allocation that can only be supported by a nonlinear (but perfectly competitive) price system. See [2] for details.

this simplification, the reader will easily verify that our no surplus definitions can be given the following special forms. (Henceforth (q_i) will represent a Pareto optimal allocation, i.e., one satisfying $\sum_i q_i = f(r)$, where $r \equiv \sum_i r_i$.)

$$(q_i) \in NS \quad \text{iff} \quad \text{for each } i,\ q^i = f^i(r^i),$$

where $q^i \equiv \sum_{h \neq i} q_h$ and $r^i \equiv \sum_{h \neq i} r_h$;

$$(q_i) \in NS(Y_i) \quad \text{iff} \quad q^i + q_i = f^i(r);$$

$$(q_i) \in NS^* \quad \text{iff} \quad (q_i) \in NS \text{ and for each } i,\ (q_i) \in NS(Y_i);$$

$$(q_i) \in RE^i \quad \text{iff} \quad f(r) = f^i(r).$$

The following definitions of marginal productivity concepts should require no elaboration; they are completely straightforward:

$$MP_i \equiv f(r) - f^i(r^i),$$

where MP_i represents the marginal productivity of individual i.

$$MP(Y_i) \equiv f(r) - f^i(r),$$

where $MP(Y_i)$ represents the marginal productivity of i's entrepreneurial abilities.

$$MP(r_i) \equiv f(r) - f(r^i),$$

where $MP(r_i)$ represents the marginal productivity of i's resources.

Note in particular that while i's entrepreneurial abilities are in some sense indivisible, $MP(Y_i)$ can be defined in a straightforward manner. It depends only on the economy's aggregate production possibilities, summarized in f, and its aggregate production possibilities without i, summarized in f^i. We now prove some equivalences between the above no surplus concepts and marginal productivity concepts. Before proceeding note that in this simple production economy assumption (A4) can be given the following special form:

(A4′) For any individual $i \in I$ there exists an $\bar{\imath} \in I$ such that $r_{\bar{\imath}} = r_i$, and for any $r \in R_+^{n-1}$ $f^{\bar{\imath}}(r) = f(r)$.

LEMMA 6 (marginal productivity characterization of no surplus). *$(q_i) \in NS$ iff for each i, $q_i = MP_i$.*

Proof. If for each i $q_i = MP_i$ then for each i $q_i = f^i(r^i) = (q^i + q_i) - f^i(r^i)$. Or, $f^i(r^i) = q^i$.

If $(q_i) \in NS$ then for each i $f^i(r^i) = q^i$. Or, for each i, $\sum_i q_i - q^i = q_i = f(r) - f^i(r^i) = MP_i$. Q.E.D.

LEMMA 7 (marginal productivity characterization of strong no surplus). *Assuming* (A4′), $(q_i) \in NS^*$ *iff for each* i, $q_i = MP_i = MP(r_i) + MP(Y_i)$.

Proof. If for each i, $q_i = MP_i = MP(r_i) + MP(Y_i)$ then by Lemma 6, $(q_i) \in NS$, and

(a) $f(r) - f^i(r^i) = (f(r) - f(r^i)) + (f(r) - f^i(r))$

But

(b) $f^i(r^i) = q^i$ since $(q_i) \in NS$ and

(c) $f(r) - f(r^i) = MP(r_i) = MP(r_{\bar{i}}) = MP_{\bar{i}} = q_{\bar{i}}$.

Therefore, substituting yields

(d) $f(r) - q^i = q_{\bar{i}} + f(r) - f^i(r)$.

Or, $q^i + q_{\bar{i}} = f^i(r)$, i.e., $(q_i) \in NS(Y_i)$.

If $(q_i) \in NS^*$ then by Lemma 6 for each i, $q_i = MP_i$, and also $q^i + q_{\bar{i}} = f^i(r)$. Since (b) and (c) of above still hold, and since (d) also still holds, substituting (b) and (c) into (d) yields (a). Or, $MP_i = MP(r_i) + MP(Y_i)$. Q.E.D.

LEMMA 8 (marginal productivity characterization of redundant entrepreneurs). *Let* $(q_i) \in NS$ *and assume* (A4′). *Then* $(q_i) \in RE^i$ *iff* $MP(Y_i) = 0$.

Proof. If $(q_i) \in RE^i$ then $f(r) - f^i(r) = 0 = MP(Y_i)$. Alternatively, if $MP(Y_i) = 0$ then, by definition, $f(r) - f^i(r) = 0$, i.e., $(q_i) \in RE^i$. Q.E.D.

The lemmas can be used to show the following generalized adding-up result:

THEOREM 4 (generalized adding-up). *Assume* (A4′). *If* $(q_i) \in NS$ *then* $f(r) = \sum_i MP_i$. *Furthermore, if* $(q_i) \in NS^*$ *then*

$$f(r) = \sum_i MP(r_i) + \sum_i MP(Y_i).$$

In addition, if $(q_i) \in NS^*$ *and for all* i, $(q_i) \in RE^i$ *then*

$$f(r) = \sum_i MP(r_i),$$

where for each i, $MP(Y_i) = 0$.

Finally, suppose (x, y, p') *is a Perfectly Competitive Equilibrium for the simple production economy, where* $p' = (p, 1) \in R^{n-1} \times R$ *(i.e.,* q *is the numeraire commodity) and* $x_i = (-r_i, q_i)$ *(i.e.,* (q_i) *is the equilibrium consumption allocation). Then, for each* i, $pr_i = MP(r_i)$ *and* $\pi_i = \sup p'Y_i = MP(Y_i)$.

Proof. Given Lemmas 5–7, we need only verify that $pr_i = MP(r_i)$ and $\pi_i = MP(Y_i)$. But if $(x, y, p') \in PC$ then for each i, $p'x_i = -pr_i + q_i = \pi_i$ and $p'x_{\bar{i}} = -pr_{\bar{i}} + q_{\bar{i}} = 0$. So $pr_i + \pi_i = q_i$ and $pr_{\bar{i}} = pr_i = q_{\bar{i}}$. Since $(x, y, p') \in PC$ implies $(q_i) \in NS^*$ by Lemmas 1 and 3, and since $MP(Y_{\bar{i}}) = 0$, Lemma 7 implies $q_{\bar{i}} = MP_{\bar{i}}(r_{\bar{i}}) = MP_i(r_i) = pr_i$ and $q_i = MP(r_i) + MP(Y_i) = pr_i + MP(Y_i)$. Or $MP(Y_i) = \pi_i$. Q.E.D.

Remark 6. Theorem 4 amounts to a complete adding-up result. First, under perfect competition:

$$\underbrace{f(r)}_{\substack{\text{total}\\\text{product}}} = \underbrace{\sum_i MP(r_i)}_{\substack{\text{factor}\\\text{earnings}}} + \underbrace{\sum_i MP(Y_i)}_{\text{profits}}.$$

And second, in the long run Euler's theorem holds—at least locally—so that factor payments exhaust the product (entrepreneurs are redundant so profits are zero):

$$\underbrace{f(r)}_{\substack{\text{total}\\\text{product}}} = \underbrace{\sum_i MP(r_i)}_{\substack{\text{factor}\\\text{earnings}}}.$$

Note in particular, that under perfect competition profits are rents to entrepreneurial ability, as observed in Remark 5 above: for each individual i,

$$\pi_i = MP(Y_i).$$

References

1. O. D. Hart, Monopolistic competition in a large economy with differentiated commodities, *Rev. Econ. Stud.* **46** (1979), 1–30.
2. L. Makowski, Value theory with personalized trading, *J. Econ. Theory* **20** (1979), 194–212.
3. L. Makowski, "A General Equilibrium Theory of Organization," SSRC Research Project on Risk and Information Discussion Paper No. 12, University of Cambridge, 1978.
4. J. Ostroy, The no-surplus conditions as a characterization of perfectly competitive equilibrium, *J. Econ. Theory* **22** (1980), 183–207.
5. J. Ostroy, Perfect competition as product exhaustion, unpublished manuscript, 1978.
6. J. Robinson, Euler's theorem and the problem of distribution, *in* "Readings in Microeconomics," 2nd ed. (William Breit and Harold M. Hochman, Eds.), Holt, Rinehart & Winston, New York, 1968.

Perfect Competition, the Profit Criterion, and the Organization of Economic Activity

LOUIS MAKOWSKI*

Department of Applied Economics, University of Cambridge, Cambridge CB3 9DE, England

Received August 6, 1979

Suppose that profit-seeking firms endogenously determine the set of traded commodities (the "commodity space"). If firms have monopoly power, it is well known that profit seeking will generally result in the marketing of an inefficient set of commodities. However, if firms are perfect competitors, it is widely believed that self-interested profit seeking will result in an efficient set of marketed commodities. That is, an economic system founded on the Profit Criterion is efficient, or "the Invisible Hand works." This moral is sometimes inferred from the fact that any standard competitive equilibrium is a Pareto optimum. But since in any standard competitive model the set of traded commodities is not a variable, the optimality of standard competitive equilibria neither proves nor disproves the efficiency of the Profit Criterion.

In the sequel we construct a competitive model which *endogenously* determines the set of traded commodities. In some sense this model completes the standard competitive model, which may be interpreted as a model in which the set of markets—whether complete *or incomplete*—is exogenously given. We use our model to examine the efficiency of the Profit Criterion. Sufficient conditions for efficiency are provided. But some counterexamples are also provided. In the latter context, themes that appear in the development literature, about the difficulties in evolving a complex well-developed economy, reappear.

To summarize the sequel, we show that:

(1) Any perfectly competitive firm will profit maximize if it is operating in accordance with its shareholders' interests (Theorem 1, Section 2).

(2) A perfectly competitive firm will always perceive positive profits to any unilateral marketing decision, e.g., innovation, which improves social welfare (Theorem 2, Section 3).

* Research for the paper was partially supported by a (U.K.) Social Science Research Council grant, which is gratefully acknowledged.

Reprinted from *Journal of Economic Theory* **22**, No. 2, 222–242 (April 1980)
ISBN 0-12-476750-8

However,

(3) Perfectly competitive firms will not, in general, introduce an efficient set of commodities, the source of market failure being the existence of inter-firm complementarities in innovation. Such complementarities give rise to potential, favorable "pecuniary externalities" in the innovation process (Theorem 3, Section 4A, and Section 4B).

(4) Perfectly competitive firms will introduce an efficient set of commodities if

(a) there are no intermediate innovations and the economy's aggregate technology is convex and differentiable (Theorem 4, Section 4C); this effectively rules out all inter-firm complementarities; or

(b) firms can become sufficiently large (e.g., by mergers or joint ventures) to internalize all potential inter-firm complementarities (Corollaries 1 and 2, Section 5; this provides a rationale for the structures of firms (Corollary 3, Section 5).

This paper is to a large degree concerned with constructing a simple model which reflects some of the principles underlying Oliver Hart's work on "monopolistic competition," principles that are obfuscated by Hart's desire to *simultaneously* ensure perfect competition by replication *and* exposit the consequences of perfect competition. It is the latter consequences that we wish to highlight here. Thus, (a) our characterization of a "perfectly competitive firm" in Section 2 below is an idealization of Hart's "small firm" in his limiting economy; (b) the unanimity result, (1), is a reformulation of Hart's unanimity result in [3], showing that it follows from firms being perfectly competitive; and (c) the optimality result, (4a), is a simplified version of Hart's optimality theorem in [2], showing that it depends crucially on convexity and differentiability assumptions.

The results mentioned in (2), (3), and (4b) are somewhat more original. A few remarks may be helpful: The optimality result, (2), may be viewed as an extension of the first basic theorem of welfare economics to competitive economies with endogenous commodity spaces. And (4b) is a corollary of (2). The nonoptimality result, (3), shows that any validation of the Profit Criterion must be qualified. Recently, Hart independently found results similar to (2) and (3); see [4]. It should also be mentioned that the model and results below are somewhat more general than those in [2–4] because they allow for innovation of intermediate inputs as well as consumption goods, and they allow for the possibility of multiproduct innovations within a firm (e.g., see Theorem 2 below).

Before closing, Ostroy's and my complementary work on the no-surplus condition should be mentioned. The explicit connections between this work and the current work will form the subject of a future paper. There it will be shown that a no-surplus condition characterizes perfectly competitive innovators. In other words, the theme in [7, 8], that no surplus (in quantity space) is the dual to perfect competition (in price space), extends to perfect competition with innovation.

1. The Preliminaries: The Basic Model[1]

The model is basically an Arrow–Debreu model with the possibility of product innovation added. There is a large, finite set of potential commodities C and a finite set of agents J. J consists of a set of individuals I and a set of firms F (i.e., $J \equiv I \cup F$). Each economic agent $j \in J$ has a trading possibility set $X^j \subset R^n$, where $n = {}^{\#}C$. Also each individual $i \in I$ has an "at least as good as" correspondence A^i from X^i to X^i that completely preorders X^i, and a "better than" correspondence B^i from X^i to X^i satisfying $y^i \in B^i(x^i)$ iff $y^i \in A^i(x^i)$ and $x^i \notin A^i(y^i)$. Finally, there are nonnegative share ownerships in the firms, $s(i, f)$, satisfying, for each $f \in F$, $\sum_i s(i, f) = 1$.

The set of potential commodities that is actually marketed is some (to be determined) subset of C, T. For any $T \subset C$, let $X^j(T) \equiv \{x^j \in X^j \colon x_c^j = 0$ for all $c \notin T\}$; it represents j's trading possibilities in T. A point $x \equiv (x^j)$ is a *T-feasible allocation* if $x \in \times_j X^j(T)$ and $\sum_j x^j = 0$.[2] For any $x^i \in X^i$ let $B^i(x^i, T) \equiv B^i(x^i) \cap X^i(T)$; it represents i's better than x^i set in T. (So, $X^j = X^j(C)$ and $B^i = B^i(..., C)$.) An allocation y *dominates* an allocation x if $y^i \in A^i(x^i)$ for all i and $y^i \in B^i(x^i)$ for some i. A T-feasible allocation x is an (unconstrained) *Pareto optimum* if there is no C-feasible allocation that dominates it.

We assume that each firm markets only personalized commodities and is sole supplier of its commodities. Specifically, letting $C(f) \subset C$ represent the set of *commodities personalized to* f, we assume $x^f \in X^f$ and $x_c^f < 0$ implies (a) $c \in C(f)$ and (b) $x_c^j \geqslant 0$ for all $x^j \in X^j$ and all $j \in J$, $j \neq f$. Note that this is not very restrictive since it is possible for different firms to market perfect substitutes.

[1] Some notation and terminology: Let $z \in E^n$, $p \in R^n$, and $B \subset R^n$. Then $pz < pB$ means $pz < py$ for all $y \in B$; cl B means the closure of B; ri B means the relative interior of B. If A is a correspondence from B to B then A "completely preorders" B means for any x, y, z in B $x \in A(x)$ (reflexivity), $x \in A(y)$ or $y \in A(x)$ (completeness), and $x \in A(y)$, $y \in A(z)$ implies $x \in A(z)$ (transitivity).

[2] More conventionally, (x^j) is written in the form $((x^i), (y^f))$, where for each f $y^f = -x^f$. Under the latter notation, py^f rather than $-px^f$ measures f's profits under prices $p \in R^n$. And the feasibility condition takes on the more usual form $\sum_i x^i = \sum_f y^f$; or $\sum_i \bar{x}^i = \sum_i w^i + \sum_f y^f$, if each "net trade set" X^i is translated to the "consumption set" $\bar{X}^i \equiv X^i + \{w^i\}$, where $w^i \in R^n$ is i's endowment. Since we shall often find it convenient to treat firms and individuals symmetrically, we find our notation more convenient.

$X^i(x, p, T) \equiv \{x^i \in X^i(T): px^i = -\sum_f s(i, f)\, px^f < pB^i(x^i, T)\}$; it represents i's demand correspondence in T given incomes derived from the allocation $x \in \times_j X^j$ and prices $p \in R^n$. Similarly, $X^f(x, p, T) \equiv \{x^f \in X^f(T): -px^f \geqslant -pX^f(T)\}$ represents f's demand correspondence in T. A *Walrasian equilibrium in* T ($W(T)$) is a pair (x, p) consisting of a T-feasible allocation and a price vector $p \in R^n$ such that for all $j \in J$ $x^j \in X^j(x, p, T)$. If (x, p) is a $W(T)$ we write $(x, p) \in W(T)$.

Since, for simplicity, in this paper we shall only allow for product innovation by firms, we shall assume that trading in commodities other than those personalized to firms is always possible. That is, letting $\mathbf{T} \equiv C\backslash(\bigcup_f C(f))$, we shall assume throughout that $\mathbf{T} \subset T$. But there exists a market for $c \in C(f)$ only if f actually markets c. That is, letting $C(x^f) \equiv \{c \in C(f): x_c^f < 0\}$ represent the *commodities personalized to f marketed in* x^f, we shall assume that $(x, p) \in W(T)$ implies $T \cap C(f) = C(x^f)$. Finally, we shall be assuming throughout that individuals are locally nonsatiated in $\mathbf{T}$. That is, for any i and any $x^i \in X^i$ there exists a $y^i \in B^i(x^i)$ such that y^i is arbitrarily close to x^i and $y_c^i = x_c^i$ for all $c \notin \mathbf{T}$.

2. The Firm's Objective and the Concept of Equilibrium

2A. *Profit Maximizing as the Perfectly Competitive Frm's Objective*

We are now in a position to observe that an arbitrary $W(T)$ has no claims to being a stable equilibrium since any firm f can move the economy from that "equilibrium" to another position by altering the set of commodities it markets. But how will a firm decide what commodities to market?

We first prove that if a firm is a perfect competitor, it will—assuming it is being operated in accordance with its shareholders' interests—make this decision based on a profit-maximizing objective.

Let $(x, p) \in W(T)$, $y^f \in X^f$, and $T(y^f) \equiv (T\backslash C(f)) \cup C(y^f)$. A *quasi-equilibrium for* y^f ($Q(y^f)$) is a pair (y, p^f) consisting of a $T(y^f)$-feasible allocation and a price vector $p^f \in R^n$ such that $y^j \in X^j(y, p^f, T(y^f))$ for each $j \in J$, $j \neq f$. If (y, p^f) is a $Q(y^f)$, we write $(y, p^f) \in Q(y^f)$. We also write $p^f \in Q(y^f)$ to indicate $(y, p^f) \in Q(y^f)$ for some y; no confusion should result. The concept of a quasi-equilibrium is useful for judging the stability of a $W(T)$. To see this, observe that if $(x, p) \in W(T)$, a firm f may try to manipulate the set of traded commodities T and/or the equilibrium prices p by altering its trade demand from x^f to some y^f. If it assumes that it cannot effect the commodities marketed by other firms (as we shall suppose that it does assume) then the change to y^f is feasible for f only if $y_c^f > 0$ only for $c \in T\backslash C(f)$. If y^f is a feasible change for f and f decides to change from x^f to y^f then the set of marketed commodities changes to $T(y^f)$. If the firm f also assumes that all other agents will still act as price takers (as we shall suppose that it does assume), then under "rational expectations" firm f will expect the change to y^f to alter prices from p to p^f, where $p^f \in Q(y^f)$. To summarize, a $W(T)$ is "stable" if no firm f would be interested in moving from it to some quasi-equilibrium $Q(y^f)$, where $y^f \in X^f$ and $y_c^f > 0$ only for $c \in T \backslash C(f)$. The set $Y^f(T) \equiv \{y^f \in X^f: y_c^f > 0$ only for $c \in T \backslash C(f)\}$ represents the set of *feasible marketing strategies* for f in $W(T)$. We assume that if $y^f \in Y^f(T)$ then $Q(y^f) \neq \varnothing$. This is obviously a strong assumption. However, without it, it is possible that a firm may not introduce an efficient innovation because the consequences of its introduction are not well defined.

A firm f is a *perfect competitor* in a $W(T)$, (x, p), if (a) it cannot influence the prices of any commodities in $T \backslash C(f)$ and (b) it cannot influence the prices of its own commodities, in the sense that it always receives the economy's reservation prices for its own commodities. That is, given any $y^f \in Y^f(T)$ and any $(y, p^f) \in Q(y^f)$, (a) $p_c^f = p_c$ for each $c \in T \backslash C(f)$ and (b) for each $j \neq f$ there exists a $y(f)^j \in X^j(y, p^f, T(y^f))$ satisfying $y(f)_c^j = 0$ for all $c \in C(f)$. The interpretation of (b) is that the prices in p^f for the commodities in $C(y^f)$ leave all agents $j \neq f$ with "no surplus" from purchasing them.

A note on notation: henceforth, given *any* allocation y, any prices $p \in R^n$, and any $T \subset C$, if $y^j \in X^j(y, p, T)$ then we write $y(f)^j$ to indicate a point in $X^j(y, p, T)$ satisfying $y(f)_c^j = 0$ for all $c \in C(f)$.

Remark 2.1. The above definition of a perfectly competitive firm is an idealization of Hart's seminal observation in [2] that if a firm is *small relative to its market* then it can essentially get the economy's reservation prices for its commodities (it faces perfectly elastic demands for its commodities at the economy's reservation prices) even if it is the *only* seller of the commodities and they have *no* close substitutes. To illustrate, suppose only one firm can produce Q's, and it can produce up to 100 Q's before its costs become prohibitive. Suppose also that Q's have no good substitutes. They are indivisible goods, and there are 10,000 people willing to pay £10 each for a Q; no one is willing to pay more than £10. Then the firm within its effective domain (100 Q's) can demand the highest-valued user's price (£10) for each of the Q's it produces. Alternatively expressed, it faces a perfectly elastic demand for Q's at £10, the price that would result from competitive bidding among the potential users. See [2] for further discussion.

We now prove a simplified version of Hart's [3] basic result.

THEOREM 1 (shareholder unanimity). *If* $(x, p) \in W(T)$ *and a firm* f *is a perfect competitor in the equilibrium then* (a) *shareholders in* f *unanimously favor profit maximizing as the firm's sole objective and* (b) *nonshareholders in* f *do not care about* f*'s behavior. That is, if* $(x, p) \in W(T)$, $y^f \in Y^f(T)$, *and* $(y, p^f) \in Q(y^f)$ *then*

(a) *for each i such that* $s(i, f) > 0$:

$$\begin{Bmatrix} y^i \in B^i(x^i) \\ y^i \in A^i(x^i) \text{ and } x^i \in A^i(y^i) \\ x^i \in B^i(y^i) \end{Bmatrix} \quad \text{as} \quad -p^f y^f \begin{Bmatrix} > \\ = \\ < \end{Bmatrix} - px^f$$

and

(b) *for each i such that* $s(i, f) = 0$:

$$y^i \in A^i(x^i) \quad \text{and} \quad x^i \in A^i(y^i)$$

(*i.e., i is indifferent between* x^i *and* y^i).

Proof. Let $(x, p) \in W(T)$, $y^f \in Y^f(T)$, and $(y, p^f) \in Q(y^f)$. Since f is a perfect competitor

$$p_c^f = p_c \qquad \text{for each } c \in T \backslash C(f). \tag{2.1}$$

Using (2.1) we know that for all $f' \in F, f' \neq f$:

$$p^f y(f)^{f'} = p^f y^{f'} = px(f)^{f'} = px^{f'}. \tag{2.2}$$

We also know that for all i

$$x^i \in A^i(x(f)^i) \quad \text{and} \quad x(f)^i \in A^i(x^i) \tag{2.3}$$

and

$$y^i \in A^i(y(f)^i) \quad \text{and} \quad y(f)^i \in A^i(y^i). \tag{2.4}$$

Finally, we know that

$$x(f)^i \in X^i(T(y^f)) \quad \text{and} \quad y(f)^i \in X^i(T). \tag{2.5}$$

For each i such that $s(i, f) = 0$, $x^i \in X^i(x, p, T)$ and $y^i \in X^i(y, p^f, T(y^f))$ implies by virtue of (2.2) and (2.5) that

$$x^i \in A^i(y(f)^i) \quad \text{and} \quad y^i \in A^i(x(f)^i). \tag{2.6}$$

Using (2.3) and (2.4) plus transitivity, (2.6) implies

$$x^i \in A^i(y^i) \quad \text{and} \quad y^i \in A^i(x^i), \tag{2.7}$$

which proves part (b) of the theorem.

Now suppose $-p^f y^f = -px^f$. Then even if $s(i, f) > 0$, $x^i \in X^i(x, p, T)$ and $y^i \in X^i(y, p^f, T(y^f))$ implies by virtue of (2.2) and (2.5) that (2.6) holds. And, as above, (2.6) implies (2.7) for each i such that $s(i, f) > 0$.

Suppose $-p^f y^f > -px^f$. Then if $s(i, f) > 0$, $px(f)^i = p^f x(f)^i < -\sum_{f' \in F} s(i, f') p^f y^{f'}$. So $y^i \in X^i(y, p^f, T(y^f))$ implies by virtue of (2.5) that $y^i \in A^i(x(f)^i)$. Or, using (2.3), $y^i \in A^i(x^i)$. But *not* $x^i \in A^i(y^i)$. To see this, observe that $p^f x(f)^i < -\sum_{f'} s(i, f') p^f y^{f'}$. And by local nonsatiation there is an $\mathbf{x}^i \in X^i(T \backslash C(f))$ such that $\mathbf{x}^i \in B^i(x(f)^i)$ and $-p^f \mathbf{x}^i < -\sum_{f'} s(i, f') p^f y^{f'}$. So, if $x^i \in A^i(y^i)$ then $\mathbf{x}^i \in B^i(y^i)$, which is impossible since $y^i \in X^i(y, p^f, T(y^f))$.

The demonstration that $-p^f y^f < -px^f$ implies $x^i \in B^i(y^i)$ for each i such that $s(i, f) > 0$ is exactly analogous to the above. Q.E.D.

2B. *A Complete Competitive Equilibrium Concept*

We have observed that a $W(T)$ is not a complete competitive equilibrium concept since firms endogenously determine T, the set of marketed commodities.

Consider instead the concept of a "Full Walrasian Equilibrium" (FWE): Suppose $(x, p) \in W(T)$. We shall say *there exist profits to innovation* by f in (x, p) if there exists a $y^f \in Y^f(T)$ and $p^f \in Q(y^f)$ such that $-p^f y^f > -px^f$. A pair (x, p) is a *Full Walrasian Equilibrium* (in T) (written $(x, p) \in$ FWE (in T)) if $(x, p) \in W(T)$ and there exist no profits to innovation by any firm $f \in F$.

A FWE is a *complete* competitive equilibrium concept insofar as it characterizes the outcome of a decentralized *innovation process* whereby the set of traded commodities is determined. Given some initial set of traded commodities (e.g., some rudimentary set of traded commodities $\mathbf{T}$), commodities are introduced into the marketplace as long as they promise the introducing firm increased profits. When no firm sees that it can increase its profits by altering its trade decision assuming the set of marketed commodities other than its own will remain the same (and all other economic agents will act as perfect competitors, i.e., price takers), the innovation process ends. Alternatively viewed, in a FWE no firm can individually manipulate prices to its advantage by altering its trading decision, either the quantities it markets or the commodities it markets. Theorem 1 characterizes the relevance of the concept of a FWE for competitive economies: in a FWE perfectly competitive firms have endogenously determined the set of marketed commodities in accordance with their shareholders' interests.

Remark 2.2. A special case of the above innovation process involves two steps at each stage of the process. In Step 1 a firm introduces a new product or set of products. Then, with a lag, in Step 2 entrants appear, introduce perfect substitute products, and compete away the profits. The two steps are repeated until no firm sees any potential profits to introducing new products. This is a Schumpeterian version of the process. In the spirit of Remark 2.1, we observe that Step 2 is not essential, in general, for perfect competition.

We should also mention that our model, with its "sneaky dynamics," is not flexible enough to permit analysis of a possibly important aspect of any Schumpeterian innovation process: In such a process there may exist "wasteful competition"[3] resulting from firms competing to innovate a product first, to appropriate monopoly profits before entrants compete them away. The inefficiency of such competition is exposed in the well-known theory of common property resources.

3. Profits to Individually Improving Welfare

Since we have assumed local nonsatiation, as is well known any $W(C)$ is a Pareto optimum. And any $W(T)$ is an "optimum relative to T:" if $(x, p) \in W(T)$ then no y can dominate x provided y is T-feasible. But an arbitrary $W(T)$ is generally not a Pareto optimum.

In the rest of the paper we shall be concerned with the question, under what conditions will a FWE be a Pareto optimum? We shall be assuming throughout the sequel that all firms are perfect competitors.

Suppose (x, p) is a FWE in T. And suppose T' is an arbitrary subset of C containing T, i.e., $T \subset T' \subset C$. We shall first show that if some allocation y dominates x, where y is T'-feasible, then more than one innovating firm is needed to move the economy from T to T'. That is, y involves innovations by more than one firm. Or, in other words, it is not the case that $T' \backslash T$ is contained in $C(f)$ (for some f). This is the import of the following benchmark result, which may be viewed as an extension of the first basic theorem of welfare economics to competitive economies with endogenous commodity spaces.

Theorem 2 (profits to individually improving welfare). *Suppose $(x, p) \in W(T)$ and suppose some T'-feasible allocation y dominates x. Then if $T' \backslash T \subset C(f)$ for some $f \in F$, there are profits to innovation by f; i.e. (x, p) is not a FWE.*

Proof. Clearly for all j, $y^j \in X^j(T(y^f))$ and $y^f \in Y^f(T)$. Let $(\bar{y}, p^f) \in Q(y^f)$, so $\bar{y}^f = y^f$. We show that $-p^f y^f > -px^f$.

Assume the contrary. Then, by Theorem 1, for all i, $x^i \in A^i(\bar{y}^i)$. Also, since y dominates x, for all i, $y^i \in A^i(x^i)$ and for some i, $y^i \in B^i(x^i)$. So, using transitivity, for all i, $y^i \in A^i(\bar{y}^i)$ and for some i, $y^i \in B^i(\bar{y}^i)$. Now this implies by a standard argument that for all i, $p^f y^i \geqslant p^f \bar{y}^i$ with strict inequality for some i. Or, using the fact that for all $f' \neq f$, $\bar{y}^{f'} \in X^{f'}(\bar{y}, p^f, T(y^f))$, $\sum_i p^f y^i > \sum_i p^f \bar{y}^i = -\sum_{f' \in F} p^f \bar{y}^{f'} \geqslant -\sum_{f' \in F} p^f y^{f'}$. But $\sum_i y^i = -\sum_{f'} y^{f'}$, a contradiction. Q.E.D.

[3] The term is Ostroy's.

4. The Efficiency of FWE in the Absence of Pecuniary Externalities

4A. *A Second Benchmark Result*

Suppose (x, p) is a FWE in T. Several innovators may be needed to move the economy from T to some $T' \supset T$. So one cannot determine from Theorem 2 whether in general x is a Pareto optimum. We now show that it is provided there would be no potential, favorable "pecuniary externalities" in the innovation process from T.

It will be convenient to first introduce some notation. Let $C^* \equiv C \backslash T$ represent the set of potential innovations from T. Then $F^* \equiv \{f: C^* \cap C(f) \neq \varnothing\}$ represents the set of potential innovators from T. And $J^* \equiv J \backslash F^*$ represents the set of potential buyers of innovated commodities. (Condition (C1) below ensures there are no potential buyers in F^*.)

Finally, $P^* \equiv \{q \in R^n: q_c = p_c$ for all $c \in T$ and for each $j \in J^*$, $x^j \in X^j(x, q, C)\}$ represents the set of price vectors which extend p to C^* so as to reflect or exceed the economy's reservation prices for the potential innovations C^* when *all* potential innovations are marketed *simultaneously* beginning from (x, p). The "minimum" $q \in P^*$ may be thought of as just reflecting the economy's reservation prices for C^*.[4]

There would be *no potential (favorable) pecuniary externalities in the innovation process from T* if

(C1) for each $f \in F^*$ $y^f \in X^f$ implies $y_c^f = 0$ for all $c \in C^*$ ("no intermediate innovations")

and

(C2) there exists a $p^* \in P^*$ with the property: for all $f \in F^*$, all $y^f \in Y^f(T)$, and all $p^f \in Q(y^f)$, $p_c^f \geqslant p_c^*$ for all $c \in C(y^f)$ ("no reservation price externalities").

The heuristics that justify giving this technical condition the title "no pecuniary externalities in the innovation process" may be explained.

Condition (C1) says that potential customers of innovators are not innovators. It rules out the possibility of "intermediate innovations": innovations by one firm that are useful to the production of other innovations by other firms. More specifically, it rules out the possibility that an innovation $c_1 \in C(f_1) \backslash T$ may be useful to the production of another innovation, $c_2 \in C(f_2) \backslash T$, where $f_2 \neq f_1$. If this possibility were not ruled out there could be favorable pecuniary externalities in the innovation process since if f_1 innovated c_1 it would reduce the shadow price of c_1 perceived by f_2 from infinity

[4] If the aggregate technology is convex and differentiable, then there exists a well-defined minimum $q \in P^*$, as will be shown in Section 4C below.

to some finite amount, aming c_1 available to him and thus perhaps enabling him to innovate c_2.[5]

Consider (C2) next, and suppose that all potential innovators cooperated and introduced all possible innovations simultaneously beginning from (x, p). Suppose further that this joint action is at a sufficiently small scale so that each $f \in F^*$ earns the economy's reservation prices for its innovations *when all other possible innovations are available.* Then each $f \in F^*$ can expect to receive the prices in p^* for its innovations, where p^* is the "minimum" $q \in P^*$. But if any $f \in F^*$ contemplates innovating a $y^f \in Y^f(T)$ independently beginning from (x, p), then it can expect to earn only the prices in p^f for its innovations, where $p^f \in Q(y^f)$.

If $p_c^f < p_c^*$ for some $c \in C(y^f)$ then there would be favorable pecuniary externalities in the innovation process since if all potential innovations were available some potential innovator could earn more for some innovation than he perceives he can earn operating independently. Or, alternatively expressed, if (C2) were not satisfied some innovator f_1 by innovating a $c_1 \in C(f_1)\backslash T$ may be able to favorably effect the reservation price perceived by another innovator, f_2, for some $c_2 \in C(f_2)\backslash T$.

THEOREM 3. *If (x, p) is a FWE in T and there are no potential pecuniary externalities in the innovation process from T then x is a Pareto optimum. Indeed, there exists a $p^* \in P^*$—namely, the p^* satisfying* (C2)*—such that $(x, p^*) \in W(C)$.*

Proof. We need only verify that $(x, p^*) \in W(C)$, since then obviously x is a Pareto optimum. Let p^* satisfy the property in (C2). Since for any $j \in J^*$ $x^j \in X^j(x, p^*, C)$, to complete the proof we need only verify that for any $f \in F^*$ and any $y^f \in X^f$, $-p^*x^f \geqslant -p^*y^f$. Since $y^f \in Y^f(T)$ by (C1), $-px^f \geqslant -p^fy^f$, where $p^f \in Q(y^f)$. But $-px^f = -p^*x^f$, so $-p^*x^f \geqslant -p^fy^f$. Since $p_c^f \geqslant p_c^*$ for all $c \in C(y^f)$, $-p^fy^f \geqslant -p^*y^f$; so, $-p^*x^f \geqslant -p^*y^f$.

Q.E.D.

Remark 4.1. The role that "no reservation price externalities" plays in this model is analogous to the role played by the "simultaneous reservation price property" in Hart [4]. Analogous to [4], we provide sufficient conditions for guaranteeing (C2) in Section 4C below. (C1) is satisfied automatically in Hart [2–4] since he studies the special case in which only consumption goods are innovated.

Violations of (C1) are quite pernicious to the optimality of any FWE, as will be illustrated in Example 4.1 below. To find sufficient conditions to

[5] Condition (C1) is slightly stronger than a perhaps more intuitive formulation of "no intermediate innovations from T": that for each $f \in F^*$ $Y^f(T) = X^f$. It is equivalent to this formulation if each potential innovator's trading possibility set is convex. The formulation in the text is favored because it greatly simplifies the exposition.

guarantee (C1) we will have to allow the structure of firms to vary endogenously; this is the program of Section 5.

4B. *Some Examples of Inefficient FWE*

The following examples are intended to give some perspective to the sequel. They illustrate the intuitive proposition that there will be no potential favorable pecuniary externalities in the innovation process from T iff there are no interfirm complementary innovations in C^*; so the availability of some $c_1 \in C(f_1)\backslash T$ does not raise the economy's demand price (or lower its supply price) for any $c_2 \in C(f_2)\backslash T$, where $f_1 \neq f_2$. That is, interfirm complementary innovations (in quantity space) correspond to favorable pecuniary externalities (in price space). Alternatively expressed, interfirm innovation complementarities and favorable pencuniary externalities are "dual" phenomena. This intuitive proposition will be useful for understanding the sufficient conditions for (C2) provided in Section 4C below.

So, we shall now provide four illustrations of how an economy can get stuck at a suboptimal FWE in the presence of interfirm complementarities. The first example involves a failure of (C1) and the other three involve failures of (C2). In all examples (x, p) is a FWE in which neither c_1 nor c_2 is traded, where $\{c_1\} = C(f_1)$ and $\{c_2\} = C(f_2)$ (i.e., there is no joint production of c_1 and c_2); and y dominates x, where y involves trading in both c_1 and c_2.

EXAMPLE 4.1 (intermediate cost-saving innovations or an example of a complementary input–output innovation). Suppose c_1 is a consumption good and c_2 is an input that significantly reduces f_1's cost of producing c_1. The unit cost of producing c_1 without c_2 exceeds any individual's reservation price for c_1. But c_2 has no significant uses other than to produce c_1; so, the reservation price of all firms including f_1 for c_2—given that the set of traded commodities T excludes c_1—is less than f_2's minimum unit cost of producing c_2.

This sort of example may occur when a new technique or, more typically, a number of new techniques are needed to economically produce a new product. This is a common occurrence. For example, consider the number of new "components" needed to produce a new type of airplane or a new type of instant-picture photo camera.

EXAMPLE 4.2 (complementary consumption innovations). Suppose that that c_1 and c_2 are consumption goods that individuals view as perfect complements (i.e., they have right angle indifference curves between the goods). An example may be nuts and bolts, as in Hart [4]. Then any individual's reservation price for c_1 in the absence of c_2 is zero, and his reservation price for c_2 in the absence of c_1 is zero. So if both goods are costly to produce, firms f_1 and f_2 will remain out of business. Yet the minimum unit cost of a c_1–c_2 combination may be significantly less than the sum of individuals' reservation prices for c_1 *and* c_2 in one-to-one combination.

EXAMPLE 4.3 (consumption complementarities arising from overhead relocation costs, or an example of underdeveloped land). Suppose c_1 (respectively c_1') is housing in location L (respectively L'), and c_2 (c_2') is a recreational service—golfing—in location L (L'). Suppose also that L is an area of undeveloped vacant land outside a city located at L', and that housing and golfing are very expensive in L' because the opportunity cost of land is high in the city. So, equivalent housing and golfing can be supplied much more cheaply at L. But if an individual only resides (golfs) in L, he has to commute to the city to work and golf (work and live), so any potential resident's reservation price for c_1, given that he must work and golf in L', is less than the unit cost of housing in L; and, similarly, any potential golfer's reservation price for such recreation at L exceeds the minimum unit cost of providing golfing services at L. So, L remains undeveloped. But the sum of the unit costs of c_1 and c_2 may be significantly less than the sum of individuals' reservation prices for c_1 and c_2 when jointly supplied.

A numerical illustration may help fix the idea underlying this example. Suppose a representative individual i has a Cobb–Douglas utility function given by $(c_0'^i)^\alpha(c_1{}^i + c_1'^i)^\beta(c_2{}^i + c_2'^i)^\gamma$, where $c_0'^i$ represents i's consumption of leisure, and the exponents α, β, γ are positive and sum to one. Note that i views c_1 and c_1' (c_2 and c_2') as perfect substitutes. Let p_1 and p_2 (p_1' and p_2') represent the prices of housing and golfing at $L(L')$. Let p_0' represent the price of leisure, i.e., the wage rate at L'; we assume that i must work in the city. Then it is easy to verify that if i lives and golfs in the city, he can attain utility

$$U' = \left(\frac{\alpha Y}{p_0'}\right)^\alpha \left(\frac{\beta Y}{p_1'}\right)^\beta \left(\frac{\gamma Y}{p_2'}\right)^\gamma,$$

where Y is the value of i's endowment (i.e., his "income"). Now also suppose that if i golfs or resides at L he must suffer a relocation cost which we assume to be merely a lump-sum loss of leisure, $\bar{c}_0'$. So, if i lives and/or golfs at L, he can attain utility

$$U(p_1, p_2) = \left(\frac{\alpha(Y - p_0'\bar{c}_0')}{p_0'}\right)^\alpha \left(\frac{\beta(Y - p_0'\bar{c}_0)}{\min(p_1, p_1')}\right)^\beta \left(\frac{\gamma(Y - p_0'\bar{c}_0)}{\min(p_2, p_2')}\right)^\gamma.$$

Individual i's reservation price for c_1 in the absence of golfing at L is given by $p_1{}^R$, where $U(p_1{}^R, \infty) = U'$. Similarly, his reservation price for c_2 in the absence of housing at L is given by $p_2{}^R$, where $U(\infty, p_2{}^R) = U'$. It is easy to verify that if $p_0\bar{c}_0 > 0$, then $p_1{}^R < p_1'$ and $p_2{}^R < p_2'$. So, if AC_1 (AC_2)

represents the minimum unit cost of c_1 (c_2), it is possible that $p_1{}^R < AC_1 < p_1'$ and $p_2{}^R < AC_2 < p_2'$; and, consequently, neither c_1 nor c_2 is produced. But if AC_1 and AC_2 are sufficiently close to $p_1{}^R$ and $p_2{}^R$, respectively, then clearly $U(AC_1, AC_2) > U'$ so c_1 and c_2 should be jointly produced.

It is of some interest to observe that the complementarity between c_1 and c_2 arises in this illustration not because of lack of differentiability or convexity in i's utility function, but because of an implicit nonconvexity in i's trading possibility set X^i: i can "spread" the overhead relocation cost $\bar{c}_0$ over both c_1 and c_2 if both are available at L.

EXAMPLE 4.4 (input complementarities arising from transportation costs, or an example of an underdeveloped region): Suppose c_1 is steel in location L and c_2 is railroad transporting services from L to L', where L is a region of largely undeveloped land (perhaps a sleepy community) and L' is a major automobile manufacturing center. Suppose also that L is an "ideal" location for producing steel because of favorable natural resources; but there is no railroad connecting L with L', so transporting steel from L to L' is prohibitively costly. As a consequence, the reservation price of the car industry, centered at L', for c_1 is significantly less than the minimum unit cost of c_1. And without a steel industry at L the economy's reservation price for c_2 is insignificant, so f_2 sees no incentive to build a road connecting L with L'. Yet if c_2 were supplied by f_2 at cost, firm f_1 could achieve significant profits from supplying c_1.

Note that in this example, a car manufacturer at L' views a unit of c_1 and a unit of (some) transporting service from L to L' as perfect complements. The above problem occurs when rail transport would be significantly cheaper than any available means of transporting steel from L to L'.

Remark 4.2. The reader may recognize Example 4.4 from [11] or [5]. Our analysis of it is consistent with that appearing there. Note that if f_2 needs c_1 to economically produce c_2, then the example involves a failure of (C1) rather than (C2). Also note that we have strained our analysis somewhat in applying it to railroad transporting services, which generally would not be small relative to f_2's market.

Remark 4.3. In addition to examples of underdeveloped regions, the above "methodology" for constructing examples of inefficient FWE can be applied to constructing examples of badly developed regions. Apropos, see the interesting "shopping center example" in [4].

4C. *Sufficient Conditions for No Reservation Price Externalities: Aggregate Convexity and Differentiability*

We show that if the aggregate technology is "convex and differentiable," assumption (A1) below—and some essentially technical assumptions, (A2)–

(A5), also hold—then (C2) will be satisfied. Thus, in view of Theorem 3, in economies satisfying (C1) (e.g., economies in which only consumption goods can be innovated), (A1)–(A5) are sufficient for a FWE to be a Pareto optimum.

To put the role of convexity and differentiability into perspective recall that all our examples of inefficient FWE (except Example 4.1 which involves a failure of (C1)) involve failures of one or the other, and that failures of differentiability are intimately connected with the existence of complementarities.

The importance of differentiability may be explained mathematically with reference to Example 4.2. As we are about to see, the key mathematical fact for intuitive understanding is that only differentiable functions have the property that their directional derivates are linear functions of their partial derivatives. Now consider Example 4.2 and, in particular, consider an individual's (nondifferentiable) utility function. At his individual optimum, being at a "corner," the sum of his partial derivatives (marginal utilities) with respect to c_1 and c_2 is less than his directional derivative for a package consisting of a unit each of c_1 and c_2. The partial derivatives (which equal zero) reflect his reservation prices for c_1 and c_2 alone, whereas the directional derivative (which is positive) reflects his reservation price for c_1 and c_2 in combination. Thus, in this example, there would be favorable pecuniary externalities to the producer of one of the commodities from the introduction of the other commodity. Alternatively expressed, only for differentiable functions, which have the property mentioned earlier, is it in general the case that experimenting in a vertical and horizontal direction (thinking about introducing one commodity at a time) gives one correct information about the profit consequences of "diagonal" experiments (thinking about simultaneously introducing several commodities).[6]

For our purpose the set-theoretic analog of differentiability at a point, at least for quasi-concave functions, is a unique support; e.g., a right angle indifference curve has an infinite number of supports at its corner. In the sequel we shall use this analog of differentiability and convexity rather than introduce quasi-concave, differentiable utility and production functions. The formal characterization follows. Let $E \subset R^n$ and $z \in R^n$. The *supports of E at z* are $S_z(E) \equiv \{q \in R^n: qz \leqslant qE\}$. $S_z(E)$ is obviously a nonempty (contains zero) convex cone. E is a *smooth, convex set* if for any $z \in \text{cl } E$ there exists a $q' \in R^n$, $q' \neq 0$, such that $S_z(E) \subset \{q: q = \lambda q' \text{ where } \lambda \in R\}$. That is, there exists a *unique* support to E at z (up to a multiplicative constant).

Let $B \equiv \sum_i B^i(x^i) + \sum_{f \in J^*} X^f$; it represents the aggregate "better than x set" net of what is realizable *without* F^*. And let $B(T') \equiv B \cap \{z \in R^n$:

[6] Differentiability is crucial to proving Grossman's characterization result [1], for exactly analogous reasons. It is also crucial for perfect competition, as shown by Ostroy in [8].

$z_c = 0$ for all $c \notin T'\}$; it represents the aggregate better than x set when trading is restricted to the subset of commodities T'. We assume

(A1) There exists a smooth, convex set $B^* \subset R^n$ such that $B = B^* \bigcap_{c \in C(F^*)} N(c)$, where $N(c) \equiv \{z \in R^n\colon z_c \geqslant 0\}$ and $C(F^*) = \bigcup_{f \in F^*} C(f)$ ("aggregate convexity and differentiability").

(A2) For any $T' \supset T$, ri $B(T') \neq \varnothing$.

(A3) For any $(x, p) \in W(T)$, $\sum_{j \in J^*} x_c^j > 0$ for all $c \in T \cap C(F^*)$.

(A4) For any $q \in R^n$ and $i \in I$, $qx^i \leqslant qB^i(x^i)$ implies $qx^i < qB^i(x^i)$ provided $q_c = p_c$ for all $c \in T$.

(A5) For any $f \in F^*$, $i \in I$, $y^f \in y^f(T)$, and $(y, p^f) \in Q(y^f)$: $s(i, f) > 0$ implies there exists an $\bar{\imath} \in I$ such that $s(\bar{\imath}, f) = 0$ but $X^{\bar{\imath}} = X^i$, $B^{\bar{\imath}} = B^i$, and $\sum_{f' \in F} s(\bar{\imath}, f')\, p^f y^{f'} = \sum_{f' \in F} s(i, f')\, p^f y^{f'}$ ("individuals are typical in any quasi-equilibrium").

Let $(x, p) \in W(T)$ and let $\bar{x} \equiv \sum_{j \in J^*} x^j$. Observe that given (A4) $q \in S_{\bar{x}}(B)$ implies $q \in P^*$ (provided $q_c = p_c$ for all $c \in T$). With this background, the role of B^* in the key assumption, (A1), may be explained. B^* "extends" B to the negative orthants in $C(F^*)$, permitting a characterization of J^*'s reservation prices for untraded commodities in $C(F^*)$, in particular for C^*. (Since the commodities in $C(F^*)$ are personalized to F^*, B does not include points in these orthants.) To illustrate, suppose $T = \{x_1\}$ and $C = \{c_1, c_2\}$. Then if B is as in Fig. 1, B may be extended to a smooth, convex B^* (see dashed

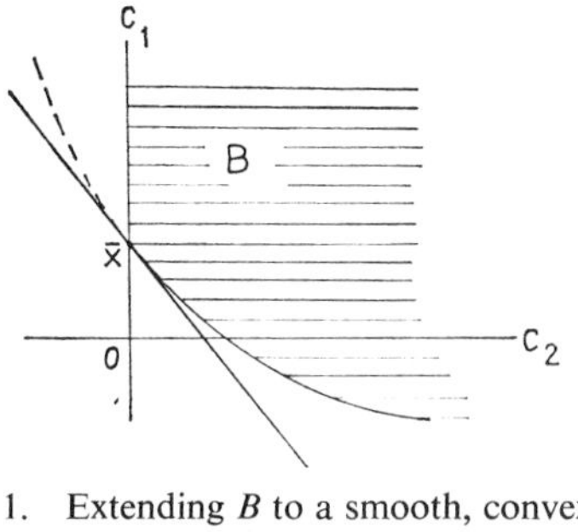

FIG. 1. Extending B to a smooth, convex set.

line) the slope of whose *unique* support at $\bar{x}$ reflects J^*'s reservation price for c_2 in terms of c_1.

Consider this analogy to the role of B^*: If an individual's consumption set is R_+^n and x^i involves zero consumption of c, then the individual's utility function defined on R_+^n may have a right-hand partial derivative with respect to c at x^i but no left-hand partial derivative unless the function can be extended to a differentiable function defined on an open set containing R_+^n.

Regarding the technical assumptions, (A2)–(A5), we make three remarks. First, (A3) and (A4) could obviously have been derived from more primitive restrictions on the technology. Second, (A3) says that any $f \in F^*$ who markets some $c \in T$ has some customers in J^* (i.e., not all buyers of any $c \in C(f) \cap T$ are potential innovators). Third, (A5) says that in any quasi-equilibrium $Q(y^f)$, any shareholder i in f has a "double" who is not a shareholder in f but has the same trading possibilities, preferences, and wealth as i. Its role is to eliminate small income effects. In particular, it ensures that when an $f \in F^*$ switches from x^f to $y^f \in Y^f(T)$ and its profits change, the resulting change in the incomes to f's shareholders will not influence the economy's reservation prices for f's innovations.

We shall now prove

THEOREM 4. *Assume the economy satisfies* (C1) *and* (A1)–(A5), *and let* $(x, p) \in W(T)$. *Then there exists a* $p^* \in P^* \cap S_{\bar{x}}(B)$ *satisfying* (C2); *i.e., there would be no reservation price externalities in the innovation process from T. Thus, if* $(x, p) \in FWE$ *then* $(x, p^*) \in W(C)$ *and x is a Pareto optimum.*

Proof. To prove the theorem we utilize the following Fact, proved in [9] as Corollary 23.8.1:

> Let $B_1 \cdots B_m$ be convex sets in R^n whose relative interiors have a point in common. Then for any $z \in R^n$
>
> $$S_z(B_1 \cap \cdots \cap B_m) = S_z(B_1) + \cdots + S_z(B_m).^7$$

To proceed, observe that $\bar{x} \in \text{cl } B(T)$. So, since $p \in S_{\bar{x}}(B(T))$, (A1) plus the Fact implies

$$p_c = p_c^* + \lambda_c \text{ for all } c \in T, \text{ where } p^* \in S_{\bar{x}}(B^*) \text{ and where } \lambda_c \geqslant 0, \lambda_c = 0 \text{ if } c \notin C(F^*) \cap \{c: \bar{x}_c = 0\}. \tag{4.1}$$

Given (A3) and (A4), clearly $p_c^* = p_c$ for all $c \in T$ and $p^* \in P^*$. Thus, in view of Theorem 3, to complete the proof we need only verify that p^* satisfies the property in (C2).

Let $f \in F^*$, $(y, p^f) \in Q(y^f)$, and $x(f) = \sum_{j \in J^*} x(f)^j$, where each $x(f)^j \in X^j(x, p, T)$. For any i such that $s(i, f) = 0$, $p^f x(f)^i = p^f y^i < p^f B^i(y^i, T(y^f)) = p^f B^i(x^i, T(y^f))$. And for any $f' \in J^*$, $p^f x(f)^{f'} = p^f y^{f'} \leqslant p^f X^{f'}(T(y^f))$. Thus, given (A5), $p^f \in S_{x(f)}(B(T(y^f)))$. So, (A1) plus the Fact implies:

$$p_c^f = q_c + \lambda_c^f \text{ for all } c \in T(y^f), \text{ where } q \in S_{x(f)}(B^*) \text{ and where } \lambda_c^f \geqslant 0, \lambda_c^f = 0 \text{ if } c \notin C(F^*) \cap \{c: x(f)_c = 0\}. \tag{4.2}$$

[7] This Fact also plays a crucial role in a proof of the Kuhn–Tucker theorem; see [6]. This is no accident. An alternate proof of Theorem 4 relies on the Kuhn–Tucker theorem. But for this proof one must assume convexity and differentiability for each agent (analogous to Hart [2]), not just aggregate convexity and differentiability.

But $p^*x(f) = p^*\bar{x}$, so $p^* \in S_{x(f)}(B^*)$. Thus, given the smoothness of B^* and the fact that $p_c^f = p_c \neq 0$ for some $c \in \mathbf{T}$ (recall $(x, p) \in W(T)$ and individuals are locally nonsatiated in $\mathbf{T}$), $q = p^*$. Substituting into (4.2) yields $p_c^f \geqslant p_c^*$ for all $c \in C(y^f)$. Q.E.D

5. The Structure of Firms

In this section we adopt another strategy for achieving optimality. We do not restrict the economy's technology so as to rule out interfirm complementarities, e.g., with (C1) and (A1). Now we allow complementarities, but we also allow firms to *integrate* or to *cooperate* in their innovation plans, i.e., to effectively change the structure of firms (as decision-making units).

It is widely believed that if there is perfect competition and constant returns to scale (or additive production sets) then the structure of firms is completely indeterminate. In particular vertical and horizontal integration, e.g., through mergers or joint ventures, is inexplicable. We show that "complete markets," or absence of interfirm complementarities in innovation, are crucial to the validity of this belief. In particular, we show that there exist incentives to vertical and/or horizontal integration—even given that there are constant returns to scale and additivity—whenever there are interfirm complementarities preventing the innovation process (under an arbitrary, fixed firm structure) from reaching an optimum.

Let us suppose that F now represents the set of basic firms in the economy, before any vertical or horizontal integration. And let us suppose that if in some $W(T)$, (x, p), firms $F' \subset F$ cooperate (e.g., by merger or joint venture) then the cooperative "firm" $f(F')$ will have trading possibilities $X^{f(F')} \equiv \sum_{f \in F'} X^f$—so there are no economies or diseconomies from cooperation—and $f(F')$'s profits will be distributed to shareholders in F' according to the "ownership shares in $f(F')$"

$$s(i, f(F')) \equiv \frac{\sum_{f \in F'} s(i, f)\, px^f}{\sum_{f \in F'} px^f}.$$

Let $\mathscr{F}^*$ be the family of *all* subsets $F' \subset F$, and let $\mathscr{F}$ be a given subset of $\mathscr{F}^*$. $\mathscr{F}$ represents the sets of basic firms $F' \subset F$ that can cooperate in (x, p). Thus, vertical and horizontal integration among firms is always (respectively, not) possible in (x, p) if $\mathscr{F} = \mathscr{F}^*$ (respectively, $\mathscr{F} = \mathscr{F}_* \equiv \bigcup_{f \in F} \{f\}$). And thus, $(x, p) \in$ FWE now only implies that (x, p) is a full Walrasian equilibrium when cooperation among firms is not possible in (x, p). Let us assume $\mathscr{F} \supset \mathscr{F}_*$. What happens when $\mathscr{F} \neq \mathscr{F}_*$?

Let $\mathscr{E}(F')$ represent the economy consisting of, as before, (a) individuals $i \in I$ with trading possibilities X^i and preferences A^i, but also, (b) firms

$f' \in F(F') \equiv F \backslash F' \cup f(F')$ with trading possibilities $X^{f'}$ and (c) ownership shares defined by the function s above from $I \times F(F')$ to R_+. Obviously our formal model of Sections 1–3 applies to any $\mathscr{E}(F')$, i.e., to *any* given firm structure $F(F')$, $F' \in \mathscr{F}^*$. Furthermore, it is easy to verify that if $(x, p) \in W(T)$, then for any $F' \in \mathscr{F}^*$ $(x(F'), p) \in W(T)$ for the economy $\mathscr{E}(F')$, where $x(F')^j \equiv x^j$ for all $j \notin F'$ and $x(F')^{f(F')} \equiv \sum_{f \in F'} x^f$.[8] This is consistent with the widely held belief mentioned earlier. But the same invariance does *not* in general apply to FWE under various firm structures, as we shall shortly see.

If $(x(F'), p) \in W(T)$ for $\mathscr{E}(F')$ and F' is a perfect competitor in $(x(F'), p)$ —i.e., when F' operates as the cooperating unit $f(F')$—then Theorem 1 says that shareholders in F' (or, equivalently, in $f(F')$) unanimously favor $f(F')$ to profit maximize in $\mathscr{E}(F')$. And, given the definition of $s(\ldots, f(F'))$ each shareholder in f, $f \in F'$, is at worst indifferent whether or not f joins F' to form $f(F')$ in the $W(T)$ (for $\mathscr{E}(\{f\})$), (x, p). Thus, given the possibilities for cooperation in the "super economy" with cooperation (these possibilities being summarized by $\mathscr{F}$), it is natural to define a *full Walrasian equilbrium given the possibilities for horizontal and vertical integration*, a FWE ($\mathscr{F}$), as an $(x, p) \in W(T)$ (for some $T \subset C$) satisfying for *each* $F' \in \mathscr{F}$ $(x(F'), p) \in$ FWE in T for the economy $\mathscr{E}(F')$. That is, there are no profits to innovation for any firm or possible coalition of firms in (x, p).

It may be helpful to remark at this point, before proceeding, that it is easiest to visualize the innovation process when $\mathscr{F} \neq \mathscr{F}_*$ in terms of the two-step sequence mentioned in Remark 2.2. Thus, if a firm leaves one coalition to enter another, it can assume that all firms outside the new coalition—including firms in the old coalition that do not enter the new one—will not change their marketed commodities (recall the definition of $T(y^f)$, and the consequent definition of $T(y^{f(F')})$): The firms in the old coalition may be visualized as being in Step 2 while the new coalition is embarking on Step 1. So, the firms in the old coalition that are not in the new one do not lose any necessary inputs by the old coalition breaking up; in Step 2 there are many available suppliers of all necessary inputs to these firms.

For the sequel, we extend our earlier assumption of perfect competition to assume that any possible coalition $F' \in \mathscr{F}$ would be a perfect competitor in any $W(T)$ in $\mathscr{E}(F')$.

COROLLARY 1 (profits to integration). *Suppose $(x, p) \in W(T)$ and some T'-feasible allocation y dominates x. Then, if $T' \backslash T \subset \bigcup_{f \in F'} C(f)$ for some*

[8] In the current context, when we simply write $(x, p) \in W(T)$, it should be understood that we mean $(x, p) \in W(T)$ for the economy $\mathscr{E}(\{f\}]$, where $f \in F$. This is consistent with our previous notation.

$F' \in \mathscr{F}$, there are profits to innovation by $f(F')$ in $\mathscr{E}(F')$; i.e., (x, p) is not a FWE($\mathscr{F}$).

Proof. Follows immediately from Theorem 2. Q.E.D.

COROLLARY 2. *If $(x, p) \in$ FWE($\mathscr{F}$) and integration is always possible (i.e., $\mathscr{F} = \mathscr{F}^*$) then x is a Pareto optimum.*

Proof. Immediate from Corollary 1. Q.E.D.

COROLLARY 3 (determinacy of firm structure). *Suppose $(x, p) \in$ FWE($\mathscr{F}$) when integration is not possible (i.e., when $\mathscr{F} = \mathscr{F}_*$). Then $(x, p) \in$ FWE($\mathscr{F}$) even when any integration is possible (i.e., when $\mathscr{F} = \mathscr{F}^*$) iff x is a Pareto optimum in $\mathscr{E}(\{f\})$.*

Proof. Given Corollary 2, we need only show that if x is a Pareto optimum then there are no profits to innovation for any $f(F')$ in $(x(F'), p)$, a $W(T)$ for $\mathscr{E}(F')$. Assume the contrary, i.e., that there exists a $y^{f(F')} \in Y^{f(F')}(T)$ such that $-p^{f(F')}y^{f(F')} > -px(F')^{f(F')} = -p \sum_{f \in F'} x^f$, where $(y, p^{f(F')}) \in Q(y^{f(F')})$ in the economy $\mathscr{E}(F')$. By Theorem 1, y dominates $x(F')$ in the economy $\mathscr{E}(F')$. So, clearly, there exists a feasible allocation y' in $\mathscr{E}(\{f\})$ that dominates x. Q.E.D.

Corollary 3 says that the firm structure is completely indeterminate (in the sense that there are no potential profits to forming any cooperative ventures) iff the innovation process without cooperation leads to a Pareto optimum. But if there are interagent complementarities leading to inefficient FWE (without cooperatives), then Corollary 1 says there exist potential profits to cooperative efforts. In particular, when there are cost-saving intermediate innovation as in Example 4.1, then there exist incentives to *vertical* integration, and when there are complementary consumption innovation as in Examples 4.2 and 4.3, then there exist incentives to *horizontal* integration. Corollary 2 says that if agents can form cooperatives that are sufficiently large to internalize all interagent innovation complementarities then the innovation process will lead to an optimum.

Remark 5.1. It is a well-known empirical fact that many firms are "too large" to be explained by economies of scale. This theory provides one explanation consistent with competitive behavior. It explains a firm's simultaneous development of several, complementary processes or innovations even in the absence of joint economies of scale. See [13, esp. Sect. III], for a somewhat different model leading to a very similar explanation.

Remark 5.2. The large, multiproduct conglomerate, replete with a massive R & D department, may be viewed as a social invention for solving potential problems involving interfirm complementarities—producing, in some sense, profit signals that the price system fails to provide. But this does not imply that complex industrialized economies, possessing this invention, have solved the underdevelopment problem (in the sense of Pareto). Since agents in one society typically innovate "ideas" that follow a common known line of development, there may exist *completely different*, Pareto dominating lines of development (e.g., different life-styles with associated organizations) that remain nonexistent just because their development requires the simultaneous introduction of *many* complementary ideas/innovations, too many for any organizer—*including* any government—to figure out. They may appear in the future as a result of "lucky coincidences."

Remark 5.3. It is well known that joint ventures and multipurpose organizations are empirically common in the early phases of innovation and development; e.g., see [14, 12].

Remark 5.4. The process of forming cooperative ventures obviously deserves further analysis beyond the casual treatment of it given here. Our approach was adopted only to make the simple point that if an economy gets stuck at a suboptimal FWE then (a) there are unexploited potential profits to innovation for some cooperative; and (b) there is at least one distribution of these profits such that all shareholders in firms constituting the cooperative benefit.

Acknowledgments

It is a pleasure to acknowledge that Earl Thompson, several years ago, pointed out to me the importance of complementarities for the innovation process, and pointed out the possibility of underdevelopment. He explicitly discusses this possibility [13]. I am also indebted to Thompson for the empirical fact mentioned in Remark 5.1. and the first observation in Remark 5.2. The empirical fact in Remark 5.1 was more recently mentioned to me by Richard Gilbert in a helpful conversation. Conversations with Joseph Ostroy were also very helpful. Finally, the work of Oliver Hart on monopolistic competition must be sighted as seminal, but for this see the text. All shortcomings of the paper are, of course, my responsibility.

References

1. S. J. Grossman, A Characterization of the optimality of equilibrium in incomplete markets, *J. Econ. Theory* **15** (1977), 1–15.
2. O. D. Hart, Monopolistic competition in a large economy with differential commodities, *Rev. Econ. Stud.* **46** (1979), 1–30.
3. O. D. Hart, On shareholder unanimity in large stock market economies, *Econometrica* **47** (1979), 1057–1083.

4. O. D. HART, Perfect competition and optimal product differentiation, *J. Econ. Theory* **22** (1980), 279–312.
5. W. P. HELLER AND D. A. STARRETT, On the nature of externalities, *in* "Theory and Measurement of Economic Externalities," Academic Press, New York, 1976.
6. L. MAKOWSKI, "A Dual Characterization of Optimal Choices Given Preference and Constraint Sets," Discussion Paper No. 20, SSRC Research Project on Risk, Information and Quantity Signals in Economics, University of Cambridge, January 1979.
7. L. MAKOWSKI, A characterization of perfectly competitive economies with production, *J. Econ. Theory* **22** (1980), 208–221.
8. J. OSTROY, The no-surplus condition as a characterization of perfectly competitive equilibrium, *J. Econ. Theory* **22** (1980), 183–207.
9. R. T. ROCKAFELLAR, "Convex Analysis," Princeton Univ. Press, Princeton, N. J., 1972.
10. J. A. SCHUMPETER, "The Theory of Economic Development," Harvard Univ. Press, Cambridge, Mass., 1934.
11. T. SCITOVSKY, Two concepts of external economies, *J. Pol. Econ.* **62** (1954), 70–82.
12. G. J. STIGLER, The division of labor is limited by the extent of the market, *J. Pol. Econ.* **59** (1951), 185–193.
13. E. A. THOMPSON, The perfectly competitive production of collective goods, *Rev. Econ. Statist.* **50** (1968), 1–12.
14. A. YOUNG, Increasing returns and economic progresss, *Econ. J.* **38** (1928), 527–542.

Small Efficient Scale as a Foundation for Walrasian Equilibrium*

WILLIAM NOVSHEK

Stanford University, Stanford, California 94305

AND

HUGO SONNENSCHEIN

Princeton University, Princeton, New Jersey 08540

Received June 6, 1979

INTRODUCTION

We are concerned with a formal description of perfect competition in which small efficient scale[1] and the entry of firms occupy a central role. The set of aggregate technological possibilities for the economy is obtained by summing the production sets of a very large number of productive units, interpreted here as firms. These units are most efficient when their output is small (infinitesimal) relative to demand, and the classical case of U-shaped average cost is admitted in the analysis. Also, because efficient scale is small, firms have only an infinitesimal effect on price when confined to the region in which they make positive profit. This enables one to capture the notion that the demand curve appears flat to a firm, while at the same time demand price may change substantially with substantial changes in aggregate quantity. The mass of firms active in an equilibrium is determined by the conditions of supply and demand. Small changes in aggregate demand will typically change the list of firms which are present in an equilibrium. Since changes in taste cause some firms to leave the market and others to enter, and since there are usually firms "on the margin" of entry, entry plays an important role in the explanation of value.

Despite the fact that our description of a perfectly competitive economy fits quite nicely with the ordinary neoclassical conception, the reader will see

* We wish to acknowledge the helpful comments of the referee and also to thank the National Science Foundation for financial support.

[1] The efficient scale of a firm is small if it takes a large number of such firms, each producing at minimum average cost (c), to satisfy demand at a market price equal to c.

Reprinted from *Journal of Economic Theory* **22,** No. 2, 243–255 (April 1980)
ISBN 0-12-476750-8

that both in detail and interpretation it differs in some important ways from modern formal competitive theory (see, e.g., Debreu [3]). For example, we will argue that the convexity of the set of aggregate production possibilities is irrelevant for the existence of competitive equilibrium. With small efficient scale and the absence of externalities, the aggregate production set is necessarily convex (by Richter's theorem, which asserts that integration with respect to a nonatomic measure yields a convex-valued correspondence), and with standard assumptions equilibrium exists. With small efficient scale and externalities, the aggregate production set is in general *not* convex, but again under general conditions equilibrium will exist. Small efficient scale, which only in the absence of externalities guarantees convexity, is the proper requirement for the existence of perfectly competitive equilibrium.

The argument of the paper proceeds as follows. We begin by defining a private ownership perfectly competitive economy $\mathscr{E} = (X_i, \omega_i, \succsim_i, Z(\cdot), s_i(\cdot))$ and defining its equilibria. Throughout the analysis, for the m consumers, preferences $\succsim_i$ are convex and initial endowments ω_i are interior to the convex consumption sets X_i.[2] The framework differs from that of standard competitive theory in that there are a continuum of productive units whose output must be integrated to generate a quantity that is significant when compared with demand. The set $Z(\beta)$ is the technology available to unit β, and $s_i(\beta)$ is the share of firm β owned by i. The notion of a variable profit assignments economy $\mathscr{E}' = (X_i, \omega_i, \succsim_i, Z, w(\cdot))$ is then introduced. In addition to the m consumers this requires a specification of the aggregate technology Z, and for each p, m numbers $w_i(p)$, which indicate how $\max p \cdot Z$ is shared among consumers: $\sum w_i(p) = \max p \cdot Z$. Variable profit assignments economies are of interest in their own right as they capture the notion of a regime in which the aggregate rent from the process of production is distributed to consumers according to a rule which depends on prices. (For example, an individual's share of $\max p \cdot Z$ may depend on his wage.) Standard techniques from competitive analysis are sufficient to show that (loosely) every variable profit assignments economy $\mathscr{E}' = (X_i, \omega_i, \succsim_i, Z, w(\cdot))$ has an equilibrium provided Z is convex and $\{w_i(\cdot)\}$ are continuous for prices at which $\max p \cdot Z$ is well defined. This is Theorem 1.

In this paper we are concerned with particular variable profit assignments economies. These economies, e.g., $\mathscr{E}' = (X_i, \omega_i, \succsim_i, Z, w(\cdot))$, are associated with perfectly competitive private ownership economies, e.g., $\mathscr{E} = (X_i, \omega_i, \succsim_i, Z(\cdot), s_i(\cdot))$, by defining Z as the integral of the correspondence $\beta \rightarrow Z(\beta)$, and for every price p, and every individual i, defining $w_i(p)$ as the integral of i's share of the profits made by each productive unit. In the absence of externalities, when Z is well defined it will be convex

[2] Rather than m consumers one may postulate m types of consumers, or with little additional difficulty, consider a continuum of consumers.

(by Richter's theorem) and mild conditions on the functions $s_i(\cdot)$ will guarantee that the functions $w_i(\cdot)$ have the continuity property necessary for the application of Theorem 1.

The central point here is that the convexity of Z does not in any way depend on the convexity of the sets $Z(\beta)$. From a descriptive point of view, the convexity of Z is a consequence of the fact that efficient increases in output require a larger number of active productive units, these units "come in" at minimum average cost, and in the order "lower minimum average cost comes in first." Thus, we have the rather classical description of increases in output being achieved by the successive addition of small scale productive units, with the necessity of using on the margin a unit which is less efficient than those which preceded it. If the production possibilities available to each firm are shared by an unbounded measure of similar firms, then constant returns to scale obtains in the aggregate. But, if firms differ greatly in their maximum efficiency, then the boundary of the aggregate production set will exhibit substantial curvature with changes in scale. In the latter case it is typical that economic rents will accrue to the productive sector. The ith agent's share of these rents is a function of price, since price determines which firms are profitable. Some price vector may make every one of the firms which an agent owns unprofitable (then his share of economic rents will be zero), while another price vector may result in high profit for several of the firms which he owns. Even in economies with only two firms and two consumers, if the firms are not identical, and if each firm is not held equally by each individual, then the share of aggregate profit which is distributed to each agent will vary with price.

Under rather mild assumption on the correspondence $\beta \to Z(\beta)$, there is a natural correspondence between the equilibria of a private ownership economy $\mathscr{E} = (X_i, \omega_i, \succsim_i, Z(\cdot), s_i(\cdot))$ and the equilibria of the associated variable profit assignments economy $\mathscr{E}' = (X_i, \omega_i, \succsim_i, Z, w_i(\cdot))$. Specifically, $(p, x, z(\cdot))$ is an equilibrium of $\mathscr{E}$ implies $(p, x, \int z(\beta)d\beta)$ is an equilibrium of $\mathscr{E}'$, and with some technical assumptions (p, x, z) for $\mathscr{E}'$ implies there exists an equilibrium of $\mathscr{E}$, $(p, x, z(\cdot))$, such that $\int z(\beta)\, d\beta = z$. Similarly, there is a natural correspondence between the Pareto-efficient allocations of $\mathscr{E}$ and the Pareto-efficient allocations of $\mathscr{E}'$. If the allocation $(x, z(\cdot))$ is Pareto efficient for $\mathscr{E}$, then $(x, \int z(\beta)\, d\beta)$ is Pareto efficient for $\mathscr{E}'$, and if the allocation (x, z) is Pareto efficient for $\mathscr{E}'$ then there exists a Pareto-efficient allocation of $\mathscr{E}$, $(x, z(\cdot))$, such that $z = \int z(\beta)\, d\beta$. With these observations in hand the existence of equilibrium for the perfectly competitive private ownership economy $\mathscr{E}$ is established; this is Theorem 2. The striking feature of the statement of the result is the absence of the assumption that the production sets $Z(\beta)$ are convex. The general argument of the proof is that (a) the production set Z of the associated variable profit assignments economy $\mathscr{E}'$ is convex (Richter's theorem), (b) equilibrium exists for $\mathscr{E}'$

(Theorem 1), and (c) an equilibrium for $\mathscr{E}'$ is naturally associated with an equilibrium for $\mathscr{E}$. Theorem 3 gives conditions under which equilibria of a perfectly competitive private ownership economy $\mathscr{E} = (X_i, \omega_i, \succsim_i, Z(\cdot), s_i(\cdot))$ are Pareto efficient. The idea of the proof is (a) every equilibrium of $\mathscr{E}$ naturally corresponds to an equilibrium of the associated variable profit assignments economy $\mathscr{E}'$, (b) equilibria of $\mathscr{E}'$ are Pareto efficient (standard), and (c) Pareto-efficient allocations of $\mathscr{E}'$ naturally correspond to Pareto-efficient allocations of $\mathscr{E}$.

Finally, Theorem 4 and its corollary establish that every Pareto-efficient allocation of a perfectly competitive private ownership economy $\mathscr{E}$ is an equilibrium subject to a suitable assignment of ownership. Again, the striking feature of the statement is the absence of the assumption that production sets are convex. The general argument of the proof is (a) each Pareto-efficient allocation of $\mathscr{E}$ naturally corresponds to a Pareto-efficient allocation of $\mathscr{E}' = (X_i, \omega_i, \succsim_i, Z, w_i(\cdot))$, (b) the production set Z is convex (Richter's theorem), (c) every Pareto-efficient allocation of $\mathscr{E}'$ is an equilibrium of $\mathscr{E}'$ for a suitable assignment of ownership (standard), and (d) every equilibrium of $\mathscr{E}'$ naturally corresponds to an equilibrium of $\mathscr{E}$. The formal analysis is followed by six remarks which explain some consequences of our formulation; included here is a reinterpretation of the classical theorems of welfare economics. Externalities and taxation are introduced into the analysis, and a potential cause of market failure is identified which does not appear in the Arrow–Debreu theory.

Define $\Delta = \{p \in R_+^l : \sum_i p_i = 1\}$; integration is in the sense of Lebesgue. For integrals of correspondences see Hildenbrand [4, Sect. D, II].

The Model

(a) A private ownership perfectly competitive economy $\mathscr{E} = (X_i, \omega_i, \succsim_i, Z(\cdot), s_i(\cdot))$ is

(a1) for each consumer $i = 1, 2, \ldots, m$, a consumption set $X_i \subset R^l$, an initial endowment vector $\omega_i \in R^l$, and a complete preference preordering $\succsim_i \subset X_i \times X_i$,

(a2) for each firm $\beta \in [0, \infty)$, a nonempty production set $Z(\beta) \subset R^l$,

(a3) for each (i, β) a nonnegative number $s_i(\beta)$ which indicates the fraction of firm β owned by individual i. For each β, $\sum_i s_i(\beta) = 1$.

(b) An equilibrium for the private ownership perfectly competitive economy $\mathscr{E} = (X_i, \omega_i, \succsim_i, Z(\cdot), s_i(\cdot))$ is a triple $(p^*, x^*, z^*(\cdot)) \in \Delta \times \Pi X_i \times$ (integrable functions from $[0, \infty)$ to R^l, where $z^*(\beta) \in Z(\beta)$ for all β) satisfying

(b1) $p^* \cdot x_i^* = p^* \cdot \omega_i + \int s_i(\beta)\, p^* \cdot z^*(\beta)\, d\beta$, $i = 1, 2, \ldots, m$, (b2) $\sum_i x_i^* \leqslant \int z^*(\beta)\, d\beta + \sum_i \omega_i$ and $p^* \cdot (\sum_i x_i^* - \int z^*(\beta)\, d\beta - \sum_i \omega_i) = 0$,

(b3) $x_i \succ_i x_i^*$ implies $p^* \cdot x_i > p^* \cdot \omega_i + \int s_i(\beta)\, p^* \cdot z^*(\beta)\, d\beta$, $i = 1, 2,..., m$,

(b4) $p^* \cdot z > p^* \cdot z^*(\beta)$ implies $z \notin z(\beta)$, for a.e. β.

(c) Given the private ownership perfectly competitive economy $\mathscr{E} = (X_i, \omega_i, \succsim_i, Z(\cdot), s_i(\cdot))$, the associated variable profit assignments A–D economy $\mathscr{E}' = (X_i, \omega_i, \succsim_i, Z, w_i(\cdot))$ is defined by

(c1) $Z = \int Z(\beta)\, d\beta$

(c2) for all $p \in \Delta$,

$$\begin{aligned} w_i(p) &= \int s_i(\beta) \sup\{p \cdot z \colon z \in Z(\beta)\}\, d\beta \qquad &&\text{if it exists and is finite} \\ &= 0 &&\text{otherwise.} \end{aligned}$$

(d) An equilibrium for the variable profit assignments A–D economy $\mathscr{E}' = (X_i, \omega_i, \succsim_i, Z, w_i(\cdot))$ is a triple $(p^*, x^*, z^*) \in \Delta \times \Pi X_i \times Z$ satisfying

(d1) $p^* \cdot x_i^* = p^* \cdot \omega_i + w_i(p^*)$, $i = 1, 2,..., m$,

(d2) $\sum_i x_i^* \leqslant z^* + \sum_i \omega_i$ and $p^* \cdot (\sum_i x_i^* - z^* - \sum_i \omega_i) = 0$,

(d3) $x_i \succ_i x_i^*$ implies $p^* \cdot x_i > p^* \cdot \omega_i + w_i(p^*)$, $i = 1, 2,..., m$,

(d4) $p^* \cdot z > p^* \cdot z^*$ implies $z \notin Z$,

(d5) $p^* \cdot z^* = \sum_i w_i(p^*)$.

(e) An allocation for the private ownership perfectly competitive economy $\mathscr{E} = (X_i, \omega_i, \succsim_i, Z(\cdot), s_i(\cdot))$ is a pair $(x, z(\cdot)) \in \Pi X_i \times$ (integrable functions from $[0, \infty)$ to R^l, where $z(\beta) \in Z(\beta)$ for all β) satisfying $\sum_i x_i \leqslant \int z(\beta)\, d\beta + \sum_i \omega_i$. The allocation $(x, z(\cdot))$ is Pareto efficient if there does not exist an allocation $(x', z'(\cdot))$ for $\mathscr{E}$ with the property that $x_i' \succsim_i x_i$ for all i and $x_k' \succ_k x_k$ for some k.

(f) An allocation for the variable profit assignments A–D economy $\mathscr{E}' = (X_i, \omega_i, \succsim_i, Z, w_i(\cdot))$ is a pair $(x, z) \in \Pi X_i \times Z$ satisfying $\sum_i x_i \leqslant z + \sum_i \omega_i$. The allocation (x, z) is Pareto efficient if there does not exist an allocation (x', z') for $\mathscr{E}'$ with the property that $x_i' \succsim_i x_i$ for all i and $x_k' \succ_k x_k$ for some k.

Theorems

For reference we state an interchangeability lemma.

Lemma 1. *If the graph of the correspondence $\beta \to Z(\beta)$ is measurable and $\int Z(\beta)\, d\beta \neq \varnothing$ then for every $p \in R^l$ $\sup\{p \cdot z \colon z \in \int Z(\beta)\, d\beta\} = \int \sup\{p \cdot z \colon z \in Z(\beta)\}\, d\beta$.*

Proof. The proof is similar to that of Proposition D, II, 6 of Hildenbrand [4] with minor modification since the measure is not a probability measure.

LEMMA 2. *Given the private ownership perfectly competitive economy* $\mathscr{E} = (X_i, \omega_i, \succsim_i, Z(\cdot), s_i(\cdot))$ *and the associated variable profit assignments A–D economy* $\mathscr{E} = (X_i, \omega_i, \succsim_i, Z, w_i(\cdot))$, *then*

(i) $(p^*, x^*, z^*(\cdot))$ *is an equilibrium of* $\mathscr{E}$ *implies* $(p^*, x^*, \int z^*(\beta)\, d\beta)$ *is an equilibrium of* $\mathscr{E}'$. *If the correspondence* $\beta \to Z(\beta)$ *is closed valued, has a measurable graph, and for each* i, $s_i(\cdot)$ *is measurable, then*

(ii) (p^*, x^*, z^*) *is an equilibrium for* $\mathscr{E}'$ *implies there exists an equilibrium of* $\mathscr{E}$, $(p^*, x^*, z^*(\cdot))$, *such that* $\int z^*(\beta)\, d\beta = z^*$.

Proof. Trivial using the interchangeability lemma for part (ii).

LEMMA 3. *Given the private ownership perfectly competitive economy* $\mathscr{E} = (X_i, \omega_i, \succsim_i, Z(\cdot), s_i(\cdot))$ *and the associated variable profit assignments A–D economy* $\mathscr{E}' = (X_i, \omega_i, \succsim_i, Z, w_i(\cdot))$, *then*

(i) *the allocation* $(x, z(\cdot))$ *is Pareto efficient for* $\mathscr{E}$ *implies* $(x, \int z(\beta)\, d\beta$ *is Pareto efficient for* $\mathscr{E}'$, *and*

(ii) *the allocation* (x, z) *is Pareto efficient for* $\mathscr{E}'$ *implies there exists a Pareto-efficient allocation of* $\mathscr{E}$, $(x, z(\cdot))$, *such that* $z = \int z(\beta)\, d\beta$.

Proof. Trivial.

THEOREM 1. *Given the private ownership perfectly competitive economy* $\mathscr{E} = (X_i, \omega_i, \succsim_i, Z(\cdot), s_i(\cdot))$, *the associated variable profit assignments A–D economy* $\mathscr{E}' = (X_i, \omega_i, \succsim_i, Z, w_i(\cdot))$ *has an equilibrium if*

(i) *for every* i, X_i *is closed, convex, bounded below,*

$\succsim_i$ *is continuous,*[3] *convex,*[4] *and there is no satiation consumption,* $\omega_i \in \text{int}\, X_i$;

(ii) Z *is closed,* $Z \cap (-Z) = \{0\}$, *and* $Z \supset (-R_+{}^l)$; *and*

(iii) *there is a compact cube* $K \subset R^l$ *such that* K^{m+1} *contains all allocations* (x, z) *in its interior*[5] *and for every* i, w_i *is continuous and nonnegative on* $\hat{\Delta} = \{p \in \Delta : \max p \cdot (Z \cap K) = \sup p \cdot Z\}$ *and for every* $p \in \hat{\Delta}$, $\sum_i w_i(p) = \max p \cdot (Z \cap K)$.

[3] $\succsim_i$ is continuous if, for every $x_i' \in X_i$, the sets $\{x_i \in X_i : x_i \succsim_i x_i'\}$ and $\{x_i \in X_i : x_i' \succsim_i x_i\}$ are closed in X_i.

[4] $\succsim_i$ is convex if $x_i' \succ_i x_i$ implies $\lambda x_i' + (1 - \lambda) x_i \succ_i x_i$ for all $\lambda \in (0, 1)$.

[5] Note that the definition of allocation requires feasibility of (x, z). By a standard argument (i) and (ii) imply that such a K exists.

Proof. By Richter's theorem $Z = \int Z(\beta)\, d\beta$ is convex, so by (ii) there is a $p \in \Delta$ such that $p \cdot Z \leqslant 0 = p \cdot 0$, and $\hat{\Delta}$ is nonempty. The set $\hat{\Delta}$ is also closed so for each i there is a continuous function $\bar{w}_i: \Delta \to R_+$ such that $\bar{w}_i(p) = w_i(p)$ for all $p \in \hat{\Delta}$ and $\sum_i \bar{w}_i(p) = \max p \cdot (Z \cap K)$ for all $p \in \Delta$. By application of a standard technique (the abstract economies approach) due to Arrow and Debreu [1] the variable profit assignments A–D economy $\mathscr{E}'_K = (X_i \cap K, \omega_i, \succsim_i, Z \cap K, \bar{w}_i(\cdot))$ has an equilibrium (p^*, x^*, z^*)which is also an equilibrium of $\mathscr{E}'$.

THEOREM 2. *The perfectly competitive private ownership economy $\mathscr{E} = (X_i, \omega_i, \succsim_i, Z(\cdot), s_i(\cdot))$ has an equilibrium if*

(i) *for every i, X_i is closed, convex, bounded below,*

$\succsim_i$ is continuous, convex, and there is no satiation consumption, $\omega_i \in int\ X_i$;

(ii) *the correspondence $\beta \to Z(\beta)$ is closed valued with a measurable graph and $0 \in Z(\beta)$ for all β;*

(iii) *$\int Z(\beta)\, d\beta = Z$ is closed,*[6] *$Z \cap (-Z) = \{0\}$, and $Z \supset (-R_+^l)$; and*

(iv) *for every i, the function s_i is measurable.*

Proof. Consider the associated variable profit assignments A–D economy $\mathscr{E}' = (X_i, \omega_i, \succsim_i, Z, w_i(\cdot))$. By (i), (iii), and a standard argument there exists a compact cube $K \subset R^l$ such that K^{m+1} contains all allocations (x, z) in its interior. Using this K, assumption (iii) of Theorem 1 holds by (ii) and (iv). By Theorem 1 there is an equilibrium of $\mathscr{E}'$ and by Lemma 2(ii) there is an equilibrium of $\mathscr{E}$.

THEOREM 3. *Suppose that the perfectly competitive private ownership economy $\mathscr{E} = (X_i, \omega_i, \succsim_i, Z(\cdot), s_i(\cdot))$ satisfies the condition that X_i contains no point of local satiation for each i. If $(p^*, x^*, z^*(\cdot))$ is an equilibrium for $\mathscr{E}$, then $(x^*, z^*(\cdot))$ is Pareto efficient.*

Proof. Consider the associated variable profit assignments A–D economy $\mathscr{E}' = (X_i, \omega_i, \succsim_i, Z, w_i(\cdot))$. By Lemma 2(i), $(p^*, x^*, \int z^*(\beta)\, d\beta)$ is an equilibrium of $\mathscr{E}'$, so by a standard argument $(x^*, \int z^*(\beta)\, d\beta)$ is Pareto efficient in $\mathscr{E}'$. Thus by Lemma 3(ii), $(x^*, z^*(\cdot))$ (and any allocation $(x^*, z(\cdot))$ such that $\int z(\beta)\, d\beta = z^*$) is Pareto efficient in $\mathscr{E}$.

[6] The closedness of Z is not implied by (ii). Additional assumptions could be made about the correspondence $\beta \to Z(\beta)$ to ensure that Z is closed. For example, if $Z(\beta)$ is the same for all β and for every nonzero y on the boundary of the least closed convex cone containing $Z(\beta)$ there is a (nonzero) multiple of y in $Z(\beta)$ then Z is closed.

THEOREM 4. *Let the private ownership perfectly competitive economy* $\mathscr{E} = (X_i, \omega_i, \succsim_i, Z(\cdot), s_i(\cdot))$ *be such that*

(i) *for every i,* X_i *is convex and* $\succsim_i$ *is continuous and convex, and*

(ii) *the correspondence* $\beta \to Z(\beta)$ *is closed valued and has a measurable graph.*

Given a Pareto efficient allocation $(x^*, z^*(\cdot))$, *where* x_k^* *is not a satiation consumption for some k, there is a nonzero price vector* $p^* \in R^l$ *such that*

(iii) *for each i,* x_i^* *minimizes* $p^* \cdot x_i$ *on* $\{x_i \in X_i: x_i \succsim_i x_i^*\}$,

(iv) *for a.e.* β, $p^* \cdot z > p^* \cdot z^*(\beta)$ *implies* $z \notin Z(\beta)$.

Proof. Consider the associated variable profit assignments A–D economy $\mathscr{E}' = (X_i, \omega_i, \succsim_i, Z, w_i(\cdot))$. The allocation $(x^*, \int z^*(\beta)\, d\beta)$ is Pareto efficient in $\mathscr{E}'$ by Lemma 3(i), and Z is convex by Richter's theorem so by a standard argument there exists a nonzero $p^* \in R^l$ such that (iii) holds and $[p^* \cdot z > p^* \cdot \int z^*(\beta)\, d\beta$ implies $z \notin Z]$. Then (iv) easily follows using (ii) and the interchangeability lemma.

COROLLARY. *If the conditions of Theorem 4 hold and* $x_i^* \in \operatorname{int} X_i$ *for each i and* $(-R_+^l) \subset Z = \int Z(\beta)\, d\beta$, *then* $(p^*, x^*, z^*(\cdot))$ *is an equilibrium for some assignment of endowments and ownership shares.*

Proof. Trivial.

Remark 1. If for each $j \in \{1, \ldots, n\}$ and $\beta \in [0, \infty)$ we define $Z(j, \beta)$ to be the production set of firm j, β (with ownership shares $s_i(j, \beta)$), then $Z_j = \int Z(j, \beta)\, d\beta$ is convex. If we let $w_i(p, j)$ be consumer i's income from industry j at prices p, and $w_i(p) = \sum_{j=1}^n w_i(p, j)$ then the variable profit assignments A–D economy $\mathscr{E}' = (X_i, \omega_i, \succsim_i, Z_1, \ldots, Z_n, w_i(\cdot))$ is quite similar to a standard Arrow–Debreu economy. However, the interpretation is different. Here Z_j is an industry production set, where the industry is made up of a continuum of infinitesimal firms, each of which has no effect on price. Thus the industry acts competitively, and as prices vary the industry output varies both because active firms change their productions and because firms enter and leave the market. This corresponds to the classical intuition about perfect competition.

Novshek and Sonnenschein [7] treated a special case where for each j, $Z(j, \beta)$ is the same nonconvex production set for all β. While each firm had efficient scale bounded away from zero (in the scale of the firm), the industry production set was a convex cone. These are the analogs of U-shaped average cost and horizontal supply in partial equilibrium. They consider a sequence of finite economies $\mathscr{E}_k$ with noninfinitesimal firms. Each economy has the same production sector with a countably infinite number of firms while the consumer sector in $\mathscr{E}_k$ is a k-fold replication of the consumer sector of $\mathscr{E}_1$. In per capita terms, as k becomes large the $\mathscr{E}_k$ converge to the perfectly competitive economy $\mathscr{E}$. In the finite economies firms set quantity in order to maximize profit, recognizing their effect on price.[7] They show that if $\mathscr{E}$ has an equilibrium satisfying a condition called DSD, then whenever the efficient scale of the firms is sufficiently small relative to the market (k is sufficiently large) a Cournot–Nash equilibrium with free entry exists for $\mathscr{E}_k$, and the set of Cournot–Nash equilibria with free entry converges to the set of (perfectly competitive) equilibria of $\mathscr{E}$ which satisfy DSD.[8] These results suggest that in the intuitive model of perfect competition, with entry and exit of many small (infinitesimal) firms producing the changes in output, only those equilibria which satisfy DSD are true equilibria. From this perspective, other equilibria are artifacts of a perfectly competitive specification in which firms are regarded as points rather than infinitesimals. For k large, no equilibria of $\mathscr{E}_k$ can exist near a Walras equilibrium of $\mathscr{E}$ at which DSD fails: entry is always profitable for additional firms.

The DSD condition is a "generalization" of Marshallian stability: at quantities "greater" than equilibrium, demand price is "less" than supply price, and thus prices provide the correct entry and exit signals. If $F(z_1, \ldots, z_n)$ is the function giving the prices that arise when industry productions are $z_1, \ldots, z_n$, and $(p^*, x^*, z_1^*, z_2^*, \ldots, z_n^*)$ is an equilibrium of $\mathscr{E}$, then $p^* = F(z_1^*, \ldots, z_n^*)$ and $p^* \cdot z_j^* = 0$ for all j since Z_j is a cone.

The DSD condition is satisfied at an equilibrium (p^*, x^*, z^*) if for each j, a "small increase in output" to $(1 + \lambda) z_j^*$ for λ small, positive, leads to prices $F(z_1^*, \ldots, (1 + \lambda) z_j^*, \ldots, z_n^*) = p(\lambda)$ such that $p(\lambda) \cdot z_j^* \leqslant 0$ so that entry is unprofitable. The DSD condition is not a pathological condition. It is satisfied at an equilibrium of $\mathscr{E}$ if a weak local version of the weak axiom of revealed preference holds at the equilibrium or if the consumer sector acts as a single consumer near the equilibrium. However, it is also not pathological for a specific equilibrium of $\mathscr{E}$ to fail to satisfy the DSD condition. Failure of DSD can occur in a two-commodity economy in which the aggregate production set is a cone and utility functions are homogeneous.

When firms in an industry do not have identical production sets the DSD condition must be carefully defined. At an equilibrium $(p^*, x^*, z_1^*, \ldots, z_n^*)$ of $\mathscr{E}$, the DSD condition must be applied to those firms which are not yet active and will therefore depend on the industry outputs z_j^*. If there is a positive measure of firms which are inactive in the equilibrium and each of which can "approximately" produce some vector y, then for DSD to be satisfied, a

[7] Prices are such that the excess demand of the price-taking consumer sector equals the asserted quantity actions of the firms.

[8] Some technical qualifications are needed; in particular the inverse demand function F must be C^2 in a neighborhood. This of course includes the requirement that F is defined in a neighborhood of the Cournot equilibrium.

small change in production of λy for λ small, positive must lead to prices $p(\lambda)$ such that $p(\lambda) \cdot y \leqslant 0$ so that entry is unprofitable. If the firms in industry j can be ordered in terms of efficiency (e.g., $Z(j, \beta) \subset Z(j, \beta')$ if $\beta > \beta'$) and only firms $[0, \beta^0]$ are active in equilibrium then DSD must be checked by "entry" of the next most efficient firms, those in $(\beta^0, \beta^0 + \epsilon)$.

Remark 2. Theorem 3 is often referred to as the first theorem of classical welfare economics; it asserts that competitive equilibria are Pareto efficient. Even with DSD added as a requirement for equilibrium, the conclusion will of course still hold. Theorem 4 is the second theorem of classical welfare economics; it asserts that Pareto-efficient allocations are perfectly competitive equilibria subject to a suitable assignment of ownership. Here the result is somewhat different than in the Arrow–Debreu theory. First, we observe that convexity of the set of aggregate production possibilities, which is one of the central hypotheses in standard treatments of the second welfare theorem, is not assumed; here it is a consequence of small efficient scale and the absence of externalities (Richter's theorem). Next we note that our definition of perfectly competitive equilibrium does not require DSD. Even if we succeed (by suitably assigning ownership) to support (in the conventional sense) a given efficient allocation as a perfectly competitive equilibrium, DSD may fail; therefore, prices may give the wrong entry signals, and in this case free entry and exit may drive the economy away from the given efficient allocation However, suppose, for example, that preferences are homothetic. If the efficient allocation is supported as a perfectly competitive equilibrium, and if endowments and ownership are distributed so as to be proportional among individuals, then the consumer sector will act as a single individual and equilibrium will satisfy DSD. This suggests that, rather than convexity, small efficient scale and the possibility of assigning ownership so that prices give the correct entry signals may be the important considerations in formulating the second welfare theorem.

Remark 3. The model can be extended to include externalities. We will indicate how the existence theorem, Theorem 2, can be modified to include production externalities such that each firm's production set depends on the aggregate production of each industry. Using the notation of Remark 1, where z_k is the aggregate production of industry k, let $Z(j, \beta, z_1, ..., z_n)$ be the production set of firm j, β when the aggregate productions are $z_1, ..., z_n$. Then the aggregate production set (by industry) $\mathscr{Z} = \{(z_1, ..., z_n): z_j \in \int Z(j, \beta, z_i, ..., z_n)\, d\beta$ for each $j\}$, $\mathscr{Z}_j = \{z_j: (z_1, ..., z_n) \in \mathscr{Z}$ for some $z_1, ..., z_{j-1}, z_{j+1}, ..., z_n\}$, and the aggregate production set $\bar{\mathscr{Z}} = \{\sum_{j=1}^n z_j: (z_1, ..., z_n) \in \mathscr{Z}\}$ may not be convex. Let $\hat{\mathscr{Z}}$ (respectively $\hat{\mathscr{Z}}_j$) be the smallest closed convex cone containing $\bar{\mathscr{Z}}$ (respectively $\mathscr{Z}_j$).

Condition (i) of Theorem 2 is unchanged while conditions (ii), (iii), and (iv) are modified to:

(ii)′ For all $(z_1, \ldots, z_n) \in R^{ln}$, $j \in \{1, \ldots, n\}$, the correspondence $\beta \to Z(j, \beta, z_1, \ldots, z_n)$ is closed valued with a measurable graph and $0 \in Z(j, \beta, z_1, \ldots, z_n)$ for all β.

(iii)′ $\mathscr{Z}$ is closed, $\hat{\mathscr{Z}} \cap (-\hat{\mathscr{Z}}) = \{0\}$, $\hat{\mathscr{Z}} \supset (-R_+^l)$, and the $\hat{\mathscr{Z}}_j$ are positively semi-independent.

(iv)′ For every i and j, the function $s_i(j, \cdot)$ is measurable.

We add a condition which is similar to condition (iii):

(v) $\sum_j \int Z(j, \beta, 0, \ldots, 0)\, d\beta \supset (-R_+^l)$ and

$$\Big(\sum_j \int Z(j, \beta, 0, \ldots, 0)\, d\beta\Big) \cap \Big(-\sum_j \int Z(j, \beta, 0, \ldots, 0)\, d\beta\Big) = \{0\}.$$

Finally we add a new condition which requires that the effect of externalities on production is continuous in the aggregate:

(vi) For all i and j, and for any nonempty compact cube $K \subset R^l$ centered at the origin, the correspondences $(z_1, \ldots, z_n) \to K \cap \int Z(j, \beta, z_1, \ldots, z_n)\, d\beta$ and $(z_1, \ldots, z_n) \to K \cap \int s_i(j, \beta) Z(j, \beta, z_1, \ldots, z_n)\, d\beta$ are continuous.

In order to prove the existence of an equilibrium with externalities under these conditions we consider an associated economy with

$$\begin{aligned} w_i(p, z_1, \ldots, z_n) &= \sum_{j=1}^{n} \int s_i(j, \beta) \sup\{p \cdot z : z \in Z(j, \beta, z_1, \ldots, z_n)\, d\beta \\ &\qquad\qquad\qquad\qquad \text{if it exists and is finite,} \\ &= 0 \qquad \text{otherwise.} \end{aligned}$$

The existence of an equilibrium for the associated economy follows, as in the proof of Theorem 1, from application of an abstract economy existence theorem, where the industry j production set (constraint set) given $(p, x_1, \ldots, x_m, z_1, \ldots, z_n)$ is $K \cap \int Z(j, \beta, z_1, \ldots, z_n)\, d\beta$. The existence of an equilibrium for $\mathscr{E}$ then follows as in Lemma 2(ii).

Remark 4. Clearly, perfectly competitive equilibria are not efficient in the presence of externalities of the type introduced in Remark 3. Even though with externalities the set of aggregate production possibilities is not convex, is it possible to state and prove a theorem that every efficient allocation is an equilibrium subject to the proper assignment of ownership shares and the appropriate Pigovian taxes?[9] This can be achieved; e.g., by applying the ideas of Shafer and Sonnenschein [8] to the specification of an economy given in Remark 3. One may conclude the convexity of the set of aggregate production possibilities has nothing to do with the second welfare theorem (with

[9] This is done in a more explicit setting by Chipman [2].

externalities and corrective taxes.) Once again, small efficient scale is the appropriate condition. As before, the possibility of not being able to distribute ownership so that DSD is satisfied remains a problem for the result; and with externalities, this may not be possible.

Remark 5. In the Arrow–Debreu theory the convexity of the set of aggregate productions Z plays a key role in establishing the existence of perfectly competitive equilibrium. As we have observed several times, without externalities, the required convexity is a consequence of Richter's theorem, and so does not have to be assumed. But with externalities present, Z may not be convex; nevertheless, the previous remark demonstrated that a general existence theorem still obtains. We assert that the convexity of the set of aggregate production possibilities is not relevant to the problem of the existence of competitive equilibrium. The existence of perfectly competitive equilibrium depends fundamentally on small efficient scale, which in any case is the economically natural condition for perfect competition to apply. Downward sloping demand in the appropriate region, so that prices give the correct entry signals, remains an additional possible requirement. These remarks are very much related to the work of Chipman [2] who makes some similar observations in a more specialized model.

Remark 6. McKenzie [5, 6] introduces a nonmarketed entrepreneurial factor which is private to the firm and owned by the owners of the firm, in order to prove the existence of equilibrium in an economy with convex, noncone production sets via an existence theorem for an economy with constant returns to scale. Application of a similar technique to the economy $\mathscr{E}$ would require the introduction of a continuum of new commodities, one for each firm.[10] On the other hand, application of the technique to the associated economy $\mathscr{E}'$ would yield "ownership shares" $w_i(p)/\sum_k w_k(p)$ which vary (perhaps discontinuously) with price.

References

1. K. Arrow and G. Debreu, Existence of equilibrium for a competitive economy, *Econometrica* **22** (1954), 265–290.
2. J. Chipman, External economies of scale and competitive equilibrium, *Q. J. Econ.* **84** (1970), 348–385.
3. G. Debreu, "Theory of Value," Wiley, New York, 1959.
4. W. Hildenbrand, "Core and Equilibria of a Large Economy," Princeton Univ. Press, Princeton N. J. 1974.
5. L. McKenzie, Competitive equilibrium with dependent consumer preferences, *in* "Proceedings, Second Symposium on Linear Programming, National Bureau of Standards and the Air Force, Washington, 1955."

[10] This was pointed out to us by A. Mas-Colell.

6. L. McKenzie, On the existence of general equilibrium for a competitive market, *Econometrica* **27** (1959), 54–71.
7. W. Novshek and H. Sonnenschein, Cournot and Walras equilibrium, *J. Econ. Theory* **19** (1978), 223–266.
8. W. Shafer and H. Sonnenschein, Equilibrium with externalities, commodity taxation, and lump sum transfers, *Int. Econ. Rev.* **3** (1976), 601–611.

The Limit Points of Monopolistic Competition*

KEVIN ROBERTS

St. Catherine's College, Oxford, England

Received August 1, 1979

1. INTRODUCTION AND SUMMARY

A standard justification for the study of perfect competition is that in large economies, the set of monopolistically competitive equilibria will be approximated by the set of perfectly competitive equilibria. It is the primary purpose of this paper to examine the general validity of this proposition.

In the present context, the distinguishing feature of monopolistic competition is that there exist agents who act in an individually rational way by exploiting the fact that their actions influence prices. However, monopolistic competition eschews the notions of group rationality that are to be found in equilibrium concepts like the core; in particular, monopolistically competitive equilibria will usually be Pareto inefficient. Thus, although the famous limit theorem of Debreu and Scarf [6], showing that core allocations are approximated by perfectly competitive equilibria in large economies, is extremely suggestive, it is not of direct relevance to the present problem.

The possible validity of the proposition rests upon the idea that in large economies, individually rational behavior is "close" to price-taking behavior. In a recent study, Roberts and Postlewaite [14] showed that under seemingly weak assumptions, this was the case. It will become clear from the present study that such a result is not so generally true as Roberts and Postlewaite have suggested.

In keeping with the literature on limit theorems for the core, this paper adopts the replication technique of Debreu and Scarf and, within this framework, investigates the limit points of monopolistically competitive equilibria. This framework of analysis is similar to that of Gabszewicz and Vial [8]. The main difference between the two analyses, and the explanation for the difference in results, is that Gabszewicz and Vial invoke very strong assumptions. In this paper, a general approach is adopted and the assumptions

* Financial support from the National Science Foundation under Grant SOC78-09084 at the Massachusetts Institute of Technology is gratefully acknowledged. I am indebted to Oliver Hart for both arousing my interest in this topic and for providing comments on an earlier version of the paper. Useful comments were also received from Glenn Loury and the referee.

Reprinted from *Journal of Economic Theory* **22,** No. 2, 256–278 (April 1980)
ISBN 0-12-476750-8

imposed are the standard ones of general equilibrium theory when studied in a differential framework. As one such assumption is the convexity of production sets, monopolistic competition with free-entry as studied by Hart [9], Novshek [12], and Novshek and Sonnenschein [13] is ruled out. Although there seems to be no conceptual difficulty in extending the analysis to cope with free-entry, it will turn out that the structure under investigation admits a sufficiently rich set of possibilities without this complication. It should be stressed that a free-entry assumption has no power in diminishing these possibilities.

As mentioned above, this paper investigates the limit points of monopolistically competitive equilibria. It is shown that if a limit point occurs where the excess demand function given fixed production levels is not at a critical point then the limit point is a perfectly competitive equilibrium. However, if the limit point occurs at a critical point then no such inference can be drawn. In this case, the limiting equilibria are called *critical equilibria.* With critical equilibria, monopolistic elements can remain important even though the economy is large; furthermore, agents may incur large losses by adopting price-taking behavior. Although the occurrence of perfectly competitive equilibria at critical points is pathological (Debreu [3]), the existence of critical equilibria is a robust feature of an economy. For without specific knowledge of production possibilities, it seems that the only way to rule out such equilibria is to impose the restriction that the excess demand function possesses no critical points. As is well known (Arrow and Hahn [2, Chap. 12]), this implies that, for fixed production levels, the economy always has a unique perfectly competitive equilibrium.

If the limit points of monopolistic competition cannot be restricted to perfectly competitive equilibria, one can at least hope that perfectly competitive equilibria will be limit points. Here the results are more satisfactory. For if a perfectly competitive equilibrium occurs at a point where the excess demand function given fixed production levels and the excess demand function including a competitive supply response are not at critical points then the equilibrium will be a limit point of monopolistic competition. Competitive equilibria without these properties are pathological (Debreu [3]) so that competitive equilibria will almost always be limit points. Of course, the existence of a limit point implies that monopolistically competitive equilibria must exist at most stages of replication. In fact, it will be shown that it is almost always the case that, beyond some stage of replication, a monopolistically competitive equilibrium exists (see also Novshek and Sonnenschein [13]).

The general organization of the paper is as follows. The problem to be investigated is formulated in the next section. Section 3 is concerned with showing that, under suitable conditions, a perfectly competitive equilibrium is a limit point and vice versa. Critical equilibria are investigated in Section 4 and their nonpathological nature is demonstrated. Pathological counterexamples are provided in Section 5. These demonstrate why only generic and not universal statements are possible. Then, in Section 6, it is shown that because of their "fragile" nature, critical equilibria, of the form studied in earlier sections, are not robust to the introduction of uncertainty. However, other, very similar, possibilities emerge when uncertainty is introduced. These results suggest that it may be difficult to find a "reasonable" specification of the economy under which it is true that when the economy becomes large, monopolistic competition always approximates perfect competition. Concluding remarks are contained in Section 7.

2. The Model

The structure of the model to be laid out is standard. As we shall be interested in the limit points that arise under monopolistic competition when an economy is replicated, we start by describing an economy E_r at stage r of replication.

There are m types of individuals in the economy and r individuals of each type. Individual $\{i, q\}$ is the q th individual of the ith type. Similarly, there are n types of firms and r firms of each type. Firm $\{j, q\}$ is the qth firm of the jth type. Firms produce and individuals consume goods.[1] There are $l + 1$ goods in the economy, good 1 being the *numeraire* (e.g., leisure). The price of good 1 is taken to be unity and the price vector for all goods is given by $p \in S = \{1\} \times \mathring{\mathbb{R}}_+{}^l$.[2] An element of $\mathbb{R}^{l+1}$ may be interpreted as a consumption (or production) bundle.

Individual $\{i, q\}$ possesses an initial endowment $\omega_i \in \mathring{\mathbb{R}}_+^{l+1}$ and receives a share $\theta_{ij} \geqslant 0$ $(\sum_i \theta_{ij} = 1)$ of the *average* profits earned by firms of type j; i.e., if π_{jq} is the profit earned by firm $\{j, q\}$ then $\{i, q'\}$ receives

$$\pi_i = \sum_j \theta_{ij} \left(\frac{1}{r} \sum_q \pi_{jq}\right). \tag{1}$$

Thus all individuals of the same type have the same endowment and receive the same level of profits. Individuals of the same type also have identical preferences. $\{i, q\}$ chooses a commodity bundle $x_{iq} \in \mathbb{R}_+^{l+1}$ (the consumption set) to make himself as well-off as possible, subject to the constraint

$$px_{iq} \leqslant \pi_i + p\omega_i, \tag{2}$$

where p is treated as exogenous, i.e., individuals are price takers. As differentiability properties of the economic structure will turn out to be of relevance,

[1] This is more restrictive than necessary. In fact, individuals are agents who are price takers and firms are agents who recognize the effect of their actions upon prices: competitive producers could be classed as individuals.

[2] $\mathring{\mathbb{R}}_+{}^l$ is the interior of the positive orthant.

it will be assumed that this choice gives rise to a twice continuously differentiable (C^2) demand function

$$f^i: S \times \mathbb{R}_+ \to \mathbb{R}_+^{l+1}. \tag{3}$$

The chosen x_{iq} is given by $f^i(p, \pi_i + p\omega_i)$ and all individuals of the same type make identical choices.

Two further restrictions will be imposed upon demand functions. First, it will be assumed that preferences embody local nonsatiation so that $pf^i(p, \pi_i + p\omega_i) = \pi_i + p\omega_i$. Second, to rule out the possibility that an equilibrium can occur where some prices are zero or infinite, it will be assumed (see Debreu [3]) that, for some type of individual, the sum of demands is unbounded as any price approaches zero or infinity. It may be noted that such an assumption effectively rules out the existence of pure intermediate goods. As the notion of monopolistic competition used in this paper is unlikely to be relevant when pure intermediate goods exist, economies with such goods demand separate attention.

Turning to the production side of the economy, firm $\{j, q\}$ chooses a production plan y_{jq} from a production set $Y_j \subseteq \mathbb{R}^{l+1}$ (negative arguments are inputs, positive arguments are outputs). The following conditions are imposed upon Y_j:

(1) $0 \in Y_j$,

(2) Y_j is closed and bounded above,

(3) Y_j is strictly convex and the boundary of Y_j possesses strict Gaussian curvature.

Apart from the assumption of strict Gaussian curvature, these conditions are standard. But given strict convexity, strict Gaussian curvature is unlikely to be a problem except at zero production. As will become clear, some relaxation of the condition at such points could be admitted without affecting the results.

The profit of firm $\{j, q\}$ is given by

$$\pi_{jq} = p\,y_{jq}. \tag{4}$$

To analyze the behavior of firms, we start by defining an exchange equilibrium.

DEFINITION. An *exchange equilibrium* in the economy E_r is an array $(p, y) \in S \times \mathbb{R}^{n(l+1)}$, where

$$\sum_i f^i\left(p, p\omega_i + \sum_j \theta_{ij} p y_j\right) - \sum_i \omega_i - \sum_j y_j = 0 \tag{5}$$

and $y = (y_j)$, $j = 1, n$.

Here, y_j is to be interpreted as the *average* production level of type j firms. Given fixed production levels $y = (y_j)$, if (p, y) is an exchange equilibrium then p is the price vector which ensures that all markets clear. With zero production, the exchange equilibrium is the perfectly competitive equilibrium of an exchange economy and this always exists (cf. Debreu [3]). Generically, such equilibria are isolated, finite, and odd in number (Debreu [3]). However, difficulties arise with nonzero production. For then there exists the problem that some individuals may not be able to attain allocations that lie within their consumption sets. This problem is alleviated in the present context because firms, through profit maximization, act to slacken attainability constraints upon individuals.

Firms in the economy have monopolistic power and recognize that a change in production will cause a change in prices which restores equilibrium. Given the possibilities of nonexistence or, more importantly, multiple equilibria of the exchange economy, some selection mechanism must be prescribed. Define $Q(y)$ by

$$Q(y) = \{p' : \{p', y\} \text{ is an exchange equilibrium}\} \subseteq S$$

and let

$$T = \{y : Q(y) \text{ is nonempty}\} \subseteq \mathbb{R}^{n(l+1)}.$$

Consider a mapping

$$P: S \times T \times T \to S \tag{6}$$

which satisfies the property that if $p \in Q(y)$ then

$$P(p, y, y') \in \{p^* : \| p^* - p \| \leqslant \| p' - p \| \; \forall p^*, p' \in Q(y')\}.$$

It will be assumed that if production levels are initially y and the price vector is p then, with a change in production to y', the new price vector is $P(p, y, y')$ (when equilibrium prices exist). This definition implies that prices change by the smallest amount necessary to restore equilibrium. Essentially, an attempt is being made to choose a well-behaved selection mechanism. However, there exist other mechanisms which are just as appealing. For instance, it could have been assumed that the price moved to the equilibrium that would result under a *tatonnement* price adjustment mechanism. In that case the characterization results would be dependent upon the local stability properties of the equilibria under investigation.

Define $Z(p, y)$ to be the last l arguments of the function

$$\sum_i f^i \Big(p, p\omega_i + \sum_j \theta_{ij} p y_j\Big) - \sum_i \omega_i - \sum_j y_j .$$

By Walras' law, if $Z(p, y) = 0$ then (p, y) is an exchange equilibrium. Z is defined on a neighborhood of (p, y) if individuals' incomes are strictly positive, i.e.,

$$p\omega_i + \sum_j \theta_{ij} p y_j > 0 \qquad \forall_i . \tag{7}$$

Equation (7) will hold if profits are nonnegative ($py_j \geqslant 0$ for all j). Thus if there are nonnegative profits, Z can be differentiated.[3] Let (p, y) be a *regular* (*resp. critical*) *exchange equilibrium* if $Z(p, y) = 0$ and the Jacobian Z_p is nonsingular (resp. singular).

By the Implicit Function Theorem (see, e.g., Dieudonné [7]), if Z_p is nonsingular then in a neighborhood of (p, y) there exists a unique C^2 function $p(\cdot)$ such that $Z(p(y'), y') = 0$. Thus for y' sufficiently close to y, the function P must be the function $p(\cdot)$.

LEMMA 1. *If (p, y) is a regular exchange equilibrium and $py_j \geqslant 0$ for all j then for all y' in some neighborhood of y, $P(p, y, y')$ is a C^2 function of y'.*

The content of Lemma 1 is that under well-defined conditions the selection mechanism will be well behaved. Of course, the conditions required are dependent upon the selection mechanism utilized. Consider again the selection mechanism induced by *tatonnement* adjustment; (p, y) will be a locally stable exchange equilibrium if the eigenvalues of Z_p have strictly negative real parts. As Z is C^2, the equilibria $(p(y'), y')$ thrown up by the Implicit Function Theorem will also be locally stable (see, e.g., Hirsch and Smale [10, Chap. 16]). Thus in this more sophisticated situation, the selection mechanism will be C^2 if (p, y) is a regular *and locally stable* exchange equilibrium with $py_j \geqslant 0$ for all j.

A monopolistically competitive equilibrium is defined as a situation of exchange equilibrium where no firm can increase its profits with the recognition that prices depend upon production levels.[4] Let $y_{-j} \equiv (y_1, ..., y_{j-1}, y_{j+1}, ..., y_n)$.

DEFINITION. A *monopolistically competitive equilibrium* (MCE) in the economy E_r is an array $(p, (y_{jq})) \in S \times \mathbb{R}^{rn(l+1)}$ such that $(p, ((1/r) \sum_q y_{jq}))$ is an exchange equilibrium in E_r,

$$y_{jq} \in Y_j \qquad \forall j, q,$$

$$py_{jq} \geqslant 0 \qquad \forall j, q,$$

[3] Differentiation of a function with respect to p is taken to mean differentiation with respect to the last l arguments of p; the price of the *numeraire* remains at unity.

[4] The fact that profit-maximization by price makers is generally not *numeraire* free is ignored. See, e.g., Gabszewicz and Vial [8].

and $\nexists\{j, q\}$ and $y'_{jq} \in Y_j$ such that

$$P(p, y, \{y_{-j}, y_j + (1/r)(y'_{jq} - y_{jq})\})\, y'_{jq} > p y_{jq}. \tag{8}$$

Equation (8) is a Cournot–Nash equilibrium assumption. However, it would be easy to admit conjectural variations, i.e., to endow firms with a belief that other firms will respond to a change in production plan in a well-specified manner. With suitably smooth functions capturing conjectural variations, the analysis of this paper goes through in a straightforward manner.

A MCE changes with replication of the economy and part of this change will be the interest of this paper. However, perfectly competitive equilibria are independent of the stage of replication.

DEFINITION. A *perfectly competitive equilibrium* (PCE) in the economy E_r is an array $(p, ((1/r) \sum_q y_{jq})) \in S \times R^{n(l+1)}$ such that $(p, ((1/r) \sum_q y_{jq}))$ is an exchange equilibrium in E_r,

$$y_{jq} \in Y_j \qquad \forall j, q,$$

and $\nexists\{j, q\}$ and $y'_{jq} \in Y_j$ such that

$$p y'_{jq} > p y_{jq}. \tag{9}$$

As Y_j is strictly convex, it may be noted that $y_{jq} = y_{jq'}$ for all j, q, q': identical firms act identically. Thus, if (p, y) is a PCE then firm $\{j, q\}$ must have y_j as its production plan. It is a simple consequence of the definition of a PCE that if (p, y) is a PCE in E_r then it is a PCE in E_s, where E_s is the economy at any other stage of replication.

At a PCE, all agents are price takers. From the assumptions that have been imposed upon production sets it can be concluded that, given a price vector p, there exists a production plan $y_j^c(p)$ which maximizes profits for type j firms. That y_j^c is a continuous function is a standard result (Arrow and Hahn [2, Chap. 3]). However, by amending the analysis of Debreu [4] to apply to producers instead of consumers (see also Laroque [11]), it may be concluded that, as the boundary of Y_j possesses strict Gaussian curvature, y_j^c will be a continuously differentiable (C^1) function. A PCE will be defined by the relation

$$Z^c(p) = Z(p, y^c(p)) = 0. \tag{10}$$

(p, y) will be a *regular* (*resp. critical*) *PCE* if Z_p^c is nonsingular (resp. singular). As in Debreu [3], Sard's theorem may be invoked to show that, for an open and dense subset of initial endowments, perfectly competitive equilibria will be regular and isolated.[5]

That a PCE exists under the assumptions that have been laid down is well known. However, because of the possibly discontinuous behavior of firms when acting monopolistically (see, e.g., Roberts and Sonnenschein [15]), the existence of a MCE must remain an open question for the present.

Finally, we shall be interested in the properties of monopolistically competitive equilibria when r becomes large. Instead of looking at the production plan of each firm, we shall be interested in the average plan of firms of each type. Define $M(r)$ as follows:

$$M(r) = \left\{ \left(p, \left((1/r) \sum_q y_{jq} \right) \right) : (p, (y_{jq})) \text{ is a MCE in } E_r \right\}.$$

We shall be interested in the limit points of monopolistic competition.

DEFINITION. A *limiting monopolistically competitive equilibrium* (LMCE) is an array $(\bar{p}, \bar{y}) \in S \times \mathbb{R}^{n(l+1)}$ which is the limit of sequence $\{(p^r, y^r)\}$ such that for all r greater than some r^*, $(p^r, y^r) \in M(r)$.

Our main interest will be the connection that exists between the set of PCEs and the set of LMCEs (note that it makes sense to ask the question whether a PCE is a LMCE and vice versa).

3. Perfect Competition and the Limits of Monopolistic Competition

The possible equivalence of PCEs with LMCEs depends upon the form of the exchange equilibrium at the point under investigation. By definition, a PCE is an exchange equilibrium. We also have

THEOREM 1. *A LMCE is an exchange equilibrium.*

Proof. Let $(\bar{p}, \bar{y})$ be a LMCE. By definition there exists a sequence $\{(p^r, y^r)\}$, $(p^r, y^r) \in M(r)$ for all r greater than some r^*, such that $p^r \to \bar{p}$ and $y^r \to \bar{y}$. As $(p^r, y^r) \in M(r)$, $r > r^*$, (p^r, y^r) is an exchange equilibrium (from the definitions of $M(r)$ and MCE). Thus $Z(p^r, y^r) = 0 \; \forall r > r^*$. Now, as $p^r y_j^r \geqslant 0$ and as the values of endowments are bounded away from zero, the demand functions, and hence Z, are defined at $(\bar{p}, \bar{y})$. Z is C^2 and thus continuous so that $Z(\bar{p}, \bar{y}) = 0$. ∎

[5] Debreu considered a pure exchange economy with price-taking individuals. However, under the assumptions that have been laid down, price-taking firms are like a special type of individual.

Given Theorem 1, we can separate out those LMCEs which occur at a regular exchange equilibrium from those which occur at a critical exchange equilibrium. In this section, we investigate the regular equilibrium case.

THEOREM 2. *If a LCME is a* regular *exchange equilibrium then it is a PCE.*

Proof. Let $(\bar{p}, \bar{y})$ be a LCME which is also a regular exchange equilibrium. If it is not a PCE then

$$\exists j, y_j^* \in Y_j, \qquad \epsilon > 0, \quad \text{such that} \quad \bar{p}y_j^* = \bar{p}\bar{y}_j + \epsilon \geqslant 0. \tag{11}$$

Here, use has been made of the fact that $\bar{y}_j \in Y_j$, which follows from the closedness and convexity of production sets. Now, as $(\bar{p}, \bar{y})$ is a LMCE, there exists a sequence $\{(p^r, y^r)\}$, $(p^r, y^r) \in M(r)$ $\forall r > r^*$, such that $p^r \to \bar{p}$ and $y^r \to \bar{y}$. If $(p^r, y^r) \in M(r)$ because $(p^r, (y_{jq}^r))$ is a MCE $(y^r = (1/r) \sum_q y_{jq}^r))$ then, from the definition of a MCE

$$\forall q\colon P(p^r, y^r, (y_{-j}^r, y_j^r + (1/r)(y_j^* - y_{jq}^r)))\, y_j^* \leqslant p^r y_{jq}^r \tag{12}$$

if P is defined.

As p^r for all $r > r^*$ and $\bar{p}$ support exchange equilibria, these vectors contain no zero arguments and are bounded above (as production possibilities are bounded). Y_j is bounded above so that y_j^* and y_{jq}^r are drawn from a bounded set, as $\bar{p}y_j^* \geqslant 0$ (from (11)) and $p^r y_{jq}^r \geqslant 0$. Thus $y_j^* - y_{jq}^r$ is bounded and as $p^r \to \bar{p}$ and $y^r \to \bar{y}$, we can choose r^* large enough so that the arguments of $P(\cdot)$ in (11) belong to any small neighborhood of $(\bar{p}, \bar{y})$. Lemma 1 applies, as $(\bar{p}, \bar{y})$ is a regular exchange equilibrium and $\bar{p}\bar{y}_j \geqslant 0$ for all j $(p^r y_j^r \to \bar{p}\bar{y}_j$ and $p^r y_j^r \geqslant 0)$, so that (12) becomes

$$P(p^r, y^r, y^r)\, y_j^* - k/r^* \leqslant p^r y_{jq}^r, \tag{13}$$

where $k \geqslant 0$ is a bounded scalar (as P is continuously differentiable in y_j and relevant production plans are bounded). Averaging (13) over q and noting that $P(p^r, y^r, y^r) = p^r$ gives

$$p^r y_j^* - k/r^* \leqslant p^r y_j^r. \tag{14}$$

Choosing $r^* \geqslant 2k/\epsilon$ and taking limits yields

$$\bar{p}y_j^* - \epsilon/2 \leqslant \bar{p}\bar{y}_j, \tag{15}$$

which contradicts (11). ∎

Remark. It may be noted that Theorem 2 requires and follows from the continuity of P. With the approach of this paper, this result requires only that demand functions be C^1 (so that the Implicit Function Theorem can be applied). An alternative approach is to assume that exchange equilibria are unique (see Gabszewicz and Vial [8]). As the limit of exchange equilibria is an exchange equilibrium (see the proof of Theorem 1), the continuity of P follows directly under the uniqueness assumption. Thus if multiple exchange equilibria are ruled out, a LMCE is always a PCE.

We now prove a partial converse to Theorem 2.

THEOREM 3. *If a* regular *PCE is a* regular *exchange equilibrium then it is a LMCE.*

Remark 1. For an open and dense subset of initial endowments, all perfectly competitive equilibria will be regular and will occur at regular exchange equilibria. Therefore, generically, all PCEs will be LMCEs.

In the present context, however, the most important remark that can be made concerning Theorem 2 is

Remark 2. If a PCE is a LMCE then, beyond some stage of replication, a MCE must exist. As a PCE exists, the existence of a MCE in a large (but finite) economy is generic.[6]

Proof. Let $(\bar{p}, \bar{y})$ be a regular PCE which is also a regular exchange equilibrium. We shall be interested in proving the existence of monopolistically competitive equilibria which are arbitrarily close to $(\bar{p}, \bar{y})$. If the economy is kept within a small neighborhood of $(\bar{p}, \bar{y})$ then Lemma 1 is applicable: given levels of production y', the price vector will be given by a C^2 function $P(y')$. Consider some firm $\{j, q\}$ in the economy E_r. If other types of firms have average production levels y^*_{-j} and other firms of the same type have an average production level y^*_j then $\{j, q\}$ chooses y_{jq} to solve the problem

$$\max \pi(y^*, y_{jq}) = P(y^*_{-j}, y^*_j + (1/r)(y_{jq} - y^*_j))\, y_{jq} \qquad \text{s.t.} \quad y_{jq} \in Y_j \tag{16}$$

(profits may be defined to be zero when there is zero production). As Y_j is bounded above and exchange equilibrium prices are always bounded away from zero and infinity, we can restrict attention to the choice of y_{jq} drawn from a bounded set. Thus, if y^* is sufficiently close to $\bar{y}$, $(y^*_{-j}, y^*_j + (1/r)(y_{jq} - y^*_j))$ will be close to $\bar{y}$ for r large enough and P in (16) will have the desirable C^2 properties alluded to in Lemma 1. The maximand in (16) is therefore C^2 and

$$\pi_{y_{jq}} = P + (1/r)\, P_{y_j} y_j\,, \tag{17}$$

$$\pi_{y_{jq} y_{jq}} = (2/r)\, P_{y_j} + (1/r^2)\, P_{y_j y_j} y_j\,. \tag{18}$$

[6] Although a similar result is provided by Novshek and Sonnenschein [13], the generic features of the economy that they utilize are not easily interpretable.

For r large enough, P being C^2 ensures that (17) will be nonzero and the curvature of the profit function (see (18)) will be less than the curvature of the boundary of the production set Y_j (as the boundary of Y_j has *strict* Gaussian curvature). Thus the same point will be chosen under a linearization of the maximand; i.e., if $\hat{y}_{jq}$ solves (16) then $\hat{y}_{jq}$ solves

$$\max \pi_{y_{jq}}(y^*, \hat{y}_{jq})\, y_{jq} \qquad \text{s.t.} \quad y_{jq} \in Y_j\,. \tag{19}$$

However, this is just the problem faced by a perfectly competitive firm when prices are given by $\pi_{y_{jq}}$. $\hat{y}_{jq}$ must therefore satisfy

$$\hat{y}_{jq} = y_j^c(\pi_{y_{jq}}(y^*, \hat{y}_{jq})), \tag{20}$$

where y_j^c is a C^1 function giving the competitive supply function.

Using (20), $(P(y^*), y^*)$ will be a MCE for E_r, r suitably large, if y^* is in a small neighborhood of $\bar{y}$ and

$$\forall j\colon y_j^* = y_j^c(\pi_{y_{jq}}(y^*, y_j^*)). \tag{21}$$

Note that this is a MCE where firms of the same type have identical production plans. Using (17), we seek to show the existence of a y^* close to $\bar{y}$ such that

$$\forall j\colon y_j^* = y_j^c(P(y^*) + \alpha P_{y_j}(y^*)\, y_j^*) \tag{22}$$

and $r = 1/\alpha$. When $\alpha = 0$ in (22), we know that, as $(\bar{p}, \bar{y})$ is a PCE,

$$\forall j\colon \bar{y}_j = y_j^c(P(\bar{y})). \tag{23}$$

As (22) is a continuously differentiable (C^1) function of y^* and α, the Implicit Function Theorem can be applied to show that in the neighborhood of $\bar{y}$ and $\alpha = 0$, there exists a unique C^1 function $y^*(\alpha)$ which solves (22) (feasibility of y^* follows from the fact that it is feasible for competitive producers at some prices). We need only check that the nonsingularity condition holds so that the Implicit Function Theorem can be applied. Stacking the vector functions in (22) and differentiating both sides with respect to y^* gives the result that, for small α, the nonsingularity condition will hold if

$$I - y_p^c(\bar{p})\, P_{y^*} \tag{24}$$

is nonsingular. If (24) is singular then there exists a $v \neq 0$ such that

$$v - y_p^c(\bar{p})P_{y^*}v = 0.$$

Premultiplying by P_{y^*} yields

$$(I - P_{y^*}y_p^c(\bar{p}))\tilde{v} = 0, \tag{25}$$

where $\tilde{v} = P_{y*}v \neq 0$ (as $v = y_p{}^c(\bar{p})\tilde{v}$). However, invoking (10) and noting that $P_{y*} = -(Z_p)^{-1}Z_y$ gives

$$(I - P_{y*}y_p{}^c(\bar{p}))\tilde{v} = (Z_p)^{-1}Z_p{}^c\tilde{v} \neq 0$$

as $(\bar{p}, \bar{y})$ is a *regular* exchange equilibrium (Z_p nonsingular) and a *regular* PCE ($Z_p{}^c$ nonsingular). This contradicts (25) and proves the nonsingularity of (24). Thus for α small enough, or r greater than some r^*, there exists a MCE and

$$\forall r > r^*: (P(y^*(1/r)), y^*(1/r)) \in M(r). \tag{26}$$

Hence there exists an infinite sequence $\{(p^r, y^r)\}$, $(p^r, y^r) \in M(r)$ for all $r > r^*$, converging along a C^1 manifold to $(\bar{p}, \bar{y})$; i.e., $(\bar{p}, \bar{y})$ is a LMCE. ∎

Remark. It has been shown that for r large but finite, there exists a monopolistically competitive equilibrium. Essentially, existence follows because the nonconcavities in firms' profit functions, as, for instance, analyzed by Roberts and Sonnenschein [15], are removed by replication of the economy. Note also that it has been shown that monopolistically competitive equilibria exist which are very close to some perfectly competitive equilibrium. Not only is this true in the aggregate (similar prices and *average* production levels), but it has also been shown that there exist equilibria where firms of the same type act identically (not just similarly). Finally, convergence is very well behaved as it takes place along a C^1 manifold.

4. Critical Equilibria

The results of the last section give a partial characterization of the connection that exists between the limit points of monopolistic competition and perfectly competitive equilibria. Generically, a set of limit points exists and this set contains the set of perfectly competitive equilibria (Theorem 3). Further, all limit points occur at an exchange equilibrium (Theorem 1) and those which occur at a regular exchange equilibrium are perfectly competitive (Theorem 2). We now need only investigate limit points which occur at a critical exchange equilibrium. Such points will be called critical equilibria.

Definition. (p, y) is a *critical equilibrium* if (p, y) is a LMCE and a critical exchange equilibrium.

One could hope to show that for an open and dense subset of initial endowments, critical equilibria could not arise. However, despite the usual implications of Sard's theorem concerning the likelihood of critical values (see Debreu [3] for an economic application), we will show that critical equilibria are a robust feature of an economy. Therefore, the set of limit points of monopolistic competition will generally be the union of the set of perfectly competitive equilibria and a set of critical equilibria: if perfect competition is studied because it is a limiting solution then critical equilibria should also be analyzed.

Our results for critical equilibria can be expressed by the following theorem.

THEOREM 4. *The existence of critical equilibria which are not perfectly competitive is nonpathological; i.e., such equilibria may exist and are not necessarily eliminated by perturbations of the excess demand function.*

To prove, it is sufficient to provide an example. First, however, it may be noted that as for almost all y exchange equilibria are regular, monopolistically competitive firms must have an incentive to "seek out" critical exchange equilibria.

It is useful first to explain the rationale of Theorem 4 and this will suggest an example. Consider a situation where firms (which are all identical) produce one good, with price p, using one input (the *numeraire*) supplied by consumers. Fig. 1 gives the excess demand function for the produced good under the assumption that each firm uses the minimum input necessary to produce the output. To give a better understanding of this function, Figs. 2 and 3 give cross-sectional cuts at different output levels and at $Z = 0$, respectively. As is well known (Debreu [5]), if the number of different types of individual m is at least as great as the number of goods $l + 1$ then, at any

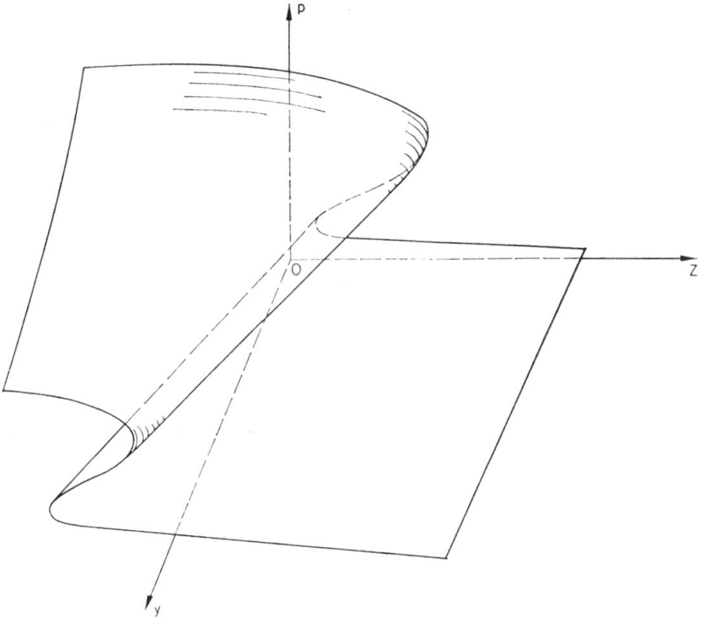

FIGURE 1

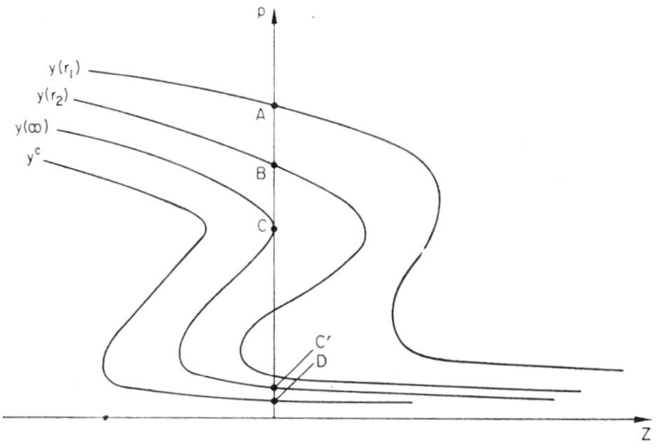

FIGURE 2

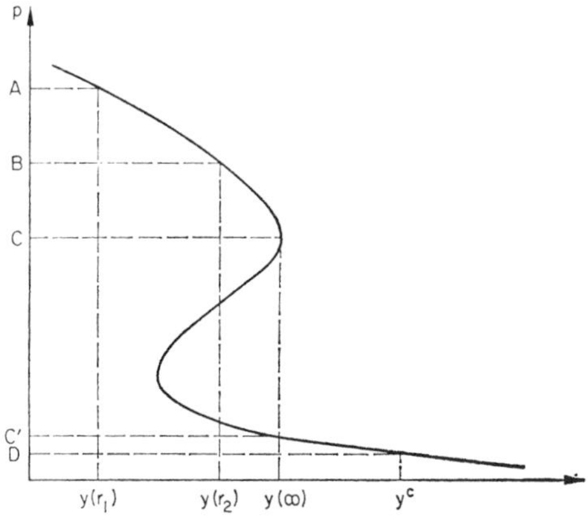

FIGURE 3

particular y, the excess demand function can take any form compatible with Walras' law and continuity.[7] In particular, the excess demand curve passing through C and C' in Fig. 2 is possible.

When there is a small number of firms (r_1), monopolistic power is recognized and a MCE occurs at $p = A$. As the economy is replicated, monopolistic power partially dissipates and a MCE occurs at $p = B$. As more firms enter, the MCE tends to the point $p = C$ and price becomes more sensitive to changes in production levels (see Fig. 3). Although there are more firms, monopolistic power is retained. Also C' may be such a low price that no firm is willing to destroy the equilibrium at C. Thus, as an economy is replicated, the MCE tends to be "held back" if critical exchange

[7] This holds over any bounded set of strictly positive prices. In fact, we have imposed a restriction on the excess demand function when prices tend to zero or infinity.

equilibria are encountered. There is therefore no reason for the economy to tend to a PCE which occurs at a point $p = D$, say, in Fig. 2.

It must now be shown that for r large, monopolistically competitive equilibria can arise at a price close to C. With r large, no firm will contemplate changing the *average* production level by more than a small amount (see the proofs of Theorems 2 and 3). Thus only local behavior around C need be analyzed. If C is a nondegenerate critical point then the Morse lemma can be applied to give the result that the excess demand function is locally quadratic in p. We shall be interested in the existence of equilibria where all firms act identically. Assume that each firm must utilize at least $F(y)$, $F' \geqslant 0$, $F'' > 0$, of the input to produce y (now a scalar). Assume that it is profitable for a firm to be technologically efficient. Then, as the input requirement will depend directly upon the output level, Z can be written as a function of price and the output level and, in a neighborhood of C, excess demand can be approximated by

$$Z = \alpha^2\beta(y^* - y) - \beta(p - C)^2 \tag{27}$$

if, at C, $Z_y < 0$. In (27), α, β, $y^* > 0$ are parameters which change with perturbations in the excess demand function (the critical point occurs at C when average output is y^*). Equating (27) to zero gives the equilibrium price as a function of average output:

$$p = C + \alpha(y^* - y)^{1/2}, \qquad y \leqslant y^*, \tag{28}$$

(the selection mechanism picks out prices which exceed C).

Given this specification, it is not difficult to show that a MCE in E_r exists, where each firm has an output y defined by

$$\alpha(y^* - y) + (C - F'(y))(y^* - y)^{1/2} - \frac{\alpha y}{2r} = 0. \tag{29}$$

This gives the point where first-order conditions of profit maximization are satisfied. Further, it is easy to check that second-order conditions are always satisfied (given only $\alpha > 0$). If $C \geqslant F'(y^*)$, so that price-taking firms would increase production, profit-maximizing output is defined by (29) and tends to y^* as r tends to infinity. From (29), output at stage r (when r is large) is given by

$$y = y^* - \left(\frac{\alpha y^*}{2r(C - F'(y^*))}\right)^2. \tag{30}$$

We have shown that a LMCE occurs at (C, y^*) if firms do not wish to, or cannot, destroy the equilibrium at C and so push the economy to C'. As is clear, if feasible output is bounded at a point just beyond y^* then it will be impossible for any firm to recuperate losses created by the price drop from C to C'. However, (30) implies that C could be destroyed by an increase in *total* production which is proportional to $1/r$. Thus, for large r, each firm *could* destroy the equilibrium at C. In particular, the equilibrium would be destroyed if any firm decided to adopt price-taking behavior. Thus, even in large economies, an agent may lose significantly by adopting price-taking behavior. It is interesting to compare this result with those obtained by Roberts and Postlewaite [14]. They reached the opposite conclusion but, in essence, this is because they ruled out, by assumption, the possibility that critical equilibria could exist.

Finally, a LMCE continues to exist at a point close to C when the excess demand function is subject to C^2 perturbations. For perturbation corresponds to small changes in α, β, and y^*: the existence analysis continues to apply. Nonperfectly competitive critical equilibria have therefore been shown to be nonpathological and Theorem 4 has been proved.

The example given to prove the theorem clearly demonstrates why a critical equilibrium can arise as a LMCE. If the excess demand function has a critical point then it is possible to converge to this point in a way that permits price responses to grow at the rate of replication.

Such a situation can also arise in an economy with many goods. Close to a critical point, firms will recognize that changes in production will significantly affect prices. Consider the form of the price response close to a critical point where Z_p is of rank $l-1$. Let z_y be the derivative of the excess demand function with respect to a change in a component of some y_j. The price response Δp will be given by

$$Z_p \Delta p + z_y = 0. \tag{31}$$

If the last row of Z_p is close to a linear combination of the other rows then (31) may be partitioned to give

$$\left[\begin{array}{c|c} z_p & z_p{}^l \\ \hline \lambda z_p + \epsilon t^{-l} & \lambda z^l p + \epsilon t^l \end{array}\right] \left[\begin{array}{c} \Delta p^{-l} \\ \hline \Delta p^l \end{array}\right] = \left[\begin{array}{c} -z_y^{-l} \\ \hline -z_y{}^l \end{array}\right]. \tag{32}$$

z_p is an $l-1 \times l-1$ matrix which, by a suitable reordering of columns, can be taken to be nonsingular (as row rank $=$ column rank $= l-1$). t is some vector and ϵ is a scalar which tends to zero as the critical point is approached.[8] Equation (32) may be solved to give an approximate result for small ϵ:

$$\epsilon \begin{bmatrix} \Delta p^{-l} \\ \Delta p^l \end{bmatrix} = \begin{bmatrix} -z_p^{-1} z_p{}^l \\ 1 \end{bmatrix} \left(\frac{\lambda z_y^{-l} - z_y{}^l}{t^l - t^{-l} z_p^{-1} z_p{}^l} \right), \tag{33}$$

[8] Superscript l denotes the lth argument (column) of a vector (matrix). Superscript $-l$ denotes the vector (matrix) with the lth argument (column) removed.

where it has been assumed that $t^l - t^{-l}z_p^{-1}z_p{}^l \neq 0$ (generically, this will be the case).

Equation (33) shows that if $\epsilon \to 0$ at a rate directly proportional to $1/r$ then each firm in the economy will retain monopolistic power. Note also that, independently of the form of z_y, the direction of price responsiveness will be the same. This is a consequence of the assumption that, at the critical point, Z_p is of rank $l - 1$. If Z_p is of rank $l - k$ then a similar analysis may be used to show that price responsiveness will lie in a k-dimensional space. Thus, although in general all firms will possess monopolistic power when convergence is toward a critical point, the extent of monopolistic power will be inversely related to the rank of Z_p.

5. Pathological Possibilities

The results that have been derived in this paper depend upon the local differentiability properties of the excess demand function around particular equilibria. This is clearly true of Theorems 2 and 4. Recalling Theorem 3, it was shown that a PCE is almost always a LMCE, nothing being said about when the PCE is critical or occurs at a critical exchange equilibrium. It is the purpose of this section to show that in these pathological cases, the theorem does not necessarily hold: only a generic, and not a universal, statement can be provided.

Three examples will be given. The economy is similar to the one in the example given in Section 4; i.e., there is one type of firm producing one output (at price p) using one input (the *numeraire*). The production technology will be assumed Cobb–Douglas in form, an output of y by a firm requiring an input of y^2.[9] Thus the competitive supply function is given by

$$y^c = p/2. \tag{34}$$

Finally, as we are investigating existence of monopolistically competitive equilibria close to a perfectly competitive equilibrium, we need only look at the economy close to this equilibrium.

Example 1. A PCE that is a critical exchange equilibrium.

Let the excess demand function for $p \in [1, 5]$ be

$$Z = (p - 2)^2 + (1 - y). \tag{35}$$

Combining (34) and (35), there are two perfectly competitive equilibria, $(p, y) = (2, 1)$ or $(5/2, 5/4)$. From (35), $(2, 1)$ is a critical exchange equilib-

[9] To conform with earlier assumptions, output may be bounded at some high level without affecting the analysis.

rium. Close to (2, 1), there are two possibilities for the price selection mechanism

$$p = 2 + (y - 1)^{1/2} \tag{36a}$$

or

$$p = 2 - (y - 1)^{1/2} \tag{36b}$$

and these are only possible when $y \geqslant 1$. When $y < 1$, assume that the economy moves to some high price ($p > 5$). The behavior of monopolistically competitive firms is easy to analyze by setting up the profit function. Under (36a), output is expanded because price rises with output. In fact, it is easy to show that a MCE cannot exist with average output below 5/4: with (36a), the LMCE is at (5/2, 5/4). Under (36b), price falls with output and each firm has an incentive to reduce output to unity. When all firms have done this there is an incentive for any one firm to destroy the equilibrium and move to an equilibrium with a high price ($p > 5$). Thus under both selection mechanisms, monopolistically competitive firms take the economy away from the PCE at (2, 1).

EXAMPLE 2. A PCE that is critical.
Around $(p, y) = (2, 1)$, let the excess demand function be given by

$$Z = p - 2y - (y - 1)^2. \tag{37}$$

Combining (34) and (37), there is a PCE at (2, 1) which is critical. Close to this point the price selection mechanism is

$$p = 2y + (y - 1)^2. \tag{38}$$

When output is close to unity, monopolistically competitive firms have an incentive to increase production. In fact, it is trivial to show that every firm wishes to produce more than the average! Thus, prices and output are driven away from (2, 1): it is impossible for (2, 1) to be the limit of monopolistically competitive equilibria.

The final example shows that pathological possibilities do not rule out the possibility that a PCE is a LMCE.

EXAMPLE 3. A PCE that is a critical PCE and a critical exchange equilibrium.

Around $(p, y) = (2, 1)$, let Z be given by

$$Z = (p - 2)^2 - 4(y - 1)^4. \tag{39}$$

At (2, 1), we have a critical exchange equilibrium and a critical PCE. An admissible price selection mechanism is

$$p = 2 - 2(y - 1)^2. \tag{40}$$

As price rises if output rises when $y < 1$ and falls if output rises when $y > 1$, it is easy to show that, *independently of the stage of replication*, a MCE exists where $(p, y) = (2, 1)$. Thus, the PCE is a LMCE in a very direct sense. The example also shows that it is possible—though unlikely—for perfectly competitive outcomes to be realizable as monopolistically competitive equilibria.

6. Uncertainty and Critical Equilibria

Despite the fact that critical equilibria are nonpathological, common sense suggests that they could not arise in "realistic" situations. The reason for such a deep-rooted belief would seem to be that, by their nature, critical equilibria are extremely fragile: if the excess demand function changes, and producers do not respond immediately to the change, then it will often be the case that there will be a jump in prices which leads to a discrete fall in firms' profits. As firms "hold back" at critical equilibria to avoid this discrete drop in profits, it may be conjectured that in situations where firms have incomplete control, the incentives for "holding back" are lost.

To investigate this conjecture, uncertainty will be introduced into the model. In particular, it will be assumed that individuals' endowments are uncertain when firms make their production decisions. Thus equilibrium prices and profits are uncertain. As for behavior toward risk, it will be assumed that firms are risk-neutral.

Consider adding a stochastic component $v_i \in \mathbb{R}$ to the endowment of the *numeraire* good held by individuals of type *i*. It will be assumed that there is an atomless probability measure ν on $v \in \mathbb{R}^m$ with support

$$V_\epsilon = \{v\colon -\epsilon \leqslant v_i \leqslant \epsilon \forall i\}.$$

Thus, as ϵ becomes small, uncertainty about endowments becomes small.

For individuals, unlike firms, uncertainty is resolved before they take decisions. If firms produce y and some v is realized then the excess demand function Z will be given by the last l arguments of

$$\sum_i f^i \Big(p, p\omega_i + \sum_j \theta_{ij} p y_j + v_i\Big) - \sum_i \omega_i - \sum_j y_i .$$

It will be convenient to write the function Z in the form

$$Z(p, y, v) \equiv X\left(p, \left\{p\omega_i + \sum_j \theta_{ij} p y_j + v_i\right\}_{i=1,m}\right). \tag{41}$$

As firms are risk-neutral, they are only interested in expected prices. If the price selection derived from equating (41) to zero is given by $P(p, y, y'; v)$ (where $Z(p, y, 0) = 0$) then expected price is given by

$$P^*(p, y, y') = \int_{V_\epsilon} P(p, y, y'; v)\, dv. \tag{42}$$

Here, p is used to define the appropriate selection. P^* is defined if and only if P is defined for almost all v.

Economies will be indexed by ϵ. For this purpose it will be assumed that for each ϵ, there exists a unique probability measure on v with support V_ϵ. Corresponding to a MCE and a PCE we have

DEFINITION. A MCE (ϵ) in the ϵ version of the economy E_r is an array $(p, (y_{jq})) \in S \times \mathbb{R}^{rn(l+1)}$ such that $(p, (1/r)\sum_q y_{jq})$ is an exchange equilibrium in the nonstochastic economy; i.e., $Z(p, y, 0) = 0$,

$$y_{jq} \in Y_j \qquad \forall j, q$$

$$P^*(p, y, y)\, y_{jq} \geqslant 0 \qquad \forall j, q,$$

and $\nexists \{j, q\}$ and $y'_{jq} \in Y_j$ such that

$$P^*(p, y, \{y_{-j}, y_j + (1/r)(y'_{jq} - y_{jq})\})\, y'_{jq} > P^*(p, y, y)\, y_{jq}\,.$$

DEFINITION. A PCE (ϵ) in the ϵ version of the economy E_r is an array $(p, ((1/r)\sum_q y_{jq})) \in S \times \mathbb{R}^{n(l+1)}$ such that $(p, (1/r)\sum_q y_{jq})$ is an exchange equilibrium in the nonstochastic economy; i.e., $Z(p, y, 0) = 0$,

$$y_{jq} \in Y_j \qquad \forall j, q,$$

and $\nexists \{j, q\}$ and $y'_{jq} \in Y_j$ such that

$$P^*(p, y, y)\, y'_{jq} > P^*(p, y, y)\, y_{jq}\,.$$

These equilibrium notions are defined relative to expected profit maximization (note that p defines the selection but is not an expected price).

The closeness in the definitions of MCE (ϵ) and PCE (ϵ) to the definitions of MCE and PCE may be noted. If (p, y) is a regular exchange equilibrium then it will be possible to apply the Implicit Function Theorem to show that

$P(p, y, y; v)$ is differentiable in v around $v = 0$. Thus, as $\epsilon \to 0$, $P^*(p, y, y) \to P(p, y, y; 0) = p$. It is then not difficult to show that if (p, y) is the limit point of PCE (ϵ)s as $\epsilon \to 0$ and (p, y) is a regular exchange equilibrium then (p, y) is a PCE (compare with Theorem 2).

Turning to critical equilibria, a LMCE (ϵ) may be defined in the ϵ version of the economy just as LMCE was defined in the standard economy. We wish to know whether a LMCE (ϵ) is a PCE (ϵ).[10] Pursuing an analysis similar to that in Theorem 2, a LMCE (ϵ) will be a PCE (ϵ) if $P^*(p, y, y')$ is continuous in y' at y. There exist two possibilities:

(1) As firms maximize expected profits, and negative profits in some states are not ruled out, there may exist v (of measure zero) under which some individuals are on the boundary of their consumption sets when production is y. When production is changed to y', y' close to y, it is possible that non-attainability will hold for a nonzero measure of states. Thus as P^* will not be defined, the notion of a continuous change will be lost. In this case it is possible for the LMCE (ϵ) to occur at a noncompetitive point where firms "hold back" their production to ensure existence. An example of this is given in Fig. 4 where, for a two-good economy, Z is plotted against p for different values of $y (Z = Z(p, y, 0))$. As the economy is replicated, production expands and price falls from A to B and then to C. At C, no firm contemplates an expansion in output because this leads to the nonexistence of an equilibrium price. However, if all firms expanded then it would be possible to move to D which, it may be assumed, is the perfectly competitive position.

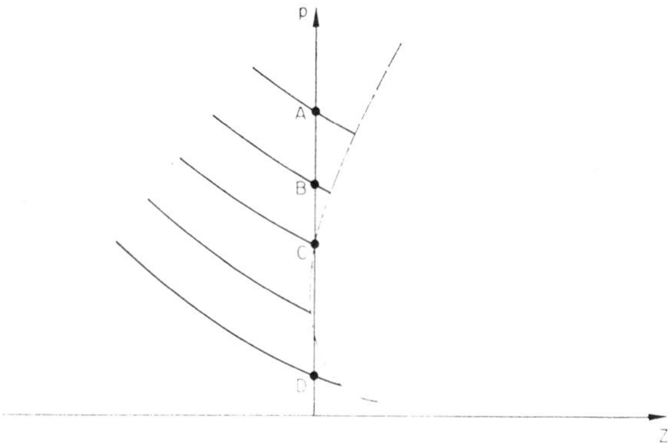

FIGURE 4

[10] An investigation of the set of PCE (ϵ) as $\epsilon \to 0$ would take us too far astray from the present analysis. It suffices to say that there can exist limit points which are not perfectly competitive for the certain economy.

Although the motivation for this type of equilibrium differs from that of a critical equilibrium, the two concepts are very close. For as expected profits are nonnegative, the nonexistence problem will not usually arise if ϵ is small and profits change continuously with y and v. This is ensured when $Z_p(p, y, 0)$ is nonsingular. However, at critical exchange equilibria, profits can fall discontinuously and the nonexistence problem is more likely to be encountered: limit points close to critical points are not unlikely.

(2) Now assume that P^* is defined for all y' close to y. Looking at (42), P^* will be C^2 in y' if $P(p, y, y'; v)$ is C^2 in y' for almost all v. When $v = 0$, P will be C^2 if Z_p is nonsingular. As Z is C^2, nonsingularity will hold for all small v so that for small ϵ, P^* will be continuous. If Z_p is singular, so that the determinant, $\det(Z_p)$, is zero, then P will still be C^2 for almost all v, ϵ small, if the differential of $\det(Z_p)$ with respect to v is nonzero. Thus, problems can only arise if there exist p, y such that

$$\begin{aligned} Z(p, y, 0) &= 0, \\ \det(Z_p) &= 0, \\ \frac{\partial}{\partial v} \det(Z_p) &= 0. \end{aligned} \tag{43}$$

Transversality theory (see, e.g., Abraham and Robbin [1]) can be applied to show that if (43) can occur then almost any small perturbation of Z will eliminate the possibility. For, by (41), Z, or alternatively X, is a function of $l + m$ variables whereas (43) is a set of $l + m + 1$ equations.

To sum up, in the ϵ version of the economy with ϵ small, critical equilibria of the form studied in earlier sections are pathological. However, in economies with uncertainty there can exist nonperfectly competitive equilibria as limit points, the incentive for adopting noncompetitive behavior being that changes in production lead to a nonexistence of equilibrium prices. Thus, the introduction of uncertainty is insufficient to ensure that the monopolistically competitive equilibria of large economies approximate a system of perfect competition.

7. Concluding Remarks

This paper has investigated and characterized the form of the limit points that arise under replication of a monopolistically competitive economy. Of particular interest has been the uncovering of critical equilibria. The non-pathological existence of these equilibria demonstrates a general point. In decentralized systems like perfect competition, there is no possibility for individual agents to exploit irregularities in the economic structure. However, when agents manipulate the system to which they belong, it is possible, and not unlikely, that irregular situations will produce beneficial outcomes. In these circumstances, equilibria cannot be properly understood without the irregularities of the economic structure being understood. In this paper, these irregularities have been critical exchange equilibria. At such equilibria, it has been shown that intuition and standard results are a poor guide to the possibilities that can exist.

REFERENCES

1. R. ABRAHAM AND J. ROBBIN, "Transversal Mappings and Flows," Benjamin, New York, 1967.
2. K. J. ARROW AND F. H. HAHN, "General Competitive Analysis," Holden–Day, San Francisco, 1971.
3. G. DEBREU, Economies with a finite set of equilibria, *Econometrica* **38** (1970), 387–392.
4. G. DEBREU, Smooth preferences, *Econometrica* **40** (1972), 603–615.
5. G. DEBREU, Excess demand functions, *J. Math. Econ.* **1** (1974), 15–21.
6. G. DEBREU AND H. SCARF, A limit theorem on the core of an economy, *Int. Econ. Rev.* **4** (1963), 235–246.
7. J. DIEUDONNÉ, "Foundations of Modern Analysis," Academic Press, New York, 1960.
8. J.-J. GABSZEWICZ AND J.-P. VIAL, Oligopoly 'a la Cournot' in a general equilibrium analysis, *J. Econ. Theory* **4** (1972), 381–400.
9. O. D. HART, Monopolistic competition in a large economy with differentiated commodities, *Rev. Econ. Stud.* **46** (1979), 1–30.
10. M. W. HIRSCH AND S. SMALE, "Differential Equations, Dynamical Systems, and Linear Algebra," Academic Press, New York, 1974.
11. G. LAROQUE, The fixed price equilibria: Some Results in local comparative statics, *Econometrica* **46** (1978), 1127–1154.
12. W. NOVSHEK, Cournot Equilibrium with Free Entry, *Rev. Econ. Stud.*, in press.
13. W. NOVSHEK AND H. SONNENSCHEIN, Cournot and Walras equilibrium, *J. Econ. Theory* **19** (1978), 223–266.
14. D. J. ROBERTS AND A. POSTLEWAITE, The incentives for price taking behavior in large exchange economies, *Econometrica* **44** (1976), 115–127.
15. D. J. ROBERTS AND H. SONNENSCHEIN, On the foundations of the theory of monopolistic competition, *Econometrica* **45** (1977), 101–113.

Perfect Competition and Optimal Product Differentiation

OLIVER D. HART

Churchill College, Cambridge, England

Received February 6, 1979

This paper considers whether a competitive economy will achieve an optimal allocation when firms produce differentiated products. In the model studied, firms market those products which maximize profit given the demand curves facing them. Markets are assumed to be open only for goods actually traded. Competitive conditions are achieved by replicating the consumer sector. It is shown that market equilibrium may be suboptimal if those products not being produced are highly complementary in consumption. Sufficient conditions on preferences and production sets for the market equilibrium to be optimal are given.

1. INTRODUCTION

Product differentiation under imperfectly competitive conditions has been the focus of a number of studies in the last few years (see, for example, Dixit and Stiglitz, 1977; Spence, 1976). Product differentiation under perfect competition has, however, received considerably less attention. One reason for this may be the widely held view that producers of nonhomogeneous goods possess monopoly power and hence that markets where products are differentiated are inherently noncompetitive. In a previous paper (Hart, 1979a), we argued that this is not the case. We showed that what causes a firm to have monopoly power is not that the firm is producing a unique commodity, but rather that the firm is a large part of the aggregate economy or, more precisely, of the potential market for its output. Of course, if a firm is producing a unique commodity, it will in general, even if it is small, earn supernormal profits or rents, i.e., it will have considerable *market* power. This, however, is quite consistent with the fact that it faces a perfectly elastic demand curve, i.e., with the fact that it has no *monopoly* power.

In Hart (1979a), we used the result that a small firm faces a perfectly elastic demand curve to show that a monopolistically competitive equilibrium, in which firms maximize profits subject to correct conjectures concerning the demand for all potential (differentiated) commodities, is approximately Pareto optimal if the economy is large. One assumption which was made in order to establish this result was that consumers' preferences are convex and

Reprinted from *Journal of Economic Theory* **22,** No. 2, 279–312 (April 1980)
ISBN 0-12-476750-8

can be represented by a differentiable utility function. This assumption may seem relatively innocuous at first sight, but on closer examination it turns out to be rather crucial. The purpose of the present paper is to explore the consequences of relaxing this assumption.

Our principal result is that if preferences are not differentiable and convex, a monopolistically competitive equilibrium may not be Pareto optimal even when the economy is large. In particular, the economy can get stuck in a situation where the set of goods being produced is socially inefficient. The reason for this is not that firms possess monopoly power. Rather, it is that, if firms' products are strongly complementary, the gain (both private and social) from several firms simultaneously producing new products may far outweigh the sum of the gains to each firm from producing a new product by itself. To take a very simple example, suppose that neither nuts nor bolts are being produced. The revenue that a bolt manufacturer would obtain from setting up in the absence of a supply of nuts might be expected to be small and hence may not cover costs. The same of course is true of a nut manufacturer who sets up in the absence of a supply of bolts. However, if the two manufacturers set up simultaneously, revenue will in general be much higher and so both manufacturers may be able to make a profit. In an atomistic economy, however, there may be no mechanism which coordinates the actions of the nut manufacturer and the bolt manufacturer. Thus, the equilibrium of the economy may involve neither nuts nor bolts being produced even though such a situation is Pareto suboptimal.

The presence of complementarities of this type captures to some extent the idea that there can be pecuniary externalities in the production process (see, e.g., Scitovsky, 1954). In particular, the profits of one firm depend on the actions of another firm even under competition. We will see that such pecuniary externalities are ruled out if consumers have convex, differentiable preferences (or if they have quasi-convex utility functions).

While a monopolistically competitive equilibrium may not be Pareto optimal if preferences are not differentiable and convex, it is possible to establish that the equilibrium is optimal in a weaker sense. We will show that, when the economy is large, it is impossible for a central planner to Pareto dominate a monopolistically competitive equilibrium allocation using only the goods which are traded in the monopolistically competitive equilibrium plus at most one new good. That is to say, a monopolistically competitive equilibrium is Pareto optimal subject to the constraint that a planner can open at most one new market.

The paper is organized as follows. The model is presented in Section 2. In Section 3, the properties of monopolistically competitive equilibria in large economies are studied. In Section 4, examples of suboptimal equilibria when preferences are not differentiable and convex are presented. In one of the examples, the nonconvexity of preferences is caused by the presence of transaction costs. Concluding remarks appear in Section 5, and proofs are contained in the Appendix.

2. THE MODEL

We consider an economy in which there are I types of consumers, J types of firms, and $(K+1)$ potential goods, indexed by $i = 1,..., I$, $j = 1,..., J$, and $k = 0,..., K$, respectively. We assume for the sake of simplicity that I, J, K are all finite (the extension to the case where I, J, K are infinite can be carried out along the lines of Hart (1979a)).

Each firm will be assumed to use good 0 as an input to produce goods $1,..., K$ as outputs.[1] In interpreting the model, we will be particularly interested in cases where not all potential goods $k > 0$ are actually produced in equilibrium. In contrast to the usual Arrow–Debreu model, we will assume that if a good $k > 0$ is not produced there is no market for it; that is, no price is quoted for it. In other words, the firms which produce a particular good "make" the market for that good. (However, we assume that there is always a market for good 0, the common input. In addition, it will be assumed that consumers have no endowments of goods $1,..., K$ and hence there is no reason for consumers to trade these goods among themselves.)

Note that our formulation is general enough to include product differentiation in the Chamberlinian or Lancastrian sense. In particular, some of the goods $1,..., K$ may represent different qualities of the same good, or the same good in different locations.

Our objective is to explain which goods are produced, i.e., which markets are open, and to explain the volume of trade in these markets.

We begin with a more precise description of the agents in the economy.

Firms

As indicated above, firms use good 0 to produce goods $1,..., K$. A type j firm $(j = 1,..., J)$ has a production set $Y_j \subset R_- \times R_+^K$, with the interpretation that $y \in Y_j$ means that it is feasible for firm j to produce the vector of outputs $(y_1,..., y_K)$ using $-y_0$ units of good 0.[2] Note that we treat inputs as nonpositive numbers. We assume that for each j:

(A.1) $0 \in Y_j$, and Y_j is closed.

[1] We do not consider the case where some goods are intermediate goods. See Makowski (1980) for a discussion of additional coordination problems which can arise when there are intermediate goods.

[2] We use the notation $x \geqslant 0$ if each component of x is nonnegative. Also we define $R_+^m = \{x \in R^m \mid x \geqslant 0\}$, $R_-^m = \{x \in R^m \mid 0 \geqslant x\}$.

(A.2) Given $y \in Y_j$ and $u \in R_-^K$,

$$y + (0, u) \in R_- \times R_+^K \Rightarrow y + (0, u) \in Y_j .$$

(A.3) There exists $\bar{y}_{j_0} < 0$ such that $y \in Y_j$ and $y \neq 0 \Rightarrow y_0 \leqslant \bar{y}_{j_0}$.

Assumption (A.2) says that there is free disposal of produced goods. Assumption (A.3) says that there is a setup cost for any firm. The existence of setup costs is consistent with the assumption that markets exist only for goods $k > 0$ which are produced (a price will be quoted only if it is profitable for a firm to set up and produce the good in question).

Subject to the payment of a setup cost, there is assumed to be free entry of type j firms, $j = 1,..., J$.

We will not place any convexity restrictions on Y_j (Y_j itself will not be convex, of course, because of (A.3); however, we will also not require $Y_j \backslash \{0\}$ to be convex). In particular, we allow for cases where a firm may be able to produce several goods, but only one at any one time (e.g., if good 1 is a Rolls Royce, and good 2 is a Volkswagen, it may be that $(y_0, 1, 0) \in Y_j$ and $(y_0', 0, 1) \in Y_j$, but there may be no $y \in Y_j$ with y_1 and $y_2 > 0$). We will assume, however, that all goods are divisible.

We will also assume that each good $k = 1,..., K$ can be produced:

(A.4) Given $k = 1,..., K$, there exists j and $y \in Y_j$ such that $y_k > 0$.

Consumers

Each type i consumer ($i = 1,..., I$) is assumed to have a continuous utility function U_i defined on his consumption set, which we will take to be R_+^{K+1}. We will assume that good 0 is desirable and that positive consumption of it is essential to get positive utility:

(A.5) For all $i = 1,..., I$: $U_i(x) > U_i(0) \Rightarrow x_0 > 0$. Furthermore, if $x \in R_+^{K+1}$, then $U_i(x + (u_0, 0,..., 0)) > U_i(x)$ if $u_0 > 0$ and

$$\lim_{u_0 \to \infty} U_i(x + (u_0, 0,..., 0)) = \infty.$$

We also assume that each good $k = 1,..., K$ is desired by some consumer:

(A.6) For each $k = 1,..., K$, there exists i such that: if $x \in R_+^{K+1}$, then $U_i(x + (0,..., 0, u_k, 0,..., 0)) > U_i(x)$ if $u_k > 0$ and

$$\lim_{u_k \to \infty} U_i(x + (0,..., 0, u_k, 0,..., 0)) = \infty.$$

We will not, however, assume that preferences are convex. As will be seen later, the possible nonconvexity of preferences will play an important role in our analysis.[3]

Each type i consumer is assumed to have an initial endowment of goods, $w_i \in R_+^{K+1}$, where $w_{ik} = 0$ for all $k > 0$ and $w_{i0} > 0$, and an initial shareholding in firms. To simplify matters, we will assume that a consumer's shareholding is the same across all firms of the same type, so that we can talk simply about a consumer's shareholding in type j firms. We will also assume that all type i consumers have the same initial shareholdings. We will denote by $\bar{\Theta}_{ij}$ the aggregate shareholding of type i consumers in type j firms, where $\bar{\Theta}_{ij} \geqslant 0$ and $\sum_{i=1}^{I} \bar{\Theta}_{ij} = 1$ for each j.

The Economy E_r

As indicated in the introduction, we are interested in analyzing whether the right mix of products is produced in a perfectly competitive environment. In order to ensure that the environment is indeed perfectly competitive, we make each firm small relative to the aggregate economy by replicating the consumer sector, at the same time keeping the characteristics (i.e., production sets) of the J types of firms $j = 1,..., J$ fixed. (Although the characteristics of the production sector remain fixed, the growth of the consumption sector allows a greater number of firms to operate since setup costs, as a fraction of the economy's aggregate endowment, become smaller.)

This leads us to consider the economy E_r consisting of r consumers of each type $i = 1,..., I$, where each type i consumer has utility function U_i and endowment w_i as indicated above. Since all type i consumers are identical, the shareholding of each type i consumer in type j firms is given by $\bar{\Theta}_{ij}/r$.

Exchange Equilibrium in E_r

In order to define an equilibrium for the economy E_r, we proceed in two stages. First, taking firms' production decisions to be already determined, we define an exchange equilibrium relative to these production decisions. Second, we turn to an analysis of how these production decisions are made.

Because of the existence of setup costs, only a finite number of firms will operate in equilibrium in the economy E_r. Suppose that n_j firms of type j choose to operate and label these $(j, 1), (j, 2),..., (j, n_j)$. Let the production decisions of these firms be given by $y_{j1},..., y_{jn_j} \in Y_j$ $(j = 1,..., J)$. Define

$$y_j = (y_{j1} + \cdots + y_{jn_j})/r \qquad (2.1)$$

[3] Some of the problems which are caused by nonconvexities in preferences also arise if consumption sets are nonconvex. To simplify matters, we will not consider the complications caused by nonconvex consumption sets in this paper.

to be the aggregate production plan of type j firms deflated by r ($y_j = 0$ if $n_j = 0$, of course), and let $y = (y_1, ..., y_J)$. Also let $\mathscr{Y}$ denote the array $(y_{jt})_{j=1,...,J, t=1,...,n_j}$.

Consider the resulting exchange equilibrium. Define $R_+^* = R_+ U\{\infty\}$, and let $p \in R_+^{*(K+1)}$ be the equilibrium price vector with the understanding that, for $k > 0$, p_k is finite if $\sum_{j=1}^J y_{jk} > 0$, i.e., if good k is actually produced, and $p_k = \infty$ if $\sum_{j=1}^J y_{jk} = 0$, i.e., if good k is not produced (we will see below that setting $p_k = \infty$ is equivalent to assuming that there is no market for good k).

We will normalize prices so that $p_0 = 1$. Let x_{it} denote the post-trade consumption bundle of the tth consumer of type i. It will be convenient to represent the consumption bundles of type i consumers by a measure. For each i define the probability measure μ_i on the Borel subsets of R_+^{K+1} as follows:

$$\mu_i(B) = \#\{t \mid x_{it} \in B\}/r \tag{2.2}$$

for each Borel subset B of R_+^{K+1}.[4] Here $\mu_i(B)$ is simply the fraction of type i consumers whose consumption bundles lie in B. Let Supp μ_i denote the support of the measure μ_i and let $\| \ \|$ denote the Euclidean norm. Also define $\mu = (\mu_1, ..., \mu_I)$. Finally, let

$$\begin{aligned} Y_r = \{ y = (y_1, ..., y_J) \mid & \text{ for each } j,\ y_j = (y_{j1} + \cdots + y_{jn_j})/r \\ & \text{for some } n_j \text{ and some } y_{j1}, ..., y_{jn_j} \in Y_j\}. \end{aligned} \tag{2.3}$$

We are now ready to define an *approximate exchange equilibrium* in the economy E_r, relative to the deflated production plans y.

DEFINITION. An ϵ-exchange equilibrium, $\epsilon \geqslant 0$, in the economy E_r is an array (μ, p, y), where $y \in Y_r$ and

$$\begin{aligned} \mu = (\mu_1, ..., \mu_I) & \text{ and each } \mu_i \text{ is a probability measure} \\ & \text{defined on the Borel subsets of } R_+^{K+1}; \end{aligned} \tag{2.4}$$

$$p \in R_+^{*(K+1)},\ p_0 = 1, \text{ and, for } k > 0,\ p_k \text{ is finite} \Leftrightarrow \sum_{j=1}^J y_{jk} > 0; \tag{2.5}$$

$$p \cdot x_i \leqslant p \cdot w_i + \sum_j \bar{\Theta}_{ij} p \cdot y_j \qquad \text{for all} \quad x_i \in \text{Supp } \mu_i \quad (i = 1, ..., I); \tag{2.6}$$

For all $x \in$ Supp μ_i,

$$U_i(x') > U_i(x) + \epsilon \Rightarrow p \cdot x' > p \cdot w_i + \sum_j \bar{\Theta}_{ij} p \cdot y_j \qquad (i = 1, ..., I); \tag{2.7}$$

[4] $\#C$ denotes the number of elements in the set C.

$r\mu_i(B)$ is integral for all Borel subsets B of R_+^{K+1} $(i = 1,..., I)$; (2.8)

$$\sum_{i=1}^{I} \int x \, d\mu_i - \sum_{j=1}^{J} y_j - \sum_{i=1}^{I} w_i = 0. \tag{2.9}$$

Condition (2.6) says that consumers satisfy their budget constraints. Condition (2.7) says that each consumer's equilibrium bundle provides utility which is within ϵ of maximum utility subject to the budget constraint. Finally, (2.9) says that demand equals supply for each good 0,..., K. We adopt the convention $\infty \cdot 0 = 0$, $\infty \cdot h = \infty$ if $h > 0$. It then follows that $x_{itk} = 0$ whenever $p_k = \infty$, so that as noted above setting $p_k = \infty$ is equivalent to assuming that there is no trading in good k.

The exchange equilibrium we have defined is an approximate one in the sense of Starr (1969) (it is exact if $\epsilon = 0$). We study approximate rather than exact equilibria because, since preferences are not necessarily convex, an exact exchange equilibrium may not exist. On the other hand, given appropriate restrictions on firms' production plans, the convexifying effects of replication will ensure the existence of an ϵ-exchange equilibrium for large enough r.[5] Note that, given ϵ, an ϵ-exchange equilibrium depends on the particular cardinalization U_i of consumer i's underlying preferences selected. However, the set of all ϵ-exchange equilibria, as we let ϵ vary, is independent of any particular cardinalization.

Note that different type i consumers will in general consume different bundles in an ϵ-exchange equilibrium.

We turn now to the determination of firms' production plans. We will assume that each firm chooses its production plan to maximize profits (measured in units of good 0).[6] We do not assume, however, that firms are price takers (this assumption would in any case be meaningless in the case of goods not being produced since there are no prices to "take"). Instead we assume that each firm, acting under the Cournot–Nash assumption that other firms' production plans are fixed, maximizes profit on the basis of a correct calculation concerning the relationship between the amount of any good it produces and the price which it will receive for this good (this calculation is made both for goods already being produced and for new goods). Such a calculation is of course in general a very complicated one, and the assumption that firms can carry it out is therefore strong. We will make this assumption because we wish to consider the misallocations which result

[5] An analysis of the existence of various different types of approximate equilibria may be found in Starr (1969).

[6] Conditions under which this objective represents the interests of the firm's owners may be found in Hart (1979b).

from the inherent characteristics of the economy rather than those which result from the mistakes of the agents.[7]

There is a problem which must be faced before we can complete the specification of a firm's behavior. In general, there will be many ϵ-exchange equilibria corresponding to a particular choice of production plan for the firm. The firm's decision whether to choose the production plan will depend on which of these equilibria is selected. In order to surmount this difficulty, we follow Novshek and Sonnenschein (1978) in assuming that an exogenous *selection* is made from the set of ϵ-exchange equilibria. Let

$$T_r = \{ y \mid y \in Y_r, \text{ and there exists an } \epsilon\text{-exchange equilibrium } (\mu, p, y) \text{ in } E_r\}. \tag{2.10}$$

Also let G be the set of all probability measures defined on the Borel subsets of R_+^{K+1}. We assume that, for each r, there is a function F_r: $T_r \to G^I \times R_+^{*(K+1)}$ satisfying, for all $y \in T_r$,

$$(F_r(y), y) = (\mu, p, y) \text{ is an } \epsilon\text{-exchange equilibrium in the economy } E_r. \tag{2.11}$$

If $F_r(y) = (\mu, p)$, we will use the shorthand $F_{r1}(y) = \mu$, $F_{r2}(y) = p$.

We are now ready to define a monopolistically competitive equilibrium in which firms maximize profits subject to the demand curves facing them. In the following definition, y_{-j} is a shorthand for $(y_1, \ldots, y_{j-1}, y_{j+1}, \ldots, y_J)$.

Definition. An ϵ-monopolistically competitive equilibrium (ϵ-MCE), $\epsilon \geqslant 0$, in E_r is an array $(\mu, p, \mathscr{Y})$, where $\mu = (\mu_i)_{i=1,\ldots,I}$ and $\mathscr{Y} = (y_{jt})_{j=1,\ldots,J, t=1,\ldots,n_j}$ such that

$$y_{jt} \in Y_j \text{ for each } t, j; \tag{2.12}$$

$$(\mu, p, y) \text{ is an } \epsilon\text{-exchange equilibrium in } E_r, \text{ where}$$
$$y = (y_1, \ldots, y_J) \quad\text{and}\quad y_j = \left(\sum_{t=1}^{n_j} y_{jt}/r\right) \text{ for each } j; \tag{2.13}$$

there does not exist (t, j), $1 \leqslant t \leqslant n_j$, $1 \leqslant j \leqslant J$, and $y'_{jt} \in Y_j$, such that $(y_{-j}, y_j - y_{jt}/r + y'_{jt}/r) \in T_r$ and

$$F_{r2}(y_{-j}, y_j - y_{jt}/r + y'_{jt}/r) \cdot y'_{jt} > p \cdot y_{jt}; \tag{2.14}$$

[7] To put it another way, whereas in the standard Arrow–Debreu model, a good entrepreneur is simply someone who knows his firm's production set well and who can therefore calculate the profit maximizing production plan, in the present context a good entrepreneur must also be skilled at market research, i.e., at calculating the way the economy's general equilibrium varies with his firm's production plan.

there does not exist j, $1 \leqslant j \leqslant J$, and $y_j' \in Y_j$, such that

$$(y_{-j}, y_j + y_j'/r) \in T_r \quad \text{and} \quad F_{r2}(y_{-j}, y_j + y_j'/r) \cdot y_j' > 0; \tag{2.15}$$

$$p \cdot y_{jt} \geqslant 0 \qquad \text{for all } t, j. \tag{2.16}$$

Condition (2.14) says that no firm which is already operating can increase its profit by moving to a new production plan, while (2.15) says that no new firm can enter and make a positive profit. Finally, (2.16) says that all operating firms break even. (It might seem as though (2.14) already implies (2.16), but this is not the case if $(y_{-j}, y_j - y_{jt}/r) \notin T_r$.)

Finally, it will be useful to define a feasible allocation in the economy E_r.

DEFINITION. A *feasible allocation* in the economy E_r is an array (μ, y), where $y \in Y_r$, satisfying (2.4), (2.8), and (2.9).

3. PROPERTIES OF MONOPOLISTICALLY COMPETITIVE EQUILIBRIA IN LARGE FINITE ECONOMIES

We study now the properties of a monopolistically competitive equilibrium (MCE) in E_r when r is large.

THEOREM 1. *Assume* (A.1)–(A.6), *and that Y_j is bounded for all j. Suppose that $\epsilon > 0$ is given. Then we can find a selection function F_r: $T_r \to G^I \times R_+^{*(K+1)}$ and a number $\bar{r}$ such that, for all $r \geqslant \bar{r}$, there exists an ϵ-MCE in E_r.*

Proof. See Appendix.

Note that Theorem 1 establishes only the existence of an ϵ-MCE for $\epsilon > 0$. Establishing the existence of an exact MCE, i.e., an ϵ-MCE with $\epsilon = 0$, is considerably more complicated and stronger assumptions are needed. See Novshek and Sonnenschein (1978).

Our main interest is to study the welfare properties of an MCE in a large economy. To this end, it is useful to introduce a measure of how far away an equilibrium allocation is from being Pareto optimal. Suppose that we are given a feasible allocation (μ_r, y_r) in E_r which satisfies $\| U_i(x) - U_i(x')\| \leqslant \epsilon$ for all $x, x' \in \operatorname{Supp} \mu_i$ $(i = 1,..., I)$ (this is an approximate equal treatment condition). Let E_r' be the economy which is identical to E_r except that the aggregate endowment of good 0 is $(r \sum_{i=1}^{I} w_{i0}) - rh$ rather than $(r \sum_{i=1}^{I} w_{i0})$, and define

$$\begin{aligned} H_r(\epsilon, \mu_r, y_r) = \sup \{\{h \mid & \text{ there exists a feasible allocation } (\mu_r', y_r') \text{ in } E_r' \\ & \text{such that } U_i(x') \geqslant U_i(x) + \epsilon \text{ for all} \\ & x \in \operatorname{Supp} \mu_{ir}, x' \in \operatorname{Supp} \mu_{ir}' \text{ and } i = 1,..., I\} \cup \{0\}\}. \end{aligned} \tag{3.1}$$

The number $H_r(\epsilon, \mu_r, y_r)$ is a measure (in per capita terms) of how far the allocation (μ_r, y_r) is from being a Pareto optimum in E_r, given that we insist that a planner makes everybody better off by at least ϵ. Note that if (μ_r, y_r) is Pareto optimal, then $H_r(\epsilon, \mu_r, y_r) = 0$ for all $\epsilon \geqslant 0$.

As well as being interested in unconstrained Pareto optimality, we will also wish to consider a notion of constrained or restricted Pareto optimality. In particular, we want to study the consequences of allowing a planner to alter firms' production plans and reallocate goods to consumers subject to the constraint that, in the new configuration of firms' production plans, *at most one new good* is being produced relative to the initial allocation (μ, y).

Given the production allocation $y = (y_1, ..., y_J)$, let $M(y) = \{k > 0 \mid \sum_{j=1}^{J} y_{jk} > 0\} \cup \{0\}$ be the set of goods which are produced at y, plus good 0. $M(y)$ represents the set of markets which are open at y. Define

$$\begin{aligned} h_r(\epsilon, \mu, y) = \sup \{\{h \mid & \text{ there exists a feasible allocation } (\mu_r', y_r') \text{ in } E_r' \\ & \text{such that } U_i(x') \geqslant U_i(x) + \epsilon \text{ for all} \\ & x \in \operatorname{Supp} \mu_{ir}, \; x' \in \operatorname{Supp} \mu_{ir}' \text{ and } i = 1, ..., I, \\ & \text{and } M(y_r') \backslash M(y_r) \text{ contains at most one element}\} \cup \{0\}\}. \end{aligned} \tag{3.2}$$

The number $h_r(\epsilon, \mu, y)$ is a measure (again in per capita terms) of how far the allocation (μ_r, y_r) is from being a Pareto optimum in E_r, given that the planner must make everybody better off by at least ϵ, and given that the planner is constrained to produce at most one new good, i.e., to open at most one new market (note that a planner is free to close markets, i.e., $M(y_r')$ can contain fewer elements than $M(y_r)$). Of course, $h_r(\epsilon, \mu_r, y_r) \leqslant H_r(\epsilon, \mu_r, y_r)$.

In Theorems 2 and 3 below, we give conditions under which $h_r(\epsilon, \mu_r, y_r)$ and $H_r(\epsilon, \mu_r, y_r)$ are small when r is large if (μ_r, p_r, y_r) is an ϵ-MCE. In order to prove these theorems, we need to assume that the limit of a sequence of production allocations $y_r \in Y_r$ is a *regular point* with respect to the selection functions F_r.

Let $\tilde{Y}_j$ be the smallest closed convex cone with vertex at the origin which contains Y_j. Then $\prod_j \tilde{Y}_j$ is the smallest closed set containing all the Y_r, $r = 1, 2, ...$, (see (2.3)). In the following definition, limits of the measure μ_r are taken with respect to the weak convergence topology (see Parthasarathy (1969)) and limits of prices with respect to the standard topology on $R_+^{*(K+1)}$.

DEFINITION. We say that $y \in \prod_{j=1}^{J} \tilde{Y}_j$ is a regular point with respect to the selection functions $F_1, F_2, ...,$ if:

(1) Given any two sequences (y_r), (y_r') of points in T_r converging to y, and limit points (μ, p), (μ', p') of the sequences $(F_r(y_r))$, $(F_r(y_r'))$, respectively, it is the case that $\mu' = \mu$ and $p_k' = p_k$ for all k such that $k = 0$ or $\sum_{j=1}^{J} y_{jk} > 0$.

(2) Given any sequence (y_r) of points converging to y, where $y_r \in Y_r$ for each r, it is the case that $y_r \in T_r$ for sufficiently large r.

In other words, y is a regular point as long as $F_r(y_r)$ changes continuously as y_r varies in a neighborhood of y. For a discussion of the importance of regularity in cases where firms take into account their effect on prices, see Novshek and Sonnenschein (1978) and Roberts (1980).

Before stating Theorem 2, we need one further assumption:

$$\text{(A.7)} \quad \tilde{Y}_j \cap R_+^{K+1} = \{0\} \qquad (j = 1,\dots, J).$$

Assumption (A.7) rules out cases where it is possible to get something for nothing in per capita terms in the limit $r \to \infty$ by operating type j firms.

THEOREM 2. *Let $\epsilon \geqslant 0$ and the selection functions $F_1, F_2, \dots,$ be given. Suppose that $(\mu_r, p_r, \mathcal{Y}_r)$ is a sequence of ϵ-MCEs in the economies E_r, $r = 1, 2, \dots,$ and, for each r, define y_r as in* (2.1). *Assume* (A.1)–(A.7), *and that each limit point y of (y_r) is regular. Assume also that for some $\eta > 0$ and r' the following is true for $k > 0$: either $\sum_{j=1}^{J} y_{jkr} > \eta$ or $\sum_{j=1}^{J} y_{jkr} = 0$ for all $r \geqslant r'$. Define $h_r(\epsilon, \mu_r, y_r)$ as in* (3.2). *Then* $\lim_{r\to\infty} h_r(\epsilon, \mu_r, y_r) = 0$.

It should be noted that the condition $\sum_{j=1}^{J} y_{jkr} > \eta$ or $= 0$ for large r rules out situations where the set of markets which are open changes discontinuously in the limit as $y_r \to y$.

Theorem 2 is proved in the Appendix. It is useful, however, to give some intuition behind the result. Suppose to simplify matters that $\mu_r \to \mu$, $p_r \to p$, $y_r \to y$. The proof proceeds by showing that the allocation (μ, y) is a competitive equilibrium allocation relative to the markets $M(y) \cup \{k'\}$ for any $k' = 1,\dots, K$ in some well-defined limit economy. In particular, in the limit, firms, subject to the constraint that they can market only goods in $M(y) \cup \{k'\}$, maximize profits as price takers at prices p^*, where $p_k^* = p_k$ for $k \in M(y)$ and $p_{k'}^*$ is chosen to be the reservation price for good k', i.e., it is the lowest price at which demand for good k' is zero even though the market for good k' is open. A standard revealed preference argument then shows that $h_r(\epsilon, \mu_r, y_r)$ must be zero in the limit.

To see why firms must maximize profits as price takers in the limit, suppose that they do not. Then this means that there exists $y' \in Y_j$ such that $p^* \cdot y' > 0$. Consider now the consequences of an additional type j firm setting up with the production plan y' in the economy E_r, starting at the ϵ-MCE (μ_r, p_r, y_r). While this action will have some effect on prices, this effect will be very small when r is large since the new prices are given by $F_{r2}(y_{-jr}, y_{jr} + y'/r)$ and this is approximately equal to $F_{r2}(y_{-jr}, y_{jr})$ when r is large. In other words, firms have a negligible effect on prices when r is large since prices depend on per capita production, $(y_{-jr}, y_{jr} + y'/r)$, and an individual firm has a very small influence on this (this argument is only formally correct if y is a regular point).

But since p_r hardly changes and since $p_r \to p^*$ as $r \to \infty$, it follows that the new firm will make positive profits by setting up with the production plan y' in E_r when r is large, which is not consistent with (μ_r, p_r, y_r) being an ϵ-MCE. This completes the proof.

It should be emphasized that Theorem 2 does not tell us that a monopolistically competitive allocation is (approximately) fully Pareto optimal when r is large, but only that it is (approximately) Pareto optimal subject to the constraint that a planner can produce at most one new good, i.e., open at most one new market. In fact, we will see in the examples of the next section that an MCE may be far from optimal in the full sense.

If we are prepared to make further assumptions, however, we can establish the full Pareto optimality of an MCE in the limit $r = \infty$. Consider first how we might try to extend the sketch of the proof of Theorem 2 given above to the case where several new goods can be produced. Define, for each good k' which is not being produced in the limiting allocation (μ, y), $p_{k'}^*$ to be the reservation price for good k'; i.e., $p_{k'}^*$ is the smallest price which is such that demand for good k' is zero if markets for goods $k \in M(y) \cup \{k'\}$ are open. It is not difficult to show that in the limit firms are maximizing profits at these prices. The problem with this approach is that if we now open markets for goods and quote prices p_k for goods k in $M(y)$ and $p_{k'}^*$ for goods k' not in $M(y)$, there is no guarantee that markets will clear! The reason is that $p_{k'}^*$ may be a reservation price for k' when only goods k in $M(y) \cup \{k'\}$ can be purchased, and $p_{k''}^*$ may be a reservation price for k'' when only goods k in $M(y) \cup \{k''\}$ can be purchased, but $p_{k'}^*$ and $p_{k''}^*$ need not be reservation prices when goods k in $M(y) \cup \{k'\} \cup \{k''\}$ can be simultaneously purchased. In particular, if k' and k'' are strongly complementary, then if only one of these goods is available, the willingness of consumers to pay for it may be low, i.e., the reservation price will be low, while if both goods are simultaneously available, the willingness to pay, and hence the corresponding reservation prices, may be much higher.

While the above is in general a problem, there are some situations in which the problem does not arise. Specifically, there are classes of preferences for consumers which have the property that goods are always sufficiently substitutable that the reservation prices of the goods taken one at a time are also reservation prices for all the goods simultaneously.

Given a subset S of $\{1, 2,..., K\}$, define $R^S = \{x \in R^{K+1} \mid x_k = 0 \text{ if } k \notin S\}$.

DEFINITION. We will say that a type i consumer satisfies the *simultaneous reservation price property* (SRPP) if given (1) any subset $\tilde{S}$ of $\{0, 1,..., K\}$ containing 0; (2) $p^* \in R_+^{*(K+1)}$ such that p_k^* is finite for all $k \in \tilde{S}$; (3) $x \in R_+^{\tilde{S}}$

such that $p^* \cdot x > 0$, and for all $S = \tilde{S} \cup \{k'\}$, where $k' = 1, \ldots, K$, $x' \in R_+{}^S$ and $U_i(x') > U_i(x) \Rightarrow p^* \cdot x' > p^* \cdot x$; then it is the case that

$$x' \in R_+^{K+1} \quad \text{and} \quad U_i(x') > U_i(x) \Rightarrow p^* \cdot x' > p^* \cdot x. \tag{3.3}$$

In the above definition, we start off with a subset $\tilde{S}$ of marketed goods, prices for these goods, and a feasible consumption bundle x containing only these goods. These prices are then extended to cover all possible goods in such a way that, if we add one new good at a time, although the consumer can now trade in the new good, the price of the good is sufficiently high that he does not wish to do so. The simultaneous reservation price property is satisfied if we may conclude that the consumer will not wish to trade when *all* goods are available.

The next theorem gives conditions for an MCE to be approximately unconstrained Pareto optimal. It applies only to exact MCEs, i.e., to ϵ-MCEs with $\epsilon = 0$.

THEOREM 3. *Let the selection functions* $F_1, F_2, \ldots,$ *be given. Suppose that* $(\mu_r, p_r, \mathscr{Y}_r)$ *is a sequence of* ϵ*-MCEs, with* $\epsilon = 0$, *in the economies* E_r, $r = 1, 2, \ldots,$ *and, for each r, define* y_r *as in* (2.1). *Assume* (A.1)–(A.7), *and that each limit point y of* (y_r) *is regular. Assume also that for some* $\eta > 0$ *and* r' *the following is true for* $k > 0$: *either* $\sum_{j=1}^J y_{jkr} > \eta$ *or* $\sum_{j=1}^J y_{jkr} = 0$ *for all* $r \geqslant r'$. *Define* $H_r(\epsilon, \mu_r, y_r)$ *as in* (3.1). *Then, if SRPP is satisfied by type i consumers for all* $i = 1, \ldots, I$, $\lim_{r \to \infty} H_r(0, \mu_r, y_r) = 0$.

Proof. See Appendix.

How strong is SRPP? The following proposition provides two conditions under which SRPP is satisfied.

PROPOSITION 4. *A type i consumer satisfies SRPP if either one of the following conditions holds*:

(1) U_i *is defined on an open subset containing* R_+^{K+1}, *and is differentiable, quasi-concave, and strictly increasing in every argument*;

(2) U_i *is quasi-convex, i.e.,* $U_i(x) = U_i(x') \Rightarrow U_i(\lambda x + (1 - \lambda)x') \leqslant U_i(x)$ *if* $0 \leqslant \lambda \leqslant 1$.

Proof. (1) Consider the SRPP definition. Since U_i is quasi-concave and differentiable, (3) of the definition implies by the Kuhn–Tucker necessary conditions that there exists $\lambda \geqslant 0$ such that $\partial U_i/\partial x_k \leqslant \lambda p_k^*$ for all $k \in S$ with equality if $x_k > 0$. Since $p^* \cdot x > 0$, $x \neq 0$ and so

$$\lambda = \max_k \left[\frac{\partial U_i}{\partial x_k} \Big/ p_k^* \right]$$

is independent of k'. Hence, by the Kuhn–Tucker sufficiency conditions, (3.3) holds.

(2) Suppose that (3.3) is violated, i.e., there exists $x' \in R_+^{K+1}$ such that $U_i(x') > U_i(x)$ and $p^* \cdot x' \leqslant p^* \cdot x$. Assume also that $p_k^* \neq 0$ for all k. For each $k' \notin \tilde{S}$, let $x(k')$ be the bundle such that $x_k(k') = x'_k$ if $k \in \tilde{S}$, $x_k(k') = 0$ if $k \notin \tilde{S} \cup \{k'\}$ and $x_{k'}(k') = (p^* \cdot x' - \sum_{k \in \tilde{S}} p_k^* x'_k)/p_{k'}^*$. Then x' is a convex combination of the $x(k')$, $k' \notin \tilde{S}$, with weights $p_{k'}^* x'_{k'}/(p^* \cdot x' - \sum_{k \in \tilde{S}} p_k^* x'_k)$. But since $p^* \cdot x(k') \leqslant p^* \cdot x$, we know from (3) of the SRPP definition that $U_i(x) \geqslant U_i(x(k'))$ for each $k' \notin \tilde{S}$. Therefore, since U_i is quasi-convex, $U_i(x) \geqslant U_i(x')$, which is a contradiction.

A contradiction can be obtained on similar lines for the case where $p_k^* = 0$ for some k.

Q.E.D.

Putting Theorem 3 and Proposition 4(1) together, we obtain a result which was also proved in Hart (1979a): if preferences are representable by a differentiable, quasi-concave utility function, an MCE is approximately Pareto optimal when r is large.

We have indicated previously that what SRPP rules out is the case where goods $k = 1, \ldots, K$ are strongly complementary, i.e., consuming two or more simultaneously is worth much more than consuming any one by itself. We see from Proposition 4 that this sort of complementarity differs substantially from the usual notion of complementarity. For complementarity in the usual sense that compensated cross elasticities of demand are negative is certainly not ruled out by differentiable, quasi-concave utility functions. Yet complementarity in the sense of this paper *is* ruled out under these conditions.

The inefficiencies that arise when the SRPP condition fails can be traced to a lack of coordination of production decisions provided by the market system. If several highly complementary goods are not being produced, then, while it may be socially desirable for these new goods to be produced simultaneously, it may not be in the interest of any single firm to produce one (or some) of these goods alone, since the price that one new good will fetch on the market in the absence of the other goods may be very low.[8] It is important to note that this coordination failure is not caused by the existence of monopoly power or by a divergence between private and social benefits. In fact, the private and social benefits from product innovation are (approximately) equal when r is large. (This follows from the fact that, as shown in the Appendix, a firm can market new goods at their reservation prices. This implies that there is no consumer surplus and hence that consumer surplus plus producer surplus equals profit.) To put it another way, the problem of coordi-

[8] A similar phenomenon has been noted by Spence (1976) in the case where firms are imperfectly competitive.

nating the production of new goods must be faced in a planned economy as well as in a market economy.

Since there is no divergence between private and social benefits, we might expect the coordination problem not to arise if it is technologically feasible for a single firm to produce all the new goods by itself on the same terms as all firms taken together.

THEOREM 5. *Let* $\epsilon \geqslant 0$ *and the selection functions* $F_1, F_2, \ldots,$ *be given. Suppose* $(\mu_r, p_r, \mathscr{Y}_r)$ *is a sequence of* ϵ*-MCEs in the economies* E_r, $r = 1, 2, \ldots,$ *and, for each* r, *define* y_r *as in* (2.1). *Assume* (A.1)–(A.7) *and that each limit point* y *of* (y_r) *is regular. Assume also that for some* $\eta > 0$ *and* r' *the following is true for* $k > 0$: *either* $\sum_{j=1}^{J} y_{jkr} > \eta$ *or* $\sum_{j=1}^{J} y_{jkr} = 0$ *for all* $r \geqslant r'$. *Then the following is a sufficient condition that* $\lim_{r\to\infty} H_r(\epsilon, \mu_r, y_r) = 0$:

$$Y_j = Y \text{ is independent of } j \text{ and } Y + Y \subset Y. \tag{3.4}$$

Proof. See Appendix.

A similar result to Theorem 5 may be found also in Makowski (1980). It should be noted that, in order to get full optimality, it is not sufficient to assume that each firm can produce every good—we require the stronger assumption that each firm can produce these goods on the same terms as the aggregate economy. An example in Section 4 will illustrate the importance of this latter assumption.

We conclude this section with a number of remarks.

(A) The failure of the market mechanism to generate an optimal allocation of resources in the absence of SRPP can be traced to the existence of pecuniary externalities. Pecuniary externalities arise when the profits of one firm depend on the actions of another firm even though perfectly competitive conditions prevail and there are no direct interdependencies through the production sets (see Scitovsky, 1954). We have seen that, if SRPP is violated, then the profits that a firm gets from marketing a new product will depend on whether other firms are marketing products which are complementary to this new product. Hence there are indeed pecuniary externalities according to the above definition. Note that, in our model, pecuniary externalities only arise with respect to the production of new commodities, i.e., the opening of new markets. This is consistent with the interpretation of pecuniary externalities given by Heller and Starrett (1976). Heller and Starrett, however, trace the existence of pecuniary externalities to firms' incorrect expectations about the prices that new products will fetch on the market. In contrast, in our model, pecuniary externalities, and the market failure that they cause, can occur even if all firms have correct expectations, i.e., even if they know the function $F_r(y)$.[9]

[9] The coordination problems arising in the absence of SRPP bear a resemblance also to those stressed in the economic development literature by Rosenstein–Rodan (1943)

(B) It is important to note that the sufficient condition for SRPP given in Proposition 4(1)—that consumers' preferences be convex and differentiable—is a condition on *individual* preferences. In particular, replicating the economy does not convexify preferences in such a way that SRPP will hold approximately in a large economy (even if preferences are differentiable). In fact, the size of the economy has no effect at all on whether a vector of prices, each of which is a reservation price for a particular nonproduced good by itself, will serve as reservation prices for all nonproduced goods taken together.

The fact that convex, differentiable preferences prevent coordination failures has been noted also in other contexts. See Marshak and Radner (1972) for examples in the theory of teams and Grossman (1977) for a discussion of planning when there are many planners.

(C) We have noted that, in the absence of SRPP, the profit which firms can make from simultaneously producing new products may outweigh the sum of the profits to each firm from producing a new product by itself. One way around this problem is for an entrepreneur to take over or merge a number of firms of different types and coordinate the production of new products. If such mergers are costless, then any production plan which can be written as $\sum_{j=1}^{J} \sum_{t=1}^{n_j} y_{jt}$ becomes feasible. Letting Y denote the set of all such plans, we see that $Y + Y \subset Y$ and hence Theorem 5 tells us that, under these conditions, the inefficiencies due to coordination failures disappear.

The assumption that mergers can occur costlessly is, however, strong. First, finding out which firms to merge and which combinations of new products to produce will in general require the use of resources. Second, a merged company may be less efficient than a collection of firms operating independently. For example, suppose that ski services and hotel services are complementary goods. Some entrepreneurs may be very good at providing the former, and other entrepreneurs may be very good at providing the latter, but nobody may be very good at providing both services. An entrepreneur who attempts to coordinate production of these two services may find that he faces a production set which is considerably less efficient than the sum of the individual production sets. Finally, note that, if mergers are easy, they may take place not to coordinate the production of new commodities but with the purpose of restricting competition and exploiting monopoly power. In this case, of course, the competitive model studied in this paper loses much of its plausibility.

This is not to deny, of course, that mergers can be important in overcoming coordination problems. In fact, it may be possible empirically to

---

and others. The latter are not traced specifically to the production of new products, however, and would seem to have more to do with imperfectly competitive conditions in the production of existing products.

explain some mergers as attempts to internalize pecuniary externalities. See Makowski (1980) on this point.

(D) It should be emphasized that the assumption that there is free entry of firms, subject to the payment of a setup cost, is not crucial to our analysis. In particular, it is not this assumption which is responsible for the realization of competitive conditions when r is large, and hence for making Theorems 2, 3, and 5 work. As we have argued in a previous paper (Hart, 1979a), perfect competition is achieved when individual agents are small relative to the aggregate economy; this is true even if an agent is the sole supplier of a particular good. Of course, an agent with unique characteristics will generally earn supernormal profits or rents, but this does not change the fact that the agent will face a flat demand curve. Hence there will be no divergence between marginal revenue and price. The role of free entry is simply to bid away these rents. In other words, free entry reduces the height of the demand curve but it does not make it any flatter.

While it is therefore possible to generalize Theorems 2, 3, and 5 to the case where there is not free entry along the lines of Hart [1979a], it should be noted that an extra assumption is now required. This is that firms' production sets are bounded. This assumption is important in showing that operating firms are maximizing profits at the prices p in the limit economy. For if an operating firm's production plan, y_r, grows in such a way that y_r/r is bounded away from zero, then by ceasing to operate this firm will have an effect on per capita supplies and hence on prices even in the limit $r = \infty$, and so competitive conditions may not prevail.

While this can also happen in the free entry case, it does not matter here. For, in this case, in order to show that operating firms are maximizing profit at prices p, it is enough to show that no new firm can make a profit from entering at a fixed scale. Since when r is large, such a firm will have a negligible effect on prices, competitive conditions do prevail in the appropriate sense even when production sets are unbounded. (So, in particular, Theorems 2, 3, and 5 apply when there are increasing returns to scale.)[10]

(E) Theorem 1 establishes the existence of an ϵ-MCE when r is large for the case $\epsilon > 0$. As we have noted, proving the existence of an ϵ-MCE for $\epsilon = 0$ is considerably more difficult and requires stronger assumptions—see Novshek and Sonnenschein (1978). Among other things, it is necessary to assume for exact existence that demand curves are downward sloping in the neighborhood of a competitive equilibrium in the limit economy. While the approximate equilibrium approach studied here therefore yields some simplifications—in the sense that weaker assumptions are needed—the

[10] I am grateful to William Novshek and Hugo Sonnenschein for helpful discussions on the relationship between free entry and perfect competition.

approach should be treated with caution. In particular, why are consumers prepared to put up with a utility level which is ϵ away from the maximal level? It may be possible to justify this assumption by appealing to transaction costs or information costs. In the absence of a rigorous justification along these or other lines, however, the approximate equilibrium approach is somewhat ad hoc in comparison with the exact approach. (Note that while the use of approximate equilibria is important for our existence result, Theorem 1, it is not important for our optimality results, Theorems 2, 3, and 5. The latter apply also to exact MCEs.)

One assumption which we require to prove the existence of even an approximate MCE is that production sets are bounded. If there are everywhere increasing returns to scale, our proof of Theorem 1 fails. It may, however, be possible to prove existence even in the increasing returns case if stronger assumptions are made on the demand side. For the problem that arises in in the usual competitive situation when there are increasing returns to scale —that firms will expand indefinitely—does not apply here. This is because, since firms are not price takers but face demand curves with finite elasticity, such expansion will not generally be profitable. We hope to analyze the question of existence of monopolistically competitive equilibrium under increasing returns to scale in future work.

4. Some Examples

We now present some examples which illustrate how Theorem 3 can break down if SRPP does not hold.

Suppose that $K = 2$ and that there is only one type of consumer, whose preferences are represented by the utility function

$$U = x_0^{1/2} + x_1^{1/2} x_2^{1/2}.$$

Let $J = 2$ and assume that $Y_1 = \{(-1, 1, 0)\} \cup \{0\}$, $Y_2 = \{(-1, 0, 1)\} \cup \{0\}$, and that the aggregate per capita endowment of the unreplicated economy $=$ $w_0 = 3$. Consider the following allocation in E_r: no firms set up, $p_0 = 1$, $p_1 = p_2 = \infty$, $x_0 = 3$ for each consumer. It is easy to see that this is an exact MCE for each r. The reason is that if a type 1 or type 2 firm starts to produce good 1 or good 2, it will make losses since

$$\left.\frac{\partial U}{\partial x_1}\right|_{x_2=0} = \left.\frac{\partial U}{\partial x_2}\right|_{x_1=0} = 0.$$

However, the allocation is Pareto dominated by one in which $x_0 = x_1 = x_2 =$ 1 and r firms of each type set up in the economy E_r.

Clearly SRPP is violated here since $p_1 = 0$ is a reservation price given the bundle $(w, 0, 0)$ when only goods 0 and 1 can be traded, $p_2 = 0$ is a reservation price when only goods 0 and 2 can be traded, but $p_1 = p_2 = 0$ is not a reservation price vector when all goods can be traded. Preferences are convex in this example. The reason that Proposition 4(1) does not apply is because U is not *differentiable* when $x_1 = x_2 = 0$. (This example corresponds to the case of nuts and bolts considered in the Introduction.)

While it is clear from the above that difficulties can arise even with convex preferences, it might be argued that problems are likely to be rare in this case, since convex preferences are almost everywhere smooth.[11] We turn now to a case where preferences are nonconvex. We will call this the shopping center example.[12]

Consider a region which is served by a single shopping center. The shopping center is assumed to be of unlimited size so that there is no limit to the number of shops which can set up in it. Consumers are located in various parts of the region and must pay a transportation cost to visit the shopping center. We will assume that this transportation cost—which may be regarded as the opportunity cost of the consumers' time—depends on the time of the day when the trip to the shopping center is made. Shops, as well as deciding what goods to sell, must also decide at what times to be open.

It will be assumed that there are n "basic" commodities which can be provided by shops and that the day is split up into a finite number of subperiods, T. Since two commodities which are available at different times of the day are different goods, the total number of possible goods available in the shopping center is Tn. To this we add the good leisure, which consumers are endowed with and which corresponds to the nonproduced good of the model of Sections 2 and 3. Thus $K + 1 = Tn + 1$.

Let us order the goods so that good 0 is leisure, goods $1, \ldots, n$ are the n basic commodities available in subperiod $t = 1$, goods $n + 1, \ldots, 2n$ are the n basic commodities available in subperiod $t = 2$, etc. Also let $e(t, j) \in R^{Tn+1}$ be the vector whose zeroth coordinate is -1, whose $((t - 1)n + j)$th coordinate is $+1$ and whose other coordinates are zero. We will assume that $J = n$ and that $Y_j = \{e(1, j), e(2, j), \ldots, e(T, j)\} \cup \{0\}$, $j = 1, \ldots, n$. In other words, a type j firm, if it sets up, uses one unit of leisure (i.e., labor) to produce one unit of commodity j, and this unit can then be sold in any one subperiod of

[11] To be more precise, Mas-Colell (1977) has shown that if preferences are convex, almost all consumption bundles have a unique supporting price vector.

[12] In the following example, not only are preferences nonconvex, but they are also discontinuous, and hence nondifferentiable, at some points. It is the nonconvexity of preferences, however, which is responsible for the breakdown of Theorem 3. Note that examples in which preferences are nonconvex but differentiable, and where Theorem 3 breaks down, can easily be constructed.

the day. We assume, however, that it is impossible for a particular shop to be open in more than one subperiod or to produce more than one unit.

To simplify matters, we will assume that there is only one type of consumer. The consumer's preferences are represented by the utility function

$$U(x) = V(x_0 - t(x), (x_1 + x_{n+1} + x_{2n+1} + \cdots + x_{(T-1)n+1}),\ldots,$$
$$(x_n + x_{2n} + \cdots + x_{Tn})), \tag{4.1}$$

where V is some function mapping R_+^{n+1} into R,

$$t(x) = \sum_{t=1}^{T} b_t \delta\left(\sum_{h=(t-1)n+1}^{tn} x_h\right), \tag{4.2}$$

and $\delta(y) = 1$ if $y > 0$, $\delta(y) = 0$ if $y = 0$.

The idea behind this is that consumers are interested only in aggregate consumption of each basic commodity and are indifferent about when the commodity is purchased except in so far as transportation costs are affected by this. Transportation costs are paid by consumers themselves out of leisure time. It is assumed that a visit to the shopping center during subperiod t uses up $b_t > 0$ units of leisure, $t = 1,\ldots, T$, but that, once the consumer is at the shopping center, the cost of shopping is zero.

The consumption set of consumers is given by

$$X = \{x \in R_+^{K+1} \mid x_0 - t(x) \geqslant 0\}. \tag{4.3}$$

In contrast to the model of Sections 2 and 3, $X \neq R_+^{K+1}$. In fact, since t is nonconvex, X is not convex. However, this difference between the models is not important; in particular, Theorem 2 can easily be generalized to the shopping center example.

What is important from our point of view is that the nonconvexity of t makes preferences nonconvex. That is, even if V is a quasi-concave (or concave) function, U will not be; in particular, if $b_1 = b_2$, consumers will be indifferent between purchasing one unit of commodity k in subperiod 1 or one unit of commodity k in subperiod 2, but will prefer either of these possibilities to purchasing half a unit in each subperiod.

Not only are preferences nonconvex, but also SRPP is in general violated.[13] Suppose, for example, that $n = 2$ and that

$$V(x_0, x_1, x_2) = x_0 + x_1^{1/2} + x_2^{1/2}. \tag{4.4}$$

[13] Note that Proposition 4(2) will not generally apply here since utilities may not be quasiconvex over consumption within subperiod t, once the transportation cost b_t has been incurred.

Consider an initial situation in which the consumer consumes only good 0. What is the consumer's willingness to pay for commodity 1 in some subperiod t? Since such a purchase involves a transportation cost of b_t, it is clear that the consumer must receive at least $(b_t)^2$ units of commodity 1 to make the transaction worthwhile. Since V is concave, it follows that the reservation price of commodity 1 in subperiod t—where we normalize so that the price of good 0 is 1—is just

$$p_1^* = \frac{\partial V}{\partial x_1} \Big/ \frac{\partial V}{\partial x_0}, \qquad \text{evaluated at some } x_1 \geqslant (b_t)^2, \tag{4.5}$$

where

$$-b_t - p_1^* x_1 + x_1^{1/2} = 0. \tag{4.6}$$

At this price the consumer is just indifferent between purchasing commodity 1 and not purchasing it. (We are assuming that the consumer's endowment of leisure is large.)

It is easy to see that (4.5), (4.6) are satisfied by

$$x_1 = 4(b_t)^2, \qquad p_1^* = 1/4b_t .$$

By symmetry, the reservation price of commodity 2 in subperiod t, p_2^*, is also $1/4b_t$.

However, if both commodities 1 and 2 are made available in subperiod t, (p_1^*, p_2^*) are not reservation prices. For if the consumer sets

$$x_1 = x_2 = 2(b_t)^2,$$

then

$$-b_t - p_1^* x_1 - p_2^* x_2 + x_1^{1/2} + x_2^{1/2} > 0, \tag{4.7}$$

and so the consumer is better off purchasing commodities 1 and 2 than not doing so. Hence SRPP is violated.

In fact it is easy to construct cases where Theorem 3 is violated in this example. Choose any subperiod t and consider the economy which is the same as the above except that the set of potential goods consists only of good 0 and commodities 1 and 2 available in subperiod t. Replicate this economy and consider a sequence of ϵ-MCE allocations in which both commodities 1 and 2 are produced. Then if $b_{t'} > \frac{1}{4}$ for all $t' \neq t$, these allocations are also ϵ-MCE allocations for the economy in which the set of potential goods consists of good 0 and commodities 1 and 2 available in all subperiods. For consider the consequences of a shop setting up and supplying one unit of commodity 1 or 2 in subperiod t'. The revenue it obtains from this cannot possibly exceed p_1^* $(= p_2^*)$. But if $b_{t'} > \frac{1}{4}$,

$$p_1^* = p_2^* = 1/4b_t' < 1,$$

and so the shop does not cover its setup cost.

However, if $b_t' < b_t$ for some t', then this sequence of ϵ-MCEs is far from being Pareto optimal since a Pareto improvement could be achieved by getting every shop which is supplying some commodity in subperiod t to supply the same commodity in subperiod t'. In other words, there is a market equilibrium in which all firms are open at the same socially inefficient hours! (There is, however, also another market equilibrium in which all firms are open at the right hours.) The reason that the economy can get stuck with firms being open at the wrong times is that, because of transportation costs, the gain (both private and social) from a single shop switching from subperiod t to t' is small, while the gain from all shops simultaneously switching is large.[14]

It is easy to generalize this example in a number of directions. For example, if we drop the assumption that it is prohibitively expensive for shops to open for more than one subperiod, and if we introduce several types of consumers, then we can construct cases where it is socially desirable for each shop to open during two subperiods, say 9 AM–5 PM and 7 PM–9 PM, but where there are monopolistically competitive equilibria in which shops open only from 9 AM–5 PM. One can also easily generate cases in which there is an inefficient monopolistically competitive equilibrium, in which no shops open at all, i.e., only good 0 is consumed, again because the gain to any single shop from opening in some subperiod is far less than the gain from all shops opening in this subperiod (for a case of this type, see the example below).

It might be thought that the above inefficiencies would disappear if we permitted shops to produce several different commodities simultaneously. The following argument shows that this is not necessarily the case.

Assume that $J = n = 2$, and let the technologies of the two types of shops now be such that, at a cost of one unit of good 0, a type 1 shop can produce the combination (1, C) of commodities 1 and 2, and a type 2 shop can produce the combination (C, 1), where $0 \leqslant C < 1$. The assumption that $C < 1$ means that shop 1 (resp. shop 2) has a comparative advantage in commodity 1 (resp. commodity 2). Assume also that $V(x_1, x_2)$ is as in (4.4).

Consider an initial situation in which no shops operate at all and so only

[14] Note that the shopping center example can be reinterpreted as a location example. Instead of thinking of goods j, $n + j$, $2n + j$,... as being the same commodity available at different times of the day, we can think of them as being the same commodity available at different locations. The transportation cost is then the cost of traveling to a particular location.

good 0 is consumed. Suppose that a shop sets up and produces the combination (y_1, y_2) in some subperiod t. Then an upper limit to the amount of revenue which the shop can obtain is given by the aggregate willingness of consumers to pay for the bundle (y_1, y_2). To evaluate the latter, assume that the (y_1, y_2) is divided equally among λ consumers (we allow λ to take nonintegral values). Then, the maximum amount which can be extracted from each consumer is given by W where

$$-W - b_t + \left(\frac{y_1}{\lambda}\right)^{1/2} + \left(\frac{y_2}{\lambda}\right)^{1/2} = 0. \tag{4.8}$$

The aggregate amount extracted is therefore

$$\lambda W = -\lambda b_t + \lambda^{1/2} y_1^{1/2} + \lambda^{1/2} y_2^{1/2}, \tag{4.9}$$

which is maximized when

$$\frac{d}{d\lambda}(\lambda W) = -b_t + \tfrac{1}{2}\lambda^{-1/2}(y_1^{1/2} + y_2^{1/2}) = 0. \tag{4.10}$$

Substituting (4.10) into (4.9), we obtain

$$R = \frac{(y_1^{1/2} + y_2^{1/2})^2}{4b_t} \tag{4.11}$$

as an upper limit to the shop's revenue.

We see that the shop makes a profit only if

$$\frac{(y_1^{1/2} + y_2^{1/2})^2}{4b_t} \geqslant 1.$$

Hence no type 1 shop will set up unless

$$(1 + c^{1/2})^2 \geqslant 4b_t,$$

and if $b_t > \frac{1}{4}$, we can always choose C small enough and positive so that this is not the case. The same argument applies of course to type 2 shops.

Thus even though both types of shops can produce both commodities, neither will find it profitable to enter even when r is large. Furthermore, this is in spite of the fact that it is socially desirable for both types of shops to set up; this can be seen from the fact that total consumer willingness to pay for one unit each of commodities 1 and 2 in subperiod t is given by

$$R = \frac{(y_1^{1/2} + y_2^{1/2})^2}{4b_t} = \frac{(1+1)^2}{4b_t} = 1/b_t,$$

which exceeds 2, the cost of setting up one shop of each type, as long as $b_t < \frac{1}{2}$.

In other words, allowing firms (shops) to market several goods does not by itself remove the possibility that the economy will get stuck in a situation where the wrong goods are being produced. In the above example, a profit could be made by a firm which produced one unit each of commodities 1 and 2 at cost less than or equal to 2. However, by assumption, there is no firm capable of doing this. Type 1 firms are able to produce only the combination (1, C) at cost 1, and type 2 firms only the combination (C, 1) at cost 1, where $C < 1$. If the firms could combine their activities, they could produce $(1 + C, 1 + C)$ at cost 2 and so would make a profit (see Theorem 5 and Remark (C) in Section 3). But, acting by themselves, they cannot. We see then that coordination problems arise even if firms can produce several goods simultaneously as long as they cannot produce them in the "right" proportions.

5. Conclusions

In this paper we have considered whether a competitive economy will provide a Pareto optimal allocation of goods when firms must choose not only what quantities of goods to produce, but also the qualities of these goods. We have shown that in general the answer to this question is no. The reason is that if the products of different firms are strongly complementary (although not in the usual sense), then the private (and social) gain from several firms simultaneously producing new products may far outweigh the sum of the gains to each firm from producing a new product by itself. The market mechanism, however, provides no obvious way for different firms' production choices to be coordinated. Thus, the economy may get stuck in a situation where the wrong (from the Pareto point of view) set of goods is being produced, but each agent is acting optimally given the actions of other agents.

One case where this problem does not arise is when consumers' preferences satisfy what we have called the simultaneous reservation price property. Under these conditions firms' products are sufficiently substitutable that uncoordinated optimizing behavior by individual agents will ensure that the market equilibrium is approximately Pareto optimal in a large economy. A sufficient condition for the simultaneous reservation price property to hold is that consumers' preferences are convex and can be represented by a differentiable utility function. (Note that the convexity condition must hold at the individual level—the existence of large numbers of agents does not convexify in the appropriate sense.) A second case where the coordination problem does not arise is if each firm has access to the production set of the whole economy. This case can occur even if the primitive production sets of individual firms differ, as long as it is possible for firms to merge costlessly so as to take advantage of the sum of their individual production possibilities.

It may be useful to contrast our results with the "first" theorem of welfare economics. This theorem says that in economies with complete markets (i.e., markets for all conceivable commodities), competitive equilibria are Pareto optimal whatever properties preferences have (transaction costs of the type considered in our example of Section 4 cause no problems for this result; see Foley, 1970, or Kurz, 1974). In the model of this paper, however, the properties of consumer preferences play a crucial role. The reason for the difference is that complete market economies provide a much richer set of signals to agents than incomplete market economies.

Consider again the example of the nuts and bolts manufacturers given in the Introduction. We argued that it might be unprofitable for either manufacturer to set up by himself, but profitable for both to set up together. Hence, without coordination, a profitable opportunity may be missed. (Furthermore, this coordination problem can arise even if there is a firm which can manufacture both nuts and bolts; see Section 4.) In a complete market model, this cannot happen. For if it is unprofitable for the bolt manufacturer to set up, it must be because the price of bolts is low and, if it is unprofitable for the nut manufacturer to set up, it must be because the price of nuts is low. But this means that consumers will be able to buy the combination of nuts and bolts at a low price and hence will register large demands for these goods on the two markets. In other words, in a complete market economy consumers can signal their demands for combinations of products which are not being produced, while in an incomplete market model they cannot.

Finally, let us compare our results with those of Drèze and Hagen (1978). Drèze and Hagen also argue that the benefits from several firms simultaneously producing new products may exceed the sum of the benefits from any one firm going it alone, and that, as a result, the market equilibrium may be suboptimal. However, they trace this phenomenon to the fact that if, as they assume, each firm can produce only one good at a time, then the set of feasible allocations of the economy is nonconvex; this in turn implies that the first-order conditions for Pareto optimality are necessary but not sufficient. In our model, however, the nonconvexity emphasized by Drèze and Hagen is unimportant. In particular, as we replicate the economy to obtain competitive conditions, the nonconvexity in the set of feasible allocations disappears (see the Appendix and also Hart (1979a)). In fact, as we have emphasized, in our model any deviations between the benefits from several firms simultaneously producing new products and from one firm going it alone are caused by the nonsatisfaction of the simultaneous reservation price property —which is a condition on preferences—rather than by nonconvexities in the feasible set.

Appendix

In this Appendix, we establish Theorems 1, 2, 3, and 5. We begin by defining the limit economy to which the economies E_r converge.

Recall that $\tilde{Y}_j$ is the smallest closed convex cone with vertex at the origin which contains Y_j. Then the limit economy E_∞ is defined as follows: it contains I types of consumers, where each type i consumer has utility function U_i, consumption set R_+^{K+1} and endowment w_i as in Section 2; and there are J "industries" where industry j has a production set given by $\tilde{Y}_j$.

An *allocation* in E_∞ is an array $(\mu, y) = (\mu_1, \ldots, \mu_I, y_1, \ldots, y_J)$, where μ_i is a probability measure defined on the Borel subsets of R_+^{K+1} and $y \in R^{(K+1)J}$. As in Section 2, $\mu_i(B)$ denotes the fraction of type i consumers whose consumption bundles lie in B for each Borel subset B of R_+^{K+1}. The allocation is *feasible* if

$$y_j \in \tilde{Y}_j \qquad \text{for each } j; \tag{1}$$

$$\sum_{i=1}^{I} \int x \, d\mu_i - \sum_{j=1}^{J} y_j - \sum_{i=1}^{I} w_i = 0. \tag{2}$$

The difference between E_∞ and E_r then is that in E_∞ we ignore the problems which arise from there having to be an integral number of firms (we replace Y_j by $\tilde{Y}_j$) and from there having to be an integral number of consumers (we drop (2.8)).

It is easy to check that every feasible allocation in E_r is also a feasible allocation in E_∞. One important effect of replacing Y_j by $\tilde{Y}_j$ and of allowing μ_i to be an arbitrary measure is to convexify the economy. In particular, it may easily be checked that the set of feasible allocations in E_∞ is convex.

We now define an approximate competitive equilibrium in E_∞ under the assumption that industries are price takers and that markets are open, i.e., finite prices are quoted, for *all* goods.

Definition. An ϵ-competitive equilibrium in E_∞, $\epsilon \geqslant 0$, is an array (μ, p, y), where $\mu = (\mu_1, \ldots, \mu_I)$, $y = (y_1, \ldots, y_J)$, such that

$$(\mu, y) \text{ is a feasible allocation in } E_\infty; \tag{3}$$

$$p \in R_+^{K+1}; \tag{4}$$

$$p \cdot x_i \leqslant p \cdot w_i + \sum_{j=1}^{J} \bar{\Theta}_{ij} p \cdot y_j \qquad \text{and}$$

$$U_i(x) > U_i(x_i) + \epsilon \Rightarrow p \cdot x > p \cdot w_i + \sum_{j=1}^{J} \bar{\Theta}_{ij} p \cdot y_j$$

$$\text{for all} \quad x_i \in \operatorname{Supp} \mu_i \quad (i = 1, \ldots, I); \tag{5}$$

$$p \cdot y_j \geqslant p \cdot y_j' \qquad \text{for all} \quad y_j' \in \tilde{Y}_j \quad (j = 1, \ldots, J). \tag{6}$$

Note that, since $\tilde{Y}_j$ is a cone, (6) implies that $p \cdot y_j = 0$ for all j. It is easy to establish

RESULT 1. *Assume* (A.1)–(A.7). *Then an* ϵ*-competitive equilibrium exists in* E_∞ *for all* $\epsilon \geqslant 0$.

Proof. Since E_∞ is a convex economy, standard techniques establish the existence of an exact competitive equilibrium in E_∞. An exact equilibrium is also an ϵ-equilibrium, however, for $\epsilon \geqslant 0$. Q.E.D.

We will say that (μ, y) is an ϵ-competitive equilibrium allocation in E_∞ if, for some p, (μ, p, y) is an ϵ-competitive equilibrium.

We now turn to the definition of Pareto optimality in E_∞. We will restrict attention to allocations with the approximate equal treatment property, i.e., $\| U_i(x) - U_i(x')\| \leqslant \epsilon$ for all $x, x' \in \text{Supp } \mu_i$ $(i = 1,..., I)$.

DEFINITION. Consider a feasible allocation (μ, y) in E_∞ satisfying the approximate equal treatment property. We say that the allocation (μ', y') ϵ-Pareto dominates (μ, y) if $U_i(x') > U_i(x) + \epsilon$ for all $x' \in \text{Supp } \mu_i'$, $x \in \text{Supp } \mu_i$ and all $i = 1,..., I$. We say that (μ, y) is ϵ-Pareto optimal if there is no feasible allocation which ϵ-Pareto dominates it.

The next proposition follows from standard arguments.

RESULT 2. *Let* (μ, y) *be an* ϵ*-competitive equilibrium allocation in* E_∞. *Then* (μ, y) *is* ϵ*-Pareto optimal in* E_∞.

So far we have assumed that all markets are open in E_∞, even markets for goods which are not produced in a competitive equilibrium. We now develop a notion of competitive equilibrium which is relevant when some markets are closed.

Recall that, given the production allocation $y = (y_1,..., y_J)$, $M(y) = \{k > 0 \mid \sum_{j=1}^{J} y_{jk} > 0\} \cup \{0\}$ is the set of goods which are produced, plus good 0. Also if S is a subset of $\{0,..., K\}$, $R^S = \{x \in R^{K+1} \mid x_k = 0 \text{ if } k \notin S\}$.

DEFINITION. The feasible allocation (μ, y) in E_∞ is said to be an *ϵ-restricted competitive equilibrium allocation relative to* $S \supset M(y)$ (ϵ-RCEA relative to S) if there exists $p \in R_+^{\#S}$ such that (μ, p, y) is an ϵ-competitive equilibrium for the economy $\hat{E}_\infty$ in which consumer i's consumption set is $R_+{}^S$ and each $\tilde{Y}_j$ is replaced by $\hat{Y}_j = \tilde{Y}_j \cap R^S$.

In other words, in a restricted competitive equilibrium, prices are quoted only for a subset of goods and both producers and consumers can supply and demand only these goods (another way of looking at this is that consumers face infinite prices for nonmarketed goods and producers face zero prices for such goods—by the free disposal assumption, producers will never wish to set $y_k > 0$ if $k \notin S$).

Note that we assume that prices are always quoted for good 0 and for all produced goods. Note also that a full ϵ-competitive equilibrium is just an ϵ-RCEA relative to $S = \{0, \ldots, K\}$.

We can also generalize the notion of Pareto optimality to cases where not all markets are open.

DEFINITION. The feasible allocation (μ, y) in E_∞, satisfying the approximate equal treatment property, is said to be an *ϵ-restricted Pareto optimum relative to $S \supset M(y)$* (ϵ-RPO relative to S) if there is no feasible allocation (μ', y'), satisfying $\sum_{j=1}^{J} y'_{jk} = 0$ for all $k \notin S$, which ϵ-Pareto dominates (μ, y).

In other words, an allocation is ϵ-RPO relative to S if a central planner who can allocate only goods in S cannot achieve a Pareto improvement.

The following is an obvious generalization of Result 2.

RESULT 3. *Let (μ, y) be an* ϵ-RCEA *relative to $S \supset M(y)$. Then (μ, y) is an* ϵ-RPO *relative to S.*

We return now to a consideration of the finite economies E_r. The following lemma will be useful in the proof of Theorem 1.

LEMMA 1. *Suppose that (μ, p, y) is an* exact *competitive equilibrium in E_r. Let (y_r) be a sequence of points converging to y, such that $y_r \in Y_r$ for each r. Then, given $\epsilon > 0$, we can find r' such that for all $r \geq r'$, there exists an ϵ-exchange equilibrium (μ_r, p_r, y_r) in the economy E_r, with $p_r = p$.*

Proof. By the definition of a competitive equilibrium in E_∞, each component of p is finite. In addition, $p_k > 0$ for all k by (A.5) and (A.6). For each r sufficienly large, choose an array $(x_{itr})_{i=1,\ldots,I, t=1,\ldots,r}$ of nonnegative consumption bundles for the r type i consumers satisfying

$$\frac{1}{r}\sum_{i,t} x_{itr} - \sum_{j} y_{jr} - \sum_{i} w_i = 0, \tag{7}$$

and such that, for each i, the distance between Supp μ_i and the set $\{x_{itr} \mid t = 1, \ldots, r\}$ tends to zero as r tends to infinity.

Although the x_{itr} satisfy feasibility, they will not generally satisfy the budget constraints

$$p \cdot x_{itr} \leq p \cdot w_i + \sum_{j} \bar{\Theta}_{ij} p \cdot y_{jr}. \tag{8}$$

Note, however, that (7) implies that

$$\sum_{i,t} p \cdot x_{itr} = r \left[\sum_i p \cdot w_i + \sum_i \sum_j \bar{\Theta}_{ij} p \cdot y_{jr} \right].$$

Therefore we may define new bundles

$$x'_{itr} = x_{itr} + \tau_{itr}, \tag{9}$$

where the $\tau_{itr} \in R^{K+1}$ are chosen so that (a) for each i, t either $\tau_{itr} \in R_+^{K+1}$ or $\tau_{itr} \in R_-^{K+1}$; (b) $\sum_{i,t} \tau_{itr} = 0$ and (c)

$$p \cdot \tau_{itr} = p \cdot w_i + \sum_j \bar{\Theta}_{ij} p \cdot y_{jr} - p \cdot x_{itr}. \tag{10}$$

(To construct such τ_{itr}, take goods away from those for whom (8) is violated and give these goods to those for whom (8) holds with strict inequality.)

Let μ_r be the measure corresponding to the bundles (x'_{itr}). We claim that, for large r, (μ_r, p_r, y_r) is an ϵ-exchange equilibrium in E_r. The only condition that remains to be established is (2.7). Suppose (2.7) is violated for large r. Then we can find sequences (x'_{itr}), (x''_{itr}) such that

$$U_i(x''_{itr}) > U_i(x'_{itr}) + \epsilon \quad \text{and} \quad p \cdot x''_{itr} \leqslant p \cdot w_i + \sum_j \bar{\Theta}_{ij} p \cdot y_{jr}. \tag{11}$$

Since the components of p are strictly positive, (11) implies that the sequence (x''_{itr}) is bounded. Assume without loss of generality (w.l.o.g.) that $\lim_{r\to\infty} x''_{itr} = x''_i$. Note also that, since $y_{jr} \to y_j$ and since each limit point of the (x_{itr}) lies in Supp μ_i, (10) implies that $\lim_{r\to\infty} p \cdot \tau_{itr} = 0$. Hence since each τ_{itr} has either all nonnegative components or all nonpositive components, it follows that $\lim_{r\to\infty} \tau_{itr} = 0$, and so the (x'_{itr}) are also bounded and each limit point of (x'_{itr}) lies in Supp μ_i. Assume w.l.o.g. that $\lim_{r\to\infty} x'_{itr} = x'_i$. Then (11) implies that

$$U_i(x'') > U_i(x'_i) \quad \text{and} \quad p \cdot x'' \leqslant p \cdot w_i + \sum_i \bar{\Theta}_{ij} p \cdot y_j, \tag{12}$$

which contradicts the fact that (μ, p, y) is an exact competitive equilibrium in E_∞. Q.E.D.

COROLLARY. *Suppose that (μ, p, y) is an exact competitive equilibrium in E_∞. Then, given $\epsilon > 0$, we can find $\delta > 0$ and r' such that, for all $r \geqslant r'$: if $y' \in Y_r$ satisfies $\| y' - y \| < \delta$, there exists an ϵ-exchange equilibrium (μ'_r, p, y') in E_r.*

Proof. If not, we can find a sequence (δ_t) tending to zero and a sequence $(y'_{r(t)})$ satisfying $\| y'_{r(t)} - y \| < \delta_t$ and $\lim_{t\to\infty} r(t) = \infty$ for which there is no

ϵ-exchange equilibrium $(\mu'_{r(t)}, p, y'_{r(t)})$ in E_r. Since $y'_{r(t)} \to y$, this contradicts Lemma 1. Q.E.D.

THEOREM 1. *For a statement of Theorem* 1, *see Section* 3.

Proof. Let (μ, p, y) be an exact competitive equilibrium in E_∞. Let $\delta > 0$ and r' be defined to satisfy the above Corollary. Choose the selection function F_r so that, whenever $r \geqslant r'$, $y' \in Y_r$, and $\| y' - y \| < \delta$, $F_r(y') =$ some (μ'_r, p'_r) with $p'_r = p$. Let F_r be arbitrary elsewhere.

By Carathéodory's theorem (see Rockafeller, 1970), and the assumption that the Y_j are bounded, we may, for each j, write $y_j = \sum_{t=1}^{K+2} \alpha_{jt} y_{jt}$, where $y_{jt} \in Y_j$ for each $t = 1,..., K+2$ and the α_{jt} are nonnegative. Choose sequences of integers (n^r_{jt}) such that

$$\lim_{r\to\infty} (n^r_{jt}/r) = \alpha_{jt} \qquad \text{for all } j, t. \tag{13}$$

Let $\mathscr{Y}_r$ represent the array of production plans where n^r_{jt} firms of type j produce y_{jt} for all j, t. For large r, $y_r = (\sum_t (n^r_{1t} y_{1t}/r),..., \sum_t (n^r_{Jt} y_{Jt}/r))$ satisfies $\| y_r - y \| < \delta$. Therefore, by the Corollary, we can find an ϵ-exchange equilibrium (μ_r, p, y_r) in E_r. We claim that, for large r, $(\mu_r, p, \mathscr{Y}_r)$ is an ϵ-MCE. We have already established (2.12) and (2.13). Condition (2.16) follows from (6) and the fact that, since $\tilde{Y}_j$ is a cone, $p \cdot y_j = 0$. Conditions (2.14) and (2.15) follow from the facts that (a) (6) holds; (b) since the Y_j are bounded, a change in one firm's production plan will, when r is large, have a very small effect on y_r, and hence will keep $\| y'_r - y \| < \delta$ and will not not affect prices. Q.E.D.

THEOREM 2. *For a statement of Theorem* 2, *see Section* 3.

Proof. Assume w.l.o.g. that $p_r \to$ some $p \in R_+^{*(K+1)}$. Since $\sum_j y_{jkr}$ is either zero or bounded away from zero for large r, p_k must be finite if $\sum_j y_{jk} > 0$. For if not, good 0's price in terms of some other good $\to 0$ as $r \to \infty$, and hence per capita demand for good $0 \to \infty$. In addition, (A.6) implies that $p_k > 0$ for all $k = 1,..., K$.

Furthermore, (2.9) and (A.7) imply that (y_r) is bounded. It follows, in view of the budget constraints (2.6), that we can find a compact set B such that $\mu_{ir}(B) = 1$ for all i, r. Hence we may assume w.l.o.g. that $(\mu_r, y_r) \to (\mu, y)$. Since (μ_r, y_r) satisfies (1) and (2), and since $\tilde{Y}_j$ is closed, it follows that (μ, y) is a feasible allocation in E_∞.

Let k' be any good 1,..., K which is not in $M(y)$ and let $S = M(y) \cup \{k'\}$. We will prove that (μ, y) is a restricted ϵ-competitive equilibrium relative to S. Theorem 2 will then follow immediately.

In order to do this, we must find prices $p^* \in R_+^{*S}$ which sustain (μ, y). The vector p will not in general do since $p_{k'}$ will be infinite. We therefore define

$p_k^* = p_k$ if $k \in M(y)$, but choose $p_{k'}^*$ as follows. Given $p_{k'}$, let $\bar{p}$ be the vector whose kth component is p_k if $k \in M(y)$ and $p_{k'}$ if $k = k'$. Define

$$p_{k'}^* = \inf \Big\{ p_{k'} \in R_+^* \mid \text{for all } i \text{ and } x_i \in \operatorname{Supp} \mu_i,\ x' \in R_+{}^S \text{ and}$$
$$U_i(x') > U_i(x_i) + \epsilon \Rightarrow \bar{p} \cdot x > \bar{p} \cdot w_i + \sum_j \bar{\Theta}_{ij} \bar{p} \cdot y_j \Big\}. \quad (14)$$

In other words, $p_{k'}^*$ is the smallest nonnegative price for good k' such that consumers who are able to trade in all goods in S actually end up choosing to consume only goods in $M(y)$; i.e., although good k' is available, the demand for it is zero.

We show now that (μ, y) is a restricted ϵ-competitive equilibrium allocation relative to S at prices p^*. We have shown that (3)–(4) hold. Since any $x \in \operatorname{Supp} \mu_i$ is the limit of a sequence of points $x_r \in \operatorname{Supp} \mu_{ir}$ and since (2.6) holds for each r, we may take limits to establish the first part of (5). The second part of (5) follows from (2.7). It remains to show that (6) is satisfied. Since (2.16) holds for the ϵ-MCE in E_r, we know that

$$p^* \cdot y_j \geqslant 0 \qquad \text{for each } j. \quad (15)$$

We will therefore have established (6) if we can show that

$$p^* \cdot y \leqslant 0 \qquad \text{for all} \quad y \in \tilde{Y}_j, \quad j = 1, \ldots, J.$$

Suppose not. Then there exists some j and $y \in \tilde{Y}_j$ such that

$$p^* \cdot y > 0.$$

But since $\tilde{Y}_j$ is the smallest closed convex cone containing Y_j, it follows that

$$p^* \cdot y' > 0 \quad (16)$$

for some $y' \in Y_j$. Otherwise, $\tilde{Y}_j \cap \{y' \mid p^* \cdot y' \leqslant 0\}$ would be a smaller closed convex cone containing Y_j.

Consider the consequences of an extra type j firm setting up and choosing the production plan y' in the equilibrium of the economy E_r. We know from the regularity assumption that, for large r, there will be a new ϵ-exchange equilibrium. Hence, by (2.15),

$$F_{r2}(y_{-jr}, y_{jr} + y'/r) \cdot y' \leqslant 0. \quad (17)$$

Take limits as $r \to \infty$. It follows from the assumption that y is a regular point that

$$\lim_{r \to \infty} F_{r2k}(y_{-jr}, y_{jr} + y'/r) = p_k = p_k^* \qquad \text{if} \quad k \in M(y). \quad (18)$$

Also

$$\liminf_{r\to\infty} F_{r2k'}(y_{-jr}, y_{jr} + y'/r) \geqslant p^*_{k'}, \tag{19}$$

since otherwise, by definition of $p^*_{k'}$,

$$0 < \lim_{r\to\infty} \sum_i \int x_{k'}\, d\mu_{ir} = \sum_j y_{jk'} + \sum_i w_{ik'} = 0,$$

which is a contradiction.

Therefore, putting (17), (18), and (19) together, we get

$$p^* \cdot y' \leqslant 0, \tag{20}$$

which contradicts (16).

This establishes that (μ, y) is a restricted ϵ-competitive equilibrium allocation relative to S at prices p^*. (Note that (A.4) and (6) imply that $p^*_{k'}$ is finite.)

Suppose now that Theorem 2 is false. Then we can (choosing subsequences if necessary) find a sequence (h_r), bounded away from zero, such that (μ_r', y_r') is feasible in E_r', ϵ'-Pareto dominates (μ_r, y_r) and $M(y_r')\backslash M(y_r)$ contains at most one element, where $\epsilon' > \epsilon$. Let (μ', y') be a limit point of (μ_r', y_r'). Then (μ', y') ϵ-Pareto dominates (μ, y), uses strictly less resources in E_∞ than (μ, y), and $M(y')\backslash M(y)$ contains at most one element. This contradicts the fact that, by Result 3, (μ, y) is ϵ-Pareto optimal in E_∞ relative to all sets of the form $M(y) \cup \{k'\}$. Q.E.D.

THEOREM 3. *For a statement of Theorem* 3, *see Section* 3.

Proof. The same argument is used as in the proof of Theorem 2. It is shown that under SRPP (μ, p^*, y) is a competitive equilibrium in E_∞, where $p^*_{k'}$ is defined as in (14) for each $k' \notin M(y)$, and where we set $\epsilon = 0$. Q.E.D.

THEOREM 5. *For a statement of Theorem* 5, *see Section* 3.

Proof. Since all industries are alike, we may take J to equal 1 and drop the subscript j. Suppose that Theorem 5 is false. Then, arguing as in the proof of Theorem 2, we may find a feasible allocation (μ', y') in E_∞ which ϵ-Pareto dominates (μ, y), where $(\mu, p, y) = \lim_{r\to\infty} (\mu_r, p_r, y_r)$.

It follows from (3.4) that $\tilde{Y}$, the smallest closed convex cone containing Y, $=\{y \mid$ there exists a sequence (y_r) of points in Y such that $\lim_{r\to\infty} y_r/r = y\}$ (for the latter is a closed convex cone containing Y). Let $y' = \lim_{r\to\infty} y_r'/r$, where $y_r' \in Y$ for each r. Consider now the consequences of a new firm setting up with the production plan $y'_{r^{1/2}}$ in E_r, starting at the ϵ-MCE (μ_r, p_r, y_r).

Since $y'_{r^{1/2}}/r = (y'_{r^{1/2}}/r^{1/2}) \cdot (1/r^{1/2}) \to 0$, we know from the regularity assumption that, for large r, there will be a new ϵ-exchange equilibrium (μ'_r, p'_r, y'_r). Hence, by (2.15),

$$F_{2r}(y_r + y'_{r^{1/2}}/r) \cdot y'_{r^{1/2}} \leqslant 0. \tag{21}$$

We can assume w.l.o.g. that $\lim_{r\to\infty} F_{2r}(y_r + y'_{r^{1/2}}/r) = p^*$. Moreover, since y is a regular point, $p_k^* = p_k$ for all $k \in M(y)$. Hence, dividing (21) by $r^{1/2}$ and taking limits, we get

$$p^* \cdot y' \leqslant 0. \tag{22}$$

In addition, again since y is regular, we know that $\mu'_r \to \mu$. It follows that

$$x \in R_+^{K+1} \quad \text{and} \quad U_i(x) > U_i(x_i) + \epsilon \Rightarrow p^* \cdot x > p^* \cdot w_i + \bar{\Theta}_i p^* \cdot y \quad \text{for all} \quad x_i \in \operatorname{Supp} \mu_i. \tag{23}$$

For otherwise, consumers will not find it optimal to choose consumption plans in the support of μ'_r when r is large. In other words, the p_k^* are reservation prices for the nonproduced goods $k \notin M(y)$ at the allocation (μ, p, y).

However, (23) and the fact that (μ', y') ϵ-Pareto dominates (μ, y) imply, by the usual revealed preference argument, that $p^* \cdot y' > p^* \cdot y$. But since the latter is nonnegative as a consequence of (2.16), this contradicts (22). Q.E.D.

Acknowledgments

I have benefited greatly from numerous helpful discussions with Louis Makowski, who has independently obtained results similar to those presented here. See Makowski (1980). I am also very grateful to Andreu Mas-Colell who suggested studying approximate equilibria. Finally, I would like to acknowledge helpful conversations with Hildegard Dierker, Bill Novshek, Joe Ostroy, and Hugo Sonnenschein, and also the comments of an anonymous referee.

References

A. Dixit and J. Stiglitz (1977), Monopolistic competition and optimum product diversity, *Amer. Econ. Rev.* **67**, No. 3, 297–308.

J. Drèze and K. Hagen (1978), Choice of product quality: Equilibrium and efficiency, *Econometrica* **46**, No. 3, 493–514.

D. Foley (1970), Economic equilibria with costly marketing, *J. Econ. Theory* **2**, 276–291.

S. Grossman (1977), A characterization of the optimality of equilibrium in incomplete markets, *J. Econ. Theory* **15**, 1–15.

O. Hart (1979a), Monopolistic competition in a large economy with differentiated commodities, *Rev. Econ. Stud.*, January, 1–30.

O. Hart (1979b), On shareholder unanimity in large stock market economies, *Econometrica* **47**, No. 5, 1057–1084.

W. Heller and D. Starrett (1976), On the nature of externalities, *in* "Theory and Measurement of Economic Externalities," Academic Press, New York.

M. Kurz (1974), Equilibrium with transaction cost and money in a single market exchange economy, *J. Econ. Theory* **7**, 418–452.

L. Makowski (1980), Perfect competition, the profit criterion and the organization of economic activity, *J. Econ. Theory* **22**, 222–242.

J. Marschak and R. Radner (1972), "Economic Theory of Teams," Yale Univ. Press, New Haven, Conn.

A. Mas-Colell (1977), A remark on a smoothness property of convex, complete preorders," **3**, No. 1, 103–105.

W. Novshek and H. Sonnenschein (1978), Cournot and Walras Equilibrium, *J. Econ. Theory* **19**, 223–266.

K. Parthasarathy (1967), "Probability Measures on Metric Spaces," Academic Press, New York.

K. Roberts (1980), The limit points of monopolistic competition, *J. Econ. Theory* **22**, 256–278.

R. Rockafellar (1970), "Convex Analysis," Princeton Univ. Press, Princeton, N. J.

P. Rosenstein-Rodan (1943), Problems of industrialization of Eastern and Southeastern Europe, *Econ. J.*, June–September.

T. Scitovsky (1954), Two concepts of external economies, *J. Pol. Econ.*, April.

M. Spence (1976), Product selection, fixed costs, and monopolistic competition, *Rev. Econ. Stud.* **43**, 217–235.

R. Starr (1969), Quasi-equilibria in markets with non-convex preferences, *Econometrica* **37**, No. 1, 25–38.

Equilibrium in Simple Spatial (or Differentiated Product) Models

WILLIAM NOVSHEK

Economics Department, Stanford University, Stanford, California 94305

Received August 11, 1979

1. INTRODUCTION

This paper is concerned with equilibrium in models where location (product) and price are strategic variables. Since Hotelling's classic paper [5] a great deal of work on spatial and related differentiated product models has been undertaken, much of it featuring the assumption of zero conjectural variation (ZCV), or zero profits in equilibrium, or symmetry in equilibrium. The difficulties created by these assumptions are sometimes noted, but are typically ignored in the analysis. Here the equilibria of a simple, standard spatial model are investigated without ignoring these difficulties. Equilibrium with free entry when firms are technologically small relative to the market is of particular interest.

It is easy to see why the ZCV assumption, that each firm views the strategies of all other firms as fixed regardless of its own strategy, is inappropriate for spatial models with price and location pairs as strategies when firms have constant marginal cost: no equilibrium at which ZCV is relevant ever exists! Suppose that for some standard spatial model with price and location pairs as strategies, a ZCV equilibrium exists. If all firms are at monopoly solutions (i.e., at locations and prices, and with demands such that if no other firms existed, the same price and location pair would remain an optimal strategy, yielding the same demand) then no firm affects any other firm, and ZCV is irrelevant. On the other hand, if some firm i is not at a monopoly solution, one of its neighbor firms, say j, must be affecting firm i's demand, and therefore firm i must be affecting firm j's demand. Without loss of generality, firm i's profit is not greater than firm j's profit, so that when firm i relocates very near firm j, and slightly undercuts firm j's price, it captures all of firm j's market at a profit arbitrarily near firm j's original profit, plus it retains some of its former market (some of the consumers "in dispute" between firms i and j, who originally purchased from i, but would purchase from j if firm i did not exist). The profit from the retained market is bounded away from zero, so firm i increases its profits by this change of strategy. Thus the only ZCV equilibria when firms have constant marginal cost are those in

Reprinted from *Journal of Economic Theory* **22**, No. 2, 313–326 (April 1980)
ISBN 0-12-476750-8

which all firms are at monopoly solutions.[1,2] Furthermore, if free entry and exit are allowed then each local monopolist must earn zero profit or an entrant, assuming ZCV, will undercut an active firm, anticipating positive profit (or, in the case of negative profit, the monopolist will exit).

In some spatial (or differentiated product) models, firms are assumed to possess a great deal of computational ability or knowledge of the behavior of others. In situations where there are many firms operating, each of which serves only a small fraction of the market, this is not a particularly appealing assumption. On the other hand, when there are only a few firms operating, a typical oligopoly problem arises: what is reasonable firm behavior, and are firms allowed to threaten or collude, etc.? Since there will be many active firms in the main situations of interest here, when firms are technologically small relative to the market and free entry and exit are allowed, only simple conjectural variations will be used.

Here, as in Eaton [1, 2] a modified ZCV is used. Each firm views the strategy of other firms as fixed so long as its own strategy does not cause its delivered price to match or undercut any other firm's price at that other firm's own location. Each firm believes that no other firm will allow itself to be undersold at its own location and that other firms will reduce price if they are undercut at their own locations. This modification effectively rules out the problem with ZCV.[3]

Modified ZCV is a minimal assumption in the sense that any assumption which will allow existence of equilibrium must effectively rule out undercutting and modified ZCV does this with a minimum change from ZCV. It may seem more reasonable to assume that firms respond whenever their profits become negative. This type of alternative conjectural variation does not affect the validity of the main results of the paper contained in Proposition 2. In a typical equilibrium of Proposition 2 all firms earn strictly positive profit and no firm is (locally) constrained by modified ZCV. For any conjectural variation in which other firms do not respond to sufficiently small changes from this equilibrium configuration each active firm will have a local profit maximum at the modified ZCV equilibrium. If the alternative conjectural variations are "well behaved" globally, the modified ZCV equilibrium will also be an equilibrium with the alternative conjectural variations. Thus the results for modified ZCV are more general than is immediately apparent.

[1] If firms have average cost curves which are very sharply U shaped, then this type of strategy change may not improve profit, since demand may substantially change.

[2] Lerner and Singer [6] discuss this type of strategy change in a duopoly context.

[3] If $(p(i), x(i))_{i=1}^{n}$ is a modified ZCV equilibrium in price-location strategies then (except for monopoly solutions) it is not a Nash equilibrium in price-location strategies. However, $(p(i), x(i), 0)_{i=1}^{n}$ is a Nash equilibrium for a corresponding game in which strategies are triples of price, location, and response price. If firm i's price is undercut so that it faces zero demand then it uses the response price (here zero) instead of $p(i)$.

(Remark 3 discusses some cases in which firms conjecture that other firms will respond to any change in price.)

The problem with the assumption of zero profits in equilibrium is that it usually leads to the generic nonexistence of equilibrium in bounded models, because the number of active firms must be an integer.[4] Free entry is usually used as the rationale for this assumption, and though the conjectural variation assumption is not always explicitly clear, the implicit assumption often appears to be ZCV, which also leads to nonexistence, even in unbounded models.[5]

There are two types of symmetry of equilibrium assumptions which cause problems. The first is the assumption that all firms will charge the same price, or will locate symmetrically. The firms are then allowed to maximize profit only with respect to one variable, without explanation as to why the equilibrium should be assumed symmetric. The second symmetry "assumption" allows firms to maximize with respect to both price and location, but considers only those equilibria which are symmetric. While this is a legitimate method for showing existence of equilibrium, the symmetric equilibria of different markets are often compared. Unless it can be shown that nonsymmetric equilibria do not exist, these comparisons are not valid comparative statics.

Here the equilibria of a simple, standard spatial model are analyzed. The market is one dimensional, bounded, and without a boundary: a circle with circumference L. All firms have identical cost functions consisting of a fixed cost F plus a constant marginal cost times output (by measuring all prices as net of marginal cost, without loss of generality the marginal cost is zero), and choose location and price. Modified ZCV is assumed, so firms believe the strategies of other firms are fixed unless a strategy change for the firm undercuts some other active firm in which case the affected firm will respond by lowering its price. A continuum of consumers is uniformly distributed on the circle with density A, and each consumer only purchases from firms with the lowest delivered price, with consumers paying transportation costs. The delivered price at x' from a firm located at x and charging price p is $p + c \mid x - x' \mid$. All consumers possess identical linear demand functions $h(p) = (a - bp)/A$ which are functions of delivered price. The demand function can be generated in the usual manner from a utility function for $l + 1$ standard commodities one of which is available from several firms at various delivered prices.

The equilibria for this model are characterized both for the case where the number of firms is exogenously fixed, and for the case of free entry and exit. Only integral numbers of firms are allowed and true free entry and exit,

[4] Salop [8] mentions this problem.

[5] Eaton [2] shows that symmetric positive profit equilibria often exist in a model using modified ZCV and free entry.

rather than a zero profit condition, is used. Except for some monopoly solutions all equilibria are symmetric. When fixed cost is small relative to the market then equilibrium with free entry and exit exists and is approximately competitive (i.e., all prices are approximately equal to marginal cost). Here (approximately) competitive results arise endogenously when technologies are small with respect to the market and there is free entry and exit, rather than exogenously as assumptions.

The paper is organized as follows. Section 2 contains results for linear demand and constant marginal cost. Section 3 contains remarks which generalize the results to include nonlinear demand, U-shaped average cost, and differentiated products. The Appendix contains the proofs, which are mainly computational.

2. Existence and Properties of Equilibrium

Let the price and location for firm i be denoted by $p(i)$ and $x(i)$ respectively. All equilibria which differ only in the "names" of firms or consumers (e.g., equilibria in which two firms interchange prices and locations, or in which all firms move clockwise by an equal amount) are identified so let $t(i) = cx(i) - cx(i-1)$. The results for exogenous n, linear demand and constant marginal cost are summarized in Proposition 1. (By measuring all prices as net of marginal cost, without loss of generality the marginal cost is zero.) For exogenous n the only n firm equilibria which exist are ones in which all active firms charge the same price. Whenever n is large enough so that all individual firms cannot be at monopoly solutions, then a unique n firm equilibrium exist, and it is symmetric in location as well as price.

PROPOSITION 1. *With linear demand, constant (zero) marginal cost, and parameters (a, b, c, A, F, L), for all positive integers n there is an n firm equilibrium (without free entry and exit).*

(a) *All firms are local monopolists if and only if $n \leqslant \max\{1, 3bcL/4a\}$:*

(i) *for $n = 1 \geqslant 3bcL/4a$ the equilibrium is unique with price $p^* = (a/2b) - (cL/8)$ and profit $\pi^*(F) = bL[(a/2b) - (cL/8)]^2 - F$;*

(ii) *for $1 \leqslant n \leqslant 3bcL/4a$ $(\neq 1)$ equilibrium is not unique unless $n = 3bcL/4a$. For all firms $t(i) \geqslant 4a/3b$, $p^* = a/3b$ and $\pi^*(F) = (4a^3/27b^2c) - F$.*

(b) *There is a nonmonopoly equilibrium if and only if $n > \max\{1, 3bcL/4a\}$. The equilibrium is unique, and symmetric with, for all firms, $t(n) = cL/n$, price $p^*(n) = (a/2b) + (3cL/4n) - (1/2) \cdot \{[(a/b) - (cL/2n)]^2 + (3c^2L^2/n^2)\}^{1/2}$ and profit $\pi^*(n, F) = (Lb/n)[(acL/8bn) - (25c^2L^2/16n^2) + (7cL/8n) \times \{[(a/b) - (cL/2n)]^2 + (3c^2L^2/n^2)\}^{1/2}] - F$.*

The equilibria for $1 < n < 3cbL/4a$ are not unique and need not be symmetric. The possible lack of symmetry does not affect the welfare properties of equilibrium, since the nonsymmetric gaps between the neighboring monopolists' markets consist of consumers who do not purchase any of the product, and the measure of consumers in this situation is independent of the arrangement of the n monopolists. However, this lack of symmetry does affect the potential for entry, with symmetric equilibria offering the smallest maximum gap and thus the lowest profit potential for entrants.

There are two properties that are important for the proof. First, in an equilibrium no active firm is (locally) constrained by modified ZCV (if any firm is locally constrained some firm is not at an optimum location). The second important property is boundary price equalization. Whenever there is a uniform density of consumers, each with identical downward sloping demand, firms maximize demand at each price they charge by locating in such a manner that the farthest consumers in each direction that purchase from the firm face the same delivered price. As the firm moves toward the center of its market, even if the measure of consumers purchasing from the firm remains constant, demand increases because the delivered prices faced by consumers in the firm's market area become lower in a statistical sense. For each price p the measure of consumers purchasing from the firm at delivered prices less than or equal to p increases (weakly for all p and strictly for some p) as the firm moves toward the center of its market. The remainder of the proof is mainly computational.

Proof of Proposition 1. See Appendix.

If we introduce free entry and exit, given parameters (a, b, c, A, F, L) the set of equilibria with free entry and exit is the union over all n of the n firm equilibria of Proposition 1 at which active firms earn nonnegative profit, and the best a potential entrant could do by entering is to earn a nonpositive profit.[6]

The following example shows that equilibrium with free entry and exit does not always exist. Let $a = b = c = 1$ and $L = \epsilon$. The monopoly price is $(4 - \epsilon)/8$ with profit $[\epsilon(4 - \epsilon)^2/64] - F$. For all n greater than one, the only possible n firm equilibrium has prices on the order of ϵ/n and firm profits which exceed $-F$ by a term on the order of $(\epsilon/n)^2$. An entrant into the monopoly market charging price $(4 - \epsilon)/8$ anticipates profit of $[\epsilon(4 - \epsilon)/32] - F$. Thus for all small ϵ there is a value of F such that the monopoly profit and the profit for an entrant given $n = 1$ are both positive, but for $n > 1$ profits are negative in every n firm equilibrium. Hence for small ϵ and appropriate F no equilibrium with free entry and exit exists.

[6] For $n = 0$ there is an n-firm equilibrium with free entry and exit if the monopoly profit in Proposition 1 is nonpositive.

Proposition 2 shows that whenever fixed costs are sufficiently small relative to the other parameters, equilibrium with free entry and exit exists and all equilibria are approximately competitive (i.e., all consumers are able to purchase the commodity at delivered prices which are approximately equal to the marginal cost-of production). Let $\mathscr{E}(a, b, c, A, F, L)$ denote the set of equilibria with free entry and exit when the parameters are (a, b, c, A, F, L).

PROPOSITION 2. *With linear demand, constant (zero) marginal cost and parameters* (a, b, c, A, L) fixed,

(a) *there exists an* $F^* > 0$ *such that for all* $F \in (0, F^*]$ $\mathscr{E}(a,b,c,A,F,L) \neq \varnothing$,

(b) *the number of equilibria is* $|\mathscr{E}(a, b, c, A, F, L)| = \mathcal{O}(F^{-1/2})$ *and*

(c) *if* $(F(k))_{k=1}^{\infty}$ *is a sequence of fixed costs such that* $F(k) \to 0$, *and for each* k, $m(k)$ *is the maximum delivered price paid by any consumer in any equilibrium in* $\mathscr{E}(a, b, c, F(k), L)$ *then* $m(k) \to 0$.

Proof. See Appendix.

3. REMARKS

(1) With constant marginal cost and linear individual consumer demand functions Proposition 1 shows that essentially all equilibria are symmetric and Proposition 2 shows that when technologies (fixed costs) are small relative to the market then equilibrium with free entry and exit exists and is approximately competitive. The results of Proposition 2 can be generalized under a variety of assumptions: if technologies are small relative to the market then equilibrium with free entry and exit exists, is symmetric, and is approximately competitive. The important requirements are that all firms have identical technologies with initial increasing returns and that there be a uniform density of consumers with identical demand functions which are downward sloping at the competitive (minimum average cost) price.

If $C(y)$ is a basic cost function with initial increasing returns to scale, for $\alpha \in (0, 1)$ let $C_\alpha(y) := \alpha C(y/\alpha)$. Then α is a measure of the technology: for the technologies of Section 2, if C has fixed cost F then C_α has fixed cost αF; if C attains minimum average cost at finite output y^* then C_α attains (the same) minimum average cost at αy^*. When $1/\alpha$ is an integer the rescaled cost function C_α can be interpreted as measuring the original cost function in "per capita" or per replication terms after a $(1/\alpha)$-fold replication of the consumer sector.

The proof technique sketched here can be applied to nonlinear demand and U-shaped average cost. The first step is to note that the boundary price equalization property discussed in Section 2 still applies. Let $p(q, \alpha)$ be the optimal price charged by a firm with cost function C_α (exit not allowed) which is located between firms at $x \pm (q/c)$ which charge a price equal to the minimum (infinum) of average cost. For each small α, $p(q, \alpha)$ and $(p(q, \alpha) + q)/2$ are invertible as functions of q for appropriate small q. Then, without allowing entry or exit, there is a symmetric n firm equilibrium if there exists a q such that $(n/c)(q - p(q, \alpha)) = L$. An entrant into this situation has optimal price $p([p(q, \alpha) + q]/2, \alpha)$. The last step is to show that for small α there exists an appropriate large n such that an n firm equilibrium exists at which active firms earn positive profit and entrants anticipate negative profit from entry ($[p(q, \alpha) + q]/2q$ is bounded away from one for appropriate (q, α) pairs so the initial increasing returns yields a situation similar to that of the proof of Proposition 2 where $[\pi_e(n, F) + F]/[\pi^*(n, F) + F] \to [9/16]$). For small α all equilibria are approximately competitive because of free entry and all equilibria are symmetric because of the invertibility of $p(q, \alpha)$ and $[p(q, \alpha) + q]/2$.

It is possible to modify the technique just sketched to apply to nonlinear transportation costs or differentiated products. For the differentiated product case there are no transportation costs but preferences vary over the differentiated products. For example suppose t is a taste parameter of consumers (distributed uniformly on $[0, L]$) and g: $[0, L/2] \to [0, 1]$ is a strictly decreasing function with $g(0) = 1$. Suppose all consumers view the differentiated products as perfect substitutes in the appropriate ratios[7] (given by g). For a consumer with parameter t let products be "named" by their distance counterclockwise (+) or clockwise (−) from t. For a consumption vector z of l standard commodities and consumption $y(x)$ for each differentiated commodity $x \in [-L/2, L/2]$, a consumer of taste t has utility $u(z, \int_{-L/2}^{L/2} g(|x|)y(x)\,dx)$, where u is a standard utility function for $l + 1$ commodities. Consumers only purchase those commodities at the lowest "effective price" $p(x)/g(|x|)$. This is similar to a situation with one characteristic where consumers differ in their subjective beliefs about the amount of the characteristic contained in each good.

(2) The results of Section 2 and Remark 1 show that with linear demand, or with downward-sloping demand, technology small with respect to the market, and free entry and exit it is legitimate to perform comparative statics using only the symmetric equilibria since no other equilibria exist (and with an appropriate dynamic the symmetric equilibria are stable). With linear demand essentially all equilibria are symmetric but with general downward-sloping demand nonsymmetric equilibria may exist when the technology is large with respect to the market. This is illustrated in Example 1.

[7] See [7] for a related discussion of this substitutability.

EXAMPLE 1. Let $L = 32/21$, $F = 3/4$, and $c = A = 1$, let there be zero marginal cost, and let consumer demand functions be

$$\begin{aligned} h(p) &= 2 - p/r \quad &\text{if } p \in [0, 1] \\ &= 1 - p/r \quad &\text{if } p \in (1, r] \\ &= \quad 0 \quad &\text{if } p \in (r, \infty). \end{aligned}$$

For every $\epsilon < 1/21$, if $r \geqslant 2[(1/21) - \epsilon]^{-1}$ and $\delta \leqslant \epsilon$ there is a two-firm equilibrium with free entry and exit which has symmetric locations and nonsymmetric prices $(13/21) - \delta$ and $(13/21) + \delta$.

In terms of the literature on spatial models the results for perfectly inelastic demand cause more of a problem. Models in which each consumer purchases one unit of the spatial commodity regardless of price (or for all prices below some reservation price) are commonly treated (see, for example, [3, 8]). With inelastic demand the boundary price equalization argument of Section 2 breaks down. With constant marginal cost, if fixed cost is small relative to the market then equilibrium with free entry and exit exists and is approximately competitive, but almost all equilibria are nonsymmetric. For each n-firm symmetric equilibrium there is an $(n - 1)$-dimensional set of nonsymmetric equilibria "near" it. Starting at an equilibrium with symmetric locations there will be an equilibrium for each small perturbation of the locations: each firm's location does not affect its own profit and for each perturbed set of locations there is a price equilibrium.

(3) The result of Section 2, proving the existence of equilibrium with free entry and exit when fixed costs are small, can be extended to a class of conjectural variation functions all of whose members include the modification to ZCV which effectively eliminated price undercutting. A simple subclass of conjectural variation functions to which the result can be extended is the class of conjectural variation functions that agree with the modified ZCV except for the belief that a neighboring firm will change its price in proportion to the change in the given firm's price, i.e., firm i believes $\Delta p(i \pm 1) = (1 - k)\,\Delta p(i)$, where $k \in (0, 1]$. For sufficiently small F, there is an n-firm equilibrium with free entry and exit in which all firms charge price approximately cL/kn, when

$$[(3/4) + \epsilon]L(ac/kF)^{1/2} < n < (1 - \epsilon)L(ac/kF)^{1/2}.$$

The above result also holds when k is replaced by a function of the original distances between the firms, $|\,\bar{x}(i \pm 1) - \bar{x}(i)| = d$, of the form kd^s for $s \in [0, 1]$. Then firm i believes that $\Delta p(i \pm 1) = (1 - kd^s)\,\Delta p(i)$ (this applies only when firms are sufficiently close that $kd^s \in (0, 1]$), and for sufficiently small fixed costs there is an equilibrium with free entry and exit.

(4) One instance in which unmodified ZCV may be reasonable is that in which firms choose location and quantities rather than prices. The difficulty in working with quantity choice models in a spatial (or differentiated products) framework arises in determining prices which correspond to a given set of location and quantity choices by firms. In the linear demand model of Section 2, if n firms are positioned symmetrically and all charge the same price, then at the corresponding quantities, q, the matrix $[\partial q/\partial p']$ has a negative dominant diagonal, and is therefore nonsingular. Thus the inverse demand function, for quantity changes with locations fixed, can be found for quantity vectors q near the original symmetric q^*. If only one firm, i, changes its quantity action, $q(i)$, then $\partial p(i)/\partial q(i)$ and $\partial p(i \pm 1)/\partial q(i)$ can be found, and, with some computation, it can be shown that

$$\frac{\partial p(i \pm 1)}{\partial q(i)} \Big/ \frac{\partial p(i)}{\partial q(i)}$$

is (locally) approximately $1 - kn^{-1/2}$, where n is the number of active firms and k is a constant determined by the parameters of the model. Quantity-setting behavior with ZCV can be thought of as price-setting behavior with a conjectural variation about neighbors' price changes which is exactly the price change (along with price changes for more distant firms) which maintains quantity levels for other firms. Locally, near a symmetric price location $2n$-vector (p, x), the necessary conjectural variation is approximately $\partial p(i \pm 1)/\partial p(i) = 1 - kd^s$, where d is the distance between firms and $s = \frac{1}{2}$. Recall that $\partial p(i \pm 1)/\partial p(i) = 1 - kd^{1/2}$ is one of the conjectural variation functions for which equilibrium with free entry and exit exists when fixed costs are sufficiently small.

(5) In a general equilibrium, differentiated products model where firms choose quantities, Hart [4] proves the convergence of equilibrium with free entry and exit to competitive equilibrium as firms become technologically small relative to the economy. However, he does not consider the question of the existence of equilibrium. The existence result of Section 2 could be easily extended to general equilibrium if the distribution of ownership shares was symmetric (i.e., each set of consumers of measure μ would own μ/AL of each firm). Substantial problems arise in both partial and general equilibrium when the symmetry assumptions of the model (uniform consumer density, identical consumer demand functions, identical ownership shares, identical cost functions) are weakened in any significant way. It is then no longer possible to treat a representative firm: each firm must be considered separately. As the technologies become small relative to the economy the endogenously determined number of firms necessarily becomes large and increases the complexity of the problem.

4. Conclusion

In spatial (or differentiated products) models in which location (product) and price are strategic variables, ZCV must be modified in order for the results to be nonvacuous. With modified ZCV, constant marginal cost production, and linear demand, essentially all equilibria are symmetric. Though equilibrium with free entry and exit does not always exist, if fixed costs are sufficiently small relative to the other market parameters, then an equilibrium with free entry and exit does exist, and all equilibria with free entry and exit are approximately competitive. The results can be generalized to cover a variety of assumptions including nonlinear demand and U-shaped average cost. In these cases, when the technology is small relative to the market, equilibrium with free entry and exit exists and is approximately competitive.

Appendix

Proof of Proposition 1

A monopolist charging price $p \leqslant a/b$ faces demand $2\int_0^r A \cdot h(p + cs)\,ds$, where $r = \min\{[(a/b) - p]/c, L/2\}$, so

$$
\begin{aligned}
D(p) &= 0 && \text{if} \quad p \geqslant a/b \\
&= (a - bp)^2/bc && \text{if} \quad a/b > p > (a/b) - (cL/2) \\
&= (a - bp)L - (bcL^2)/4 && \text{if} \quad (a/b) - (cL/2) \geqslant p.
\end{aligned}
$$

Maximizing profit, $\pi(p, F) = pD(p) - F$, the monopolist's optimal price is $a/3b$ if $3cbL/4a > 1$ and is $(a/2b) - (cL/8)$ if $3cbL/4a \leqslant 1$. When $3cbL/4a \leqslant 1$, the single monopolist serves the entire market, and earns profit $bL((a/2b) - (cL/8))^2 - F$. When $3cbL/4a > 1$, the single monopolist serves a market of length $4a/3bc < L$, and earns profit $(4a^3/27b^2c) - F$. When $3cbL/4a > 1$, for any $n \leqslant 3cbL/4a$, n firms can operate as local monopolists, each charging price $a/3b$, as long as the distance between any two firms is at least $4a/3bc$. These equilibria (with $1 < n \leqslant 3cbL/4a$) need not be symmetric in location since location does not affect the monopolist's profit (as long as the distance $4a/3bc$ is maintained between monopolists).

Now consider an n-firm equilibrium in which some firm is not at a monopoly solution. The demand faced by firm i, from consumers located between firms i and $i + 1$ is the integral of individual consumer demands (which are functions of the delivered price from firm i) for consumers between i and $i + 1$ whose lowest delivered price is from i,

$$\int_0^r A \cdot h(p(i) + cs)\,ds,$$

where

$$r = \min\{[p(i+1) - p(i) + t(i+1)]/2c,\ [(a/b) - p(i)]/c\}$$

or $(1/8c)(p(i+1) - p(i) + t(i+1))(4a - b[3p(i) + p(i+1) + t(i+1)])$ if $p(i+1) + p(i) + t(i+1) \leqslant 2a/b$, and $(a - bp(i))^2/2bc$ otherwise, while the demand from consumers located between firms $i - 1$ and i is $(1/8c)(p(i{-}1) - p(i) + t(i))(4a - b[3p(i) + p(i{-}1) + t(i)])$ if $p(i{-}1) + p(i) + t(i) \leqslant 2a/b$, and $(a - bp(i))^2/2bc$ otherwise.

With firm i's price fixed, demand (and hence profit) is maximized by locating in such a manner that the farthest consumers in each direction that purchase from firm i face the same delivered price.

Therefore in a nonmonopoly equilibrium, for all i,

$$p(i) + p(i+1) + t(i+1) = p(i-1) + p(i) + t(i)$$

and every firm is at an interior (unconstrained) profit-maximizing solution, so the first- and second-order conditions for profit maximization can be used to characterize equilibrium. For the following analysis, constrain firm i to remain between firms $i - 1$ and $i + 1$, so a "global" solution is only global in that restricted domain.

The unique global profit-maximizing solution for location, $x(i)$, satisfies $p(i+1) - p(i-1) + cx(i+1) + cx(i-1) - 2cx(i) = 0$ (this is the location that equalizes the boundary-delivered prices). Taking the partial derivative of profit with respect to price, $p(i)$, after the optimal value of $x(i)$ has been substituted into the profit function, the first-order condition requires that $(b/16c)\{36p^2(i) - 8p(i)(s + 4a/b) + (8sa/b) - s^2\} = 0$, where $s = p(i+1) + p(i-1) + cx(i+1) - cx(i-1)$. Note that the second-order condition is only satisfied at the smaller of the two solutions to this equation. Substitute $t(i) = cx(i) - cx(i-1)$ into the two systems of first-order conditions. The n first-order conditions for locations yield only $n - 1$ independent equations, but $1^{*\prime}t = cL$,[8] so, solving for t as a function of p,

$$\begin{bmatrix} 0 & 1 & 0 & \cdots & 0 & -1 \\ -1 & 0 & 1 & 0 & \cdots & 0 \\ \vdots & \ddots & \ddots & \ddots & \ddots & \vdots \\ 0 & \ddots & & \ddots & \ddots & 0 \\ \vdots & \ddots & -1 & & 0 & 1 \\ 0 & \cdots & 0 & & 0 & 0 \end{bmatrix} p + \begin{bmatrix} -1 & 1 & 0 & \cdots & & 0 \\ 0 & -1 & 1 & 0 & \cdots & 0 \\ \vdots & \ddots & \ddots & \ddots & \ddots & \vdots \\ \vdots & & \ddots & \ddots & \ddots & 0 \\ 0 & \cdots & & 0 & -1 & 1 \\ 1 & 1 & \cdots & & 1 & 1 \end{bmatrix} t = \begin{pmatrix} 0 \\ \vdots \\ \vdots \\ \vdots \\ 0 \\ cL \end{pmatrix}$$

[8] 1^* is the n vector of ones and $'$ denotes transpose. The vector t has ith component $t(i)$ for all i.

and

$$t = (cL/n)\, 1^* + (2/n)\, 1^* 1^{*\prime} p - \{I + D\} p, \qquad (1)$$

where D is the $n \times n$ matrix with all zero entries except for ones just below the diagonal ($i-1$, i entries) and in the upper right corner (1, n entry). Substituting this expression into the n equations corresponding to the first-order conditions for prices, and simplifying,

$$48 \begin{bmatrix} p(1) & 0 & \cdots & 0 \\ 0 & p(2) & \ddots & \vdots \\ \vdots & \ddots & \ddots & 0 \\ 0 & \cdots & 0 & p(n) \end{bmatrix} p - 8((6a/b) + k)\, p + ((16a/b)\, k - 4k^2)\, 1^* = 0, \qquad (2)$$

where $k = (cL + 2(p'1^*)/n$. Thus every $p(i)$ must satisfy the same quadratic equation, and a computation shows that the larger solution fails to satisfy the second-order condition for profit maximization. Thus all prices are the same, and letting $p^*(n)$ be this common price, substituting $p = p^*(n)\, 1^*$ into (2) yields further simplification to

$$p^{*2}(n) - ((a/b) + (3cL/2n))\, p^*(n) + (acL/bn) - (c^2L^2/4n^2) = 0$$

with the correct solution being

$$p^*(n) = (a/2b) + (3cL/4n) - \tfrac{1}{2}\{[(a/b) - (cL/2n)]^2 + (3c^2L^2/n^2)\}^{1/2}. \quad (3)$$

For large values of n, this is approximately $(cL/n) - (3c^2L^2b/4n^2a)$, or approximately cL/n. Since all the prices are equal, from (1), $t = (cL/n)\, 1^*$.

This result was based upon the assumption that in the equilibrium, some firm was not at a monopoly solution. Now check to see which values of n satisfy that condition by finding those values of n for which the borderline consumer between neighboring firms faces a delivered price less than a/b; i.e., $p^*(n) + (cL/2n) < a/b$. Substituting (3) into this inequality, this condition holds if and only if $n > 3cLb/4a$. Thus for $n \leqslant \max\{3bcL/4a, 1\}$, the only possible equilibria are the previously discussed monopoly equilibria, and for $n > \max\{3bcL/4a, 1\}$, all equilibria are symmetric, with prices and locations equal to the just-computed values, and firm demands and profits

$$D^*(n) = (Lb/n)[(a/2b) - (cL/n) + \tfrac{1}{2}\{[(a/b) - (cL/2n)]^2 + (3c^2L^2/n^2)\}^{1/2}]$$

and

$$\begin{aligned}\pi^*(n, F) = (Lb/n)[(acL/8bn) - (25c^2L^2/16n^2) + (7cL/8n) \\ \times \{[(a/b) - (cL/2n)]^2 + (3c^2L^2/n^2)\}^{1/2}] - F,\end{aligned}$$

respectively.

It remains to show that each firm is at a true global profit-maximizing solution. This is obvious for monopoly solutions. By the symmetry of all nonmonopoly equilibria no firm can improve profit by jumping between two firms separated by a gap of L/n (as compared to its present position in a gap of $2L/n$). It is always most profitable to retain location $x(i)$ because of the boundary price equalization property and modified ZCV. At location $x(i)$ it is not possible to undercut any other firm since $p^*(n) - (cL/n) < 0$. Q.E.D.

Proof of Proposition 2

Since in every equilibrium, all firms charge the same price, the best location for a potential entrant is exactly between two firms which are at least as far apart as all other neighboring pairs of firms. An optimal location for the entrant is $(x(i) + x(i + 1))/2$, where $x(i + 1) - x(i) \geqslant x(j + 1) - x(j)$ for all j (if $n = 1$, $x(1) + (L/2)$ is the optimal location). If $3cbL/4a > 1$ and $x(i + 1) - x(i) \geqslant 8a/3bc$, then the entrant can be at a monopoly solution, just as all other firms. When $n = 1$ and $L \leqslant (4a/69bc) \times [(73)^{1/2} - 2]$ then the optimal price for the entrant, $[(a/2b) - (5cL/8)]^+$, "almost undercuts" the monopolist and the entrant faces demand $bL[(a/2b) + (3cL/8)]^-$ and earns profit $\{(bL/4)[(a^2/b^2) - (acL/2b) - (15c^2L^2/16)] - F\}^-$. In all other cases, using the first- and second-order conditions for profit maximization, the optimal price, demand, and profit for the entrant are

$$(s/9) + (4a/9b) - (1/18)[(64a^2/b^2) - (40sa/b) + 13s^2]^{1/2},$$

$$(b/216c)\{(56sa/b) - 11s^2 - (32a^2/b^2) + [s + (4a/b)] \cdot [(64a^2/b^2) - (40sa/b) + 13s^2]^{1/2}\},$$

and

$$(b/3888c)\{-35s^3 + (12s^2a/b) + (480sa^2/b) - (512a^3/b^3) + [(64a^2/b^2) - (40sa/b) + 13s^2]^{3/2}\} - F;$$

respectively, where $s = 2p^*(n) + cx(i + 1) - cx(i)$.

(a) For active firms $F + \pi^*(n, F) = (acL^2/n^2) + o(n^{-2})$ and for entrants $F + \pi_e(n, F) = (9acL^2/16n^2) + o(n^{-2})$. Thus there exists an integer $N > \max\{1, 3bcL/4a\}$ such that for all $n \geqslant N$, $F + \pi^*(n, F) > (0.81)(acL^2/n^2)$ and $F + \pi_e(n, F) < (0.64)(acL^2/n^2)$. Let $F^* = \min\{(acL^2/100), \frac{1}{2}\min_{n \leqslant N} \{\pi_e(n, F) + F\}\}$. To show that $\mathscr{E}(a, b, c, F, L) \neq \varnothing$ for all $F \in (0, F^*]$, fix $F \in (0, F^*]$. Then by the choice of F^*, $(0.64)(acL^2/N^2) - F > \pi_e(N, F) \geqslant 2F^* > F$. Let n be the smallest integer greater than N such that $(0.64)(acL^2/n^2) - F \leqslant 0$. By the choice of F^*, $(0.64)[acL^2/(n-1)^2] - F > 0$ implies $(0.81)(acL^2/n^2) - F > 0$ so $\pi^*(n, F) > (0.81)(acL^2/n^2) - F > 0 \geqslant (0.64)(acL^2/n^2) - F > \pi_e(n, F)$ and there is an n-firm equilibrium with free entry and exit.

(b) It is clear from the proof of part (a) that for any $\epsilon > 0$, for each sufficiently small F there will be an n-firm equilibrium with free entry and exit for each integer $n \in [(\frac{3}{4} + \epsilon)L(ac/F)^{1/2}, (1 - \epsilon)L(ac/F)^{1/2}]$, and there will be no n-firm equilibrium with free entry and exit for each integer $n \in [0, (\frac{3}{4} - \epsilon)L(ac/F)^{1/2}]$ or $n \in [(1 + \epsilon)L(ac/F)^{1/2}, \infty)$.

(c) For all n, $F + \pi_e(n, F) > 0$ so there exists an $F_n > 0$ such that $\pi_e(n, F) > 0$ for $F < F_n$ ($F_n = (9acL^2/16n^2) + o(n^{-2})$). Thus as $F(k)$ converges to zero, $n(k)$, the smallest number of active firms in any equilibrium in $\mathscr{E}(a, b, c, F(k), L)$, becomes arbitrarily large. Hence for large k the maximum delivered price $m(k) = p^*(n(k)) + (cL/2n(k)) < (3cL/2n(k))$ and $m(k)$ converges to zero. Q.E.D.

Acknowledgments

Comments by Hugo Sonnenschein and a referee have improved the presentation of this paper. All errors are of course my own.

References

1. B. C. Eaton, Spatial Competition Revisited, *Canad. J. Econ.* (1972), 268–278.
2. B. C. Eaton, Free entry in one dimensional models: Pure profits and multiple equilibria, *J. Regional Sci.* **16** (1976).
3. B. C. Eaton and R. G. Lipsey, The principle of minimum differentiation reconsidered: Some new developments in the theory of spatial competition, *Rev. Econ. Stud.* **42** (1975), 27–49.
4. O. Hart, Monopolistic competition in a large economy with differentiated products, *Rev. Econ. Stud.* **46** (1979), 1–30.
5. H. Hotelling, Stability in competition, *Econ. J.* **39** (1929), 41–57.
6. A. P. Lerner and H. W. Singer, Some notes on duopoly and spatial competition, *J. Pol. Econ.* (1937), 145–186.
7. W. Novshek and H. Sonnenschein, Marginal consumers and neoclassical demand theory, *J. Pol. Econ.* **87** (1979), 1368–1376.
8. S. Salop, Monopolistic competition with outside goods, *Bell J. Econ. Manage.* **10** (1979), 141–156.

Entry (and Exit) in a Differentiated Industry*

J. JASKOLD GABSZEWICZ AND J.-F. THISSE

Center for Operations Research & Econometrics, Université Catholique de Louvain, Louvain-la-Neuve 1348, Belgium

Received August 6, 1979

The entry process in an industry embodying more or less close substitutes is considered. One examines whether the increase in the number of substitutes induces pure competition when prices are chosen noncooperatively. It is shown that there exists an upper bound on the number of firms which can compete in the market: when this upperbound is reached, any further entry entails the exit of an existing firm. In spite of this fact, new entries imply the decrease of prices to the competitive ones.

Since Cournot [3], there has been a long-standing tradition according to which entry into a homogeneous market, where oligopolists use quantity strategies, restores pure competition (see, for instance, [5] or [7]). Intuitively, when the number of firms increases, the ability of each oligopolist to alter the value of the inverse demand function through his own strategic choice must necessarily diminish, and vanishes at the limit. By contrast, if the firms use price strategies on the same market, it has been known since Bertrand [1] that pure competition obtains already with two firms. Clearly the loss induced by undercutting the competitor's price is broadly compensated by capturing the whole demand. With Hotelling [4] and Chamberlin [2], the idea was developed that firms operate through product differentiation in order to avoid price competition "à la Bertrand." Nevertheless, within such a context, the problem remains open whether, by analogy with the homogeneous case, the increase in the number of substitutes in the industry induces pure competition when prices are chosen noncooperatively.

In order to deal with this problem, the approach employed for the homogeneous case suggests starting out with an entry process where the entrants arrive in the industry with products which are more or less close substitutes for the existing ones, and then studying the asymptotic behavior of noncooperative prices when the number of entrants tends to infinity. It is the purpose of this article to show through an example that this procedure

* The major part of this work was done while the first author was visiting Bonn University. Financial support from the Sonderforschungsbereich 21 is gratefully acknowledged.

Reprinted from *Journal of Economic Theory* **22,** No. 2, 327-338 (April 1980)
ISBN 0-12-476750-8

cannot be transposed as such to the case of a differentiated industry with price strategies.

Our example suggests that *the number of firms which can coexist in a differentiated industry cannot exceed a finite value* n^* (in our example, the number n^* is determined by a set of parameters which describe our simple economy, inspired by a previous work of the authors [6]). Surprisingly, if more than n^* firms try to remain on the market, they will necessarily jostle each other, and this struggle will provoke the exit of one of them. Still more surprising is that *this upper bound on the number of firms does not preclude that entry reinforces the tendency toward pure competition.*

In fact, the entry process decomposes into three successive phases. The first one corresponds to the situation where the number of firms is such that the whole market is not supplied at the equilibrium prices. The second obtains when the whole market is served, but where room is left for the entry of some additional firms. In the third, and last, phase, the number of potential firms is larger than n^*. It will be shown that in both the first and second phases, new entries entail decreases in prices of the products already sold on the market. As for the third phase, a new entry is now necessarily accompanied by the exit of another firm. But, in spite of the fixed number of firms still allowed on the market, equilibrium prices must necessarily decrease to the competitive ones when the number of entrants increases.

Finally, it must be noted that competition can also be restored with means other than the number of firms, because product differentiation adds a new dimension to the rivalry among firms. Our example suggests that, more than from the number of firms, perfect competition could emerge from the close substitutability among the products, thus confirming the "objection péremptoire" of Bertrand against Cournot.

The authors have recently proposed a model for dealing with a situation of differentiated duopoly [6]. Its extension to an arbitrary number of firms can provide a natural framework for settling an example in which the above questions can be discussed.

Imagine an industry constituted by n *firms*, indexed by k, $k = 1,\ldots, n$; firm k sells, at no cost, product k; all these products are more or less close substitutes for each other. Let $T = [0, 1]$ be the set of *consumers*, which are assumed to be ranked in T by order of increasing income, and let the income $R(t)$ of consumer $t \in T$ be given by

$$R(t) = R_1 + R_2 t, \qquad R_1 > 0,\ R_2 \geqslant 0.$$

Consumers are also assumed to make indivisible and mutually exclusive purchases. Thus if consumer t decides to buy one of the products, k, he buys that product only, and a single unit of it.

Let us denote by $u(k, R)$ the utility of having one unit of product k and an income R, and by $u(0, R)$ the utility of having no unit of any product and an income R. In our example we take the further specification[1]

$$u(k, R) = u_k \cdot R = u_1 \cdot [1 + \alpha(k-1)] \cdot R, \qquad \alpha \geqslant 0, \tag{1}$$

and

$$u(0, R) = u_0 \cdot R \tag{2}$$

with $u_1 > u_0 > 0$.

In this specification, u_k is a "utility index" which ranks the quality of the products: if $k > h$, product k is more desired than product h. The parameter α is a measure of the substitutability between products k; thus, for $\alpha = 0$ all products are perfect substitutes, and substitutability decreases when α increases.

Let p_k be the price quoted by oligopolist k; product k would be bought by customer t rather than product j, $j \neq k$, if and only if

$$\begin{aligned} u(k, R(t) - p_k) &= u_1 \cdot [1 + \alpha(k-1)](R_1 + R_2 t - p_k) \\ &\geqslant u_1 \cdot [1 + \alpha(j-1)](R_1 + R_2 t - p_j) = u(j, R(t) - p_j). \end{aligned} \tag{3}$$

To be sure that t buys product k, we must further have

$$\begin{aligned} u(k, R(t) - p_k) &= u_1 \cdot [1 + \alpha(k-1)](R_1 + R_2 t - p_k) \\ &\geqslant u_0 \cdot (R_1 + R_2 t) = u(0, R(t)). \end{aligned} \tag{4}$$

(The consumer must prefer to buy product k rather than nothing.)

In what follows we want to characterize a noncooperative price equilibrium for the above framework. By this we mean an n-tuple of prices such that no firm can increase its profit by any unilateral deviation and such that each of the n products obtains a positive market share. To this end, let us derive the contingent demand function for each oligopolist, under the assumption that each of the n firms has a positive market share. Let $M_k(\bar{p}_1, \ldots, p_k, \ldots, \bar{p}_n)$ be the *market share* of firm k defined by

$$M_k(\bar{p}_1, \ldots, p_k, \ldots, \bar{p}_n) = \{t \mid t \text{ buys product } k \text{ at prices } (\bar{p}_1, \ldots, p_k, \ldots, \bar{p}_n)\},$$

and let (t, τ) be a pair of consumers such that $t < \tau$ (which implies that t is poorer than τ). Using (1), it is easily seen that if t chooses to buy product k, then τ will not choose to buy a product $k - j$ of lower quality, with $j \in$

[1] Note that this formulation does not imply any restriction with respect to our analysis in [6], when $n = 2$.

$\{1,..., k-1\}$. Similarly, again using (1), if τ chooses to buy product k, then t will not choose to buy a product $k+j$ of higher quality, with $j \in \{1,..., n-k\}$. It follows that $M_k(\bar{p}_1,..., p_k,..., \bar{p}_n)$ is defined by an interval I_k of [0, 1] and that the intervals I_k are ranked from the left to the right of [0, 1] in an increasing order. Given our hypothesis that each consumer of brand k buys only a single unit of that product, the contingent demand function of oligopolist k is equal to the length of the interval I_k. To determine that length, it is sufficient to identify both extremities of I_k. First, let k be a product such that $1 < k < n$. The lower extremity of I_k is given by the consumer who is just indifferent between buying product k or product $k-1$, since by assumption all the firms are on the market. Similarly the upper extremity is defined by the consumer who is just indifferent between purchasing product k or product $k+1$. According to (3), the lower and upper extremities of I_k are consequently given by

$$t_k(\bar{p}_1,..., p_k,..., \bar{p}_n) \underset{\text{def}}{=} \frac{u_k p_k - u_{k-1} p_{k-1}}{(u_k - u_{k-1}) R_2} - \frac{R_1}{R_2} \tag{5}$$

and

$$t_{k+1}(\bar{p}_1,..., p_k,..., \bar{p}_n) \underset{\text{def}}{=} \frac{u_{k+1} p_{k+1} - u_k p_k}{(u_{k+1} - u_k) R_2} - \frac{R_1}{R_2}, \tag{6}$$

so that the demand function $\mu[M_k(\bar{p}_1,..., p_k,..., \bar{p}_n)]$ is equal to

$$\mu[M_k(\bar{p}_1,..., p_k,..., \bar{p}_n)] = t_{k+1}(\bar{p}_1,..., p_k,..., \bar{p}_n) - t_k(\bar{p}_1,..., \bar{p}_n). \tag{7}$$

Let us now consider the case of product n. Since no brand of higher quality exists, the upper extremity of I_n is provided by the richest customer $t = 1$, so that the demand function of oligopolist n is given by

$$\begin{aligned}\mu[M_n(\bar{p}_1,..., \bar{p}_k,..., p_n)] &= 1 - t_n(\bar{p}_1,..., \bar{p}_k,..., p_n)\\ &= 1 - \frac{u_n p_n - u_{n-1} p_{n-1}}{(u_n - u_{n-1}) R_2} + \frac{R_1}{R_2}.\end{aligned} \tag{8}$$

Finally let us envision the case of product 1. Since no brand of lower quality is offered and if the whole market is not served, the lower extremity of I_1 is provided by the consumer who is just indifferent between buying product 1 or buying nothing, i.e., using (4) with $k = 1$,

$$t_1(p_1,..., \bar{p}_k,..., \bar{p}_n) \underset{\text{def}}{=} \frac{u_1 p_1}{(u_1 - u_0) R_2} - \frac{R_1}{R_2}; \tag{9}$$

the demand function of oligoplist 1 is then given by

$$\mu[M_1(p_1,..., \bar{p}_k,..., \bar{p}_n)] = t_2(p_1,..., \bar{p}_k,..., \bar{p}_n) - t_1(p_1,..., \bar{p}_k,..., \bar{p}_n). \tag{10}$$

On the other hand, if the whole market is served, the lower extremity of I_1 is defined by the poorest customer $t = 0$, so that the demand function of oligopolist 1 is then equal to

$$\mu[M_1(p_1, \ldots, \bar{p}_k, \ldots, \bar{p}_n)] = t_2(p_1, \ldots, \bar{p}_k, \ldots, \bar{p}_n). \tag{11}$$

Denote by $P_k(\bar{p}_1, \ldots, p_k, \ldots, \bar{p}_n) = p_k \cdot \mu[M_k(\bar{p}_1, \ldots, p_k, \ldots, \bar{p}_n)]$ the profit function of firm k. A *noncooperative price equilibrium* is defined as an n-tuple of prices $(p_1^*, \ldots, p_k^*, \ldots, p_n^*)$ such that no firm k can increase its profit by any unilateral deviation from p_k^* when other firms j stick to prices $p_j^*, j \neq k$, and $\mu[M_k(p_1^*, \ldots, p_k^*, \ldots, p_n^*)] > 0, \forall\, k = 1, \ldots, n$.[2]

Let us now determine the equilibrium prices, successively, when the whole market is not served $(\sum_{k=1}^{n} \mu[M_k(p_1^*, \ldots, p_n^*)] < 1)$ and when it is entirely served $(\sum_{k=1}^{n} \mu[M_k(p_1^*, \ldots, p_n^*)] = 1)$. In the first case, the demand functions are described by (7), (8), and (10). Assuming that there exists a noncooperative price equilibrium, the following first-order conditions must be satisfied:

$$\left.\frac{\partial P_1}{\partial p_1}\right|_{(p_1^*, \ldots, p_n^*)} = \frac{(1 + \alpha)\, u_1 p_2^* - 2u_1 p_1^*}{\alpha u_1 R_2} - \frac{2u_1 p_1^*}{(u_1 - u_0)\, R_2} = 0,$$

$$\left.\frac{\partial P_k}{\partial p_k}\right|_{(p_1^*, \ldots, p_n^*)} = \frac{(1 + \alpha k)\, u_1 p_{k+1}^* - 2[1 + \alpha(k-1)]\, u_1 p_k^*}{\alpha u_1 R_2} - \frac{2[1 + \alpha(k-1)]\, u_1 p_k^* - [1 + \alpha(k-2)]\, u_1 p_{k-1}^*}{\alpha u_1 R_2} = 0,$$

$$k = 2, \ldots, n-1,$$

$$\left.\frac{\partial P_n}{\partial p_n}\right|_{(p_1^*, \ldots, p_n^*)} = 1 - \frac{2[1 + \alpha(n-1)]\, u_1 p_n^* - [1 + \alpha(n-2)]\, u_1 p_{n-1}^*}{\alpha u_1 R_2} + \frac{R_1}{R_2} = 0,$$

[2] The contingent demand functions we have derived above are only valid in the restricted domains of price strategies for which all the n oligopolists obtain a positive market share. Without this assumption the possibility should indeed be recognized that, for any group of products, n-tuples of prices can be found which would cancel the demand for any product in that group. Nevertheless, it can be shown that the equilibrium prices calculated in the restricted domains are in fact equilibrium prices over the whole domains. The reason is that the profit function of each oligopolist is quasi-concave over the whole domain of its strategies, so that a local best reply is also a global one. This subject will be dealt in a forthcoming paper.

which reduce to the system of difference equations:

$$(1 + \alpha)(u_1 - u_0)\, p_2^* - 2[(u_1 - u_0) + \alpha u_1]\, p_1^* = 0,$$
$$(1 + \alpha k)\, p_{k+1}^* - 4[1 + \alpha(k - 1)]\, p_k^* + [1 + \alpha(k - 2)]\, p_{k-1}^* = 0,$$
$$k = 2,\ldots, n - 1,$$
$$-2[1 + \alpha(n - 1)]\, p_n^* + [1 + \alpha(n - 2)]\, p_{n-1}^* = -\alpha(R_1 + R_2).$$

Using the change of variables defined by

$$x_k = [1 + \alpha(k - 1)]\, p_k^* \tag{12}$$

the above system can be rewritten as

$$\begin{aligned} &(u_1 - u_0)\, x_2 - 2[(u_1 - u_0) + \alpha u_1]\, x_1 = 0,\\ &x_{k+1} - 4x_k + x_{k-1} = 0, \qquad k = 2,\ldots, n - 1,\\ &-2x_n + x_{n-1} = -\alpha(R_1 + R_2), \end{aligned} \qquad \{1\}$$

the solution of which is

$$x_k = A_n(2 + 3^{1/2})^k + B_n(2 - 3^{1/2})^k$$

with

$$A_n = \frac{\alpha(2 - 3^{1/2})[3^{1/2}(u_1 - u_0) + 2\alpha u_1](R_1 + R_2)}{\left((3u_1 - 3u_0 + 2 \cdot 3^{1/2}\alpha u_1)(2 + 3^{1/2})^{n-1} - (3u_1 - 3u_0 - 2 \cdot 3^{1/2}\alpha u_1)(2 - 3^{1/2})^{n-1}\right)}$$

and

$$B_n = \frac{\alpha(2 + 3^{1/2})[3^{1/2}(u_1 - u_0) - 2\alpha u_1](R_1 + R_2)}{\left((3u_1 - 3u_0 + 2 \cdot 3^{1/2}\alpha u_1)(2 + 3^{1/2})^{n-1} - (3u_1 - 3u_0 - 2 \cdot 3^{1/2}\alpha u_1)(2 - 3^{1/2})^{n-1}\right)}.$$

Given (12), we finally obtain

$$p_k^* = \frac{1}{[1 + \alpha(k - 1)]}\,[A_n(2 + 3^{1/2})^k + B_n(2 - 3^{1/2})^k]. \tag{13}$$

These prices are only valid when the whole market is not served. In order to guarantee that this condition is satisfied, we must have, in particular, that the equilibrium price p_1^* for oligopolist 1 obtained from (13) is larger than $[(u_1 - u_0)/u_1]\, R_1$ (by (4) with $k = 1$), i.e.,

$$\frac{R_1}{R_2} < \frac{2u_1\alpha\, 3^{1/2}}{\left(3(u_1 - u_0)[(2 + 3^{1/2})^{n-1} - (2 - 3^{1/2})^{n-1}] + 2u_1\alpha\, 3^{1/2}[(2 + 3^{1/2})^{n-1} + (2 - 3^{1/2})^{n-1} - 1]\right)}. \tag{14}$$

In the case where the whole market is served, the demand functions are defined by (7), (8), and (11). Hence an interior noncooperative price equilibrium must verify the first-order conditions

$$\left.\frac{\partial P_1}{\partial p_1}\right|_{(p_1^*,\ldots,p_n^*)} = \frac{(1+\alpha)\,u_1 p_2^* - 2u_1 p_1^*}{\alpha u_1 R_2} - \frac{R_1}{R_2} = 0,$$

$$\left.\frac{\partial P_k}{\partial p_k}\right|_{(p_1^*,\ldots,p_n^*)} = \frac{(1+\alpha k)\,u_1 p_{k+1}^* - 2[1+\alpha(k-1)]\,u_1 p_k^*}{\alpha u_1 R_1}$$

$$- \frac{2[1+\alpha(k-1)]\,u_1 p_k^* - [1+\alpha(k-2)]\,u_1 p_{k-1}^*}{\alpha u_1 R_2} = 0,$$

$$k = 2,\ldots, n,$$

$$\left.\frac{\partial P_n}{\partial p_n}\right|_{(p_1^*,\ldots,p_n^*)} = 1 - \frac{2[1+\alpha(n-1)]\,u_1 p_n^* - [1+\alpha(n-2)]\,u_1 p_{n-1}^*}{\alpha u_1 R_2}$$

$$+ \frac{R_1}{R_2} = 0,$$

which, for the change of variables (12), are equivalent to the system of difference equations

$$\begin{aligned} x_2 - 2x_1 &= \alpha R_1, \\ x_{k+1} - 4x_k + x_{k-1} &= 0, \qquad k = 2,\ldots, n-1, \\ -2x_n + x_{n-1} &= -\alpha(R_1 + R_2), \end{aligned} \tag{\{2\}}$$

whose solution is given by

$$x_k = A_n'(2+3^{1/2})^k + B_n'(2-3^{1/2})^k$$

with

$$A_n' = \frac{(3 - 2\cdot 3^{1/2})[\alpha(2-3^{1/2})^{n-1} R_1 - \alpha(R_1+R_2)]}{3[(2+3^{1/2})^{n-1} - (2-3^{1/2})^{n-1}]}$$

and

$$B_n' = \frac{(3 + 2\cdot 3^{1/2})[\alpha(2+3^{1/2})^{n-1} R_1 - \alpha(R_1+R_2)]}{3[(2+3^{1/2})^{n-1} - (2-3^{1/2})^{n-1}]}$$

so that p_k^* is defined by

$$p_k^* = \frac{1}{[1+\alpha(k-1)]}\,[A_n'(2+3^{1/2})^k + B_n'(2-3^{1/2})^k]. \tag{15}$$

These prices are only valid when the market is entirely served and when each oligopolist gets a positive market share. To this effect, the equilibrium price p_1^* of oligopolist 1 given by (15) must be smaller than or equal to $[(u_1 - u_0)/u_1]\, R_1$, i.e.,

$$\frac{2u_1\alpha\, 3^{1/2}}{\left(\begin{array}{l}3(u_1 - u_0)[(2 + 3^{1/2})^{n-1} - (2 - 3^{1/2})^{n-1}] \\ \qquad + u_1\alpha\, 3^{1/2}[(2 + 3^{1/2})^{n-1} + (2 - 3^{1/2})^{n-1} - 2]\end{array}\right)} \leqslant \frac{R_1}{R_2} \tag{16}$$

and $\mu[M_1(p_1^*,\ldots, p_k^*,\ldots, p_n^*)]$ must be positive, i.e.,

$$\frac{R_1}{R_2} < \frac{2}{(2 + 3^{1/2})^{n-1} + (2 - 3^{1/2})^{n-1} - 2}\,. \tag{17}$$

So far, we have characterized equilibrium prices in an industry embodying n firms selling products whose respective utility indices satisfy relationship (1). Equipped with this framework, we may now study the change in prices and market shares when the number of firms increases. To proceed in that direction, we shall assume that new firms always enter the market with higher-quality products, namely, that the $(n + 1)$st firm enters the market with a utility index u_{n+1} equal to $(1 + \alpha n)\, u_1$.[3]

To begin with, let us assume that the starting number n of firms is such that the whole market is not served. In this case, we know that condition (14) must hold and that equilibrium prices are given by (13). Defining $\bar{n}$ as the largest integer for which condition (14) is verified, it means that $n \leqslant \bar{n}$. If a new firm enters, then either $n + 1$ is still smaller than or equal to $\bar{n}$, or $n + 1$ is greater than $\bar{n}$. In the first alternative, it is easily verified that *the "after-entry" equilibrium prices for existing firms*, still given by (13), *are smaller than the "pre-entry" equilibrium prices*. Consequently, as long as the whole market is not served, equilibrium prices form a decreasing sequence of the number of the new entrants. In the second alternative, the whole market is served. Assuming that an interior noncooperative price equilibrium is observed with $(\bar{n} + 1)$ firms (which is fulfilled if condition (16) holds for $\bar{n} + 1$), the equilibrium prices are then given by (15). Computing $\partial p_k^*/\partial n$ from (15), we obtain the result that, as soon as the whole market is served, equilibrium prices again form a decreasing sequence when the number of entrants increases.

Our major finding is that this entry process cannot allow a continuously increasing number of firms with a positive market share. Indeed, for all the firms already on the market to maintain a positive share, we know that condition (17), among others, must be satisfied. As the right-hand side of (17) is a decreasing function of n, there exists a maximal number, say n^*, of firms for

[3] Although the use of this particular entry process entails some loss of generality, that loss is comparable with the loss of generality which follows from assuming that all firms are identical, a hypothesis usually made in the theory of entry with homogeneous products. Moreover, analogous processes are considered in the recent literature in location theory (see, for instance, [8]).

which (17) can still hold. For $n > n^*$, the converse of (17) must be verified: income disparities, as expressed in our model by the value of R_2, are no longer sufficient to sustain an industry embodying a larger number of firms. In other words, *the income distribution determines endogenously the maximal number of products which defines the industry.* It is our belief that the number n^* can be viewed as a kind of long-run equilibrium number of firms in the sense that, when this number is reached, no room is left for a larger number of products.

Does it mean that no other firm with a higher-quality product can enter when the long-run equilibrium number n^* is reached? The answer is no. Indeed the entry of a new firm can take place, provided, however, that it is accompanied by the exit of another. Assume that a firm selling a product with utility index $u_{n^*+1} = (1 + \alpha n^*)\, u_1$ decides to enter. It then follows from the definition of n^* that at least one other firm must necessarily obtain a null market share at the after-entry equilibrium. In fact, it can be shown that only one firm must exit at the after-entry equilibrium and that it can be only firm 1 (see the proposition given in the Appendix). Consequently, after entry of firm $n^* + 1$, the industry again embodies n^* firms, but now with indices $\{2,..., n^* + 1\}$. More generally, the entry of firm $n^* + m$, with utility index $u_{n^*+m} = [1 + \alpha(n^* + m - 1)]\, u_1$, would similarly lead to an industry profile defined by the firms $\{m + 1,..., n^* + m\}$. Interestingly, *the after-entry equilibrium prices form a sequence decreasing to the competitive prices as the number m of new entrants increases.* Indeed, the equilibrium price of firm k is given by

$$p_k^* = \frac{1}{1 + \alpha(k - 1)} [A'_{n^*}(2 + 3^{1/2})^{k-m} + B'_{n^*}(2 - 3^{1/2})^{k-m}],$$

with $k = m + 1,..., m + n^*$ (again see the proposition of the Appendix). Among other things, this result implies that we may observe low prices in an industry embodying a fixed, and possibly small, number of firms provided m is large enough.

Let us illustrate the whole process we have just described when the long-run equilibrium number n^* is equal to 2. Let firm 1 initially be a monopolist in the industry and sell a product with utility index u_1. By the choice rule (4) with $k = 1$, one easily checks that the market share $M_1(p_1)$ is defined by the interval I_1 whose lower and upper extremities are respectively given by

$$t_1(p_1) = \text{Max} \left\{0, \frac{u_1 p_1}{(u_1 - u_0) R_2} - \frac{R_1}{R_2}\right\}$$

and 1. The demand function $\mu[M_1(p_1)]$ faced by firm 1 is then

$$\text{Min} \left\{1, 1 - \frac{u_1 p_1}{(u_1 - u_0) R_2} + \frac{R_1}{R_2}\right\}.$$

Assuming $R_1/R_2 < 1$, a simple calculation shows that the monopoly price is equal to $\frac{1}{2}[(u_1 - u_0)/u_1](R_1 + R_2)$. Since, at this price, all the consumers are not served, room is left for entry of firm 2 with utility index $u_2 = (1 + \alpha) u_1$. Assuming also that condition (16) holds for $n = 2$, namely,

$$\frac{\alpha}{3(u_1 - u_0) + \alpha u_1} \leqslant \frac{R_1}{R_2},$$

we deduce from the above that the whole market is supplied at the equilibrium prices

$$p_1^* = \frac{\alpha(R_2 - R_1)}{3} \quad \text{and} \quad p_2^* = \frac{\alpha(2R_2 + R_1)}{3(1 + \alpha)};$$

consequently, $\bar{n} = 1$.[4] Suppose further that condition (17) is not fulfilled for $n = 3$, namely, that $\frac{1}{6} \leqslant R_1/R_2$; accordingly, $n^* = 2$. Hence under the hypothesis

$$\max \left\{ \frac{\alpha}{3(u_1 - u_0) + \alpha u_1}, \frac{1}{6} \right\} \leqslant \frac{R_1}{R_2} < 1,$$

two firms, and only two firms, may remain in the industry forever. If firm 3 with utility index $u_3 = (1 + 2\alpha) u_1$ would in turn enter the market, then a new equilibrium would emerge at which firm 1 has been enforced to exit, with prices

$$p_2^* = \frac{\alpha(R_2 - R_1)}{3(1 + \alpha)} \quad \text{and} \quad p_3^* = \frac{\alpha(2R_2 + R_1)}{3(1 + 2\alpha)}.$$[5]

It remains to study the role of substitutability among the products at the equilibrium. First note that, whatever the fixed number of products, a value of α sufficiently small exists for condition (16) to be satisfied. In this case, equilibrium prices are then given by (15). Second, these equilibrium prices form a decreasing sequence which converges to zero as the substitutability between products increases, that is, as α tends to zero. As stated above, pure competition is the limit of a process where products become more and more homogeneous. At the limit this is nothing else but the "objection péremptoire" of Bertrand against Cournot.

Appendix

PROPOSITION. *Let q and m be two arbitrary integers such that $q \leqslant m + 1$ and let the firms defined by the set of indices $\{q, \ldots, n^*, \ldots, n^* + m\}$. A non-*

[4] A more extensive discussion of the market solution for $n = 2$ is contained in [6].

[5] This illustration shows that the long-run equilibrium number is not necessarily very large. A priori, to any value of n, there corresponds an income distribution which authorizes a number of firms at most equal to this value. Possibly, with a high degree of income dispersion, a large number of products will be observed.

cooperative price equilibrium involves exactly n^* firms given by the set of indices $\{m + 1,..., n^* + m\}$. Furthermore, the equilibrium price of firm k, with $k = m + 1,..., n^* + m$ is given by

$$p_k^* = \frac{1}{1 + \alpha(k-1)} \cdot [A'_{n^*}(2 + 3^{1/2})^{k-m} + B'_{n^*}(2 - 3^{1/2})^{k-m}]. \quad (18)$$

Proof. Assume that the firms defined by $\{q,..., n^* + m\}$ have a positive market share at the equilibrium and that the firms defined by $\{1,..., q - 1\}$ have been put out of business. In this case, the equilibrium prices must verify the following first-order conditions:

$$(1 + \alpha q)\, p_{q+1}^* - 2[1 + \alpha(q-1)]\, p_q^* - \alpha R_1 = 0,$$

$$(1 + \alpha k)\, p_{k+1}^* - 4[1 + \alpha(k-1)]\, p_k^* + [1 + \alpha(k-2)]\, p_{k-1}^* = 0,$$
$$k = q + 1 \cdots n^* + m - 1,$$

$$\alpha(R_1 + R_2) - 2[1 + \alpha(n^* + m - 1)]\, p_{n^*+m}^*$$
$$+ [1 + \alpha(n^* + m - 2)]\, p_{n^*+m-1}^* = 0.$$

Using the change of variables defined by (12), we obtain

$$\begin{gathered} x_{q+1} - 2x_q - \alpha R_1 = 0, \\ x_{k+1} - 4x_k + x_{k-1} = 0, \qquad k = q + 1,..., n^* + m - 1, \\ \alpha(R_1 + R_2) - 2x_{n^*+m} + x_{n^*+m-1} = 0. \end{gathered} \quad \{3\}$$

Furthermore, setting $j = k - q + 1$ yields the system

$$\begin{gathered} x_2 - 2x_1 - \alpha R_1 = 0, \\ x_{j+1} - 4x_j + x_{j-1} = 0, \qquad j = 2,..., n^* + m - q, \\ \alpha(R_1 + R_2) - 2x_{n^*+m-q+1} + x_{n^*+m-q} = 0. \end{gathered} \quad \{4\}$$

This system is identical to system {2}, with $n = n^* + m - q + 1$, so that its solution is given by

$$x_j = A'_{n^*+m-q+1}(2 + 3^{1/2})^j + B'_{n^*+m-q+1}(2 - 3^{1/2})^j,$$
$$j = 1,..., n^* + m - q + 1,$$

i.e.,

$$x_k = A'_{n^*+m-q+1}(2 + 3^{1/2})^{k-q+1} + B'_{n^*+m-q+1}(2 - 3^{1/2})^{k-q+1},$$
$$k = q,..., n^* + m,$$

which leads to

$$p_k^* = \frac{1}{1 + \alpha(k-1)} \cdot [A'_{n^*+m-q+1}(2 + 3^{1/2})^{k-q+1} + B'_{n^*+m-q+1}(2 - 3^{1/2})^{k-q+1}]. \quad (19)$$

By definition of a noncooperative price equilibrium, each firm must have a positive market share. In particular, this must be true for firm q, so that

$$u_{q+1} p_{q+1}^* - u_q p_q^* > \alpha R_1 .$$

The latter condition is verified if and only if condition (17) holds for $n^* + m - q + 1$, which is impossible as long as $q < m + 1$. Consequently, firm q cannot afford a positive market share. As a similar argument applies to firms $k = q + 1, ..., k = m$, *exactly* n^* firms, namely, the firms defined by $\{m + 1, ..., n^* + m\}$, remain on the market and the corresponding equilibrium prices are provided by (19), where $q = m + 1$, i.e., by (18). Q.E.D.

Acknowledgments

We thank J. Drèze and an anonymous referee for their helpful comments.

References

1. J. Bertrand, Théorie mathématique de la richesse sociale, *J. Savants* (1883), 499–508.
2. E. H. Chamberlin, "The Theory of Monopolistic Competition," 7th ed., Harvard Univ. Press, Cambridge, Mass. 1956.
3. A. A. Cournot, "Recherches sur les principes mathématiques de la théorie des richesses," Librairie des Sciences politiques et sociales, M. Rivière et Cie, Paris, 1838.
4. H. Hotelling, Stability in competition, *Econ. J.* **39** (1929), 41–57.
5. J. Jaskold Gabszewicz and J. P. Vial, Oligopoly "à la Cournot" in a general equilibrium analysis, *J. Econ. Theory* **4** (1972), 381–400.
6. J. Jaskold Gabszewicz and J.-F. Thisse, Price competition, quality and income disparities, *J. Econ. Theory* **20** (1979), 340–359.
7. W. Novshek and H. Sonnenschein, Cournot and Walras equilibrium, *J. Econ. Theory* **19** (1978), 223–266.
8. E. C. Prescott and M. Visscher, Sequential location among firms with foresights, *Bell J. Econ.* **8** (1977), 378–393.

Efficiency Properties of Strategic Market Games: An Axiomatic Approach*

PRADEEP DUBEY

Yale University, New Haven, Connecticut 06520

ANDREU MAS-COLELL

University of California, Berkeley, California 94720

AND

MARTIN SHUBIK

Yale University, New Haven, Connecticut 06520

Received July 23, 1979

The paper investigates the conditions under which an abstractly given market game will have the property that if there is a continuum of traders then every noncooperative equilibrium is Walrasian. In other words, we look for a general axiomatization of Cournot's well-known result. Besides some convexity, continuity, and nondegeneracy hypotheses, the crucial axioms are: anonymity (i.e., the names of traders are irrelevant to the market) and aggregation (i.e., the net trade received by a trader depends only on his own action and the mean action of all traders). It is also shown that the same axioms do not guarantee efficiency if there is only a finite number of traders. Some examples are discussed and a notion of strict noncooperative equilibrium for anonymous games is introduced.

1. INTRODUCTION

In this paper we shall attempt an axiomatization of a central theme of economic theory, namely, the idea that the noncooperative equilibria of

* This paper brings together and supersedes Dubey and Shubik (1978) and Mas-Colell (1978). We are indebted for discussion, suggestions, and amendations to K. Arrow, W. Heller, L. Hurwicz, Ch. Kahn, E. Maskin, A. Postlewaite, and W. Thomson. The usual caveat applies. A. Mas-Colell's research was supported by NSF Grant SOC76-19700A01 and SOC77-06000. The latter grant was at the Institute for Mathematical Studies in the Social Sciences, Stanford University. The work of Dubey and Shubik relates to Department of the Navy Contract N00014-77-C-0518, issued by the Office of Naval Research under contract authority NR047-006.

Reprinted from *Journal of Economic Theory* **22**, No. 2, 339–362 (April 1980)
ISBN 0-12-476750-8

market-like economies with many relatively small traders are Walrasian (hence efficient) or, in other words, that price-taking behavior is, in a mass market, the natural consequence of "message taking" behavior. The classical partial equilibrium reference is, of course, Cournot's (1838). Two modern general-equilibrium version of Cournot's model are represented by Shubik (1973) [see also Shapley (1976), Shapley and Shubik (1977), Jaynes, Okuno, and Schmeidler (1978)] and by Gabszewicz–Vial (1972) [see also Hart (1979) and Novshek–Sonnenschein (1978)]. The work reported here develops from the Shubik line.

We take as our conceptual starting point the notion of Strategic Market Game, to be understood as a complete specification of trading rules and transaction constraints with respect to which a noncooperative equilibria is reached. This is to be contrasted with the theory of the core of a market, [which originated in Edgeworth (1881); see Hildenbrand (1974) and his references] where final outcomes are completely unconstrained by institutional mechanisms of trade.

The game being played in real economic life is quite complex. It is clear that there is not a unique, somehow given, way to formalize it as a strategic market game. So it is sound research strategy to build a gallery of models emphasizing different important features, their fine structure reflecting the host of institutional features of the economy not usually taken into account by the economic theorist, but of importance in the understanding of marketing and transaction technologies. Nevertheless, experience with different models indicates that a number of facts are quite robust to changes of specification. Among them: the noncooperative equilibria of markets with a finite number of traders tend (this is a suitably vague verb) to be inefficient, and the noncooperative equilibria of markets with many relatively small participants tend to be (almost) efficient. Thus, it seems justified in order to bring out the robustness of these phenomena to engage in axiomatics.

We proceed by sidestepping the modeling problem and assuming (admittedly, this is quite a lot to assume) that a strategic market game is given to us in an abstract manner. We then try to identify general principles yielding the efficiency results. Our axiomatization will be fairly transparent and, from the mathematical point of view, trivial. The basic principles turn out to be:

(i) convexity: traders have available a convex set of strategies.

(ii) anonymity: from the point of view of the market, only the message sent by the trader matters.

(iii) continuity: of outcomes with respect to strategies.

(iv) aggregation: the trading possibilities of any player are influenced by the messages of the other players only through the *mean* of those messages (and not, say, through the variance).

(v) nondegeneracy: it must be possible for individual players to influence to a substantial extent their trading possibilities in the market.

With the given axioms we first prove some inefficiency results for the finite number of traders case and then establish efficiency for the large number of small traders case. As in Aumann (1964) for "large number of small traders," we shall adopt the idealization of the continuum. We do this merely for convenience and in order to sharpen the essential facts. We will, however, devote one section to the asymptotic, in contrast to limit, theory. It is fortunate that the consideration of a large number of small traders (in the limit a continuum) has simplifying implications for noncooperative analysis. Indeed, under general conditions, if individual players are, in whichever is the relevant sense, very small relative to the size of the game, the only sensible expectations (at "equilibrium" or at "disequilibrium" plays) of individual players is that the rest of the players will not react (or react very little) to changes of their actions. Thus, in contrast to games among few, simple Cournot–Nash equilibrium emerges as the natural noncooperative solution. Our treatment of Cournot–Nash equilibrium in the continuum builds on a paper of Schmeidler (1973) which deserves to be better known.

There are clear similarities and connections between our formal structure and the extensive literature growing out of Hurwicz's (1960) seminal contribution on the designing of resource allocation mechanism. But it is important to keep in mind that the spirit of our work is very different. In particular, we do not attach normative significance to our results. For us, the market mechanism is given, and we merely analyze its properties.

The paper is organized as follows: Sections 2–5 present the basic model. Section 6 enumerates the axioms. Section 7 looks at the continuum as a limit of the finite but large situation. Section 8 discusses a nondegeneracy issue for equilibria. Sections 9 and 10 present efficiency results for the finite and continuum cases, respectively. Section 11 looks at examples; and, finally, Section 12 defines and discusses a type of noncooperative equilibria of special relevance to market situations.

2. Commodities, Agents, Assignments

The commodity space is R^l.

We let I, the set of agents names, be either a finite set equipped with the counting measure or the interval [0, 1] with Lebesgue measure (denoted λ). This will allow us to treat simultaneously the finite and the continuum cases.

An *assignment* is an integrable map $\mathbf{x}\colon I \to R^l$ such that $\int \mathbf{x}(t)\, dt = 0$. Note that we are concerned only with net trades.

3. Economies

We now look at the agents in I as the traders of an economy.

A *trader* is characterized by:

(i) a closed, convex, nonempty set $X \subset R^l$ of net trades, interpreted as the set of contracts the trader can honor, and

(ii) a complete and transitive preferences relation $\succsim \subset X \times X$. Every X is assumed to satisfy *free disposability*, i.e., if $x \in X$, then $x + R_+^l \subset X$. Preferences $\succsim$ are taken to be continuous, convex, and *monotone*. The set of characteristics is $\mathscr{A} = \{(X, \succsim)\}$. As in Hildenbrand (1974), one can view $\mathscr{A}$ as a measurable space by endowing it with the σ-field derived from the closed convergence topology on the closed subsets of R^l.

We define an economy à la Aumann (1963), i.e., as a (measurable) map $\mathscr{E}: I \to \mathscr{A}$. We denote $\mathscr{E}(t)$ by $(X_t, \succsim_t)$.

An assignment $\mathbf{x}: I \to R^l$ is *feasible* if $x(t) \in X_t$ for a.e. $t \in I$.

The existence of two types of trade constraints is a basic distinction in our treatment. We have the *public constraints* embodied in the fact that the sum of net trades must be zero (i.e., markets should clear) and the *private constraints* requiring that individual net trades belong to the individual trading sets. As a matter of interpretation we take that the private constraints are not publicly observable.

A feasible assignment $\mathbf{x}$ is efficient if there is no other feasible assignment $\mathbf{x}'$ such that $\mathbf{x}'(t) \succsim_t x(t)$ for a.e. $t \in I$ and $x'(t) \succ_t x(t)$ for a set of t's of positive measure.

A feasible assignment $\mathbf{x}$ is *Walrasian* if there is $p \in R^l$ such that for a.e. $t \in I$, $\mathbf{x}(t)$ is $\succsim_t$ maximal on $\{x \in X_t : p \cdot x \leqslant 0\}$. It is, of course, well known that, with the hypothesis made, a Walrasian assignment is efficient.

Remark 1. Note that (i) individual production (i.e., firms with a single owner) is encompassed by the model, (ii) consumption or technological externalities are not permitted.

4. Strategic Markets Games

We now look at the set of agents I as a set of players.

There is given a nonempty set S called the message, action, or strategy space. We assume that S is a *subset of a separable Banach space*. It will be conceptually simpler if the reader thinks of S as lying in a finite-dimensional space, i.e., a subset of some R^m.

A *play* is an integrable function $\mathbf{s}: I \to S$.

A *strategie market game* is specified by the *set of players* I, the *strategy space* S and an *outcome rule* Φ, which associates with every play $\mathbf{s}$ an assignment $\Phi(\mathbf{s})\colon I \to R^l$. If Φ is understood, we write $\mathbf{x_s}$ for $\Phi(\mathbf{s})$.

For the measure theoretic treatment to be sensible, we should require that the outcome rule satisfies the following property: *if* $[\mathbf{s}] = [\mathbf{s}']$, *then* $[\mathbf{x_s}] = [\mathbf{x_{s'}}]$. The symbol [ ] denotes the equivalence class of the function (i.e., all functions which are a.e. equal to the given function). Informally speaking, this property, which is nonvacuous only for the case $I = [0, 1]$, has the implication that (again for $I = [0, 1]$) individual actions do not have a macroscopic influence on market outcomes (i.e., pecuniary externalities are absent), which is a well-known heuristic requirement for a competitive process to yield efficient outcomes.

Let us illustrate with some examples. They will be discussed with more detail in Section 11, from where, especially for Example 1, a clearer understanding of the underlying economics will be gained.

EXAMPLE 1. [Shubik (1973)]. There are two commodities. The strategy space is R_+^2. A message (s_1, s_2) is to be interpreted as follows: s_1 (resp. s_2) is the amount of commodity 1 (resp. 2) a trader proposes to deliver to the market. Let $\mathbf{s}$ be a play. Suppose first that $\int \mathbf{s}_1, \int \mathbf{s}_2 > 0$. Then the outcome is given by

$$\mathbf{x_s}(t) = \left(\frac{\int \mathbf{s}_1}{\int \mathbf{s}_2}\, \mathbf{s}_2(t) - \mathbf{s}_1(t), \frac{\int \mathbf{s}_2}{\int \mathbf{s}_1}\, \mathbf{s}_1(t) - \mathbf{s}_2(t)\right).$$

If either $\int \mathbf{s}_1 = 0$ or $\int \mathbf{s}_2 = 0$, we put $\mathbf{x_s} \equiv 0$.

In the next two examples the strategies are whole demand-supply functions.

EXAMPLE 2. Again $l = 2$. The strategy set is $S = \{f \in C([0, r]) : f(0) \geqslant 0, f(r) \leqslant 0\}$, where r is some large number and for $p \in [0, r]$ one interprets $f(p)$ as a proposal to buy ("sell" if negative) $f(p)$ units of the second commodity in exchange for $pf(p)$ units of the first commodity. Let $\mathbf{s}$ be a play. Define

$$p = \max\left\{p \in [0, r]\colon \left(\int \mathbf{s}\right)(p) = 0\right\}.$$

Then the outcome is given by

$$\mathbf{x_s}(t) = (-p\, \mathbf{s}(t)(p), \mathbf{s}(t)(p)).$$

This example shows that there is substance in the implicit hypothesis that to every play $\mathbf{s}$ there corresponds a unique assignment. The rule for choosing one among the possibly many price equilibria is completely arbitrary. In the next example, the equilibrium is naturally unique.

EXAMPLE 3. Identical to Example 2 except that now $S = \{f \in C([0, r]) : f(0) \geqslant 0, f(r) \leqslant 0 \text{ and } f \text{ is decreasing}\}$.

Remark 2. In the case where S is infinite dimensional (which shall not be emphasized), "integrable" is taken to mean Pettis integrable [see, for example, Yosida (1971)].

Remark 3. We could in the definition of a play require simply that **s** be measurable, thus allowing for nonintegrable plays. But not much would be gained, since in fact we will have a need to integrate.

Remark 4. In the present approach the outcomes of a play are not necessarily feasible assignments. This is in keeping with the modelling of market institutions as blind to private characteristics. Any player is free to send any message to the market although the outcome of a play can be realized only if almost every trader can honor the proposed contract without going bankrupt. Thus, our strategies are more in the nature of proposals than actual actions, and to that extent the use of the term "game" may be a little abusive. A modeling via Debreu's Generalized Games (1952) would have been possible. The present situation can be contrasted with the well-known price tâtonnement. Here public constraints are always satisfied, but private ones need not be. There private constraints do hold, but not necessarily the public ones (i.e., at given arbitrary prices, there may be excess demand or supply).

Remark 5. The concept of strategic market games introduced in this section is formally related to the concept of allocation mechanism growing out of Hurwicz's (1960) approach to the *design* of resource allocation methods. [See, for example, Hurwicz (1979) and Schmeidler (1978)].

5. NONCOOPERATIVE EQUILIBRIA

For fixed I let an economy $\mathscr{E} : I \to \mathscr{A}$ and a strategic market game Φ with message space S be given.

DEFINITION. A play **s** is a Cournot–Nash (CN) equilibrium if $\mathbf{x_s}$ is feasible and for almost every $t \in I$, $\mathbf{x_s}(t)$ is $\succsim_t$ maximal on $X_t \cap \{\mathbf{x_{s'}}(t) : \mathbf{s}'(t') = \mathbf{s}(t') \text{ for all } t' \neq t\}$.

The assignment $\mathbf{x_s}$ corresponding to a CN play will be called a CN assignment.

Since we will very quickly specialize our model, we shall not dwell on a discussion of this definition.

Remark 6. For the continuum, i.e., $I = [0, 1]$, the definition of CN equilibrium has taken inspiration in Schmeidler's (1973) work on the non-cooperative theory of games with a continuum of players.

6. Axioms

Let the strategic market game Φ on a set of players I be given.

We shall restrict our consideration to strategic market games whose outcomes depend only on the strategies played and not on the names of the players. More precisely: (i) if two traders choose the same action, they get assigned the same net trade, and (ii) for a given fixed action of a trader, the net trade assigned depends only on the distribution of the strategies of all traders. Those are particular conditions, but they embody the anonymity principles of well-functioning markets: the trading possibilities of any particular economic agent are limited *only* by their availability of commodities to trade.

Our wish to impose an anonymity axiom explains two aspects of our treatment of strategic market games: the strategy sets of different players were assumed equal and the outcome of a play was not required to satisfy the private feasibility constraints.

Let $\mathcal{M}$ be the set of probability measures on S with finite mean. To every $\mathbf{s} : I \to S$ there corresponds an $\nu_{\mathbf{s}} = \lambda \circ \mathbf{s}^{-1} \in \mathcal{M}$.

Anonymity Axiom. There is a function $G : S \times \mathcal{M} \to R^l$ such that, for all plays $\mathbf{s}$, $x_{\mathbf{s}}(t) = G(\mathbf{s}(t), \nu_{\mathbf{s}})$ for all $t \in I$.

Clearly, for I finite, the function G is not unique, while for $I = [0, 1]$, it is trivially so.

Under the Anonymity Axiom, a play $\mathbf{s}$: $I \to S$ is a CN equilibrium if $G(\cdot, \nu_{\mathbf{s}}) : I \to R^l$ is a feasible assignment and, for a.e. $t \in I$, $G(\mathbf{s}(t), \nu_{\mathbf{s}})$ is $\succsim_t$ maximal on $X_t \cap \{G(s, \nu_{\mathbf{s}}) : \mathbf{s} \in S\}$.

A second, important axiom is:

Continuity Axiom. The function G given by the Anonymity Axiom is jointly continuous when $\mathcal{M}$ is endowed with the topology of the weak convergence [see (Hildenbrand, 1974, p. 48), for a definition].

Under the continuity axiom the uniqueness of G in the continuum case (i.e., $I = [0, 1]$) can be sharpened to: if for all $\nu \in \mathcal{M}$, G and G' are continuous and coincide on supp(ν), then $G = G'$.

A third axiom will be:

Convexity Axiom. The strategy set S is convex.

Given the previous axioms, our key hypothesis is:

Aggregation Axiom. For any $\nu, \nu' \in \mathscr{M}$ if $\int i d\nu = \int i d\nu'$, then $G(\cdot, \nu) = G(\cdot, \nu')$. The symbol i denotes the identity map.

In words: the net trade proposed to a player by the strategic market game does only depend on the message sent by this player and the mean message of all players. Particular as this condition is, we would argue that it reflects well the aggregate nature of the impact of demand and supply in organized markets. To be sure, it is quite possible that an economic trading situation may be most succinctly and naturally described in a way which does not satisfy the Aggregation Axiom. The point is, however, whether or not it can be described in some way for which it does, even if it perhaps involves a much expanded, but still convex, strategy space. For example, a typical competitive problem among firms may involve as individual strategies, price and quality (suppose there are only m possible qualities). The concept of mean quality is then irrelevant to the equilibrium problem. It may not even be defined. So, the Aggregation Axiom is not satisfied. On the other hand, if we view as the set of messages the much larger set of supply (and demand) functions for the m quality goods (with arguments the m vector of prices), then the Aggregation Axiom will hold.

We will postpone a more detailed discussion of the role of the different axioms until after the statement of the efficiency results in Section 10.

If the four axioms of this section are satisfied, it will be simpler to describe the strategic market game Φ by the continuous function $F: S \times S \to R^l$ such that $G(s, \nu) = F(s, \int i d\nu)$.

7. The Continuum as a Model for a Large Number of Participants

Suppose we have a continuum of traders $I = [0, 1]$, an economy $\mathscr{E}: I \to \mathscr{A}$ and a strategic market game Φ, with player set I, which satisfies the Anonymity, Continuity, Convexity, and Aggregation Axioms of the previous section, i.e., the strategic market game can simply be defined by a continuous function $F: S \times S \to R^l$. In which sense does this amount to a model for an economy and strategic market game with a large number of participants? We address this question now. Given the limited nature of the strategic games we deal with (anonymous, aggregable), this is not a difficult problem. Even so we shall not attempt to obtain the most general possible results.

Suppose we are given a sequence of trader sets I_n, $\#I_n < \infty$, economies $\mathscr{E}_n : I_n \to \mathscr{A}$, and strategic market games Φ_n with player set I_n and a common convex strategy space S. We assume that $\#I_n \to \infty$.

As in Hildenbrand (1974), we say that $\mathscr{E}_n \to \mathscr{E}$ if the distribution of characteristics induced by $\mathscr{E}_n$ converges weakly to the distribution of characteristics of $\mathscr{E}$.

For the sequence of strategic market games we assume: (i) there is a function $H : S \times \hat{S} \to R^l$, where $\hat{S}$ is the cone spanned by S, such that for all n, plays $\mathbf{s} : I_n \to S$ and $t \in I_n$, $\Phi_n(\mathbf{s})(t) = H(\mathbf{s}(t), \sum_{t \in I_n} \mathbf{s}(t))$ and (ii) the function H is homogeneous of degree zero in its second arguments, i.e., $H(s, \lambda b) = H(s, b)$ for all $\lambda > 0$. This could be called the Homogeneity Axiom.

We say that $\mathscr{E}_n$, Φ_n *converges to* $\mathscr{E}$, F if (i) $\mathscr{E}_n \to \mathscr{E}$ and

(ii) $F = H \mid S \times S$. Since H, F remain fixed, we identify $(\mathscr{E}_n, \Phi_n)$ with $\mathscr{E}_n$.

A comment to this definition may be useful. The requirement that H be common to all terms of the sequence is in order since we want to formalize the idea that the number of participants in some *fixed* market institutions increases. For the same reason, i.e., the market institutions do not depend on the number of participants, the function H is given in an unnormalized way. Thus the homogeneity axiom emerges as fundamental since it is this axiom which allows us to replace sums by averages and therefore to define a meaningful continuum model embodying the notion of the negligibility of individual participants. The sequences generated as in Examples 1–3 satisfy the axiom.

If assertions about CN equilibria in the continuum are to be relevant, then it should at least be true that the "limits" of CN equilibria for $\mathscr{E}$ are CN equilibria for the limit $\mathscr{E}$. But what is a limit of CN equilibria? We borrow the notion of equilibrium distribution introduced by Hart, Hildenbrand, and Kohlberg (1974). Given a (Borel) distribution μ on $\mathscr{A} \times S$, let $\mu_{\mathscr{A}}$, μ_S be the respective marginals. We say that μ is a CN distribution for $\mathscr{E}_n$ (resp. $\mathscr{E}$) if (i) $\mu_{\mathscr{A}}$ is the characteristic distribution of $\mathscr{E}_n$ (resp. $\mathscr{E}$) and (ii) for all $(X, \succsim, s) \in \text{supp}(\mu)$, $F(s, \int i\mu_S)$ is $\succsim$-maximal on $X \cap \{F(s', \int i d\mu'_S) : \text{all } s' \in S\}$, where i is the identity map on S and μ' is the distribution obtained by transferring a total mass of $1/n$ from $(X, \succsim, s)$ to $(X, \succsim, s')$ (resp. $\mu = \mu'$). Note that the concept of CN distribution captures everything essential in the definition of CN equilibria in the sense that if two CN equilibria have the same distribution, then they are identical up to a relabeling of the traders' names.

Then we have:

PROPOSITION 1. *Assume that for all n and $t \in I_n$, $X_t = R^l$. Let μ_n be a CN distribution for $\mathscr{E}_n$ and $\mu_n \to \mu$ weakly. Then μ is a CN distribution for $\mathscr{E}$.*

Proof. If $\mu_n \to \mu$, then $\mu_{n\mathscr{A}} \to \mu_{\mathscr{A}}$ and $\mu_{nS} \to \mu_S$. So the first condition in the definition of CN distribution is satisfied for μ. Now let $(\succsim, s) \in \text{supp}\,(\mu)$ (we can forget about X as $X = R^l$). Take $(\succsim_n, s_n) \to (\succsim, s)$, $(\succsim_n, s_n) \in$ supp. (μ_n). Call $x = F(s, \int i d\mu_S)$ and for arbitrary $s' \in S$ let $y = F(s', \int i d\mu_S)$. By the continuity of F, $x_n \to x$ and $y_n \to y$, where $x_n = F(s_n, \int i d\mu_{nS})$ and

$y_n = F(s', \int i\mu'_{nS})$. Hence $x \succsim y$ as $x_n \succsim_n y_n$ for all n. So, the second condition is also satisfied. ▮

Proposition 1 is a closed graph property for the CN equilibrium correspondence (defined from distribution on $\mathscr{A}$ to distribution on $\mathscr{A} \times S$). It is well known that in order to prove results of this sort it is essential that constraint sets correspondences be continuous. To guarantee this we take $X_t = R^l$ in Proposition 1. Of course, more general conditions could be given.

A stronger result than Proposition 1 would be the upper hemicontinuity of the equilibrium correspondence. Only then can we assert that the equilibria of large economies are near the equilibria of the continuum. Upper hemicontinuity obtains under the hypothesis of Proposition 1 and, for example, the very strong assumption that S be compact (this is trivial to prove). If upper hemicontinuity fails (as it may well be the case in the context, for example, of an Example 3), then the behavior of the equilibria in arbitrarily large economies may differ markedly from the continuum situation. See Thompson (1978) for examples where precisely this happens. This is an important point which does surely deserve closer investigation.

8. Proper and Full Cournot–Nash Equilibria

Our aim is to establish efficiency properties for CN equilibria. It is clear that, informally speaking, a necessary condition for efficiency is that individual net trades be responsive enough to individual actions. Indeed, if all markets are closed, every play is a CN equilibrium. It will be useful to distinguish two types of not totally unrelated local rigidities. The first would arise if in some markets there were quantitative limits on trades and some traders had reached them. The second would arise if some markets were effectively closed at the CN equilibrium. This motivates the following definitions.

Let the agents set I, economy $\mathscr{E}$ and strategic market game Φ be given. Suppose that $\mathbf{s}$ is a CN equilibrium. For every t let $B_t = \{\Phi(\mathbf{s}')(t) : \mathbf{s}'(t') = \mathbf{s}(t')$ for all $t' \neq t\}$.

We say that the CN equilibrium $\mathbf{s}$ is *proper* if for some $n \leqslant l$ and a.e. $t \in I$, a neighborhood of $\mathbf{x}_\mathbf{s}(t)$ on B_t is homeomorphic to R^n. If we can take $n \geqslant l - 1$, we say that the equilibrium is *full.*

Note that the notion of proper equilibrium is compatible with traders being at the boundary of their private trading sets.

We shall see in Section 11 that it is quite possible, and even typical, that for the same economy a strategic market game exhibit both full and nonfull CN equilibria. Improper equilibria would appear to be more pathological in "flexible prices" models, but they would be typical in rationing models.

9. ON THE EFFICIENCY OF THE CN NET TRADE ALLOCATIONS IN THE FINITE NUMBER OF TRADERS CASE

Let $F: S \times S \to R^l$ represent a strategic market game satisfying the four axioms of Section 7. It is fairly clear from the usual examples that if F acts on an economy with a finite number of traders, there is no reason to expect the CN equilibrium allocations to be efficient. We shall here illustrate this point by proving, under a number of simplifying but reasonable hypotheses, that given F and $n \geqslant 2$, there are economies with n traders exhibiting nonefficient full CN equilibria (which, further, cannot be perturbed away).

Let I be a traders index set with $\#I = n$. Given a play $\mathbf{s}: I \to S$ and $t \in I$, it is convenient to define: $\bar{s}_t = 1/(n-1) \sum_{t' \neq t} \mathbf{s}(t')$. Let also H: $S \times S \to R^l$ be given by $H(s, s') = F(s, (1/n)((n-1)s' + s))$. Then $B_{s'} = H(S, s')$ is the public budget of any $t \in I$ at any play $\mathbf{s}$ with $s' = 1/(n-1) \sum_{t' \in I\, t' \neq t} \mathbf{s}(t')$.

We shall make the following hypothesis:

(I) S is open and H is C^1.

(II) For all s, s', rank $D_s H(s, s') = l - 1$ and Range $D_s H(s, s') \cap R_+{}^l = \{0\}$.

(III) For some s and s' rank $D_{s,s'} H(s, s') = l$.

These are very reasonable hypotheses. Assumption (II) asserts that it is not possible by an infinitesimal displacement to get something from nothing, but that, subject to this fact, rank $D_s H(s, s')$ is maximal, i.e., $l - 1$. This is a clear requirement if there is to be any hope that the allocations induced by the CN equilibria of the strategic market game be efficient. Assumption (III) asserts that at some combination of actions the strategic market game allows, if cooperation prevails, for (local) unrestricted variation of an individual allocation (i.e., cooperation makes it possible for some individual to get something from nothing). It is satisfied if, for example, $H(S \times S)$ contains an open set.

PROPOSITION 2. *If H satisfies* (I), (II), *and* (III), *there is an economy $\mathscr{E}: I \to \mathscr{A}$ and a play $\mathbf{s}: I \to S$ such that*:

(i) $\mathbf{s}$ *is a CN equilibrium*,

(ii) *the net trade allocation of* $\mathbf{s}$ *is not efficient*.

Proof. Let s and s' be as in Assumption (III). With $I = \{1,..., n\}$, we consider the play $\mathbf{s}(1) = s$, $\mathbf{s}(j) = s'$ for $2 \leqslant j \leqslant n$. We let $s_i = \mathbf{s}(i)$, $s_i = \bar{s}_i$. By (II), for every i there is a unique $p_i \geqslant 0$, $\|p\| = 1$, such that $p_i \cdot D_s H(s_i, s_i') = 0$. Let $\mathbf{x}: I \to R^l$ be the net trade induced by $\mathbf{s}$. If $\mathbf{x}$ is to be efficient for any economy which satisfies our hypothesis and makes **s** into a CN equilibrium, then p_i must be the same for all i. Indeed, for every i, we can take $X_i = R^l$ and choose monotone preferences $\succsim_i$ representable by a C^1 utility function and such that $\mathbf{x}(i)$ is $\succsim_i$ maximal on $B_{s'_i}$. By Assumption (II) this can be done (it is easy to verify that at any s' and $x \in B_{s'}$, $B_{s'} \cap (\{x\} + R_+{}^l) = \{x\}$. See Fig. 1), and it makes **s** into a CN equilibrium. By

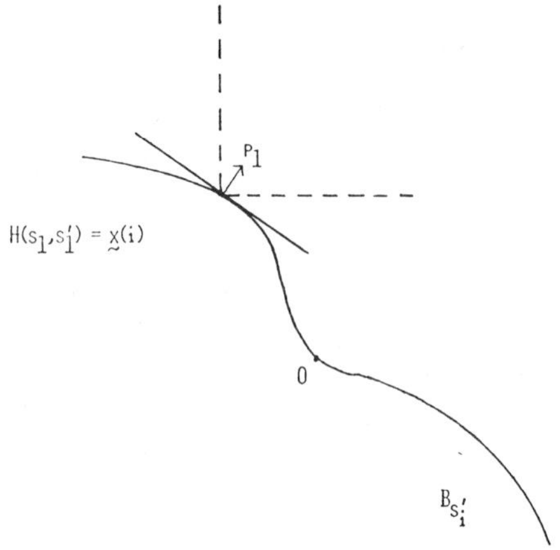

FIGURE 1

the usual efficiency conditions, if **x** is efficient, then the normalized gradients of utility functions, which equal the p_i's must be the same.

So, let $p_1 = \cdots = p_n = p$. Differentiating $\sum_{i=1}^n H(s_i, s'_i)$ with respect to s_j, we get $D_s H(s_j, s'_j) + \sum_{i \neq j} D_{s'} H(s_i, s'_i) = 0$ for all j. Therefore, $\sum_{i \neq j} p \cdot D_{s'} H(s_i, s'_i) = 0$ for all j. As $p \cdot D_{s'} H(s_j, s'_j) - p \cdot D_{s'} H(s_{j'}, s'_{j'}) = \sum_{i \neq j} p \cdot D_{s'} H(s_i, s'_i) - \sum_{i \neq j'} p \cdot D_{s'} H(s_i, s'_i) = 0$ for all j, j', we conclude that $p \cdot D_{s'} H(s_i, s'_i) = 0$ for all i. In particular, $p \cdot D_{s'} H(s_1, s'_1) = p \cdot D_{s'} H(s, s') = 0$. But then $p \cdot D_{s,s'} H(s, s') = 0$, which implies rank $D_{s,s'} H(s, s') \leqslant l - 1$ and contradicts Assumption (III). Therefore not all p_i's are the same, and we are done. ∎

Remark 7. Proposition 2 is a weak result as it asserts only the existence of an economy exhibiting a nonefficient CN equilibrium. We would surmise that the general picture is as follows:

Postulate Hypothesis (III) for all s, s'. Then restricting ourselves to the class of smooth economies, it would be the case that, but for some exceptional economies (i.e., "generically"), the set of efficient net allocations is a codimension one smooth manifold in the space of net trades allocations and the set of CN allocations induced by the strategic market game is also a smooth manifold. Further both manifolds intersect transversally. This means that if a particular noncooperative theory of market allocation is deterministic in spirit (i.e., generically the set of CN equilibria is finite), then but for coincidental cases, no CN allocation will be efficient. This we have verified for the case dim $S = l - 1$ [see Dubey (1980), where a particular model is thoroughly analyzed]. More generally, the efficient CN allocations will form a lower-dimensional submanifold of the CN manifold. The investigation of this topic, which does require the methods of differential topology, we have not pursued at much length although we think its clarification is of importance. For a study of the generic properties of CN equilibria in a purely game theoretic context, see Dubey (1978).

Remark 8. Without the Continuity Axiom the conclusions of Proposition 2 may well fail [see, for example, Dubey (1979) and Schmeidler (1978)] The same is true for the Aggregation Axiom [see Hurwicz (1979) model, where the CN equilibria are efficient, but outcomes depend on the squares of the messages].

10. On the Efficiency of the CN Net Trade Allocations in the Continuum of Traders Case

We now take up an examination of efficiency of CN allocations in the continuum of traders-players situation. We will be led to qualitatively different results from those in the finite case.

From now on $I = [0, 1]$, and we have given a strategic market game satisfying the Anonymity, Continuity, Convexity, and Aggregation Axioms. So, the mechanism is summarized by function $F: S \times S \to R^l$. After stating our main results, we will discuss the role of each of the axioms.

The first obvious consequence of being in the continuum of agents is that all traders face the same public budget set, as no single trader can affect the average action and anonymity holds. For every $s' \in S$ let $B_{s'} = F(S, s')$. Then given a play $\mathbf{s}: I \to S$, the common public budget set is $B_{\bar{\mathbf{s}}}$ where $\bar{\mathbf{s}} = \int \mathbf{s}$. Of course, a play $\mathbf{s}$ is a CN equilibrium if for a.e. $t \in I$ $F(\mathbf{s}(t), \bar{\mathbf{s}})$ is $\gtrsim_t$ maximal on $B_{\bar{\mathbf{s}}} \cap X_t$.

The second and fairly obvious consequence of being in the continuum of agents is that for every $s' \in S$, $B_{s'}$ is in fact a convex set. Aggregation is the crucial axiom here.

Proposition 3. *Under the Anonymity, Continuity, Convexity, and Aggregation Axioms, $B_{s'}$ is a convex set for every s'.*

Proof. Let $s' = c$ be given. By the continuity axiom, we can assume without loss of generality that c belongs to the relative interior of S. We proceed to show that $F(\cdot, c): S \to R^l$ is then linear. Let $f_c: S \to R$ be any of the coordinate functions of $F(\cdot, c)$. We know that if **s** is a play with $\int \mathbf{s} = c$, then $\int (f_c \circ \mathbf{s})\, dt = 0$. If f_c, which is continuous, is not linear, then an easy argument shows the existence of $s_1, s_2 \in S$ and $0 \leqslant \alpha \leqslant 1$ such that

$$\alpha f_c(s_1) + (1 - \alpha) f_c(s_2) \neq f_c(\alpha s_1 + (1 - \alpha) s_2).$$

Let $c : I \to S$ be a play with $\int \mathbf{c} = c$ and such $\lambda(\mathbf{c}^{-1}(s_1)) > 0$, $\lambda(\mathbf{c}^{-1}(s_2)) > 0$. Such a **c** exists because c belongs to the relative interior of S. Now let **c**′ be as **c** except that for a small $\epsilon > 0$ an amount of mass equal to $\alpha\epsilon$ (resp. $(1 - \alpha)\epsilon$) is transferred from $\{s_1\}$ (resp. $\{s_2\}$) to $\alpha s_1 + (1 - \alpha) s_2$. We still have $\int \mathbf{c}' = c$. Therefore, $\int (f_c \circ \mathbf{c})\, dt \neq \int (f_c \circ \mathbf{c}') dt$. But this is impossible because $\int (f_c \circ \mathbf{c}) dt = 0 = \int (f_c \circ \mathbf{c}) dt$.

Hence, $F(\circ, c)$ is linear and since S is convex, $B_c = F(S, c)$ is convex. ▮

For all s' we also have $0 \in B_{s'}$, since the constant play $\mathbf{s}'(t) = s'$ should yield, by anonymity and aggregation, the null set trade. Let $L_{s'}$ be the linear subspace spanned by $B_{s'}$. Then we have:

PROPOSITION 4. *Under the Anonymity, Continuity, Convexity, and Aggregation Axioms, if* $\mathbf{s} : I \to S$ *is a proper CN play, then for a.e. t.* $F(\mathbf{s}(t), s')$ *is* $\succsim_t$ *maximal on* $L_{s'} \cap X_t$, *where* $s' = \int \mathbf{s}$.

Proof. The proof is trivial. Since **s** is a CN equilibrium, it is true that for a.e. t $F(\mathbf{s}(t), s')$ is $\succsim_t$-maximal on $B_{s'} \cap X_t$. As the CN equilibrium is proper and $B_{s'}$ is a convex set containing 0, we have that for a.e. $t \in I$, $F(\mathbf{s}(t), s')$ belongs to the relative interior of $B_{s'}$. Now suppose that for some of those t we had $x \in L_{s'} \cap X_t$, $x \succ_t F(\mathbf{s}(t), s')$. As preferences are convex, we could take x in $B_{s'}$, but this is impossible. Hence the proposition is proved. ▮

Proposition 4 could be interpreted as saying that proper CN equilibria yield Walrasian allocations relative to the set of markets which, given the equilibrium strategies, are open. This is particularly clear if $L_{s'}$ belongs to a coordinate subspace. It can well happen (see Section 11) that the set of open markets is different at different CN equilibria.

One could ask about the efficiency properties of proper CN equilibria. Taking a cue from the previous paragraph, one could assert the efficiency of the equilibrium allocations relative to a properly defined subset of net trades allocations. It is not clear, however, if this would amount to much, as the really interesting property would be the efficiency of the CN net trade allocation relative to the net trade allocations which are feasible *within the given strategic market game*. Unfortunately, it is easy to convince oneself that proper CN equilibria are not necessarily efficient in this sense.

So, we are left with the following corollary of Proposition 5, which, being the main result of this paper, we call a theorem:

THEOREM 5. *Under the Anonymity, Continuity, Convexity, and Aggregation Axioms, every full* CN *equilibrium allocation is Walrasian, hence efficient.*

Remark 9. Let's restrict ourselves to strategic market games on $I = [0, 1]$ satisfying the Anonymity and Continuity Axioms. It will be convenient and admissible to identify a game with the continuous function $G : S \times \mathcal{M} \to R^l$. As we are in the continuum case, the public budget set is common to all traders. So, if the game G is understood, we let $B_\nu = G(S, \nu)$ for any $\nu \in \mathcal{M}$.

We show now how given any interval $T \subset R$, continuous function $g : T \to R$, and nondegenerate probability measure $\bar{\nu} \in \mathcal{M}$ satisfying $\int id\bar{\nu} = 0$ and $\int gd\bar{\nu} = 0$, we can construct an anonymous strategic market game G for a two-commodity world with $I = [0, 1]$ and $B_{\bar{\nu}} = \text{Graph } g$.

Indeed, it suffices to define

$$G(s, \nu) = \left(\int |s| \, d\nu \Big/ \int |s| \, d\bar{\nu}\right) \times \left(s - \frac{|s|}{\int |s| \, d\nu} \int s \, d\nu, \; g(s) - \frac{|s|}{\int |s| \, d\nu} \int g \, d\nu\right).$$

If $\int |s| \, d\nu = 0$ put $G(s, \nu) = 0$. The Continuity and Convexity Axioms are satisfied, but the Aggregation one is not. Also, if $g(0) = 0$, then $0 \in B_\nu$ for all $\nu \in \mathcal{M}$. Obviously, this G does not have any particular economic interpretation, which is not surprising, given the failure of aggregation.

It is therefore possible to have strategic market games satisfying the Anonymity, Continuity and Convexity Axioms and generating CN equilibria as the ones depicted in Figs. 2a, b, c, d. In every case, the economy is formed by two equal weight types with $X = R^2$ and the indicated preferences. The play distribution is in all cases $\nu(\{s_1\}) = \nu(\{s_2\}) = \frac{1}{2}$.

Figure 2a exhibits an improper equilibria. Figure 2b gives a proper, but not full equilibria. Both equilibria are inefficient. It is obvious that both pictures could be sustained by strategic market games satisfying the Aggregation Axiom. Figures 2c and 2d provide examples of full equilibria failing to be efficient on account of the lack of aggregation.

Remark 10. It is important to notice the interplay between the Aggregation axiom and the convexity hypothesis on the strategy space S. It is the latter which gives force to the first. Indeed, it is always formally possible, by expanding S, to satisfy approximately the aggregation axiom. But the expanded S may fail to be convex. For example, if $S = [0, 1]$ and the outcome net trades depend on plays through the mean and the variance of the message distribution, we could extend the message space to $S' = \{(s, s^2) : s \in [0, 1)\} \subset [0, 1]^2$. Then, the Aggregation Axiom is satisfied, but the Convexity Axiom is not.

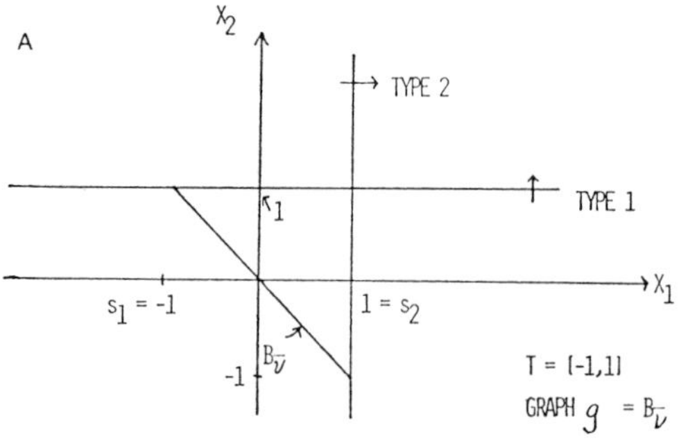

FIGURE 2a

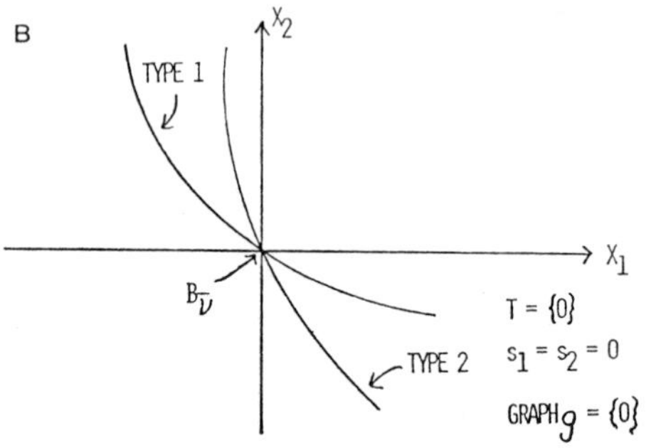

FIGURE 2b

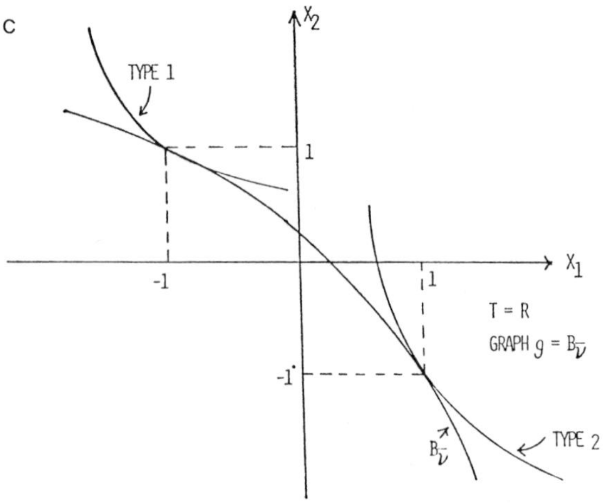

FIGURE 2c

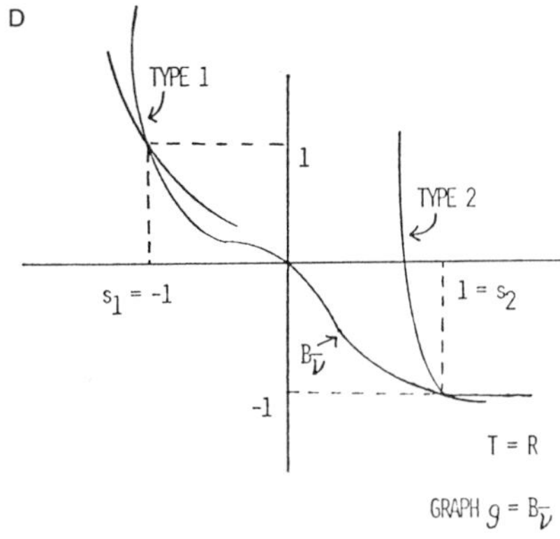

FIGURE 2d

Remark 11. Under the hypothesis made, the Theorem concludes that CN allocations are not just efficient, but in fact Walrasian. Essentially, this is a consequence of the Anonymity Axiom. Under quite general circumstances, it is the case that if the allocation derived from an anonymous continuum strategic market game is efficient then it is Walrasian. See Hammond (1979) for this point. Ch. Kahn (1979) has succeeded in formulating and proving an analog of the Theorem without the Anonymity Axiom. He gets that CN allocations are still efficient but not necessarily Walrasian. A common price system and linear budget sets still obtain, but lump-sum transfers at equilibrium are possible.

Remark 12. The Continuity Axiom is troublesome. It is basic to our approach since, as we saw in Section 7, we need something like it if the continuum model is to be of any use as a representation of a finite but large situation. But there is no denying that there are sensible economic models for which this axiom poses problems. As an instance, the outcome rule may be naturally multivalued (as in Example 2; more generally, this will tend to be the case if the outcome is itself the result of some equilibrium process). Or think of price competition along strict Bertrand lines, or on retaliation strategies, etc. See Green (1980) for a discussion and analysis of the continuity problem in a different (dynamic) context.

At any rate, if continuity fails the properties of equilibria for both the finite and the finite but large models may be very different from the conclusions of this paper. We may have models where equilibria are always efficient, even in the finite case (Bertrand-like models, for example) and models where there is no tendency for the equilibria to become efficient even if the economy is very large [see Green (1980)].

Once we place ourselves in the continuum, the Continuity Axiom plays only a minor role in the proofs of efficiency of a CN play $\mathbf{s}$. It is obvious from the proofs that it could be replaced by either of the hypotheses "$\int \mathbf{s} \in \text{Int } S$" or "$F$ is continuous on $S \times \{\int \mathbf{s}\}$".

Remark 13. It is easy to convince oneself that we cannot dispense with the convexity of preferences. It is this hypothesis which, for each trader, makes a local optimum (and this is all we can prove for a CN equilibrium with our axioms) into a global maximizer in the budget set.

11. Some Examples

We shall now examine some specific examples in the direction of the ones introduced by Shubik (1973). See also Shapley (1976) and Shapley and Shubik (1977).

The space of traders is I, finite or infinite.

As a first step, let there be only two commodities, $h = 1, 2$.

The simplest model calls for strategies which are nothing more than the single act of sending messages promising delivery of a certain amount of goods to either side of a single market, i.e., $S = R_+^{\,2}$ where by $(s_1, s_2) \in S$ we understand a commitment to supply s_h, $h = 1, 2$, of good h.

Let $\mathbf{s} : I \to S$ be a play. Which rules should we specify for the disbursal of $\bar{s}_1 = \int \mathbf{s}_1$, $\bar{s}_2 = \int \mathbf{s}_2$? Or, in other words, which conditions shall we impose on the outcome $\mathbf{x} : I \to R^2$ of the play? Consider the following three (postulated to be valid for every possible play *and* players space):

(i) Suppose we create a fictitious player space $[0, 2]$—endowed with Lebesgue measure—and a play $\hat{\mathbf{s}} : [0, 2] \to S$ defined by letting $\hat{\mathbf{s}}(r) = (\mathbf{s}_1(r), 0)$ if $r \leqslant 1$ and $\hat{\mathbf{s}}(r) = (0, \mathbf{s}_2(r - 1))$ if $1 \leqslant r \leqslant 2$. Let $\hat{\mathbf{x}}$ be the outcome of this play. Then $\mathbf{x}(t) = \hat{\mathbf{x}}(t) + \hat{\mathbf{x}}(t + 1)$. In words, there is complete separation of buying and selling and we can, without loss of generality, assume that $I = I_1 \cup I_2$ where

$$I_1 = \{t \in I : \mathbf{s}_2(t) = 0\},\ I_2 = \{t \in I : \mathbf{s}_1(t) = 0\}.$$

(ii) If $t \in I_h$, $h = 1, 2$, then $\mathbf{x}_h(t) = -\mathbf{s}_h(t)$, i.e., the supply of a commodity offered to the market is always taken.

(iii) With the convention that 0/0 qualifies as any number, the ratio $\mathbf{x}_1(t)/\mathbf{x}_2(t)$ (resp. $\mathbf{x}_2(t)/\mathbf{x}_1(t)$) is independent of $t \in I_2$ (resp. $t \in I_1$). This can be interpreted as a kind of anonymity cum arbitrage-freeness.

Then, of course, the outcome is

$$\mathbf{x}(t) = \left(\frac{\bar{s}_1}{\bar{s}_2}\, \mathbf{s}_2(t) - \mathbf{s}_1(t),\ \frac{\bar{s}_2}{\bar{s}_1}\, \mathbf{s}_1(t) - \mathbf{s}_2(t)\right).$$

If $\bar{s}_2 = 0$ (resp. $\bar{s}_1 = 0$) we put the first (resp. the second) entry equal to $-\mathbf{s}_1(t)$ (resp. $-\mathbf{s}_2(t)$). This is nothing but Example 1 in Section 4 (with an inessential difference: to enforce that $\mathbf{x}$ be always an allocation, we required there that $\mathbf{x} = 0$ whenever $\bar{s}_1 = 0$ or $\bar{s}_2 = 0$ while here if, say $\bar{s}_1 \neq 0$ and $\bar{s}_2 = 0$, $\mathbf{x}$ will not be an allocation, since $\bar{s}_1$ is not redistributed to anyone). Note that the Anonymity, Convexity, and Aggregation Axioms are satisfied while Continuity may fail only at the point $\bar{s}_1 = \bar{s}_2 = 0$. It is Condition (iii) which yields anonymity and aggregation. Alternatively, we could have assumed the latter and derive the former. For example, if there was a function $F : S \times S \to R$ such that $\mathbf{x}(t) = F(\mathbf{s}(t), \bar{s})$ for every possible play and players space, then, by Theorem 5, F will have to be linear on the first argument and we recover Condition (iii).

A multicommodity extension of the previous example is readily available. Let there be l commodities. We may define a *simple market* as one in which quantities of a single commodity i are exchanged for another single commodity j. A *market structure* composed of simple markets can be represented by a graph where the points represent commodities and the edges simple markets. See Fig. 3. We could call the edges of the graph *open markets* (and the nonexisting edges *closed markets*). A market structure is *complete* if its graph is connected. A commodity is a *money* if in the market structure there is an edge to every other commodity. So, every market structure with a money is complete. In Fig. 3, Structure 3a is not complete, while the rest are. Structures 3c, 3d, 3e have, respectively, 1, 2, and 4 money commodities.

Given a market structure M we could assume, to focus on the simplest case, that every market functions as the simple market previously discussed. Then the strategy space is $S = R_+^{2M}$ where for every $k \in M$ s_{1k}, s_{2k} represent the quantities offered to the market k of the two commodities transacted in that market. For a given play $\mathbf{s}$ we could let $M_\mathbf{s} \subset M$ be the active markets

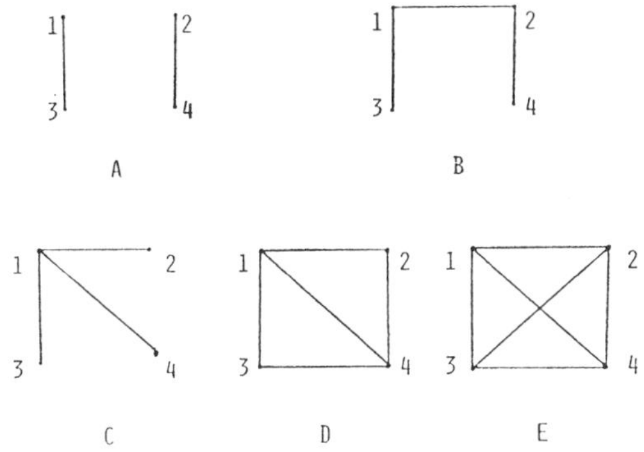

FIGURE 3

at $\mathbf{s}$, i.e., $M_\mathbf{s} = \{k \in M\colon \int \mathbf{s}_{1k}, \int \mathbf{s}_{2k} > 0\}$ and $S_\mathbf{s} = R_+^{2M_\mathbf{s}}$ the "active" strategy set.

Suppose $\mathbf{s}$ is a CN play. If we forget about nonactive strategies, i.e., imagine that our strategy set is $S_\mathbf{s}$ then each one of our axioms is satisfied (see end of Remark 12). So, the efficiency Theorem 5 applies if the equilibrium is full (note that the equilibrium is always proper). Now, the equilibrium will be full if and only if the market structure formed by the *active* markets $M_\mathbf{s}$ is complete. For this type of model an inactive market is no better than a closed one.

The reader familiar with Shubik's original model (1973) and with the multicommodity extensions due to Shapley (1976), Jaynes, Okuno and Schmeidler (1976), Postlewaite and Schmeidler (1978), Dubey and Shapley (1977), may wonder why we get efficiency of equilibria in the continuum case merely out of the connectedness of active markets when this was not at all the case in the previous references. The reason lies in the feasibility constraint we are presently using. We completely abstract from transactions problems and for equilibrium we only require the *net* trade to be individually feasible. So, it is possible to use the receipts in one market to buy in another market. If we visualize our simple markets as taking place simultaneously, this amounts to the absence of a liquidity constraint, i.e., to the presence of a perfect credit system.

Another observation is that the previous model will typically have multiplicity of equilibria. In fact if an existence theorem is available (it is, see references of the previous paragraph), we will have an equilibrium for every a priori specification of inactive markets.

The market strategies so far considered are rather extreme. They are commitments to supply a given amount of commodity i to the market in exchange for any quantity of commodity j. More generally, we could envision a supply message (interpretable, perhaps, as a decision rule) to a simple market as being a function $s_i(x_j)$ to be read as a promise to deliver $s_i(x_j)$ units of commodity i in exchange for x_j units of commodity j. In line with Conditions (i), (ii), and (iii) for the simpler case, we could require of market clearing and disbursal rules that at the transactions outcome of a play we had that for all i and j, $s_i(x_j)/x_j$ be independent of the particular supplier. Of course, this is nothing but market clearing at a price system, and if we further constrain every s^i to be nondecreasing and concave, we put ourselves in the anonymous and aggregate situation of Example 3 in Section 4. Indeed, it suffices to redefine a selling strategy as a 0-homogeneous function $\hat{s}_i(p_i, p_j)$ promising to deliver $\hat{s}_i(p_i, p_j)$ units of commodity i in exchange for $1/p_j\ p_i\hat{s}_i(p_i, p_j)$ units of commodity j. Clearly, every s_i strategy induces a $\hat{s}_i$ strategy and equilibrium prices are determined by the condition

$$p_j \int \hat{s}_j(p_i, p_j) = p_i \int \hat{s}_i(p_i, p_j). \qquad \text{See Fig. 4.}$$

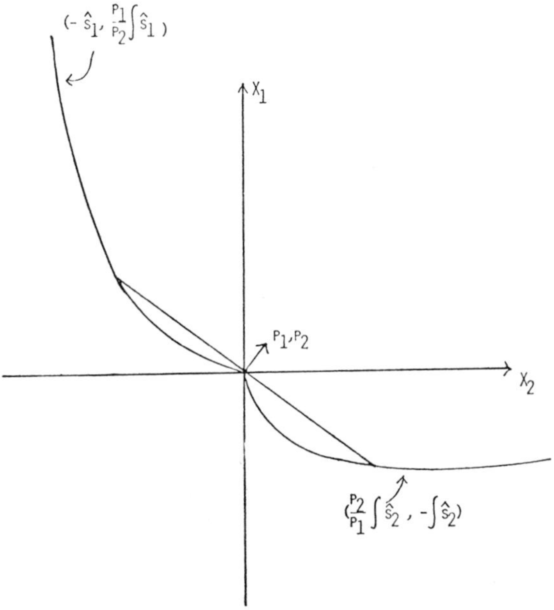

FIGURE 4

The example at the beginning of this section is a limit (the Cournot case) of this latter model. It corresponds to the case $s_i(x^j) = c$. The other limit, $s^i(x_j)$ linear homogeneous, is the Bertrand case. Since outcomes are in this case highly discontinuous on strategies, it is not easily amenable to our analysis.

12. ON THE CONCEPT OF STRICT COURNOT–NASH EQUILIBRIUM IN CONTINUUM ECONOMIES

Suppose that for $I = [0, 1]$ we have given an economy $\mathscr{E} : I \to \mathscr{A}$ and an anonymous trading game $G : S \times \mathscr{M} \to R^l$. From a noncooperative game theoretic standpoint, a CN play $\mathbf{s} : I \to S$ will be rather fragile if there were traders (strictly speaking, a nonnull set of traders) that could obtain a better net trade by pretending to be n different players (n finite but otherwise arbitrary). Indeed, in an anonymous mass market it may not be possible to prevent an individual trader from entering it several times or simply, using proxies. This observation prompts the following

DEFINITION. A play $\mathbf{s} : I \to S$ is a *strict Cournot–Nash equilibrium* if $x_{\mathbf{s}}$ is feasible and for a.e. $t \in [0, 1]$ $G(\mathbf{s}(t), \nu_{\mathbf{s}})$ is $\succsim_t$ maximal on $X_t \cap \bigcup_{n=1}^{\infty} nB_{\nu_{\mathbf{s}}}$.

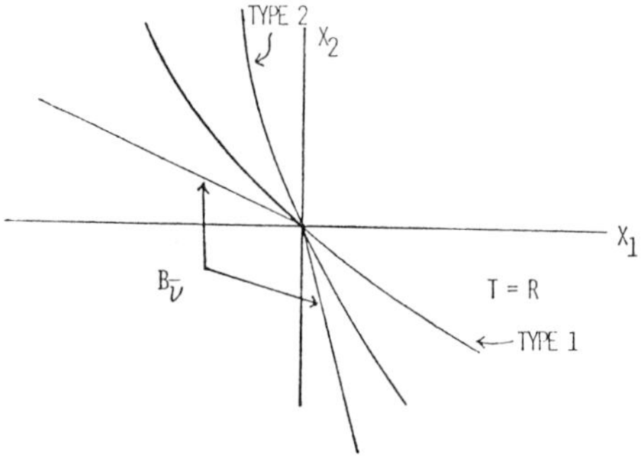

FIGURE 5

From Proposition 4 it is clear that

PROPOSITION 6. *If the Anonymity, Continuity, Convexity, and Aggregation Axioms are satisfied, then every proper CN equilibrium is strict.*

Without the Aggregation Axiom a proper CN equilibrium needs not to be strict. For example if at a CN distribution we have that $B_\nu \cap R^l_{++} \neq \varnothing$ (as in the example of Fig. 2c) then by the monotonicity of preferences, the distribution cannot be a strict CN.

Without the Aggregation Axiom, is every strict Cournot–Nash equilibrium Walrasian? Not necessarily. In Fig. 5 we can see an example where the CN equilibria are proper and full but not Walrasian (the two types indicated have the same weight). By using the technique of Remark 9 we can without difficulty construct economies and strategic market games supporting the figure. In the figure, $B_{\bar{\nu}}$ fails to be smooth. An obvious result is:

PROPOSITION 7. *Suppose that $X_t = R^l$ for a.e. t and that the Anonymity Axiom holds. Let* **s** *be a strict CN equilibrium. If* $0 \in B_{\nu_{\mathbf{s}}}$ *and* $B_{\nu_{\mathbf{s}}}$ *is a* $(l-1)$ C^1 *manifold, then the equilibrium is Walrasian.*

Proof. Let T be the $(l-1)$ tangent plane to $B_{\bar{\nu}_{\mathbf{s}}}$ at 0. It is easy to verify that for any $z \in T$, $\bigcup_{n=1}^{\infty} nB_{\nu_{\mathbf{s}}}$ contains net trades arbitrarily close to z. Henceforth by the continuity of preferences, for a.e. $t \in [0, 1]$, $\mathbf{x}_{\mathbf{s}}(t) \succsim_t z$ for any $z \in T$. Because of monotonicity of preferences, $T \cap R^l_{++} = \varnothing$. Hence we can pick $p \geqslant 0$ such that $T = \{z \in R : p \cdot z = 0\}$. With p as the candidate Walrasian price, the proof proceeds from this point on as in Proposition 4. ∎

As the example of Fig. 2d shows, Proposition 6 holds for strict CN equilibria but not for ordinary ones.

Remark 14. Given an anonymous strategic market game $G : S \times \mathscr{M} \to R^l$ it is possible to build a new one $G^* : S^* \times \mathscr{M}^* \to R^l$ in such a manner that the concept of ordinary and strict CN equilibria coincide in G^* and the ordinary equilibria of G^* correspond to the strict equilibria of G.

One would proceed as follows. Let S be a complete, separable subset of a Banach space. Denote by S^* the set of finite, nonnegative integer valued measures on S. Endow S^* with the weak-star topology and corresponding Borel σ-field. Let $\mathcal{M}^*$ be the (Borel) probability measures on S^* with bounded mean. A play is now an integrable $\mathbf{s}^* : I \to S^*$. The integral is defined by $(\int \mathbf{s}^*)(V) = \int \mathbf{s}^*(t)(V)$ for every Borel set $V \subset S$. It is a nonnegative finite measure on S [see (Mas-Colell, 1975, Sect. 3.1) for the mathematical technicalities of this remark]. Given $\mathbf{s}^*$ we let $\nu^*_{\mathbf{s}^*} \in \mathcal{M}^*$ be the Borel probability measure induced by $\mathbf{s}^*$ on S^*. An element $\nu^* \in \mathcal{M}^*$ induces a distribution ν on A by letting

$$\nu(V) = \frac{1}{\int s^*(A)\, d\nu^*} \int s^*(V)\, d\nu^*.$$

Given a play $\mathbf{s}^*$, one let $\nu_{\mathbf{s}^*}$ be the measure in S corresponding to $\nu^*_{\mathbf{s}^*}$. Clearly,

$$\nu_{\mathbf{s}^*} = \frac{1}{(\int \mathbf{s}^*)(A)} \left(\int \mathbf{s}\right).$$

Finally, one defines

$$G^*(s^*, \nu^*) = \int G(s, \nu)\, ds^*.$$

Note that in this new game the Aggregation Axiom is satisfied but S^* is not convex. Also, a proper strict CN equilibrium of G is an ordinary, but not necessarily proper, CN equilibrium of G^*. (See Fig. 5) where B_{ν^*} is the convex hull of B_ν).

References

1. R. Aumann, Markets with a continuum of traders, *Econometrica* **32** (1964), 39–50.
2. A. Cournot, "Recherches sur les Principes Mathématiques de la Théorie des Richesses," Hachette, Paris, 1838. Translated as "Researches into the Mathematical Principles of the Theory of Wealth," Macmillan, New York, 1929.
3. G. Debreu, A social equilibrium existence theorem, *Proc. Nat. Acad. Sci. USA* **38** (1952), 886–893.
4. P. Dubey, "Finiteness and Inefficiency of Nash Equilibria," Cowles Foundation Discussion Paper 508R, 1978.
5. P. Dubey, Nash equilibria of market games: Finiteness and inefficiency, *J. Econ. Theory* **22** (1980), 363–376.
6. P. Dubey, "Price-Quantity Strategic Market Games," Cowles Foundation Discussion Paper 520 (1979).

7. P. DUBEY AND L. SHAPLEY, Non-cooperative exchange with a continuum of traders," Cowles Foundation Discussion Paper 447 (1977).
8. P. DUBEY AND M. SHUBIK, "Strategic Market Games and Market Mechanisms," Cowles Foundation Preliminary Paper CF-80915, 1978.
9. F. Y. EDGEWORTH, "Mathematical Psychics," Kegan Paul, London, 1881.
10. J. GABSZEWICZ AND J. P. VIAL, Oligopoly à la Cournot in general equilibrium theory, *J. Econ. Theory* **4** (1972), 381–400.
11. E. GREEN, "Non-cooperative Price Taking in Large Dynamic Markets," *J. Econ. Theory* **22** (1980), 155–182.
12. P. HAMMOND, "Straightforward Individual Incentive Compatibility in Large Economies," *Rev. Econ. Stud.* **46** (1979), 263–282.
13. O. HART, Monopolistic competition with differentiated commodities, *Rev. Econ. Stud.* **46** (1979), 1–30.
14. S. HART, W. HILDENBRAND, AND E. KOHLBERG, On equilibrium allocation as distributions on the commodity space, *J. Math. Econ.* **1** (1974), 159–167.
15. W. HILDENBRAND, "Core and Equilibrium of a Large Economy," Princeton Univ. Press, Princeton, N. J., 1974.
16. L. HURWICZ, Optimality and informational efficiency in resource allocation processes, *in* "Mathematical Methods in the Social Sciences" (Arrow, Karlin, and Suppes, Eds.), pp. 17–47, Stanford University Press, Stanford, Calif., 1960.
17. L. HURWICZ, Outcome functions yielding walrasian and lindhal allocations at Nash equilibrium points," *Rev. Econ. Stud.* **46**, No. 2 (1979), 217–227.
18. J. JAYNES, M. OKUNO, AND D. SCHMEIDLER, Efficiency in an atomless economy with fiat money, *Internat. Econ. Rev.* **19** (1978), 149–157.
19. CH. KAHN, "An Extension of the Axiomatic Characterization of Non-cooperative Equilibria in Economies with a Continuum of Traders," manuscript, Harvard University, Cambridge, Mass., 1979.
20. A. MAS-COLELL, A model of equilibrium with differentiated commodities, *J. Math. Econ.* **2** (1975), 263–295.
21. A. MAS-COLELL, "An Axiomatic Approach to the Efficiency of Non-Cooperative Equilibrium in Economies with a Continuum of Traders," Technical Report 274, Economics, IMSSS (1978), Stanford University, Stanford, Calif.
22. W. NOVSHEK AND H. SONNENSCHEIN, Cournot and Walras Equilibrium, *J. Econ. Theory* **14** (1978), 223–267.
23. E. PAZNER AND D. SCHMEIDLER, "Non-Walrasian Equilibria and Arrow-Debreu Economies," mimeograph, University of Illinois, Urbana, Ill., 1976.
24. A. POSTLEWAITE AND D. SCHMEIDLER, Approximate efficiency of non-Walrasian Nash Equilibria," *Econometrica* **46** (1978), 127–137.
25. D. SCHMEIDLER, Equilibrium Points of Non-Atomic Games, *J. Stat. Phys.* **7** (1973), 295–309.
26. D. SCHMEIDLER, "Walrasian Analysis via Strategic Outcome Functions," mimeograph, Tel-Aviv University, Tel-Aviv, Israel, 1978.
29. L. SHAPLEY, "Non-cooperative General Exchange," *in* "Theory and Measurement of Economic Externalities" (S. A. Y. Lin, Ed.), Academic Press, New York, 1976.
30. L. SHAPLEY AND M. SHUBIK, Trade using one commodity as a means of payment, *J. Pol. Econ.* **85** (1977), 937–968.
31. M. SHUBIK, Commodity money, oligopoly, credit and bankruptcy in a general equilibrium model, *Western Econ. J.* **11** (1973), 24–38.
32. W. THOMSON, "Nash Equilibria of Walras and Lindhal mechanism," mimeograph, University of Minnesota, Minneapolis, Minn. 1978.
33. K. YOSIDA, "Functional Analysis," 3d ed., Springer–Verlag, Berlin/New York, 1971.

Nash Equilibria of Market Games: Finiteness and Inefficiency*

PRADEEP DUBEY

Cowles Foundation for Research in Economics, Yale University, New Haven, Connecticut 06520

Received August 1, 1979

1. INTRODUCTION

In this paper we make good the promise [6, Sect. 9] that, under appropriate conditions, the Nash Equilibria of finite-player strategic market games are generically inefficient. Our conditions are: (a) the dimension of each trader's strategy set is at most $l - 1$, where l is the number of commodities, (b) the mapping from strategies to net trades is sufficiently smooth, (c) so are the traders' preferences. For concreteness we work out a specific model—the so-called "sell-all" model, explored in [9]. But the same proof can easily be adapted to the general case.

Condition (c) is quite standard and not particularly restrictive (e.g., see [7]); Condition (b) is necessary and without it our conclusion may well fail. Indeed see [8, 5] for models with price-cutting strategies where the Nash and Walras Equilibria coincide. For a discussion of (a), see again Section 9 of [6].

Needless to say we take our cue from the analogous finiteness results obtained for the Walras Equilibria of markets by Debreu [2], Smale [11], and others. For a similar analysis of strategic games in general, see [4].

For any integer r, let $I_r = \{1, 2,..., r\}$, and let Ω^r be the nonnegative orthant of the Euclidean space of dimension r. Let I_n be the set of traders and I_{k+1} the set of commodities in which they trade. Each trader $i \in I_n$ is characterized by an initial endowment $a^i \in \Omega^{k+1}$ and a utility function $u^i : \Omega^{k+1} \to R$. (Here a_j^i is the quantity of commodity j held by trader i.) We assume that $\sum_{i=1}^n a^i > 0$ and that $a_{k+1}^i > 0$ for all[1] $i \in I_n$.

To recast the market as a game in strategic form, we single out the $(k + 1)$st commodity as a money. There are k trading posts, one for each of the other commodities. Traders are required to put up all of their first k commodities

* The research reported in this paper was partially supported by grant No. SOC77-27435 from the National Science Foundation, and by Contract N00014-77-C0518 issued by the Office of Naval Research under Contract Authority NR-047-006.

[1] If $a_{k+1}^i = 0$, then trader i is a "strategic dummy" in our game and can be ignored.

Reprinted from *Journal of Economic Theory* **22**, No. 2, 363–376 (April 1980)
ISBN 0-12-476750-8

for sale in these trading posts, and use their endowment of commodity money for bidding on them. The strategy set S^i of trader i consists of bids on the k trading posts, but he is constrained to bid within a^i_{k+1} :

$$S^i = \left\{ b^i \in \Omega^k : \sum_{j \in I_k} b_j{}^i \leqslant a^i_{k+1} \right\}.$$

Given a choice of strategies $b = (b^1, \ldots, b^n)$, $b^i \in S^i$, prices $p(b) \in \Omega^k$ are formed in the trading posts and the markets cleared, with the final bundle x^i(b) accruing to i, according to the rules:

$$p_j(b) = \frac{\bar{b}_j}{\bar{a}_j} \qquad \left(\text{where } \bar{b}_j = \sum_{i \in I_n} b_j{}^i, \text{ etc.}\right)$$

$$x_j{}^i(b) = \frac{b_j{}^i}{p_j(b)} \qquad \text{if } \; p_j(b) > 0$$

$$= 0 \qquad \text{if } \; p_j(b) = 0$$

for $j = 1, \ldots, k$; and

$$x^i_{k+1}(b) = a^i_{k+1} - \sum_{j=1}^{k} b_j{}^i + \sum_{j=1}^{k} p_j(b)\, a_j{}^i.$$

(We may interpret $x_j{}^i(b) = 0$ to be a confiscation of goods in the absence of any bid. Consider a $\hat{b} = (\hat{b}^1, \ldots, \hat{b}^n) \in S = S' \times \cdots \times S^n$. $\hat{b}$ is called a *Nash Equilibrium* (N.E.) of this game if, for all $i \in I_n$,

$$u^i(x^i(\hat{b})) \geqslant u^i(x^i(\hat{b} \mid b^i)), \qquad b^i \in S^i,$$

where $(\hat{b} \mid b^i)$ is the same as $\hat{b}$ but with $\hat{b}^i$ replaced by b^i ; it is called an *efficient* point of the game if there is no $b \in S$ such that

$$u^i(x^i(b)) \geqslant u^i(x^i(\hat{b})) \qquad \text{for all } \; i \in I_n ,$$

$$u^l(x^l(b)) > u^l(x^l(\hat{b})) \qquad \text{for some } \; l \in I_n .$$

2. Finiteness and Inefficiency

In our analysis we will, for convenience (see Remark 3, however), hold the traders' endowments fixed and vary their utilities only. Put $Q = \{x \in \Omega^{k+1} : x_j \leqslant \bar{a}_j\}$. Let U denote the linear space of all C^2 functions[2] from Q to R, endowed with the C^2-norm.[3] Thus we may think of a market game as

[2] That is, those which can be extended to a C^2 function on R^{k+1}.

[3] That is, $\| u \| = \sup\{\| u(x)\|, \| Du(x)\|, \| D^2u(x)\| : x \in Q\}$, where $\| \;\; \|$ denotes the maximum norm.

given by a point $u = (u^1,\ldots, u^n) \in (U)^n$. Denote the set of its N.E. by $\eta(u)$, and the set of its efficient points by $\epsilon(u)$.

We will focus our attention on certain open sets of $(U)^n$. Let e be the unit vector in Ω^{k+1}, i.e., $e_j = 1$ for each j. Take two positive numbers σ and σ', $\sigma < \sigma'$. Define $U(\sigma, \sigma') = \{u \in U : \sigma e < Du < \sigma' e\}$. The manifold of games which we will consider will be open sets of the type $(U(\sigma, \sigma'))^n$. Finally let $S' = \{(b^1,\ldots, b^n) \in S : b^i$ is a vertex of S^i for at least one $i \in I_n\}$. We are now ready to state our main result:

THEOREM. *Fix σ and σ', $0 < \sigma < \sigma'$. There is an open dense set E of $(U(\sigma, \sigma'))^n$ such that, for any $u \in E$,*

(a) *$\eta(u)$ is a finite set,*

(b) *$\eta(u) \cap \epsilon(u) \subset S'$.*

Remark 1. To obtain generic inefficiency, we could, for instance, confine our attention to $u = (u^1,\ldots, u^n) \in (U(\sigma, \sigma'))^n$ such that:[4]

for any i in I_n, there exist at least two distinct $j_1(i)$ and $j_2(i)$ in I_k with the property $u^{i^{-1}}(r) \cap \{x \in \Omega^{k+1}\colon x_{j_1(i)} = 0\} = \varnothing$ and $u^{i^{-1}}(r) \cap \{x \in \Omega^{k+1}\colon x_{j_2(i)} = 0\} = \varnothing$, whenever $r > u^i(0)$.

Such u form an open set $\tilde{E}$ in $(U(\sigma, \sigma'))^n$, and clearly imply $\eta(u) \cap S' = \varnothing$. Thus the theorem could be restated with $\tilde{E}$ in place of $(U(\sigma, \sigma'))^n$ and "$\eta(u) \cap \epsilon(u) = \varnothing$" in place of (b).

3. PROOF OF THEOREM

LEMMA 1. *Fix σ and σ', $0 < \sigma < \sigma'$. Then there exists a $\mu > 0$ such that for any $u \in (U(\sigma, \sigma'))^n$,*

$$\eta(u) \subset S_\mu = \{b \in S : \bar{b}_j > \mu \quad \textit{and} \quad b_j^i < \bar{b}_j \quad \textit{for all} \quad i \in I_n, j \in I_k\}.$$

Proof. Let $u \in (U(\sigma, \sigma'))^n$ and $b = (b^1,\ldots, b^n) \in \eta(u)$. Then clearly $\bar{b}_j > 0$ for $j \in I_k$. Otherwise, if $\bar{b}_j = 0$ for some j, then any trader could bid an arbitrarily small ϵ on the jth trading post (if necessary by reducing some other bid). By this change of strategy, he acquires $\bar{a}_j$, while his other holdings change by amounts that go to zero with ϵ. Hence for small enough ϵ this improves his payoff, a contradiction.

Next, it is also clear that $b_j^i < \bar{b}_j$ for all i and j. For if $b_j^i = \bar{b}_j$, then i could reduce b_j^i and improve his payoff, a contradiction.

[4] Intuitively this says that each trader "sufficiently desires" at least two commodities.

To establish the lower bound on $\bar{b}_j$ we consider two cases.

Case I. $\sum_{r=1}^{k} b_r^h < a_{k+1}^h$ for all $h \in I_n$. Let i be such that $b_j^i/\bar{b}_j < 1/2$. Now if i bids ϵ more on j, his increase in payoff for small ϵ is approximately:

$$\epsilon \cdot \left[\frac{\partial u^i}{\partial x_j}(x^i(b)) \cdot \frac{\bar{a}_j}{\bar{b}_j}\left(\frac{\bar{b}_j - b_j^i}{\bar{b}_j}\right) - \frac{\partial u^i}{\partial x_{k+1}}(x^i(b))\left(1 - \frac{a_j^i}{\bar{a}_j}\right)\right]$$

$$\geqslant \epsilon \cdot \left\{\frac{\sigma}{2} \cdot \frac{\bar{a}_j}{\bar{b}_j} - \sigma'\left[1 - \frac{a_j^i}{\bar{a}_j}\right]\right\}.$$

For b to be a N.E. we must have $a_j^i < \bar{a}_j$, and

$$\frac{\sigma \bar{a}_j}{2\bar{b}_j} \leqslant \sigma'\left[1 - \frac{a_j^i}{\bar{a}_j}\right],$$

i.e.,

$$\boxed{\bar{b}_j \geqslant \frac{\sigma \bar{a}_j}{2\sigma'\left[1 - \frac{a_j^i}{\bar{a}_j}\right]}}\ .$$

Case II. $\sum_{r=1}^{k} b_r^h = a_{k+1}^h$ for some $h \in I_n$. Then there is a $r^* \in I_k$ such that $b_{r^*}^h \geqslant a_{k+1}^h/k$. If $r^* = j$, then

$$\boxed{\bar{b} \geqslant \frac{a_{k+1}^h}{k}}\ .$$

If $r^* \neq j$, choose $i \in I_n$ to ensure that $b_j^i/\bar{b}_j < 1/2$. Now if i reduces his bid on r^* by ϵ and increases his bid on j by ϵ, then his increase in payoff for small ϵ is approximately:

$$\epsilon \cdot \left\{\frac{\partial u^i}{\partial x_j}(x^i(b)) \cdot \frac{\bar{a}_j}{\bar{b}_j}\left(\frac{\bar{b}_j - b_j^i}{\bar{b}_j}\right) - \frac{\partial u^i}{\partial x_{r^*}}(x^i(b)) \cdot \frac{\bar{a}_{r^*}}{\bar{b}_{r^*}}\left(\frac{\bar{b}_{r^*} - b_{r^*}^i}{\bar{b}_{r^*}}\right)\right.$$

$$\left. - \frac{\partial u^i}{\partial x_{k+1}}(x^i(b))\left(\frac{a_{r^*}^i}{\bar{a}_{r^*}} - \frac{a_j^i}{\bar{a}_j}\right)\right\}.$$

Now note

$$\frac{\partial u^i}{\partial x_{r^*}}(x^i(b)) \cdot \frac{\bar{a}_{r^*}}{\bar{b}_{r^*}}\left(\frac{\bar{b}_{r^*} - b_{r^*}^i}{\bar{b}_{r^*}}\right) \leqslant \sigma' \frac{\bar{a}_{r^*}k}{a_{k+1}^h},$$

$$\frac{\partial u^i}{\partial x_{k+1}}(x^i(b))\left[\frac{a_{r^*}^i}{\bar{a}_{r^*}} - \frac{a_j^i}{\bar{a}_j}\right] \leqslant \sigma' \frac{a_{r^*}^i}{\bar{a}_{r^*}},$$

$$\frac{\partial u^i}{\partial x_j}(x^i(b))\, \frac{\bar{a}_j}{\bar{b}_j}\left(\frac{\bar{b}_j - b_j^i}{\bar{b}_j}\right) \geqslant \frac{\sigma \bar{a}_j}{2\bar{b}_j}.$$

Hence the increase in i's payoff is at least:

$$\epsilon \cdot \left\{\frac{\sigma \bar{a}_j}{2\bar{b}_j} - \sigma' \left[\frac{a^i_{r*}}{\bar{a}_{r*}} + \frac{\bar{a}_{r*}k}{a^h_{k+1}}\right]\right\}.$$

This must be nonpositive, from which we get

$$\boxed{\bar{b}_j \geqslant \frac{\sigma \bar{a}_j}{2\sigma' \left[\frac{a^j_{r*}}{\bar{a}_{r*}} + \frac{\bar{a}_{r*}k}{a^h_{k+1}}\right]}}\ .$$

Let

$$M^1 = \min\{\bar{a}_j : j \in I_k\}$$

$$M^2 = \min\{a^i_{k+1} : i \in I_n\}$$

$$M^3 = \max\left\{1 - \frac{a_j^i}{\bar{a}_j} : i \in I_n,\ j \in I_k,\ a_j^i < \bar{a}_j\right\}$$

$$M^4 = \max\left\{\frac{a_j^i}{\bar{a}_j} + \frac{k\bar{a}_j}{a^h_{k+1}} : i \in I_n,\ h \in I_n,\ j \in I_k\right\}.$$

Set

$$\mu = \min\left[\frac{M^1}{2M^3\sigma'}, \frac{M^1}{2M^4\sigma'}, \frac{M^2}{k}\right]. \qquad \text{Q.E.D.}$$

Lemma 1 enables us to steer clear of the discontinuity in the payoff functions at $\bar{b}_j = 0$ for $j \in I_k$. This is important—see Remark 5—because in order to show the openness of E in the theorem we need to be able to extend the payoff functions smoothly in a neighborhood of S_μ.

Given Lemma 1, it suffices to prove the

AUXILIARY THEOREM. *There is an open dense set E of $(U(\sigma, \sigma'))^n$ such that for any $u \in E$*

(a) *$\eta(u) \cap S_\mu$ is a finite set*

(b) *$\eta(u) \cap \epsilon(u) \cap S_\mu \subset S'$.*

We proceed to prove the Auxiliary Theorem through a sequence of lemmas. Unfortunately, first we need to introduce some fairly cumbersome notation

$$V^i = \text{the set of all the } k + 1 \text{ vertices of } S^i,$$

$$\tilde{V}^i = \text{the set of all nonempty subsets of } V^i,$$

$$\tilde{V} = \tilde{V}^1 \times \cdots \times \tilde{V}^n.$$

For any $T^i \in \tilde{V}^i$, $T_0{}^i = T^i/\{0^i\}$, where 0^i is the zero vertex of S^i.
For any $T = \{T^1,\dots, T^n\} \in \tilde{V}$ and $i \in N$:

$$S^i(T) = \text{convex hull of } T^i,$$

$$\dot{S}^i(T) = \text{relative interior of } S^i(T),$$

$$\dot{S}(T) = \dot{S}^1(T) \times \cdots \times \dot{S}^n(T),$$

$$\tilde{S}(T) = \dot{S}(T) \cap S_\mu\,,$$

$$S_j{}^i = \left\{b \in S\colon a_j{}^i(\bar{b}_j - b_j{}^i) + \bar{a}_j b_j{}^i \left(\frac{a_j{}^i}{\bar{a}_j} - 1\right) = 0\right\},$$

$$\tilde{S}_j{}^i(T) = \tilde{S}(T) \cap S_j{}^i,$$

$$N(T) = \{i \in N\colon |\, T^i \,| > 1\},$$

$$\hat{T} = \bigcup \{T_0{}^i\colon i \in N(T)\},$$

$$t^i = |\, T_0{}^i \,|,$$

$$\hat{t} = \sum_{i \in N(T)} t^i,$$

$$t = |\, N(T)|,$$

$R^{N\hat{T}}$ = Euclidean space of dimension $t\hat{t}$ whose axes are indexed by pairs $(i, j) \in N(T) \times \hat{T}$.

For any $v \in R^{N\hat{T}}$, $v_j{}^i$ will be its (i, j)th component. Also for any $L \subset \hat{T}$, $v_L{}^i$ will be the vector in R^L (whose axes are indexed by elements of L) with components $\{v_j{}^i : j \in L\}$.

Note that there is a natural correspondence between elements of $V_0{}^i$ and the variables $\{b_j{}^i : 1 \leqslant j \leqslant k\}$. Thus, without confusion, we will speak sometimes of the variable x_l, $l \in \hat{T}$.

We construct a mapping[5]

$${}_T\psi : (U(\sigma, \sigma'))^n \times \tilde{S}(T) \to R^{N\hat{T}}\,,$$

which will enable us to study $\eta(u)$ and $\epsilon(u)$. Letting $u = (u^1,\dots, u^n) \in (U(\sigma, \sigma'))^n$ $b \in \tilde{S}(T)$, define (for $i \in N(T)$, $j \in \hat{T}$)

$${}_T\psi^i(u, b) = \left(\frac{\partial u^i}{\partial x_l}\right)(b), \qquad i \in N(T), \quad l \in \hat{T}.$$

It is easy to compute that:

$${}_T\psi_j{}^i(u, b) = \frac{\partial u^i}{\partial x_j}(x^i(b)) \cdot \left[\frac{\bar{a}_j(\bar{b}_j - b_j{}^i)}{(\bar{b}_j)^2}\right] + \frac{\partial u^i}{\partial x_{k+1}}(x^i(b)) \left[\frac{a_j{}^i}{\bar{a}_j} - 1\right]$$

[5] Assuming $\tilde{S}(T)$ is not empty.

if $j \in T_0^i$; and

$$_T\psi_j^i(u, b) = -\frac{\partial u^i}{\partial x_j}(x^i(b)) \cdot \left[\frac{\bar{a}_j b_j^i}{(\bar{b}_j)^2}\right] + \frac{\partial u^i}{\partial x_{k+1}}(x^i(b)) \left[\frac{a_j^i}{\bar{a}_j}\right]$$

if $j \notin T_0^i$.

Using $_T\psi$ we now define some other mappings. First, define the subspace $R^{\hat{T}}$ of $R^{N\hat{T}}$ by $R^{\hat{T}} = \{v \in R^{N\hat{T}} : v_j^i = 0 \text{ if } j \notin T_0^i\}$. Then define $_T\tilde{\psi} : (U(\sigma, \sigma'))^n \times S(T) \to R^{\hat{T}}$ by setting $_T\tilde{\psi}_j^i = 0$ if $j \notin T_0^i$. Finally define

$$_T\varnothing : (U(\sigma, \sigma'))^n \times \tilde{S}(T) \to R^{N\hat{T}} \times \tilde{S}(T)$$

and

$$_T\tilde{\varnothing} : (U(\sigma, \sigma'))^n \times \tilde{S}(T) \to R^{\hat{T}} \times \tilde{S}(T)$$

by

$$_T\varnothing(u, b) = (_T\psi(u, b), b),$$
$$_T\tilde{\varnothing}(u, b) = (_T\tilde{\psi}(u, b), b).$$

We next need to define two subsets of $R^{N\hat{T}}$. To this end, first let

$$T_a = \{i \in N(T) : 0^i \in T^i\},$$
$$T_b = \{i \in N(T); 0^i \notin T^i\}.$$

Then let

$$\Delta^1(T) = \{v \in R^{N\hat{T}} : \text{the projections of the } v^i, i \in N(T), \text{ on } S(T) \text{ are linearly dependent}\},$$

$$\Delta^2(T) = \{v \in R^{N\hat{T}} : v^i_{T_0^i} = 0 \quad \text{for} \quad i \in T_a; \quad v_j^i = v_l^i \quad \text{for} \quad i \in T_b, j \in T_0^i, l \in T_0^i\}.$$

LEMMA 2. *Let M be any submanifold of $R^{\hat{T}} \times \tilde{S}(T)$. Then $_T\tilde{\varnothing}$ is transversal*[6] *to $M((_T\tilde{\varnothing} \pitchfork M))$.*

Proof. Consider any $(u, b) \in (U(\sigma, \sigma'))^n \times \tilde{S}(T)$ such that $_T\tilde{\varnothing}(u, b) = y \in M$. Take any $v \in R^{\hat{T}}$ and any $w \in$ Tangent space of $\tilde{S}(T)$. We will show that there is a differentiable path $\{(_\tau u, {}_\tau b)\}_{\tau=0}^{1}$ in[7] $(U)^n \times \tilde{S}(T)$ such that

$$(_0u, {}_0b) = (u, b),$$

$$\frac{d}{d\tau}[_T\tilde{\varnothing}(_\tau u, {}_\tau b)]\bigg|_{\tau=0} = (v, w).$$

[6] For the definition of "transversal," see Appendix.

[7] Clearly, for sufficiently small τ, this path will lie in $(U(\sigma, \sigma'))^n \times \tilde{S}(T)$.

To do this, let $\{_\tau b\}_{\tau=0}^{1}$ be a path in $\tilde{S}(T)$ such that[8]

$$_0 b = 0,$$

$$\frac{d}{d\tau}\, _\tau b \Big|_{\tau=0} = w$$

and then let $_\tau u = \{_\tau u^i : i \in N(T)\}_{\tau=0}^{1}$ be given by:

$$_\tau u^i(x) = u^i(x) + \sum_{j \in T_i^0} \tau \alpha_j{}^i x_j\,,$$

where

$$\alpha_j{}^i = \frac{1}{A_j{}^i}\,[v_j{}^i - A_j{}^i L_j{}^i - B_j{}^i Q_j{}^i - D_j{}^i],$$

$$A_j{}^i = \frac{\bar{a}_j(\bar{b}_j - b_j{}^i)}{(\bar{b}_j)^2}\,,$$

$$L_j{}^i = \lim_{\tau \to 0^+} \frac{d}{d\tau}\left[\frac{\partial u^i}{\partial x_j}\,(x(_\tau b))\right],$$

$$B_j{}^i = \lim_{\tau \to 0^+} \left[\frac{\partial u^i}{\partial x_j}\,(x(_\tau b))\right],$$

$$Q_j{}^i = \lim_{\tau \to 0^+} \frac{d}{d\tau}\left[\frac{\bar{a}_j(_\tau \bar{b}_j - {}_\tau b_j{}^i)}{(_\tau \bar{b}_j)^2}\right],$$

$$D_j{}^i = \left(\frac{a_j{}^i}{\bar{a}_j} - 1\right) \lim_{\tau \to 0^+} \frac{d}{d\tau}\left[\frac{\partial u^i}{\partial x_{k+1}}\,(x(_\tau b))\right].$$

($A_j{}^i \neq 0$ since $b \in S''$, and these limits exist because u^i is C^2.) It is straightforward to verify that this path has all the requisite properties.

To complete the proof of the lemma, we need to establish that $(T_{(u,b)}\, {}_T\tilde{\varnothing})^{-1}$ $(T_y M)$ splits. Since we have established that the derivative map is surjective, this follows from the finite dimensionality of the range $T_y M$.

Q.E.D.

LEMMA 3. *There exists an open dense set $E(T)$ in $(U(\sigma, \sigma'))^n$ such that, for any $u \in E(T)$,*

(a) $\eta(u) \cap \tilde{S}(T)$ is a finite set,

(b) $\eta(u) \cap \tilde{S}_j{}^i(T)$ *is empty (for $i \in N(T), j \in T^i$).*

Proof. For any fixed u, denote by ${}^u_T\tilde{\varnothing}$ the mapping from $\tilde{S}(T)$ to $R^{\hat{T}} \times \tilde{S}(T)$ given by ${}^u_T\tilde{\varnothing}(b) = {}_T\tilde{\varnothing}(u, b)$. Consider the submanifold $(\Delta^2(T) \cap R^{\hat{T}}) \times \tilde{S}(T)$ of $R^{\hat{T}} \times \tilde{S}(T)$, and call it Z. By the Transversal Density and Openness

[8] Clearly such a path exists.

Theorems,[9] there is an open dense set $\hat{E}(T)$ of $(U(\sigma, \sigma'))^n$ such that for each $u \in \hat{E}(T)$, ${}^{u}_{T}\tilde{\varnothing} \pitchfork Z$. But (letting $t_b = | T_b |$) codim $Z = \hat{t} - t_b = \dim \tilde{S}(T)$. Hence, for such u, ${}^{u}_{T}\tilde{\varnothing}^{-1}(Z)$ has dimension zero. Being bounded, it must be a finite set.[10]

Next let $Z_j^i = (\Delta^2(T) \cap R^{\hat{T}}) \times \tilde{S}_j^i(T)$. Again there is an open dense set $E_j^i(T)$ of $(U(\sigma, \sigma'))^n$ such that for any $u \in E_j^i(T)$, ${}^{u}_{T}\tilde{\varnothing} \pitchfork Z_j^i$. But codim $Z_j^i > \hat{t} - t_b = \dim \tilde{S}(T)$. Hence, for such u, ${}^{u}_{T}\tilde{\varnothing}^{-1}(Z_j^i) = \varnothing$.

Let $E(T)$ be the intersection of $\hat{E}(T)$ and all the $E_j^i(T)$. Since $\eta(u) \cap \tilde{S}(T) \subset {}^{u}_{T}\tilde{\varnothing}^{-1}(Z)$ and $\eta(u) \cap \tilde{S}_j^i(T) \subset {}^{u}_{T}\tilde{\varnothing}^{-1}(Z_j^i)$, we have proved the lemma.

Q.E.D.

In Lemmas 4, 5, and 6 we will assume that $N(T) = N$. Consider $M(T) = \tilde{S}(T)/\cup\{\tilde{S}_j^i(T) : i \in N, j \in T^i\}$. Then $M(T)$ is a manifold of dimension $\hat{t} - t_b$.

LEMMA 4. *Consider any* $M(T)$, *and the mapping* ${}_T\varnothing : (U(\sigma, \sigma'))^n \times M(T) \to R^{N\hat{T}} \times M(T)$. *Then, for any* $b \in M(T)$, *and* $i \in N$,

(a) $L_T^i(b) = \{{}_T\varnothing^i(u, b) : u \in (U(\sigma, \sigma'))^n\}$ *is a manifold of dimension* $t^i + 1$.

(b) $L_T^i(b) \cap R^{T_0^i}$ is an open set in $R^{T_0^i}$ (where $R^{T_0^i} = \{v \in R^{N\hat{T}} : v_j^l \neq 0$ *if, and only if,* $l = i$ *and* $j \in T_0^i\}$).

Proof. (a) Take any $j \in T_0^i$ (w.l.o.g. $j = 1$) and consider the $(k + 1) \times (k + 1)$ matrix:

$$\begin{pmatrix}
\dfrac{\bar{a}_1(\bar{b}_1 - b_1^i)}{(\bar{b}_1)^2} & 0 & 0 & \cdots & 0 & 0 & \dfrac{a_1^i}{\bar{a}_1} - 1 \\
-\left(\dfrac{\bar{a}_1 b_1^i}{(\bar{b}_1)^2}\right) & 0 & 0 & \cdots & 0 & 0 & \dfrac{a_1^i}{\bar{a}_1} \\
0 & -\left(\dfrac{\bar{a}_2 b_2^i}{(\bar{b}_2)^2}\right) & 0 & \cdots & 0 & 0 & \dfrac{a_2^i}{\bar{a}_2} \\
\vdots & \vdots & \vdots & & \vdots & \vdots & \vdots \\
0 & 0 & 0 & \cdots & 0 & -\left(\dfrac{\bar{a}_k b_k^i}{(\bar{b}_k)^2}\right) & \dfrac{a_k^i}{\bar{a}_k}
\end{pmatrix}$$

[9] See Appendix.

[10] This sentence is made rigorous in Remark 5.

Since $b \notin S_j^i(T)$ for any $j \in T_0^{\,i}$,

$$\det \begin{vmatrix} \dfrac{\bar{a}_1(\bar{b}_1 - b_1^{\,i})}{(\bar{b}_1)^2} & \dfrac{a_1^{\,i}}{\bar{a}_1} - 1 \\ -\left(\dfrac{\bar{a}_1 b_1^{\,i}}{(\bar{b}_1)^2}\right) & \dfrac{a_1^{\,i}}{\bar{a}_1} \end{vmatrix} \neq 0$$

from which it is easily deduced that the rank of the matrix is $t^i + 1$. To prove (a) note (i) the mapping from $(U(\sigma, \sigma'))^n$ to $R^{N\hat{T}}$ given by ${}_T\varnothing^i(u, b)$ for fixed b is linear, (ii) the image of the mapping is obtained by linear combinations[11] of $(t^i + 1)$ nonzero vectors each with $\hat{t}$ components, (iii) the matrix displayed above (after removal of columns j, $j \notin T_0^{\,i}$) is a submatrix of the matrix (which, for future reference, will be denoted by $C_T^{\,i}(b)$) of these vectors.

(b) This is obvious.

Q.E.D.

By Lemma 4, ${}_T\varnothing((U(\sigma, \sigma'^n)) \times M(T))$ is a manifold $\tilde{M}(T)$ in $R^{N\hat{T}} \times M(T)$ (of dimension $\hat{t} + n + \hat{t} - t_b$). From now on, view the range of the mapping ${}_T\varnothing$ as $\tilde{M}(T)$.

LEMMA 5. *Consider* ${}_T\varnothing : (U(\sigma, \sigma'))^n \times M(T) \rightarrow \tilde{M}(T)$. *Let* M' *be any submanifold of* $\tilde{M}(T)$. *Then* ${}_T\varnothing \pitchfork M'$.

Proof. This is along the same lines as the proof of Lemma 2. Let ${}_T\varnothing(u, b) = (v, b) \in \tilde{M}(T)$. Consider any differentiable path $({}_\tau v, {}_\tau b)$ in $\tilde{M}(T)$ for $\tau \in [0, 1]$, with $({}_0v, {}_0b) = (v, b)$. We will show that there is a differentiable path $({}_\tau u, {}_\tau b')$ in [12]$(U(\sigma, \sigma'))^n \times M(T)$ such that ${}_T\varnothing({}_\tau u, {}_\tau b') = ({}_\tau v, {}_\tau b)$ for $\tau \in [0, 1]$, and $({}_0u, {}_0b) = (u, b)$.

Write ${}_\tau v = ({}_\tau v^1, \ldots, {}_\tau v^n)$, ${}_\tau u = ({}_\tau u^1, \ldots, {}_\tau u^n)$. Since each $C_T^{\,i}({}_\tau b)$ has full rank there exists a unique $(t^i + 1)$-vector, ${}_\tau\alpha^i = \{{}_\tau\alpha_j^{\,i} : j \in T_0^{\,i} \text{ and } j = k + 1\}$ such that $C_T^{\,i}({}_\tau b)_\tau\alpha^i = {}_\tau v^i$. Now construct the path $({}_\tau u, {}_\tau b')$ as follows:

$${}_\tau b' = {}_\tau b,$$

$${}_\tau u^i(x) = u^i(x) + \sum_{j \in T_i^{\,0}} {}_\tau\delta_j^{\,i} x_j + {}_\tau\delta_{k+1}^i x_{k+1},$$

where

$${}_\tau\delta_j^{\,i} = {}_\tau\alpha_j^{\,i} - \frac{\partial u^i}{\partial x_j}(x^i({}_\tau b))$$

for $j \in T_0^{\,i}$ and $j = k + 1$.

[11] Where the coefficients of the combination are picked from an open set in R^{t^i+1}.
[12] Again, for small enough τ, this path lies in $(U(\sigma, \sigma'))^n \times M(T)$.

It is easily checked that this path has the requisite properties. The rest of the proof is concluded as in Lemma 2. Q.E.D.

LEMMA 6. *For any T there is an open dense set $V(T)$ of $(U(\sigma, \sigma'))^n$ such that for $u \in V(T)$, $\eta(u) \cap \epsilon(u) \cap M(T)$ is empty.*

Proof. Define $M^*(T) = [R^{N\hat{T}} \cap \Delta^1(T) \cap \Delta^2(T)] \times M(T)$. Recall that $\Delta^1(T)$ is a finite union of submanifolds of $R^{N\hat{T}}$, each of which has codimension $\geqslant 1$. Piecing this with the previous lemma, we see that $M^*(T)$ is then a finite union of submanifolds of $\tilde{M}(T)$, say $M_1^*(T), \ldots, M_{r(T)}^*(T)$, with codimension $M_i^*(T) > \hat{t} - t_b$. But Lemma 5 again implies that there exist open dense sets $V_i(T)$ $(i = 1, \ldots, r(T))$ of $(U(\sigma, \sigma'))^n$ such that for any $u \in V_i(T)$, ${}^u_T\varnothing \pitchfork M_i^*(T)$. But then codim ${}^u_T\varnothing^{-1}(M_i^*(T)) =$ codim $M_i^*(T) >$ dim $M(T)$; hence ${}^u_T\varnothing^{-1}(M_i^*(T)) = \varnothing$. On the other hand, using the proposition from [10] $[\eta(u) \cap \epsilon(u) \cap M(T)] \subset {}^u_T\varnothing^{-1}(M_1^*(T) \cup \cdots \cup M_{r(T)}^*(T))$. Put $V(T) = \cap \{V_i(T) : i = 1, \ldots, r(T)\}$. Q.E.D.

Proof of Auxiliary Theorem. Put

$$E = [\cap\{E(T) : T \in \tilde{V}] \cap [\cap\{V(T) : T \in \tilde{V}, N(T) = N\}].$$

The proof follows from the observation that $\{\eta(u) \cap \tilde{S}(T) : T \in \tilde{V}\}$ constitutes a partition of $\eta(u) \cap S_\mu$. Q.E.D.

4. CONCLUDING REMARKS

Remark 2. Let $\hat{U} = \{[u^1, \ldots, u^n) \in (U(\sigma, \sigma'))^n$: each u^i is concave$\}$. Then it can be shown—see [9]—that $\eta(u) \neq \varnothing$ for any $u \in \hat{U}$. Since $\hat{U}$ contains an open set of $(U(\sigma, \sigma'))^n$—for instance, consider those u^i which are strictly concave—our theorem is not vacuous.

Remark 3. We could have let the space of games be $(U)^n \times (\text{Int}\, \Omega^{k+1})$, allowing for the endowments to vary also. However, it would become necessary to restrict this variation to ensure that the N.E. are bounded away from the zero-price strategies, as in Lemma 1. Thus, for instance, we could state the theorem with $(U(\sigma, \sigma'))^n \times (\hat{Q})^n$, where $\hat{Q}$ is the interior of a cube which itself is in the interior of Ω^{k+1}.

Remark 4. The generic inefficiency of the N.E. attenuates in this model as the player-set is increased in the direction of a nonatomic continuum. For the continuum itself, the N.E.—under appropriate conditions (see [3])—are efficient, and coincide with the Walras Equilibria of the market.

Remark 5. We have been somewhat slipshod in parts of the proof in order to keep the main ideas clear. Now we redress this. Let $\hat{Q}$ be an open neighborhood of Q in R^{k+1} and $\hat{U}$ the manifold of all C^2 functions on $\hat{Q}$ whose restriction to Q is an element of $U(\sigma, \sigma')$. Note that if $\hat{E}$ is open (or dense) in $\hat{Q}$, then E, obtained by restricting the functions in $\hat{E}$ to the domain Q, is open (or dense) in E. This follows from the well-known fact that there is a $K > 0$ such that: each $u \in U(\sigma, \sigma')$ can be extended to a $\hat{u} \in \hat{U}$ with $\| u \| \leqslant K \| \hat{u} \|$. Next let $\hat{S}_\mu$ be an open neighborhood of S_μ in Ω^{nk} such that[13] $\hat{S}_\mu \cap \{(b^1,..., b^n) \in \Omega^{nk} : \bar{b}_j = 0, \text{ some } j \in I_k\} = \varnothing$. $\hat{S}(T) = (\text{Aff } \tilde{S}(T)) \cap \hat{S}_\mu$, where Aff stands for "affine hull." Then define the mappings ${}_T\psi$, ${}_T\tilde{\psi}$, ${}_T\varnothing$ and ${}_T\tilde{\varnothing}$ on $(\hat{U})^n \times \hat{S}(T)$ exactly as before.[14] By adjusting $\hat{Q}$ to be large enough, and $\hat{S}_\mu$ to be small enough, there is no problem of definition. (There would have been a problem if $\hat{S}_\mu$ was not bounded away from points where $\bar{b}_j = 0$. Hence the importance of Lemma 1.)

Lemma 2, in fact, holds—and the proof really shows this—for this bigger mapping ${}_T\varnothing : (\hat{U})^n \times \hat{S}(T) \to R^{\hat{T}} \times \hat{S}(T)$. Now the proof of Lemma 3 may be reread as follows. First we apply the Transversal Density and Openness Theorems (see Appendix) to this ${}_T\tilde{\varnothing}$ with $A \equiv (\hat{U})^n$, $X \equiv \hat{S}(T)$, $K \equiv$ Closure of $\tilde{S}(T)$, etc. This gives us the open dense set in $(\hat{U})^n$, which in turn induces the desired open dense set $\hat{E}(T)$ in $(U(\sigma, \sigma'))^n$, as explained above. Also $\eta(u) \cap \tilde{S}(T) \subset {}^u_T\varnothing^{-1}(Z) \cap K$, and the latter set is clearly finite since it is the intersection of a compact set and a 0-dimensional manifold.

Lemmas 4, 5, and 6 can similarly be reread to make the proof rigorous.

Appendix

We recall the results from [1] used in this paper.

"Let X and Y be C^1 manifolds, $f : X \to Y$ a C^1 map, and $W \subset Y$ a submanifold. We say that f is *transversal to W at a point* $x \in X$, in symbols : $f \pitchfork_x W$, iff, where $y = f(x)$, either $y \notin W$ or $y \in W$ and

(1) the inverse image $(T_x f)^{-1}(T_y W)$ splits, and

(2) the image $(T_x f)(T_x)$ contains a closed complement to $T_y W$ in $T_y Y$.

We say f is *transversal to W*, in symbols: $f \pitchfork W$, iff $f \pitchfork_x W$ for every $x \in X$.

Let $\mathscr{A}$, X, and Y be C^r manifolds, $\mathscr{C}^r(X; Y)$ the set of C^r maps from X to Y, and $\rho : \mathscr{A} \to \mathscr{C}^r(X, Y)$ a map. For $a \in \mathscr{A}$ we write ρ_a instead of $\rho(a)$; i.e., $\rho_a : X \to Y$ is a C^r map. We say ρ is a *C^r representation* iff the evaluation map

$$\text{ev}_\rho : \mathscr{A} \times X \to Y$$

[13] This is clearly possible.

[14] I.e., by the same formulas.

given by

$$\mathrm{ev}_\rho(a, x) = \rho_a(x)$$

for $a \in \mathscr{A}$ and $x \in X$ is a C^r map from $\mathscr{A} \times X$ to Y.

TRANSVERSAL DENSITY THEOREM. *Let $\mathscr{A}$, X, Y be C^r manifolds, $\rho : \mathscr{A} \to \mathscr{C}^r(X, Y)$ a C^r representation, $W \subset Y$ a submanifold (not necessarily closed), and $\mathrm{ev}_\rho : \mathscr{A} \times X \to Y$ the evaluation map. Define $\mathscr{A}_W \subset \mathscr{A}$ by*

$$\mathscr{A}_W = \{a \in \mathscr{A} \mid \rho_a \pitchfork W\}.$$

Assume that:

(1) *X has finite dimension n and W has finite codimension q in Y;*

(2) *$\mathscr{A}$ and X are second countable;*

(3) $r > \max(0, n - q)$;

(4) $\mathrm{ev}_\rho \pitchfork W$.

Then $\mathscr{A}_W$ is residual (and hence dense) in $\mathscr{A}$.

Openness of Transversal Intersection. Let $\mathscr{A}$, X, and Y be C^1 manifolds with X finite dimensional, $W \subset Y$ a closed C^1 submanifold, $K \subset X$ a compact subset of X, and $\rho : \mathscr{A} \to C^1(X, Y)$ a C^1 pseudorepresentation. Then the subset $\mathscr{A}_{KW} \subset \mathscr{A}$ defined by

$$\mathscr{A}_{KW} = \{a \in \mathscr{A} \mid \rho_a \pitchfork_x W \quad \text{for} \quad x \in K\}$$

is open. This holds even if X is not finite dimensional, provided that ρ is a C^1 representation."

For our purposes, it is enough to note that every C^1 representation is a C^1 pseudorepresentation. Also $T_y W$ is the tangent space to W at y; $T_x f : T_x X \to T_y Y$ is the derivative map of f at x. See [1] for detailed definitions.

REFERENCES

1. R. ABRAHAM AND J. ROBBIN, "Transversal Mappings and Flows," Benjamin, New York, 1967.
2. G. DEBREU, Economies with a finite set of equilibria, *Econometrica* **38** (1970), 387–392.
3. P. DUBEY AND L. S. SHAPLEY, Non-cooperative exchange with a continuum of traders, Rand Report P-5964.
4. P. DUBEY, "Finiteness and Inefficiency of Nash Equilibria," Cowles Foundation Discussion Paper No. 508R, 1978.
5. P. DUBEY, "Price-Quantity Strategic Market Games," Cowles Foundation Discussion Paper No. 515, Yale University, 1979; *Econometrica*, 1981, in press.

6. P. Dubey, A. Mas-Colell, and M. Shubik, Efficiency properties of strategic market games: An axiomatic approach, *J. Econ. Theory.* **22** (1980), 339–362.
7. R. Howe, "Most Convex Functions are Smooth," Cowles Foundation Discussion Paper No. 524, Yale University, 1979.
8. D. Schmeidler, "Walrasian Analysis via Strategic Outcome Functions," mimeograph, Tel Aviv University, Tel-Aviv, Israel, 1978; *Econometria*, in press.
9. L. S. Shapley and M. Shubik, Trade using one commodity as a means of payment, *J. Pol. Econ.* **85** (1977), 937–968.
10. S. Smale, Optimizing several functions, *in* "Proceedings, Tokyo Manifolds Conference, 1973."
11. S. Smale, Global analysis and economics IIA, extension of a theorem of Debreu, *J. Math. Econ.* **1** (1974), 1–14.

Printed in Belgium

Index

ECONOMIC THEORY, ECONOMETRICS, AND MATHEMATICAL ECONOMICS

Consulting Editor: Karl Shell

UNIVERSITY OF PENNSYLVANIA
PHILADELPHIA, PENNSYLVANIA

Franklin M. Fisher and Karl Shell. **The Economic Theory of Price Indices: *Two Essays on the Effects of Taste, Quality, and Technological Change***

Luis Eugenio Di Marco (Ed.). **International Economics and Development: *Essays in Honor of Raúl Presbisch***

Erwin Klein. **Mathematical Methods in Theoretical Economics: *Topological and Vector Space Foundations of Equilibrium Analysis***

Paul Zarembka (Ed.). **Frontiers in Econometrics**

George Horwich and Paul A. Samuelson (Eds.). **Trade, Stability, and Macroeconomics: *Essays in Honor of Lloyd A. Metzler***

W. T. Ziemba and R. G. Vickson (Eds.). **Stochastic Optimization Models in Finance**

Steven A. Y. Lin (Ed.). **Theory and Measurement of Economic Externalities**

David Cass and Karl Shell (Eds.). **The Hamiltonian Approach to Dynamic Economics**

R. Shone. **Microeconomics: *A Modern Treatment***

C. W. J. Granger and Paul Newbold. **Forecasting Economic Time Series**

Michael Szenberg, John W. Lombardi, and Eric Y. Lee. **Welfare Effects of Trade Restrictions: *A Case Study of the U.S. Footwear Industry***

Haim Levy and Marshall Sarnat (Eds.). **Financial Decision Making under Uncertainty**

Yasuo Murata. **Mathematics for Stability and Optimization of Economic Systems**

Alan S. Blinder and Philip Friedman (Eds.). **Natural Resources, Uncertainty, and General Equilibrium Systems: *Essays in Memory of Rafael Lusky***

Jerry S. Kelly. **Arrow Impossibility Theorems**

Peter Diamond and Michael Rothschild (Eds.). **Uncertainty in Economics: *Readings and Exercises***

Fritz Machlup. **Methodology of Economics and Other Social Sciences**

Robert H. Frank and Richard T. Freeman. **Distributional Consequences of Direct Foreign Investment**

Elhanan Helpman and Assaf Razin. **A Theory of International Trade under Uncertainty**

Edmund S. Phelps. **Studies in Macroeconomic Theory, Volume 1: *Employment and Inflation.* Volume 2: *Redistribution and Growth.***

Marc Nerlove, David M. Grether, and José L. Carvalho. **Analysis of Economic Time Series: *A Synthesis***

Thomas J. Sargent. **Macroeconomic Theory**

Jerry Green and José Alexander Scheinkman (Eds.). **General Equilibrium, Growth and Trade: *Essays in Honor of Lionel McKenzie***

Michael J. Boskin (Ed.). **Economics and Human Welfare: *Essays in Honor of Tibor Scitovsky***

Carlos Daganzo. **Multinomial Probit: *The Theory and Its Application to Demand Forecasting***

L. R. Klein, M. Nerlove, and S. C. Tsiang (Eds.). **Quantitative Economics and Development: *Essays in Memory of Ta-Chung Liu***

Giorgio P. Szegö. **Portfolio Theory: *With Application to Bank Asset Management***

M June Flanders and Assaf Razin (Eds.). **Development in an Inflationary World**

Thomas G. Cowing and Rodney E. Stevenson (Eds.). **Productivity Measurement in Regulated Industries**

Robert J. Barro (Ed.). **Money, Expectations, and Business Cycles: *Essays in Macroeconomics***

Ryuzo Sato. **Theory of Technical Change and Economic Invariance: *Application of Lie Groups***

Iosif A. Krass and Shawkat M. Hammoudeh. **The Theory of Positional Games: *With Applications in Economics***

Giorgio Szegö (Ed.). **New Quantitative Techniques for Economic Analysis**

John M. Letiche (Ed.). **International Economic Policies and Their Theoretical Foundations: A Source Book**

Murray C. Kemp (Ed.). **Production Sets**

Andreu Mas-Colell (Ed.). **Noncooperative Approaches to the Theory of Perfect Competition**

In preparation

Victor A. Canto, Douglas H. Joines, and Arthur B. Laffer. **Foundations of Supply-Side Economics**

Jean-Pascal Benassy. **The Economics of Market Disequilibrium**

Tatsuro Ichiishi. **Game Theory for Economic Analysis**

David P. Baron. **The Export-Import Bank: *An Economic Analysis***